THE
RICE BOOK

SRI OWEN

St. Martin's Griffin
New York

THE RICE BOOK. Copyright © 1993 by Sri Owen.
Illustrations copyright © 1993 by Soun Vannithone.
"A Rice Landscape" Copyright © 1993 by Roger Owen.

Library of Congress Cataloging-in-Publication Data

Owen, Sri.
The rice book : the definitive book on the magic of rice, with
hundreds of exotic recipes from around the world / Sri Owen.
        p.   cm.
          ISBN 0-312-14132-7
  1. Cookery (Rice)   2. Cookery, International.   I. Title.
            TX809.R5095   1996
        641.6'318—dc20   95-43664   CIP

First published in England by Doubleday, a Division of
Transworld Publishers Ltd.

First St. Martin's Griffin Edition: February 1996
        10 9 8 7 6 5 4 3 2 1

CONTENTS

To the memory of
HAIKAL SALAM

Acknowledgements

To mention every single person who helped us with this book would fill many pages with small print, and gratify no one. We want to express our particular thanks to the people named below, and also, in very many cases, to their colleagues, spouses, friends and relations who did so much for us. If we have negligently omitted any name that should be included, we hope the person concerned will still feel assured of our gratitude.

The names of many writers whose recipes have (with their permission) been used in the book appear in the introductions to those recipes, and their books are listed in the Bibliography. We have attempted to group everyone else under two main heads, and then to arrange the names in what we hope is alphabetical order.

First, the information providers, many of whom helped in other ways as well:

In Britain, at the Natural Resources Institute (Overseas Development Administration) at Chatham, P.A. Clarke, Claire Coote, Angus Hone and David Twiddy. At the University of Kent, Professor Roy Ellen. In London, Vincent Donatantonio and Mr Parmigiani of the firms that bear their names, and Marcello Serafino of Alivini Ltd; Dr Ian Glover of the Institute of Archaeology of University College, London; Maggie Black; Alan Davidson; Roz Denny; Dr John and Dr Jatmi Dransfield, of the Royal Botanic Gardens, Kew; Bea Green; Geraldene Holt; John Maidment; Gerald and Valerie Mars; María José Sevilla and her colleague, Janine Gilson of Food From Spain, Spanish Embassy Commercial Office; Ann Watson; Sami Zubaida.

In Singapore: at the National University of Singapore, Dr Ian Caldwell, of the Department of Malay Studies, and Dr Victor Savage, of the Department of Geography; Low Lee Yong, of Ng Nam Bee Marketing Pte Ltd; Violet Oon of *The Food Paper*.

In Indonesia: Alida; Ali Achmad Hidrus; Iskandar; Murni; Anak Agung Gede Rai, of the Hotel Indonesia International Corporation; my sisters, Ratnasari and her late husband Haikal Salam, Roslina and her husband Usman Beka, and many other members of my own family.

In the Philippines: Lydia Arribas; Professor Doreen G. Fernandez; Professor Angelita Malagday del Mundo; Dr Carmen Paule; Dr Santiago R. Obien, the Director of the Philippines Rice Research Institute; at the International Rice Research Institute (IRRI), Dr Michel Arraudeau, Dr Thomas Hargrove, Dr Keith Ingram, Dr G.S. Khush, Salvador C. Labro, Dr Moo Sang Lim, Thelma Paris, Dr LaRue Pollard, Dr Graeme Quick, William H. Smith, Dr Duncan Vaughan, Dr Virmani, and a visitor, Mark W. Rosegrant of the International Food Policy Research Institute, Washington.

In Taiwan (Republic of China): Dr Jenny Chang, and colleagues at the China Grain Products Research and Development Institute; in the Council of Agriculture Executive Yuan, Chen Wen-Deh, Bret J.C. Lin; in the Food Industry Research and

Development Institute, Wen-Lian Chen, C.P. Huang, Dr Tin-Yin Liu, Dr Jiing-Yang Wu, and many colleagues; and Professor Cheng-Yi Lii, of the National Taiwan University.

In Japan: at Hokuriku National Agricultural Experiment Station, Joetsu, Dr and Mrs Kiichi Fukui, Yoshimichi Fukuta, Dr Ken'ichi Ohtsubo, Dr Masahiro Yano and colleagues; Professor Naomichi Ishige of the National Museum of Ethnology, Osaka; Professor Richard Hosking of Shuda University, Hiroshima.

In South Korea: at the Crop Experiment Station, Rural Development Administration, Suwon, Dr Choi Hae Chune, Dr Jekyu Kim, Dr Ki-Joon Shin, Dr Kyu-Won Kim.

In Spain: Alicia Ríos; in Valencia, José Garrigues, and in Murcia, Angel González, of the Spanish Institute for Foreign Trade; Ali Zamani Valian, of Ibérica de Arroces SA, Oliva.

In India: Dr A. Alam and Dr D.P. Singh of the Indian Council of Agricultural Research; Dr F.U. Zaman of the Indian Agricultural Research Institute; Arvindpal Singh Chatha and Jasbir Singh Chatha; J. ('Jiggs') Inder Singh Kalra; Madan Lal Jaiswal, Master Chef of the Bukhara Restaurant, and Mohammed Rais, Master Chef, Maurya Sheraton Hotel, New Delhi; Arvind Saraswat of the Taj Palace Hotel, New Delhi.

In Thailand: Sombat Bhuapirom; Kamolvan Punyashthiti ('Noot'); Chanpithya Shimpalee and colleagues, Agricultural Extension Department; Rakesh Sodhia of G. Premjee Ltd; Niphond Wongtrangan and Opas Akardviphat, of Thai Rice Mills Association.

In Australia: at the Rice Growers' Co-operative, Leeton, NSW, Chris Black, Lindsay Bramall and Karen Inge; at Yanco Agricultural Institute, Yanco, NSW, Anthony Blakeney, Linsey Welch and colleagues; Cherry Ripe, of *The Australian*, Sydney.

In Malaysia: Dr Supaad Mohd. Amin, Dr Chew, Dr Adinan Husein and Dr Ahmad Zamzam, of MARDI (Malaysian Agricultural Research and Development Institute); Mohammad Dashilah, of LPN (Lembaga Padi dan Beras Negara: National Padi and Rice Board).

In the United States: at the USA Rice Council, Houston, Texas, Bill Farmer, Mary Jo Hogue, Kristen O'Brien, James W. Willis and colleagues; in Beaumont, Texas, Dr Bill Webb; in Crowley, Louisiana, Leonard Hensgens, President of the Louisiana Rice Growers' Association and Past President of the USA Rice Council; at Mer Rouge, Louisiana, Larry G. Tubbs; in Washington, Donna Jo Denison, Patsy Guyer and Laura Hudson, in the office of Senator J. Bennett Johnston of Louisiana.

The other group is of people and organizations equally vital to our work; they helped with travel, accommodation, contacts and communications, and made the gathering of material not only possible but enjoyable. We are glad to thank many of them for their hospitality.

Some hotel people: in Hilton International, James A. Smith in Hong Kong; Michael Schuetzendorff in London; André Bossard in Seoul; Armin H. Schroecker in

Kyongju; Wolfgang Schack and Elizabeth Soo in Kuala Lumpur. At the Dorchester Hotel, London, David Wilkinson and Willi Elsener. In Park Hyatt Hotels, Michael Gray in London and Paul J. Limbert in Washington, DC. At the Conrad Hotel in London, John W. Serbrock and Jaideep Mazumdar; and at the Hong Kong Conrad, Judi Arundel and Jenny Lee. At the Oriental Hotel, Bangkok, Kurt Wachtveitl, Eric Brand, Mrs Pornsri Luplaiboon, Mrs Ankana Gilwee and Norbert A. Kostner. At the Golden Sands Resort, Penang, Wong Wai Ling. In the Taj Group of Hotels, Subhash N. Thaker in London, Surjit Dhillon and Rajiv Dutta in Jaipur, and many others in New Delhi and Agra. At the Maurya Sheraton Hotel, New Delhi, Shona Adhikari. In the Hotel Indonesia International Corporation, the Vice President, A.A. Gede Rai, who also organized our stay in Bali, his home island, and welcomed us there. Also in Bali, F. Purwono and A.A.G. Agung at the Putri Bali Hotel in Nusa Dua, and Suryasih Mudita and many of her colleagues at the Bali Beach Hotel. And a special thank you to the friendly and efficient staff at the IRRI Guesthouse, Los Baños.

Other organizations and individuals: Aishah Ali of the *New Straits Times*, Kuala Lumpur; Bill Barsana, of IRRI; Jan Boon and her team at the Australian Gas Cooking School in Sydney; Margaret and Richard Clarke, Melbourne; Silvija Davidson and Hugo Dunn-Meynell of the International Wine and Food Society; Elizabeth Gabay; Soekarno Hadian, Jakarta; Michael Harrison, Head of Indonesian Section, BBC World Service; Alan Kenny; at Books for Cooks, Heidi Lascelles and Clarissa Dickson-Wright; Professor Kenneth Lendon of Waseda University, Tokyo; Yekti and Alan Morris, Melbourne; David Natt; Zahara Othman; our sons, Irwan and Daniel; Roma Satara, Dipak Deva, and staff of Travel Corporation (India) Ltd in India, and Pal Sakhuja at the TCI office in London; Swan and Rena Sarumpaet, Melbourne; Harlan Walker, Birmingham; Professor and Mrs Donald Weatherbee, Columbia, South Carolina.

Our special thanks go to Dr J.M. Allen, our family doctor, and Dr C.S. McIntosh, Consultant Physician, Queen Mary Hospital, Roehampton, who helped overcome health problems; and to the President of the Ladder Publishing Company in Taipei, Shawn-Wu Yen, and his secretary, Mrs Shirley C.H. Hsieh, who made contacts and arranged meetings for us with government officials and scientists; without their help, our visit to Taiwan would have achieved very little.

Finally, we want to say thank you to Sri's agent, Caroline Davidson, who found a helpful publisher and who has taken a close interest in the manuscript throughout its development; to the Commissioning Editor, Sally Gaminara, who had the courage to let us loose for two years in the belief that the book would eventually be finished; as well, of course, to everyone at Doubleday who has worked so hard on it since. And to Soun Vannithone, the artist, because his skill, and his delight in everything that he draws, illuminate so many pages.

Rice: A Recipe for Good Living

I love rice, and I want everyone to share my enjoyment of it. That is my real reason for writing this book. I grew up among rice fields, with people who did not consider rice at all exotic, though it still had traces of magic. Today I find rice, in a dozen or more varieties, in Western supermarkets, and no one any longer thinks of it as foreign. For me, the magic is as strong as ever.

This book is above all one of recipes and advice on cooking and eating rice. What we eat, how we grow and prepare it, and what we think about our food, are essential parts of our culture. Rice is grown in more than a hundred countries, and the recipes in this book are from every continent. The cultivation of rice is one of humanity's best claims to possess some kind of collective wisdom.

In the old societies of Asia, rice is a link between Earth and Heaven. It shapes our landscapes and the way we live, as it has done for many centuries. It is also at the root of our political and economic life, present and future. These seem to me very good reasons for finding out more about rice, not just in my own country of Indonesia but in some of the hundred or so other lands where it is cultivated. The first part of this book looks at what is happening to rice, as it passes from tradition to a high-technology future.

Sri Owen

A Rice Landscape

In this opening section, there is something to be said not just about rice as a food but also about other aspects of this extraordinary plant: its origins, its life-cycle and cultivation, its power over the lives of those who live by it. To enjoy rice, it helps to know how to shop for it as well as how to cook it. We ought to understand what it offers us as a food. And to appreciate rice fully, we need to have some idea of its status in different countries today, and of how it came to be where it is.

RICE ON EVERY SHOPPING LIST

What do people think about rice? The contrast between the old rice of the Asian peasant farmer and the new rice of the supermarket shelf is reflected in the contradictory images that exist in people's minds – often, I'm sure, in the same minds at the same time. In different contexts, it may be seen as the food of Third World peoples living at subsistence level, or as an expensive gourmet item from the delicatessen. It's fattening (practically all starch), and polished rice is low in proteins (pictures of children with beri-beri), but it's healthy, pure, natural, non-allergenic and seems to be included in a lot of slimming diets.

Rice, like any other staple, started as a wild plant and in domesticating it during, perhaps, ten millennia, men and women have shown they are willing to pay almost any price to get it. Asians don't eat rice because they can't get anything else. There are almost always other foods they can fall back on in bad years, and there are often other crops which would feed them more easily and cheaply. They go to the enormous trouble of cultivating rice because, in flavour, texture and general satisfaction, no other staple food comes anywhere near it.

For the shopper in the supermarket or the local store, the rice fields are far away, and the work of breeding, selecting, growing, harvesting, milling and marketing has all been done. Any rice that has got this far has been checked, inspected and graded so many times, by such experienced humans and such sophisticated machines, that we can be confident it's good. But this knowledge makes the products on the shelves still more bewildering. How can something as basic as rice need to be packaged under so many different names? Does it really matter which I choose?

Yes, it matters. You need to get it more or less right, and as your rice knowledge and experience widen you will become more discriminating. However, the selection is not really too critical. There is a difference between, say, Basmati and Texmati (the Texas variety doesn't have quite the aroma of the real thing), but if you happen to be shopping in Houston, then Texmati will do just as well. If your local mini-supermarket in a London suburb only has something labelled 'American long grain', then buy it. If you're miles from anywhere and all you can find is an old packet of pudding rice, use that. The final result will still be edible and nourishing and will still taste good.

In the recipes in this book, the most suitable type of rice is usually indicated. You aren't, except in a few recipes, obliged to have exactly this type, but it's worth trying to get something near it.

GETTING TO KNOW RICE BY NAME

In this section, I shall talk about the rice you find in your supermarket or so-called 'ethnic' store. Obviously the selection is going to vary quite a bit from country to country, but the major types are likely to be represented in most places, under one brand name or another. Australians, for example, will look for Sunrice where Americans will expect to find Uncle Ben's.

There are several different ways of classifying rice as a product, and some of the types overlap. So this section is based on an attempt to classify the classifications.

> 1   *By physical appearance: long, medium, or short grain, patna, rose, pearl, red, black.*

Broadly, **long** and **medium grain rices** are used in, or eaten with, savoury and main-course dishes. **Short grain rice**, in Western countries, is traditionally used for rice puddings. Many Japanese rices, however, are short grain and sticky, which makes them suitable for sushi. Some European rices are short grain and are used in savoury dishes such as paella. In any case, these descriptions are relative. The lengths of grains of different varieties make up a continuous spectrum. Since width also varies, professionals grade rice not only by length but by the ratio of length to width. The shortest rices are almost spherical, the longest look like little zeppelins. The shortest grain rice we have come across is an expensive Spanish variety, marketed as Bomba. The longest is Basmati, which exists in many varieties. Basmati rices have the peculiarity that, in cooking, the grains become longer but not wider. In Italy, where the rice business has since 1931 been regulated by the Ente Nazionale Risi, milled rice is graded by length as follows:

comune	less than 5.2 mm
semifino	5.2–6.4 mm
fino, superfino	6.4 mm and above

However, size isn't the same thing as quality; all Italian rices are good, but they are not all equal and *superfino* is clearly above *fino*. Vincent Donatantonio, an Italian rice importer in London, tells me that Arborio, one of the best known, is rated a premium rice only because it is large grained; the very best, at any rate for risotto, are Carnaroli and Vialone Nano.

Some American millers still use the words **patna**, **rose**, or **pearl** to describe their products; these are taken to mean long, medium and short grain respectively.

Another way of describing rice varieties is by the colour of the grains. These colours affect only the pericarp, the outer layer of the milled grain. **Red rice** is really brownish, but 'brown rice' is something different (see below). Most red rices are considered inferior in quality, and farmers generally treat them as weeds, but some are cultivated. A red variety is the regional speciality of the Camargue, the wetlands near the delta of the river Rhône. Rice has long been grown there, but the industry has only taken off in the last twenty years or so; the area planted to rice has quadrupled since 1980, and Camarguais rice is beginning to be exported. Red rice needs extra cooking time (page 102).

Black rice, which is in fact a deep blackberry-purple, is highly regarded and is obtainable in some Western shops that specialize in Far Eastern produce. There is a recipe for Black Rice Sorbet on page 335.

> 2 By *how it has been milled and processed: white, brown (or whole), enriched, parboiled, boil-in-the-bag, popped (or expanded), flaked, ground (rice flour, rice powder); also 'convenience' rices − pre-cooked (or instant), frozen part-cooked, easy-cook.*

White rice has been 'fully milled'; the bran coat has been completely removed from the grains. The grains are pure white and semi-translucent, though part or all of each grain may be opaque and 'chalky' (because it contains tiny air bubbles). White rice is often described as 'polished', though in the trade this word is associated with the use of glycerine, talc, or even a light mineral oil to make the grains glossy and slippery. It's like waxing supermarket fruit to make it shine. Whether talc or oil, the amounts anyone would ingest in a lifetime would be extremely small; but this kind of cosmetic operation is much rarer than it used to be. Californian and other millers sometimes print on their rice bags 'no talc'.

Brown rice, also called **whole rice** or in Italian *semigreggio*, still has the bran on, and is therefore a more nutritious food than white rice. Virtually all brown rice sold in Western countries is long or medium grain. It has normally been heat-treated to stop the bran oils going rancid in storage. It takes longer to cook than white rice, and is very chewy, with a mild nutty bran flavour. In rice-growing countries, it is bought only for small children and invalids. Wherever you are, brown rice always costs more because there is less demand for it and because the bran, if it had been milled off, would have been sold separately.

6

As a health food, brown rice is good, but quite unnecessary if you are eating a normal well-balanced diet. It's good for slimmers because you eat less: you feel full more quickly, partly because the work of chewing it makes you think you've eaten more than you have. As a food treat, you may find that it makes a nice change from time to time, especially if you don't eat rice of any kind regularly. Personally, I wouldn't want to eat brown rice very often, but some people get really hooked on it.

In between, but closer to white than to brown, is a range of semi-milled rices which have a little of the bran left on the grains; in Italy these are described as *semilavorato*. In cooking, treat these as white rice but be prepared to give them a little more time to boil or steam.

Enriched or **fortified rice** has vitamins, proteins and/or trace elements added to make up for those that nature neglected to put in or that the miller has already taken out. It would be unnecessarily expensive to fortify every grain, so fortified grains are coated very thinly with a soluble plastic and then mixed with unfortified ones in a proportion, usually, of 1 to 20. Most of the rice processed in the United States is enriched with iron, niacin and thiamin; some states actually forbid the sale of non-enriched milled rice.

Parboiled rice is both very ancient and very modern. Parboiling probably originated in India about 2,000 years ago (some writers say 4,000 years). Today, many northern Indians like their rice treated in this way, and many Middle Easterners insist on it. I suspect that Americans and Europeans often eat it without realizing they are doing so, for the most famous brand of American rice, Uncle Ben's, is parboiled; within North America, Uncle Ben's uses the term 'converted rice' as a registered trademark. In Britain, Uncle Ben's costs up to twice as much as ordinary rice because the consumer has to pay the packaging, distribution and advertising costs plus the EC tariff, which is much bigger for milled rice. Most people in South-East Asia, as far as I know, dislike parboiled rice; they say it has less flavour than 'ordinary' rice and is rather chewy. Parboiled rice is normally long or medium grain.

The technique of parboiling varies from country to country, and in a modern factory has become very sophisticated. Basically there are two stages. The paddy, which has been threshed from the stalk but is still in the husk, is first soaked in water for several hours, then steamed for perhaps ten minutes. It is then dried, and is milled in the usual way.

Parboiling has two advantages. Some of the nutrients in the bran are made to 'stick' to the starchy endosperm – the part we eat – or are even pushed right into it, so that less protein and other nutrients are lost in milling. And because the grains have become less brittle, milling is easier and cheaper, with fewer 'brokens'.

Parboiled rice usually has a slightly yellowish colour when you buy it, but this disappears in cooking. It takes longer to cook than ordinary rice, because parboiling has made the grains harder.

Note that **boil-in-the-bag rice**, nowadays, is almost always parboiled. This is a sore

7

point with us, as you will see if you refer to the recipe for Compressed Rice on page 107. The only purpose of the bag, as far as I know, is to keep rice grains from sticking to your saucepan; it's a very tiny advantage to pay good money for, but it does mean slightly less waste and easier washing-up.

Popped or **expanded rice** is short grain rice that has been cooked with sugar, then subjected to high pressure which is suddenly released; the water inside each grain turns to steam and expands violently. The grains are then quickly toasted to prevent them collapsing into a mush, which of course is what they soon become if you leave your Rice Krispies standing too long after you pour the milk over them. In 1991 we met a food scientist in Taiwan who was working on popped rice that you could make yourself in a microwave. The Australians, Americans and Scandinavians make excellent popped-rice biscuits which are marketed as a health food and for portable meals.

Flaked rice is just parboiled rice that has been flattened under heavy rollers. It is used by the food-processing industry in Europe and America, who turn it into breakfast cereals, snacks and confectionery, but if you want to buy some you will have to go to an Oriental shop; people in Asia use it as a cooking ingredient, either for stuffing poultry or for making sweets. For the latter purpose it may be dyed light green.

Ground rice (rice flour or **rice powder)** is used in making the sticky, coconutty cakes and sweets that in Asian countries are usually offered to guests who call around teatime. It is occasionally used to thicken sauces, but only in very small quantities. It makes excellent batter. It is no good for making leavened bread, because it contains no gluten and therefore cannot hold the little air bubbles produced by the action of the yeast. If you bake your own bread, however, try substituting rice flour for up to a quarter of the total weight of wheat flour. (You may find you need a little more water than usual.) The bread has an agreeably ricy flavour and the texture is a little more crumbly.

Rice powder is exceedingly fine rice flour, and in Britain is only obtainable in Chinese or other Asian shops. Some recipes in this book, e.g. Rempeyek (page 144), specify it because ordinary rice flour is not fine enough.

'Convenience' rices (described below) are perfectly satisfactory in every way – just as nutritious as 'ordinary' rice, comparable in flavour and texture, certainly quicker to cook. A short cooking time is, however, their only advantage, and you pay what I regard as an excessively high premium for it. Once you start to eat rice regularly, you may well prefer to buy regular white or brown rice. In any case, you'll want to try all the different varieties and flavours that are on the market, not limit yourself to the same old rice all the time.

Pre-cooked (or **instant**) **rice** has been cooked until ready to eat, then dried and packaged. All it needs is to be heated and rehydrated – the water must be put back into the grains. The main reasons for applying heat are to speed up the process, and to leave you with hot rice, which is usually more appetizing than cold. The Australians market a brand of pre-cooked rice which 'cooks in the fridge' overnight when it's soaked in

8

Rice fields: Japan

water. Don't try to do this with other brands of pre-cooked rice – different manufacturing processes have different results. Follow the instructions on the packet. If you have a cook-in-the-fridge rice and intend to rehydrate it in this way, use boiled water and put the rice in the fridge as directed – this is to prevent infection from *Bacillus cereus*, an organism that dies below 4°C/39°F and above 60°C/140°F. In between these temperatures, it multiplies rapidly and can give you a nasty tummy upset.

There are several processes for manufacturing **frozen cooked** or **part-cooked rice** and **easy-cook rice**, but they lead to more or less similar products. If you follow the instructions on the packet, you can't go wrong.

Microwaving rice: manufacturers tend to splash the word 'microwave' on their packs as though this meant that the contents could be cooked in the magic oven in a very short time. In fact, any kind of rice can be cooked in a microwave, but there is little, if any, advantage to be gained by it; see page 100.

3   *By taste or texture: sticky or glutinous rice (sometimes called waxy rice),
    sweet rice.*

No rice contains any gluten whatever, and certainly no wax; **'glutinous rice'** is either bad English or bad science, but the term is used so often that we have to live with it.

Stickiness comes from starch. There are two kinds of starch in a cereal grain: one is amylose, the other is amylopectin. **Sticky rice** is high in amylopectin. In every starch granule, molecules of both types exist together, and every molecule contains many thousands of units of glucose strung together in long chains. Amylopectin molecules have many branches, and are therefore relatively compact. Amylose starch molecules are long, single chains, and as a result bond easily with surrounding water molecules and with each other; this makes them useful for thickening sauces. It takes a much larger number of amylopectin molecules to achieve the same effect. When rice is cooked, amylose molecules make a gel, enclosing the water in their long strands. Amylopectin molecules tend to remain separate, producing the soft, rather sticky consistency of cooked glutinous rice.

This food chemistry is clearly and fascinatingly explained for us laypersons by Harold McGee in his book *On Food and Cooking*. As with length of grain, so with stickiness: there is a continuous spectrum, from hardly-sticky-at-all to very-sticky-indeed, and a particular rice variety may be anywhere between these extremes. All rices, however, have an amylose content somewhere between about 17 and 28 per cent, so amylopectin is always in a large majority, even in the non-stickiest Basmati.

Almost all the very sticky rices are short grain. Most of the world's rice-eaters regard non-sticky rice as their staple food and use the sticky stuff mainly for sweets, but a few – for example, in the mountains of Laos, Cambodia and Vietnam – eat sticky rice all the time. Most rice-based alcohol is brewed from sticky rice. But glutinous rice accounts for less than 2 per cent of the world's annual rice harvest.

Sweet rice is a descriptive name for short grain glutinous Japanese-style rice.

4   *By what the rice is intended for: pudding rice, curry rice.*

There's really very little to say about these; **pudding rice** is short grain, **curry rice** is long grain.

5   *By some generic name which confers prestige and may also suggest where
    the rice comes from: Basmati, Patna, Thai Fragrant, Arborio.*

These are not brand names, though their use may be controlled (there is even one Spanish rice labelled *denominación de origen*, like a wine). They are often, in effect, varieties; most Italian rices are labelled with their variety names, and there are over forty of them, so Italian shoppers have a real choice. But the British have no way of knowing which among the many varieties of Basmati they are buying. Our friend 'Jiggs' Inder Singh Kalra, a food writer and consultant in New Delhi, told us that the top Basmatis in India carry the brand names Lalkilah and Red Fort, but that the absolutely best grows in Rambirsingpura, a little village in the Indian state of Punjab. Why there? No one knows; it is the combination of soil, water, even air. **Basmati** is grown in North India, mainly in Punjab, and also across the border in Pakistan, in *the* Punjab. Other well-known north Indian rices which are exported include **Dehra Dun** and **Patna**, both long grain non-sticky types which are good for pilafs, curries and biryanis.

Our own favourite rice in Britain is **Thai Fragrant**, also called **Jasmine** rice. It is long grained, slightly sticky when cooked, wonderfully aromatic as the steam rises from it, and it remains delicious when cold or reheated.

6 *By a brand name.*

In a supermarket, this may be the only real difference between one rice and the next. The marketing director of a Singapore firm of rice importers said disarmingly that he and his competitors were all selling the same half-dozen or so grades of rice, and the only way to increase his market share was to keep up a barrage of brand advertising. This is understandable, I suppose; Singapore, which never grew much rice, has now abandoned rice cultivation completely, just as Hong Kong has done. I don't think it would be useful to try to list brand names here.

7 *By the way the rice has been grown: organic, biodynamic; wild rice.*

Organically grown rice has been grown without the use of any synthetic fertilizers, herbicides, or pesticides. This approach to agriculture is much to be desired and admired, but the end product is just ordinary rice at a rather high price. Even rarer is rice grown on **biodynamic** principles, which were formulated by Rudolf Steiner in the 1920s and summed up by sceptics in the one word 'witchcraft'. Biodynamic farmers and gardeners have achieved impressive results with all sorts of crops, including Australian rice. Biodynamically grown products are marketed under the brand names Biodyn and Demeter.

Wild rice is a grass, *Zizania aquatica* or *Z. palustris*, quite closely related to *Oryza* but growing wild only in the shallows of a few North American lakes, where it used to be picturesquely harvested by native American Chippewa in canoes. Probably it still is, but most of what reaches the market is grown in the same area in irrigated fields. So the long black shiny grains are not really rice, and not really wild either, but they look and taste good, for example in a Wild and White Rice Pilaf (page 313). Note that wild rice takes much longer to cook (page 102).

Storing Rice

Whenever you buy rice in London that has obviously been milled and bagged in its country of origin, the words 'new crop' are quite likely to be found somewhere on the bag, especially if it is a Japanese-style rice from California. Well, every crop is new at the time it's harvested. How long will rice keep?

Different people give you different answers, but a general consensus seems to be that paddy (rice in the husk) keeps perfectly well for at least a year. After that, it slowly begins to turn yellow and becomes a little more brittle; it is perfectly good to eat but it is no longer marketable except at very low prices and it would not be likely, when milled, to reach your local supermarket. The Bontoc people in northern Luzon, in the Philippines, traditionally stored rice in wooden granaries with thatched roofs, where it remained in perfect condition for up to ten years. Modern Bontoc use brick granaries with corrugated iron roofs, and the rice tastes bitter after three years.

For the miller and dealer, the moisture content of the grain is a key factor. When the rice is harvested, this is quite high, perhaps above 20 per cent. Drying brings this down to 14 per cent; if the moisture content is above 15 per cent, the grains will go mouldy in store. Thereafter, assuming the rice is kept in a dry place, the moisture level very slowly falls, and very old rice may need extra water in cooking because it will absorb so much. But it's safe to say that, once milled and polished, rice is good for at least three years, and thereafter deteriorates very slowly. Aromatic rice gradually loses its aroma.

Storing cooked rice is another matter. If you store cooked rice for more than a few hours, you should either refrigerate it or, before serving, reheat it to at least 60°C/140°F. This will frustrate the growth of *Bacillus cereus* (see page 9). Electric rice cookers that keep rice warm indefinitely always heat it above the 60/140-degree threshold, so they are perfectly safe; the only trouble is that, after two or three hours, they spoil the texture of the rice by repeatedly heating it up.

RICE IN YOUR DIET

In Australia and North America, rice is marketed as a healthy food, richer than perhaps we thought in vitamins and fibre. In particular, the appeal is to sports people because rice gives a controlled long-term supply of energy to the muscles. By contrast, people in many Asian countries are turning to bread, meat and dairy products because rice is thought to be fattening and they want to eat what Americans eat. I have based this section on a wide variety of sources, and have tried to be impartial and as scientific as possible. Is rice really good for you, and how good?

Nowadays, negative virtues are often highly rated, especially in food. To start with, therefore: rice does *not* contain any 'bad' cholesterol, gluten or extrinsic sugar. Extrinsic sugar is what makes teeth decay. Quite a lot of people are allergic to gluten, and therefore cannot eat bread, pasta, or other wheat products; allergy to rice is practically unknown. I shall say more about cholesterol under the heading of rice bran.

On the positive side, rice is very low in fats and salt; and it does contain appreciable amounts of the useful things discussed below.

Carbohydrate

The most important thing rice has to give us is starch. A grain of rice, whether brown or polished, is about 80 per cent starch. Food writers love to point out that milling and polishing remove the bran and outer layers, and with them much of the dietary fibre, vitamins and minerals. This is true, but it is no reason to avoid white rice, which is healthy and nutritious in its own right; its deficiencies are amply made up for by all the other foods in the average person's diet – even in the diets of poor people in developing countries. The current UK recommendation is that intrinsic and milk sugars (the sort that don't attack your teeth) and starch should account for 37 per cent of our daily calorie intake. Starch is good for us, and don't let anyone put you off it merely because somebody else has eaten too much and got fat.

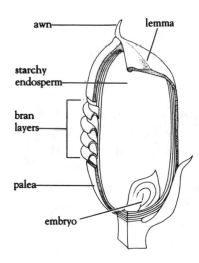

Rice grain

Rice is medium on calories: 120 grams/4 ounces/1 cup of cooked brown rice contains 270 kilocalories, equivalent to 1,130 kilojoules or three medium-sized potatoes. Most of this energy comes from carbohydrates – that is, from starch.

The rice grain is, of course, the fruit of the plant, the food store on which the seed depends while it germinates and until it can get its roots into nourishing soil. Baby plants, like babies of any species, need energy, which means they need sugar – or, to be precise, glucose. Sugar and starch are both made up of atoms of carbon, hydrogen and oxygen. A starch molecule is a long chain of glucose molecules, strung together to make a sugar polymer or polysaccharide. Breaking these down into glucose molecules is one of life's basic chemical processes.

There are (at any rate for our purposes) three kinds of starch in most starchy food plants. Two of them, amylose and amylopectin, are bundled together in layers to make starch granules. The cooking and eating qualities of the rice depend partly on the exact proportions of these (page 10). They absorb water easily and become mushy, so to keep them dry and safe every starch granule is encased in a layer of the third form of starch, cellulose. Cellulose is extremely tough. Only a few animal species have bacteria in their guts that can digest it; cows and other cud-chewing animals do, we humans certainly don't. We therefore cook our starchy foods, shattering the cellulose walls of the granules and releasing their contents.

The starches that we eat pass fairly quickly through the stomach and into the small intestine, where the complex polysaccharide molecules are broken down into relatively simple molecules of glucose. These pass through the wall of the intestine into the bloodstream, which takes them to the muscles and deposits them in the form of glycogen. Glycogen is muscle fuel. When it has been burnt as energy, the muscles need time to rebuild their stocks; it takes between 24 and 48 hours for them to do this from rice starch. In other words, rice delivers a steady medium-term supply of energy, not a quick fix. This is why rice is promoted as a stamina-giving food for athletes.

The fragments of cellulose from the shattered cell walls are much too tough to be broken down and absorbed in this way. They continue on down the digestive tract, to fulfil their natural function as dietary fibre – see below.

Vitamins

Rice contains no Vitamin A or C. It is, however, a source of several B group vitamins, and here there is quite a big difference between brown and white rice. This is not, by itself, a sufficient reason for choosing brown rice. You get plenty of vitamins in the rest of what you eat.

In what follows, 'an average helping' means 120 grams/4 ounces/1 cup of cooked rice. Please remember that percentages of daily requirements are very approximate, and that the quantity of each nutrient that your body needs depends on your sex, age, weight, and activity level. My figures are based on the requirements of a 40-year-old moderately active woman weighing around 55 kilos/120 pounds.

Thiamine (or thiamin; vitamin B1) is vital in the chemistry of turning nutrients into energy. In cereal grains, it lives very near the outside layer, which gets stripped off in milling. Lack of thiamine causes beri-beri; an average helping of brown rice contains about 30 per cent of your daily requirements, the same amount of white rice about 2 per cent or less.

Riboflavin (vitamin B2) is likewise concerned with transforming nutrients; deficiency affects the skin and eyes. A helping of white rice contains a little over 1 per cent of your daily needs, the same helping of brown rice about 2.5 per cent.

14

Niacin (or nicotinic acid; vitamin B3) is also vital to release of energy in the body; lack of it causes pellagra. A portion of brown rice gives you about 20 per cent of your daily needs, of white rice perhaps 10 per cent.

Vitamin B6, sometimes known as *pyridoxine*, indirectly helps to control amino acids in the body. A severe shortage of it would have bad effects on your central nervous system and make you more liable to infection. However, B6 is found in a wide range of foods and deficiency is rare. A helping of white rice gives you about 6 per cent of what you need in a day.

Folate (folic acid) is needed in the manufacture of DNA and haemoglobin. In conjunction with other vitamins it helps run the nervous system. Dark-leafed vegetables are our main source. A severe lack of it can cause anaemia. A portion of brown rice will supply 8 per cent of daily requirement, of white rice 2.5 per cent.

From the above, you will see that rice is a useful source of vitamins; any deficiencies are amply made up for by the vitamin-rich foods that we eat with it. Some processed rice, and rice products such as breakfast cereals, are fortified or vitamin-enriched. Full details will no doubt be prominently displayed on the packet.

Proteins

These, plus water, are what we are mostly made of. They are complex chemical products built up from amino acids – twenty of them in human beings, of which adults require eight in their diet, growing children one or two extra ones. The rest are produced inside our bodies. The proteins that we eat have to be broken down into their constituent amino acids, and used again in the construction of bone, muscle, blood, skin, and so on. Plant proteins are almost all incomplete – missing a few vital amino acids. Vegetarians can thrive, however, by eating plants whose proteins are complementary: they make up for each other's deficiencies. Many Javanese people who cannot afford much meat live on rice and soya beans (page 288), whose proteins complement each other very effectively.

Proteins fill the spaces between the starch granules of the rice grain, so white and brown rice contain roughly similar proportions of protein: 3.3 grams per 155 grams of cooked white rice, 3.9 grams for the same quantity of cooked brown rice. And 3.3 grams is about 6 per cent of a man's daily protein requirement, 7.3 per cent of a woman's; putting it another way, 120 grams/4 ounces/1 cup of cooked rice supplies about 9 per cent of the protein that an average adult needs.

Minerals

The presence of these in our bodies may be a distant memory of the primitive seas in which life first evolved on Earth; or maybe not. Anyway, they regulate the balance of water and other fluids in the body, moving molecules through cell walls as required. Rice contains small but useful amounts of phosphorus, zinc, selenium, copper and iodine, among others.

Fibre

Nutritionists often refer to this as NSP, which stands for non-starch polysaccharides. (A polysaccharide is a long chain of sugar molecules; most polysaccharides are starches.) Brown rice contains at least twice as much fibre as polished rice, and this is one of the reasons people choose it. Brown rice certainly has the edge here; but a 155 gram portion, even of cooked brown rice, will give you only 7 per cent of the fibre you need in a day. And a similar portion of cooked white rice gives you only about 1.5 per cent – mainly the fragments of cellulose that have been broken down in cooking.

It's worth remembering, however, that cooked rice, white or brown, also contains RS (resistant starch). This is made up of starch molecules that have been squeezed so tightly together in the saucepan that they act as fibres – they become indigestible and pass into the colon where they provide bulk and get waste matter moving, as fibre should. The Australians claim that cooked rice is one of the very best sources of RS, provided it is high in amylose – that is, a medium or long grain rice which remains firm when cooked. Nearly 80 per cent of the fibre to be found in boiled white rice is said to be resistant starch, which implies that boiled white rice contains much more fibre than was once thought.

Rice Bran

Every rice mill produces large quantities of brown, powdery bran – the outer seed-coat that is rubbed off between the rollers of the milling machines. Bran accounts for roughly 5 per cent of the weight of an unmilled grain, so the world's total 'rough rice' production of 480 million tonnes a year includes nearly 24 million tonnes of bran. Most of this is milled off and fed to animals, which are then eaten by people, so the bran is by no means wasted. But since the bran contains most of the vitamins and some excellent oils, we can eat it ourselves and save the animals the trouble.

One way to get your health-giving rice bran is to eat brown rice, but in some countries you can buy processed bran. The problem with unprocessed bran is that the oils in it go rancid very quickly after milling. The Australians have overcome this problem by gently heating the bran and extruding it to form grains, looking something like light-coloured instant coffee granules. The heat destroys the enzymes that make the oils rancid. A similar product is manufactured in the USA.

The Australians make large claims for their product, which you sprinkle over your breakfast or add to your cooking. It absorbs five times its own weight of water and is therefore a good thickener for casseroles, sauces and soups, if you think they need thickening. Two tablespoons of rice bran and two cups of brown rice each day, in addition to your normal diet, will give you all the fibre you need. As a laxative, it is as good as wheat bran fibre. But rice bran can also help to keep your heart healthy.

This is because bran and brown rice can lower your cholesterol level. Cholesterol is a fatty substance that our bodies need for the production of hormones and cell membranes. Being fatty, it won't dissolve in blood; so to get it into the bloodstream and transport it to where it is needed, it has to have a carrier, called a lipoprotein. There are two main types of lipoprotein: high-density (HDL) and low-density (LDL). HDL, which diet books often refer to as 'good' cholesterol, is broken down and excreted after use. LDL stays in the body, builds up on artery walls and can cause hardening of the arteries and heart disease. Rice bran, which contains no cholesterol whatever, has been shown to increase the proportion of HDLs to LDLs in the body.

The oils contained in rice bran are high in HDLs, mono- and polyunsaturates. According to the FAO and US Department of Health, Education, and Welfare, they contain up to 72 per cent unsaturated fatty acids against 19 per cent saturated. There is no evidence that they reduce the likelihood of cardiovascular disease, but it does appear that they reduce that of ischemic heart disease.

Rice bran oil itself is somewhat difficult and expensive to extract, but it is marketed in Japan and some other Far Eastern countries as a cooking oil.

RICE IN THE WORLD

All rice statistics are suspect. They change from one source to another, from one viewpoint to another. Governments massage their figures to present whatever case is being argued at the moment. The people who provide the figures have positions to keep up and protect. Different countries define their terms differently or count in different units. But published figures are still useful, as long as we regard them as no more than approximate.

The world produces each year about 480 million tonnes of paddy. Paddy, from the Malay-Indonesian word *padi,* is rice that is growing in the field, or rice that has been cut but not threshed, or cut and threshed but not husked. Paddy that has been threshed but is still in the husk is known in the trade as **rough rice**. This goes to be milled, either directly or after being parboiled (page 7). At the mill, the husk is first removed, revealing the seed-coat of bran. We now have **brown rice** or **whole rice**,

Major Rice-Growing Areas of the World

★ 1,000,000 tonnes per annum
● Less than 1,000,000 tonnes per annum

known to shippers as **cargo rice** because this is how it is usually exported. In the next stage of milling, the bran is rubbed away so that we reach the stage of **white rice**, and finally the grains are polished. What comes to market is therefore **polished** or **fully milled rice**, though the label on the bag will say 'white rice' or simply 'rice'.

Milling is obviously a fairly violent business, at least from the point of view of the rice grain. In a small mill, it may be a one-step pass between abrasive discs that remove husk and bran together; in a large modern establishment the rice will be conducted through a series of machines, passing from abrasives to rubber rollers and cones. A skilled operator must set his machines to ensure that as many as possible of the grains survive the experience intact as **head rice**. Some will always crack up; these **brokens** are worth much less. A proportion of the larger ones may be mixed back into the head rice, but the rest will be sold off cheap to the food processors or the brewers.

In its progress through the mill, each grain has lost up to a third of its weight as its husk and bran are removed; so the world paddy harvest of 480 million tonnes ends up as perhaps 350 million tonnes of rice ready to cook. The 24 million tonnes of bran go mostly for animal feed, and the 100 or so million tonnes of husks tend to hang around as a problem of a familiar kind: they are too good (and too bulky) to throw away but it's hard to find a sensible use for them.

Most of this huge crop is still cultivated and harvested by hand. Machines are becoming more important every year, but it is hard to say just what percentage of the rice-growing effort is mechanized. At one extreme – in Louisiana or New South Wales – germinated seed is sown from low-flying aircraft straight into fields levelled by laser-controlled scrapers. Inputs of water and fertilizer are carefully controlled, with computers playing their inevitable role. Massive combines are contracted to come on a certain date to cut and thresh the grain and bulk-load it into trucks that take it straight to the mill. In this way one man or one family, working hard, can run a farm of 300 hectares* and produce between 2,500 and 3,500 tonnes of paddy in a season.

At the other end of the scale, in India or the Philippines, a similar labour force may have half a hectare of land or less and be quite satisfied with a hard-won crop of 2 or 3 tonnes once, twice, or perhaps three times a year – enough for their own needs, and with some left over to take to market. Machines, where they are used, are often simple. On a typical farm in Thailand or Korea, you may find a farmer tending a hectare of his own land and renting a few more, often from relatives; he owns, or rents, small machines to prepare the soil, transplant seedlings, and cut the ripe grain. But in some rice areas, parts of Malaysia for example, the changeover is taking place from peasant farming to capital-intensive commercial growing, a development which may be inevitable and in the long run good, but which is bound to be a painful experience for a generation or two.

This shift from a subsistence crop to a commercial one, from a peasant economy to one

---

* 1 hectare = approximately 2½ acres.

obedient to the laws of the market, from tradition and ritual to the management of agribusiness – this is one of the huge shapes that loom out from the murky columns of statistics. Another is that of changes in people's tastes, so that rice-staple countries, as they get richer, are eating less rice per head of population, while rice-importing countries, or those where rice is a secondary crop, are eating more. A third mysterious shape, whose outline is especially difficult to make out in the activity of the international rice trade, is that of the changing world market, the big exporters and importers.

The latest figures we have from the International Rice Research Institute – which should at least be impartial – show that a little over 12 million tonnes of milled rice is traded between countries each year – less than 4 per cent of world production. (The corresponding figure for wheat is nearer 50 per cent.) Over half of all rice is still estimated to be consumed within 50 kilometres of the farm where it was grown. The big exporters are Thailand, 4.3 million tonnes, and the USA, 2.3 million tonnes. Yet in the world production league, Thailand ranks fifth and the USA twelfth. The fourth biggest importer in the world – China – is also the third biggest exporter; it sells high-grade rice to earn foreign exchange, and buys low-grade rice to feed its people. The Philippines, on a much smaller scale, does the same.

Malaysia, on the other hand, imports rice as a matter of policy; it can use national resources more profitably than in growing a staple food. The world's biggest rice importer is the European Community, followed by Brazil and Iran, both of which are quite substantial rice producers. Brazil grows almost as much rice as Japan; but between 1989 and 2020 it is forecast that Brazil's needs will double, whereas Japan's will fall by more than 20 per cent. Nigeria, whose population growth rate is among the fastest in Africa, is expected to treble its rice consumption in the same period. At the moment it depends on imports for almost one-third of the rice it eats.

Half-an-hour with the statistics can soon make the head spin. One bleak estimate stands out. In 1989 the world produced a surplus of about 18 million tonnes of rough rice, the bonus of the 'Green Revolution' of the 1960s. By 2020, the demand for rice will increase from 455 million tonnes to over 780 million tonnes. That is an increase of 60 per cent in thirty-one years, during which time the available rice land in the world will become significantly less.

What is this plant we are going to ask so much of?

THE RICE PLANT

Rice is grass, related to wheat, oats, barley and the other grass-descended cereals that trace their ancestry back to some genetic accident on the ancient continent of Gondwana perhaps 130 million years ago. In botanist's terms, it is a species, *sativa*, of the genus *Oryza*, of the family Gramineae, or Poaceae. There are plenty of other species of rice, about twenty-five altogether; one of these, *Oryza glaberrima*, has for a long time been a staple food in West Africa (though there, too, its place is being taken by *O. sativa*).

Some of these 'wild' species are gathered and eaten by the very poor, and samples of their seeds are carefully preserved in gene-banks because they may contain valuable genetic traits, but all of them are a potential nuisance to growers. They have the bad habits of their ancestors, habits that the farmer has spent generations breeding out of their cultivated cousins: they shatter, or drop their grain as soon as it is ripe, and they lodge, or fall over and lie in the mud. They lurk on the edges of fields as wild plants – 'volunteer' rice, the old American farmers used to call them – and release their pollen just when the cultivated rice is flowering. As a result, the farmer's carefully selected seed gets crossed with bad blood from the roadside.

Cultivated rice, then, is a single species, but its subspecies and varieties are almost endless. Top botanists met at Valencia in 1914 to try and agree on their classification, but their successors are still arguing. Even the major subdivisions are fuzzy. Many of the books say that *O. sativa* varieties fall into two groups: indica and japonica. These were defined and named by a Japanese scientist in 1928, but the Chinese had for centuries called them *xian* and *geng* respectively. Indica rices are long grained and not sticky. Japonica are short grained and show varying degrees of stickiness. The differences reflect the areas where these groups originated: indicas in India, japonicas not in Japan but at any rate in the Far East.

This classification doesn't really account for all the South-East Asian rices that are long grained and rather sticky, so there is now a third group for them, called javanica because they may have originated in Java.

Rice plant

Rice obviously has a lot in common with the other cereal food crops. It is more interesting, however, to look at its differences. Its flowering heads are long, many-branched and very flexible, so that under the weight of the mature grains they bend over and hang head down, as if to show you how heavy and rich they are. Rice grains, unlike wheat but like barley and oats, are enclosed in hard protective husks which can only be broken open and removed by force. Rice needs high temperatures and long hours of sunshine to flourish – compared, at any rate, with most other cereals. In origin, however, it is not a tropical plant and man has had to spend thousands of years breeding varieties that will tolerate equatorial conditions.

The one really obvious thing about rice is that it needs lots of water. It is not an aquatic plant, and must keep its head above the surface; its roots breathe through microscopically narrow tubes that run the whole length of the stem, taking in air and releasing carbon dioxide and methane to the world outside. Rice will tolerate a few days' total immersion without coming to any harm; seedlings can put up with longer.

Less well known, but more remarkable, is the range of conditions and environments that the different varieties of rice can get accustomed to. Upland rices grow in forest clearings or on unterraced hillsides, asking only for generous rainfall. Swamp or deepwater rices are happy in flood conditions near river mouths, able to grow 10–15 centimetres a day to keep pace with the rising water level. Some rices like salty ground, though most don't. Some will tolerate the chill of high mountains, up to 3,000 metres in the Himalayas, or the uncertain weather of a Czech or Russian summer. Some are indifferent to the length of the daylight hours, others measure them so precisely that they can tell the exact date on which to begin flowering in order to give the grain time to mature before summer ends. Traditional rice varieties reach maturity in anything from 140 to 240 days; some modern ones mature in 90 days, allowing a quick-moving farmer to grow two, three, or even four crops a year.

That is another astonishing characteristic of irrigated rice. You can grow it in the same field, year after year, indefinitely – some rice fields are believed to have been continuously cropped for 2,000 years or more. Some have been diligently manured and composted by their owners, but not all. Naturally, without some sort of fertilizer the yield soon starts to drop, but it settles down at a fairly low level and then keeps going, apparently for ever. Even the most prolific new high-yield varieties, although they need fertilizer if they are to work miracles, can produce a fair harvest without it.

The Flooded Field

But why all that water? An Italian writer calls it *la coperta termica*, a kind of thermal blanket which insulates the crop against excessive heat and cold. Other people say that the water is there mainly to drown the weeds. These may be coincidental advantages, but they don't explain why rice evolved as a water-loving species of a non-water-dwelling genus. From transplanting to harvest, a typical field needs between 1 and 2 metres depth of it – not all at once, of course; on any one day, the water is likely to be between 5 and 50 centimetres deep. Each kilogram of rice has been irrigated by anything from 3,000 to 10,000 litres of water.

Water brings nutrients to rice plants, but rice doesn't depend on these. A healthy old-fashioned rice field has been compared to an aquarium, in which a complex ecological system maintains a natural balance. But this can really only be true at the level of bacteria and suchlike micro-organisms, because the field is never flooded for more than a few weeks, or months at most. You will find ducks, frogs, fish, shellfish and other creatures in it, but they are just passing through, not permanent residents.

Farmers realized many centuries ago that irrigated or flooded rice would support a much larger population than upland rice ever could, but that once they had chosen to live by it they could not turn back. Their success, ever since that moment, has been demonstrated by their understanding and use of water. Rice will grow perfectly well in still or even stagnant water, but efficient farmers who have adequate supplies will change the water at intervals, and in many areas the water is constantly on the move from one field to the next one lower down. It is an old saying that the best man to put in charge of the local water system is the one whose fields are at the bottom of the hill.

The best water is fresh from the river, as long as it is not too cold, and it should be carrying particles of clay and organic matter, frog spawn and tadpoles, a fish from time to time to provide a farmer's family with some extra protein. Stagnant water is better than none, but water that stands in the field for too long may heat up and damage young plants if their leaves are too small to shade the surface, and it may allow malarial mosquitoes to breed. Rice fields were for many years forbidden near Spanish and Italian cities, and the tidal swamps of South Carolina were notorious.

Approaching Harvest

As the rice seedling gets a grip on life and consumes the last of its starchy endosperm, it starts to produce leaves and tillers – the stems that will flower and bear fruit. Tillers grow from the main stem, but secondary and even tertiary tillers may grow from these primary ones. The tendency in the past twenty or thirty years has been to breed for a large number of tillers, producing a bushy plant that bears a good weight of grain. This plant type is now going a little out of fashion, and we shall probably see leaner and meaner rice plants in future, planted much closer together so that the total yield per square metre is higher. The narrow green spears of leaves grow from the main stem and tillers, each leaf wrapping its lower part tightly around its stem, then breaking free at a node or junction. At the top of the main stem the plant tops out with a narrow pennon of green, the blade of the flag leaf. On every lower stem a similar flag, sharp and erect, appears. A dense mat of hairy roots develops on the surface of the soil to extract additional oxygen from the water.

About two months after sowing, the stem-tops begin to develop their flowering heads, the panicles. By this time the rice field is a dense mass of green, the plants 50–60 centimetres tall, the space under their canopy a closed environment that creates its own micro-climate; air trapped under the leaves amasses heat radiated from the water, and a fresh early morning temperature of 9–10°C above a rice field may conceal a sultry 16–18°C near the water's surface. This warm blanket of air can help plants through an unseasonably cool night just at the critical moment of flowering, for florets that develop outside their temperature range, too hot or too cold, are likely to be sterile.

The panicles branch and branch again into delicate spikelets, on each of which a flower-bud develops. When temperature and humidity are exactly right, usually around mid-morning, the flowers, green and tiny, open suddenly, but not all at once. The seventy or so flowers on a single panicle may take up to a week to pop, the ones nearest the panicle-tips going first, those nearest the main stem sometimes waiting too long and never opening at all. Each flower stays open for between ten minutes and two hours, in the hottest part of the day. At this time, if you are downwind of a field of fine rice, you will be aware of a perfume of most subtle and refined sweetness, a breath of heaven that you may need to train yourself at first to detect; you will meet it again in the kitchen, when the rice is cooking. I think it was this perfume that put the first successful rice farmers in mind of the feminine spirits of rice. When they caught it in their nostrils they knew that, barring accidents or the whims of fate, their crop was assured.

As soon as a rice flower springs open, its male anthers are thrust out into the sunlight and its pollen dries and falls, or is blown away. At least a grain or two, with luck, will fall on the stigma which is waiting just below, or on the stigma of a neighbouring flower. Soon the flower shuts again, and the ovary at its base starts to develop into the rice seed,

Harvesting with *ani-ani*, Indonesia: see page 77

accumulating starch from the leaves and stem. The bowl-shaped lemma and palea, that were the green petals of the flower, become fibrous and confine the starch under some pressure; at first soft and doughy, the starchy endosperm gradually dries and hardens. If it fails to plump out the available space fully, which may happen in unusually warm weather, little air-bubbles will be left in the grain which will make it, as rice millers say, 'chalky'. Around the starch the inner skin of bran is built up; when the seed germinates, it will feed on the starchy granules that lie nearest it, the proteins between these granules, and the vitamins and minerals of the bran.

As harvest approaches, the plant begins to dry out and the green to become tawny – though combine harvesting, which works best when the moisture content of the rice is still high, often starts before this stage is reached. It makes no difference; the plant's work is done. The lemma and palea, old now, harden as the grain ripens and become the husk. From the tip of the lemma a single thin spike grows, the awn: sometimes so short as to be hardly visible, but in some rice varieties long and yellow like the beard on a grain of barley.

A rice field after harvest is a rather melancholy sight. The stubble is not golden and even, as it is after the wheat harvest, but stands in little clumps of rotting straw above the fast-drying mud of the drained field. If the field has been combined and the stubble is long and reasonably dry, fire may be set to it and clouds of black smoke go billowing away just as, until recently, they did in the English countryside in late August. In some parts of the world the farmer may leave the plants in the ground and let them shoot again next season, so that he gets a second crop, sometimes a third, here and there even a fourth, with very little extra investment beyond, perhaps, a dressing of nitrogen. These are called ratoon crops; with each one the yield diminishes, but ratooning is not altogether a thing of the past, even in the United States. Modern fast-growing varieties actually encourage it. In southern Louisiana, farmers will take a ratoon crop if the summer has been good and their main crop, sown in early April, is harvested by 10 July. Whereas 300 kilometres to the north, the growing season is just never quite long enough to do this, so the fields are left to the crawfish, that live most of the year underground. Then, in January, the fields are flooded again, the crawfish come up to swim, and are trapped and sent to market to play leading roles in Cajun cuisine.

Otherwise, everything is just ploughed under.

THE CROP

Harvest time comes and goes; the rice is cut and gathered in. Now the paddy is to be threshed, dried and milled, and in these processes it may be bought and sold more than once and may travel across oceans; or it may go no farther than the storeroom of the family who grew it.

The old-fashioned way to thresh rice or most other grains is to grab a handful of the cut stems, raise them above your head and bring them down forcefully on something hard. In Bali, a woman fills a bamboo sieve with what her husband has just threshed. Standing sideways to the wind, she raises the sieve gracefully above her head and shakes it so that the grains fall at her feet and the straw, if it is not trapped in the sieve, blows away.

Rice which is for the farmer's own use then goes into the family storehouse. Rice barns are a beguiling subject of study. They are holy places, where the rice spirit lives until it is time for the next sowing or the next harvest, so they must be fit dwellings for a supernatural being. They are often beautifully carved and decorated, like the Toraja rice barn that was built for the Museum of Mankind in London a few years ago. They may denote their owner's rank, as the three traditional types of rice barn did on the island of Lombok, next door to Bali. There are almost always strict rules about who may enter them to take rice for the family, and how this is to be done. In parts of Indonesia, for example, only a woman may go into the barn, and only once a day. If unexpected guests arrive, she must turn the ladder over so that the spirit inside will not

Old Japanese rice barn

know she has invaded the privacy of the rice twice on the same day.

But the rice that the farmer sells comes, one way or another, to the mill, while the straw goes for animal feed, composting, growing paddy-straw mushrooms, making bricks or coarse paper, or still, in a few places, weaving straw sandals and ropes. Milling rice involves two processes: first, the husk has to be removed, then the bran. The old way is to pound the rice by hand, with a heavy wooden pestle and a mortar of wood or stone. Rice was milled like this in some parts of the United States until the middle of the nineteenth century, and it still is today in remote parts of many Asian countries. It fetches good prices in local markets, because a little of the bran is left on the grain and this improves the flavour and the nutritional value.

But hand-pounding will survive only as a fad or a tourist attraction. In Kalimantan (Indonesian Borneo) we visited an area which was recently settled by migrant farmers from Java. They had set up a tiny but very noisy mill in a wooden shed. It was driven by a diesel engine and could polish 10 kilos of rice an hour, 1 kilo of which went to the miller as his fee. In Asia, thousands of small mills like this one serve local needs; they are obviously not commercial, but they produce enough polished rice for a small community.

Commercial mills are as various as the people who run them. Some are located close to the area of production, others near the retail market. Asian and American rice is usually imported into Europe as unmilled 'cargo rice', because EC tariffs on this are much lower than on polished rice. (This is another reason why premium rices like Thai Fragrant, milled in Thailand, or Kokuho Rose, milled in California, are expensive in Britain.) There are a number of millers in the UK, such as Joseph Heap in Liverpool and Tilda in Essex, but by far the largest European rice mills are in the Netherlands; their sheer size, with their advanced technology and commanding market share, makes a challenge from new mills anywhere else in the EC seem unlikely at the moment.

Modern large-scale milling is a highly skilled job, and the skills depend at least as much on experience as they do on book learning. In a modern mill, the machinery is controlled from a massive console of lights and switches that would not look out of place in a power station. We visited one in Spain that looked as if it could handle any situation, though a small crucifix had prudently been sellotaped just above the rows of blinking lights. Although the miller (or his customer) is aiming at a standardized product, his raw material comes in batches and is unpredictable in grain size, quality and moisture content. When he has run all his laboratory tests on samples, he must still make his final decisions by what his eyes and long-practised instinct tell him, rubbing the grains in the palm of his hand, biting into a few, or, with milled grains, pushing them about on a standard blue inspection table (blue highlights any variation in whiteness). In particular, the exact setting of machines is vital. An error of judgement means more broken grains, and these are worth far less than whole or 'head' rice. A miller in Amritsar told me that top-quality Basmati, 100 per cent whole grains, fetched 30 to 36 rupees a kilo; brokens were worth 5 rupees.

28

FARMERS, TRADERS, SCIENTISTS

The Small Agribusinessman

The farmer's first decision is which seeds he will sow. The freedom to choose may be limited by circumstance and sometimes by the authorities: I don't recall ever seeing, in any declaration of human rights, any affirmation of the farmer's freedom to grow whatever crops he wants to. I have heard that Balinese farmers are 'discouraged' from growing favourite traditional rices because of their low yields, so they grow them in secret in small fields hidden in valleys. There certainly is commercial pressure on farmers to grow a standard crop, especially if it is going to be sold abroad.

On the other hand, if every farmer in a neighbourhood grows the same variety, the whole crop may be at risk if its weak point is found by a pest or freak weather conditions. A Malaysian government official told me that his organization issues a list of approved varieties and advises farmers to grow different ones in adjoining fields; but as long as they keep to the approved list it cannot prevent them all growing the same variety if they wish to. Because today's farmer does not entirely trust his own

Rice mill: Amritsar

judgement in the matter of these new miracle rices, he and his neighbours all plant whatever is fashionable that season.

Another snag of a monoculture is that, unless planting dates are staggered by careful organization, everyone will want to harvest his rice at the same time and all the workers (or all the machines) in the neighbourhood won't be able to cope. In the rich rice fields of West Malaysia, planting schedules are advertised on notice boards in each village, and a farmer who fails to observe them endangers everyone's harvest timetable; he may find that his supply of free water or subsidized fertilizer is cut off.

Lucien Hanks, an American researcher, wrote an excellent book with the rather grandiose title *Rice and Man*. In fact it is a detailed study of a small village of rice farmers about 20 kilometres outside Bangkok (I suspect that by now the village has been totally absorbed within the city limits). He shows how, in less than 120 years, the land was brought into cultivation for rainfed rice; then irrigated, so that two crops a year could be taken; but then, as the incentive to grow rice diminished after the First World War, much of the land returned to a rainfed system and one crop of rice a year.

Marking the field for transplanting: Lombok

Farmers, in other words, adapt to the demands of the market, if they are growing for the market.

When I visited an area not far from Hanks's village about twenty years after him, I found that farmers had given up transplanting and were sowing seed directly on to the fields – broadcasting it by hand, just as we see European farmers doing in medieval illuminated manuscripts. But the farmers I talked to were getting two harvests a year; the modern varieties they grow now mature so fast that there is no need to gain extra time by sowing in nurseries, and chemical weedkillers do away with the need to give seedlings a head start over weeds.

One problem with broadcasting is that the seeds are bound to be unevenly scattered, though with so much practice the Thai farmers are very skilful. It also makes it impossible to weed between rows, but this can be overcome by reverting to transplanting for a season or two if weeds start to get the upper hand. The Australians and Americans broadcast their seed, where the ground is soft enough, from low-flying aircraft. However you sow, seeds have to be soaked overnight and then left damp for two days so that they germinate and are ready to put down roots the moment they find themselves on soft warm mud. The exception to this is when the soil is hard, as it is in the forest-clad hills of many Asian countries, where the seed is dibbled by a line of men with pointed sticks, or in Arkansas, which has the largest rice acreage of the United States, where rice is sown with a drill, as wheat is.

As we have seen, irrigated rice fields do not have to be fertilized; if they are well managed their fertility will remain at a fixed, fairly low level indefinitely. But farmers have been giving them a helping hand for centuries, ploughing in the rice stubble after harvest (often after burning it), pushing weeds under the mud to rot them, composting straw and dung, spreading marl or lime or good black mud brought from a nearby stream-bed, turning their animals into the fields after harvest to manure the ground, or – especially around old Chinese cities – carting and spreading human waste. In the Philippines and elsewhere, farmers sow quick-growing plants like *Sesbania* as 'green manure'; these plants, rich in nitrogen, are ploughed back into the soil they have grown from.

Even rice husks are used as fertilizer. The farmer first spreads them over his chicken run, then carts them off to the fields a few months later, enriched with chicken droppings. Unfortunately this gets rid of only a little of the vast quantity of rice husks that are threshed off the grain each year. Another small percentage is burnt and the ash scattered on the soil.

Chemical fertilizers are more scientific, more precise, more productive than all of these, and of course more complex in their effects. They are expensive, their prices fluctuate unpredictably, they are ecologically unsound if used ignorantly or carelessly, they make farmers dependent on them, they encourage the production of surpluses, they may be another way in which rich countries, or multinational companies, exploit poor countries. Worst of all, they break the chain by which flooded rice land renews –

however inadequately – its natural fertility; once you have started using chemicals, it is difficult to stop. The counts against them are formidable, but we cannot do without them now and certainly won't be able to in the future.

Herbicides, pesticides and fungicides are a quite different problem. The old-time farmer expected to see a large fraction of his crop – often half, sometimes all – taken by pests and disease; there was not much he could do about it, except join organized rat-hunts with his neighbours, or rig up bells and clappers, worked by small children pulling strings, to scare the birds as harvest-time approached.

It is often the most successful farmers who use chemicals most sparingly, because they have been trained to apply them scientifically. In Australia, the system of rotating crops makes fertilizer almost unnecessary, and the isolation of their rice-growing areas protects them from disease and pests. The key to higher yields is not more money to subsidize synthetic products, but better education for farmers.

National rice research institutes as well as international bodies consider such extension services to be just as important as their scientific work. One organization that proclaims itself non-political is the International Rice Research Institute. It is also the body that everyone seems to have heard of, partly, perhaps, because it has a pleasing and memorable acronym: IRRI. IRRI's headquarters are at Los Baños, 65 kilometres south of Manila. We spent ten days there, talking to some of the world's leading rice experts and going on long car rides into the hills of northern and central Luzon to look at IRRI projects.

IRRI field office: Carosucan

32

One of these was in a village in Pangasinan province, where farmers' wives were growing paddy-straw mushrooms. IRRI grinds no ideological axes, but it is concerned about the role of women in rice-farming – more generally, about the lives of women in Third World economies. In most South-East Asian countries women do about 40 per cent of the farm work, including, as a rule, all the transplanting and harvesting and often the threshing as well. (In India, the women do anything up to 80 per cent.)

We were introduced to the women of Carosucan village, and we talked away the afternoon in the little yard outside the project office, laughing at stories of grandiose outsiders' projects that had come to nothing. All these flat lands, a few kilometres inland from the sea, had been irrigated at one time by a system of electric pumps; on our evening walk we saw the empty concrete channels and cisterns, dry for years because after the 1974 oil shock electricity cost more than the second rice crop was worth. There was no electricity in the village itself. 'Before the elections, people from the government come and put up poles and tell us the electricity will come. After the elections, they send a truck round to take the poles away again.' More hilarity.

The Terraces of Banaue

Our second trip was farther, right up into the mountains where the Ifugao people still maintain and cultivate their famous terraces that rise like stairways up almost vertical hillsides. We left Los Baños soon after sunrise, passed through the smoggy heart of Manila, apoplectic with rush-hour traffic, and drove northwards through the endless flat lands of Nueva Ecija. North of San José, the hills that had rested all morning on the horizon, seeming to laugh at us by never coming any nearer, suddenly closed in and we were driving up a long river valley. All the traffic was using the same side of the road, regardless of which way it was going.

'These are timber trucks,' our driver explained. 'When they go north, they're empty – so the road surface is still good. When they come back, they're carrying big trunks of trees, many tonnes. The road couldn't take it. You see the big holes now on that side.' It was soon clear that not only the road had suffered the activities of the timber men. The hillsides above us were almost completely bare of trees. 'Twenty-five years ago,' he said, 'I remember all these hills covered in big trees – in my lifetime, everything has gone.' The valley was like a textbook example of the reasons why a tropical forest should not be cut down. The slopes were eroded, the river choked with soil brought down by the rains. The farmers in the plain were paying for the loggers' greed. The river had once given them two rice harvests a year. Now, without irrigation, they only get one.

We reached Banaue at dusk. The next morning the sun went up like a rocket into the clear air and filled the valley with an almost tangibly cold, liquid light. We were

33

introduced to the young research officer in charge of the IRRI cold tolerance station. We were about 2,000 metres above sea level, and special varieties of rice are needed to survive the cool nights, though it never freezes here. The IRRI office was in a small room overlooking a pocket of green rice shoots, which were surrounded by a rather flimsy fence. The fence was supposed to keep out the rats, which are among the rice farmer's oldest and deadliest enemies.

A plaque by the roadside drew our attention, as if it needed to be drawn, to the wonders of the Banaue terraces: 2,000 years old, the eighth wonder of the world . . . All this landscape is indeed exceedingly fine. I am glad that the Ifugao treasure their forest as well as their fields, and the high slopes are still tree-covered. The skills of building and repairing earthworks survive strongly too, so the terraces themselves and their watercourses are in good condition.

But are they really as old as the plaque and the guidebooks want you to believe? If they were built 2,000 years ago, why did early Spanish explorers, who came through here in the 1660s and reported everything they saw in meticulous detail, not mention them?

Still more enigmatic is the problem of why anyone went to so much trouble. The

Rice terraces: Banaue

region is not excessively overpopulated (as most areas with terraced rice fields are); there was never any compelling pressure on the Ifugao to live in this fatiguing way. True, they may have wanted irrigated terraces originally to grow taro rather than rice. Taro, a rather unappetizing root, requires much more land to feed the same number of people. Or the Ifugao may once have been farmers in the plains, and have been driven into the hills by invaders . . . But no explanation clears up all the problems neatly. The terraces exist, they are there, they work and they are beautiful, whatever complex reasons drove men and women to make them.

A Lunch-box on the Shinkansen

Back in the IRRI Guesthouse we were making all the contacts we could with other visiting foreigners, particularly from countries where we knew we were going but didn't know many people. Two Japanese men came into breakfast one morning, and expressed polite interest in our research project. There was the obligatory exchange of name cards, and they suggested we might visit their institute when we came to Japan the following month.

Lunch-box on a Japanese train

Japanese people's attitude to rice goes a long way towards explaining their government's rigid protection of Japanese farmers. The national origin-myth binds the founding of Japan closely to the gift from heaven of the secrets of rice cultivation; the first Emperor was also the first rice farmer. There is perhaps no country, certainly no techno-economic world power, that still holds rice in such mystical esteem. At the same time, because Japanese parliamentary constituencies retain more or less the boundaries they were given in 1946, the declining rural population continues to return more members to the Diet than the hugely swollen urban areas. Japanese politicians therefore have every reason to treat rice farmers with great respect, to keep farming subsidies high and resolutely to ban all rice imports.

Japanese housewives express their feelings about rice by consistently buying the best quality available, regardless of price. However deep the recession in the West, everywhere we went in Asia we found an unshakeable confidence that the boom would continue.

Over almost every great Asian city hangs a smog that speaks of success as surely as the smoke over Bradford or Sheffield did 150 years ago. They all look to Japan as the power that first set in motion this Pacific-rim commercial flywheel. But we found people in Japan who were less confident than we expected.

'In the next ten years, maybe the Japanese economy will go like *that*,' said one, moving his hand like an aeroplane across his body till it nose-dived over the arm of his chair. 'We say we have to feed ourselves, but the farmers are going into the cities. Their land is not used, or people grow only vegetables.' He said that in the whole of Japan about 30 per cent of rice land had been lost. 'Also, subsidies are less, so it is not so attractive now to be a part-time farmer. Land is more and more expensive in the cities, demand for land is less in the countryside. In a few years, land values everywhere can collapse. Then our economy will be in trouble.'

Farms here are small, like rice farms almost everywhere. Japanese law, when a landowner dies, divides the property among all the children, and if some of them want to relinquish their shares to the one who actually wants to farm the land, they pay a tax for doing so. Traditional attitudes to rice do not extend to the selection of seed; all the rice grown in Japan today is from 'new' varieties, carefully tailored to suit local conditions and micro-climates. The Japanese government is determined to increase rice consumption, which is already down to about 65 kilos per person per year and which even IRRI predicts will fall further. In the Plant Breeding Laboratories we were shown the complex forms on which every new variety is assessed for over forty different characteristics, including its cooking quality. Much of the assessment is done by instruments, but we asked the head of the department how his team filled in the last part of the form, which was about the taste of the rice. 'Oh, we just sit around the table in the lab and eat some,' he said. We found this reassuring.

I asked one of the senior scientists who he thought ought to organize the rice-breeding programme. 'That's simple,' he said, 'because about 100 per cent is

36

decided by the government.' The Japanese government was the first in Asia to plunge into scientific plant-breeding, before the twentieth century had even started. However, a new variety takes up to ten years to perfect, test and release for general use, even using the latest hybridization techniques or laboratory tissue cultures. Before a new rice can be registered all sorts of people must accept it: government departments, local bodies, farmers' representatives. 'There's room for local government politics,' he said tactfully. He thought rice would go on being the staple food of Japan for a long time to come, 'but it's a problem for agriculture because the number of farmers is rapidly decreasing. Maybe in five or ten years there will be drastic change.' Yet he said it is virtually impossible for anyone who is not a rice farmer already to acquire land for growing rice, just as it is in the USA.

We decided to go to Tokyo on the express train rather than the *shinkansen*; Japanese expresses often go quite slowly and you can see much more than you can at 200 kilometres an hour. The line from Joetsu winds its way between the mountain vertebrae of Honshu, through a landscape in which the wild and the intensively cultivated are often separated by no more than a wire fence. The forests we passed through seemed to be doing their job of holding the soil to the mountain sides, but even these, according to our friend in the Experiment Station, had problems. All the old trees, the primary forest, had been cut down for timber during the war, and though they had been replanted the forests had not been properly managed; there was not enough skilled labour to thin out the trees as they grew. So now everything was growing up together, and overcrowded trees were becoming stunted and diseased.

We could see for ourselves the truth of what he had said about arable land: rice fields going out of use, some abandoned, others filled with cabbages. In Taipei a week or two earlier we had been told how the Taiwan government was tackling the problem of falling rice consumption: 'through the children's lunch-boxes', according to an official of the Council of Agriculture. A publicity campaign had been launched to encourage mothers to send their offspring to school with traditional packed lunches instead of giving them money for hamburgers.

Much the same has happened in Japan. You can only do this sort of thing successfully, of course, if the art of the lunch-box has never been allowed to die out, and on the express from Kyoto we had already seen and tasted how exquisitely even a cheap lunch for travellers is put together. In fact it was so beautiful that we had to photograph it before we could bear to mess it up by eating it: sushi (with the seaweed wrappers in a separate pack, so they would remain crisp), tempura (prawns and vegetables), rice, pickles (daikon radish, lotus root and others) and pieces of fruit as dessert.

Ricebowls of West Malaysia

Malaysia and Japan have some of the same problems where rice is concerned, though they have come up with very different solutions. In both, the government is fully involved in planning, allocating resources, managing the rice economy with subsidies. Both look after their farmers well, and in both countries the farmers are rewarding this attention by leaving the land more or less as fast as they can go. The official Malaysian attitude, however, is that the country should not attempt to be self-sufficient in food; its industries will make it rich enough to import up to half the rice it needs (at the moment the figure is about 40 per cent).

The richest Malaysian rice bowl is in the north-west of the peninsula, up towards the Thai border, in the states of Kedah and Perlis. Here you see the classic rice landscape: an ocean of grain, stretching to the horizon, rippling like lime-green waves in the breeze. You would say that rice had been grown in Kedah since the dawn of time. In fact the oldest of these fields dates from the late seventeenth century – about the same time that the first rice was being grown in South Carolina.

Nearly 100,000 hectares are irrigated by water from the Muda river, administered by MADA, the Muda Agricultural Development Authority. Farmers, too, are closely controlled: they plant varieties chosen from an official list, following exactly a fixed timetable. Anyone who steps out of line disorganizes everyone else. This close synchronization used to mean that at transplanting or harvest-time there were too few

Combining in West Malaysia

38

people to do the work, and labourers had to be hired; but as machines have taken over, opportunities for the rural poor to find casual employment have become fewer and fewer.

In some areas, the government has set up rice 'estates', grouping small farmers together so that they can afford machines and chemicals. One wonders: are peasants becoming government agents? Rice growers in Kedah get free water for their fields, in return for which they surrender most of their freedom to make management decisions, but they still own their land. A day or two earlier we had been in the headquarters of MARDI, the Malaysian Agricultural Research and Development Institute. The people we talked to said that without 'estatization', the consolidation of small farms, the land would be abandoned or would be farmed by foreign labour. 'So the idea came out, why didn't the government organize a sort of estate where the farmers are workers, paid for their labour, and are also paid for the yield of their plots? So they can pay for mechanical planting and harvesting.'

My question about government agents was gracefully sidestepped. 'The government help the farmers as much as they can because the farmers are mostly poor, and now they are at least above the poverty line.' This means a family income of $375

Malaysian a month (about £95 or US$145). To achieve this, the family needs about 4.5 hectares of rice land, up to three or four times the size of the average property. So the farmer must rent from neighbours or relatives who have moved to the city. This is becoming a common pattern in most Asian rice-growing countries, but the resulting farms are still not big enough to be really profitable. 'It's hard of course for them to become rich like they are in Australia.'

I could imagine what reception this remark would get in New South Wales, where we had seen an isolated group of rice-farming families – isolated geographically and economically – putting up a dogged and successful fight for survival. We asked Tony Blakeney, a cereal chemist at the Yanco Agricultural Institute, what made the difference between a good and a not-so-good farmer. 'Management decisions,' he said without hesitation. 'The man who should have ordered his seed for this week but leaves it till next week and doesn't sow it till the week after – he's the fellow who gets 7 tonnes.' Seven tonnes of paddy from each hectare is regarded as an indifferent harvest in New South Wales; some farmers get 12 or 13.

'A Crop of Extraordinary Fickleness'

The story of rice in New South Wales looks quite logical with hindsight, but must have seemed bizarre to those who watched it unfolding. The rice-growing area is the Riverina – the broad, shallow valleys of the Murrumbidgee and Murray rivers, where the land is almost as flat and as green as a billiard table. John Oxley, Government Surveyor, passed through here in 1817 and wrote: 'I am the first white man to see it and I will undoubtedly be the last. There is a uniformity in the barren desolation of this country that wearies one more than I am able to express . . .' By 1900, however, there were sheep stations in the area, drawing water from the Murrumbidgee, whose name means 'never-failing water'; the rivers are fed all year round from the Snowy Mountains. A Scottish farmer saw the potential of an irrigation system that would stop the rivers running to waste, and the state government, which was keen to encourage people to move inland from the coast, set the project going.

By 1913 there were 3,000 kilometres of canals, and settlers began to take up the new land. They were supposed to buy water from the project, thereby enabling the state of New South Wales to pay off the loans it had raised to meet the development costs. But they all grew fruit, which took up much less water than the state needed to sell, though for years the fruit growers and the local cannery made a fair living, and indeed still do.

The possibility of rice seems to have occurred to landowners and the state government fairly early on, but no one had the knowledge or skills to grow rice even in ideal conditions, and the Riverina was far from ideal. One heroic figure who may have known something about rice landed in Melbourne in 1905: Jo Takasuka. His father had been a chef with an aristocratic Japanese family who had awarded him the rank of samurai. Jo studied economics in Japan and the United States, and for a while was a member of the Japanese House of Representatives. His wife was the daughter of a judge. Jo was 40 years old when he brought his family to Australia. He could have had a comfortable life at home in Matsuyama. Instead, he dedicated the remainder of his life, and all the family's resources, to trying to grow rice in the Murray river valley, on the Victoria side of the border with New South Wales.

In an early report to the state government, he made no bones about the difficulties: 'rice culture is very difficult and requires special knowledge . . . In my native country the cultivation is in the hands of farmers who for generations have followed this culture for their living. It is a crop of extraordinary fickleness.' He struggled against flood, drought, frost, heatwave, pests, diseases, government hostility and apathy, the racism of those days, and of course the uncertain attention of the rice goddess. At the end he achieved a modest livelihood and the respect and affection of his neighbours. One year, he sold a few bags of seed rice to the Yanco Experimental Farm, a new variety which he named Takasuka. In his seventies, he sailed back to Japan for a holiday and died of a heart attack in his family home.

Though 'management decisions' were perhaps not Jo Takasuka's strong point, I find his story moving, not just in itself but as a reminder of the uncountable forgotten farmers and their families who have given their lives to 'a crop of extraordinary fickleness' and prospered, or starved, at the goddess's whim. It would be nice to relate that from the seed Jo sold to Yanco were descended the rice varieties that produce 12 tonnes to the hectare in the Murrumbidgee valley today. But in the four seasons his seed was sown, everything went against it: heat, locusts, failure to germinate, finally frost.

Meanwhile, in about 1920, the director of the Letona Fruit Cannery, N.C. Brady, went on a trip to the United States and happened to see Japanese rice varieties being successfully grown in California. Because of all the money the New South Wales government had invested in the Murrumbidgee Project, the Riverina at this time was under close control by government departments. Many of the farmers were First World War veterans, settled on virgin land in a 'dry' area; that is, it had lots of water but no alcohol. Brady bought three sacks of rice and shipped them home; they were labelled 'Caloro', 'Caluso' and 'Watrambune'. Tony Blakeney told us what happened to them.

'These were probably just cargo rices that had been exported from Japan, and someone said this'll do for seed. So those three arrived and spent nine months in a shed, and then somebody decided to put them in and they split the seed in two. Half was grown on this station, the other on a commercial farm.' The yields were quite good, but this was not an official government project. 'The government did almost nothing. But in with that seed came a bit of the dreaded red rice, and that started to build up, particularly in the Watrambune, and the Caluso started to have other problems.' With rice as with any plant grown from seed, constant vigilance is needed to keep the seed pure, to stop the variety backtracking genetically to its wild forebears.

41

Red rice is particularly unwelcome since the gene that gives redness is closely linked to one that causes shattering – the premature shedding of seed.

In spite of the conservatism of the New South Wales government and farmers, things went on reasonably well. I was beginning to get a picture of how crop varieties are developed. 'They introduced Calrose from California; a well-adapted variety, one of its parents was Caloro, the short grain we're talking about, and the other was a Caloro cross, Caloro by Lady Wright. So Caloro by Lady Wright was Callady, and Callady by Caloro was Calrose.' This is not the Calrose that is now grown in California, however. 'A modern breeder would have given it a new name, but we went on calling it Calrose. When Okinawa was a market, Australian Calrose was the preferred rice that went to Okinawa, to the despair of the Americans.'

Up to then, Tony explained, the Australians, being mostly Anglo-Saxons, had always eaten short grain rice – in rice puddings. 'Then Asian immigrants and foodlore from SE Asia started to create a demand for long grain rice. In the early 1960s, people tried to grow southern US long grains like Bluebonnet 50; they got abysmal yields but they started a hybridizing programme and eventually released the variety Kulu; pretty terrible for growers and for quality, but at least yield was good enough to justify a long grain rice industry. It had milling problems so they got into parboiling to overcome the milling problems, so that's where our parboiling industry comes from.

'Kulu was replaced by Inga in 1972, about when I started work here. I selected Inga from several possibilities – I thought it was the best of a bad lot. It had excellent appearance but I thought it was too soft. I didn't realize that in South-East Asia people prefer soft rice; the experts (there weren't many) said we needed a firmer-cooking rice from America. It was only when Inga was a big success in Hong Kong and other places and was well accepted by the Australian market that we decided that we would have a soft-cooking long grain from then on – it's become an Australian style.'

The high yields are obtained by careful management of a rather loosely structured, infertile soil. 'From the start, they grew by rotation, a five-year rotation: they had a lot of sheep in the early days, four years of clover, then a year of rice.' Today, the rotation is two years of rice followed by five years of pasture and clover. This nourishes the soil and prevents the build-up of pest populations by interrupting their life-cycles. It means that on any farm, in any one year, only two-sevenths of the land is under rice. But farms are big: about 300 hectares/750 acres on average, fifty times the size of the army veteran's farm at Carosucan. No wonder our friends in Malaysia thought Australian farmers were rich.

However, unlike the Malaysians, they still pay for their water; it is metered by a large metal wheel, called a Dethridge wheel, set in the inlet channel of each farm. I asked Chris Black, of the Ricegrowers' Cooperative in Leeton, a few kilometres down the road from Yanco, what it was really like to be a rice farmer in Australia in the early 1990s.

'Living on the edge of survival. Australian farmers are the last free traders in the world,' he said. 'They are unsubsidized, unprotected against competition from imports

– yet we export between 80 and 90 per cent of our rice, and in the last two years our sales in Australia have gone up by 20 per cent. We're already breeding new rices ready for the Japanese market when it opens up.' He was especially pleased that a variety had just been released for commercial use which would compete against imported Thai Fragrant rice.

Water, water, but not everywhere

Whatever the future, water will continue to be a key factor in rice farming, and one that will defy assessment in money terms, though the question, 'Who's paying?' will still be prominent. Especially where farms are small, there will be tension among neighbours, and between farmers and the authorities who control the supply. Small farms tend to use water less economically than large ones, partly because they don't usually have to pay for it, but mainly because a landscape of small farms has a great number of inflows and outflows, small ponds, reservoirs and sluices; half-a-dozen large farms need relatively few. Water is one reason why rice farms are going to get bigger.

Traditionally, water has been paid for by work, and one of the most convincing and best-documented instances of this is the Balinese *subak*. We were driving through the

Dethridge wheel: New South Wales

43

hills near Ubud when we caught sight simultaneously of a view so breathtaking and a lay-by so inviting that we stopped. Our parking place was next to a bridge, over a canal about two metres wide. The canal was filled with flowing, crystal water; its edges were meticulously dressed with well-squared concrete, and on it swam a flock of extremely smart ducks, smugly preening themselves as if aware that they were ornaments in a thoroughly well-kept landscape. Facing the road was a wooden board on a post, spick and span and neatly painted, to inform us that 'anyone fouling this waterway will pay a fine of 5000 rupiah to the subak of Bangbang.' That is to say, about £1.50 ($2.50); or, in other terms, the local retail price of about 10 kg of rice.

Beyond, the rice fields had recently been harvested, or were ready to cut; here and there a small stone shrine, wrapped in coloured cloth, showed that the rice goddess was still honoured. A hundred metres away, the fields plunged into a deep, serpentine valley whose far side shone green in the afternoon sun, with the mountains rising blue beyond it.

It is from these mountains, often dark with cloud and the dense curtain of tropical storms, that the water for this green landscape comes, rushing down steep-sided valleys to waste itself, if it is not caught, in the sea. The Balinese mastered the technology of harnessing water many centuries ago – no one is sure quite when, perhaps in the 16th

Water pump, to a design by IRRI

century AD, around the time the last Hindu kings fled from Java before the advance of Islam, or perhaps much earlier.

But water control in Bali has developed in ways unknown in Java. The subak is a water-users' club, to which members pay an annual subscription and give their services, as required and agreed by the monthly meeting of the club. Balinese society is a complex of associations and obligations; you are a member of a family, and a member of a village, but your family ties and your village ties may not overlap – may indeed conflict. You are also a member of a caste, a member of a trade or profession, and, if you are a farmer, a member of a subak. The subak is based not on a village or a group of farms but on a water-system, often a stream whose source may be far away in the hills.

Since the Balinese until recently made little distinction between religious and secular things, the subak has a sacred existence, expressed in its two temples – one near the source of the water, the second near the point where the stream splits into the main canals that will take the water, eventually, to the fields. Everyone in the subak is responsible for making sure that each member gets his fair share of water when he needs it, that the system is kept in good working order, and that worship is properly conducted at the temples.

It sounds idyllic, and I fear is probably too good to last. Some bureaucrat will decide that water can be better organised from an office with a computer. Of course, the Balinese are no better than the rest of us, and water-theft is as common there as in most other rice areas. In the old days, this was often a matter for open war between villages, and there is a long tradition of the farmer spending the night – especially at crucial times, such as when the rice grains are swelling and ripening – parading round his fields in the moonlight to make sure no one is cutting holes in his dykes. The fact that the subak's boundaries were different from those of the village or the clan, and therefore everyone's loyalties were divided, may have helped to defuse the situation.

There are two basic problems with water. You have either too much, or not enough; and it is moving either too fast or too slowly. And of course the problems are never constant; there are wet seasons and dry seasons, the rice needs most water just after flowering but the fields need to be drained dry before harvest. The classic way to deal with fast-flowing excess is to cut feeder canals so that you can take from the main streams only what the local system needs.

A spectacular example, which has been working efficiently since 230 BC, is at Guanxian, in Sichuan, at the foot of the Tibetan plateau. The river Min rushes down, swollen with melted snow, on its way to the Yangzi. It has scoured out a deep channel, which prevents it flooding the plain, but it carries a good deal of silt, and to dam the river at this point would be disastrous because the silt would pile up behind the dam. Between 250 and 230 BC, two governors of Sichuan, father and son, organised the building of an artificial island in midstream, with a massive pile of rocks at its head called the Fish Snout. The Fish Snout divides the waters, sending them into two irrigation feeder canals, one of which is diverted into a flood relief channel when the river is at its height. Each feeder canal system is closed off, in turn, during the winter, so that it can be cleared of silt. About five million people now live on the land that is irrigated from this one source of water. And over the centuries, the silt that might have blocked the river has been spread over the land to improve it.

Water disputes must be as old as farming itself. In the principal rice-growing district of Spain, the three-man Tribunal de las Aguas, the court of waters, still meets outside the *Puerta de los Apostoles* of Valencia cathedral. Its members are themselves farmers, so at least they should understand what each case is about. The court is said to have been started by the Moors, which I find easy to believe since it was they who introduced rice to Spain and built irrigation canals that are still in use around Valencia and up in the hills behind Murcia. The court meets at noon every Thursday, the day before the Moslem holy day, always an auspicious time to do important things, and the cathedral itself stands on the site of the old Friday Mosque. The proceedings are entirely oral, and there is no appeal against the court's decision.

The Green Revolution

Like most revolutions, the famous, or infamous, Green Revolution of the late 1960s and 70s was a long time coming to the boil. Its success was only partly due to advances in rice breeding, but without genetics it would not have taken place and it was inevitably the 'miracle rice' that snatched the glamour and the headlines. Farmers and gardeners have been improving their stock by selecting the best plants for next year's seed for thousands of years, but until quite recently they depended on chance mutations or cross-breedings that they did not understand and could not direct.

In fact, in 1898 the head of the Shiga Agricultural Experiment Station in Japan had already managed to breed a new rice variety by hybridization, fertilizing the seed of one plant with pollen from another, a tricky operation in a self-pollinating species. Within fifteen years, Japanese farmers were growing twenty newly created varieties, each representing years of patient work and the exercise of great technical skill. Japan also had the administrative energy to teach and encourage farmers to plant new varieties, and the infrastructure to deliver seed and fertilizer to remote villages and finance the farmer who wanted to buy them. In short, it possessed the elements of what Dr Swaminathan, a director-general of IRRI, would later call 'symphonic agriculture'.

By 1940, some progress had been made in increasing rice production in India, and more in Java, where the Dutch had introduced daylength-insensitive rice from China. This was necessary if farmers were to grow more than one crop a year; rice that hangs around waiting

46

for the day to be exactly the right length before it will flower is no good if you are trying to get harvests in several different seasons. They had also completed many irrigation projects, most of which are doing good service today. But as the war ended, and first the Japanese and then the Europeans left, it became clear that little had survived apart from the irrigation canals and sluices. The land was there, the farmers were there, but these basic resources could not cope with the explosive growth in population.

The key problem was to find medium and long grain indica rices that would respond to fertilizer as vigorously as the short grain japonicas did. Most of the indicas had never been given any fertilizer at all – not even the straw from the previous crop ploughed under. If they were dosed with nitrogen, most of them grew tall, put out a lot of tillers whose heads became too heavy for their stems, and then lay down in the water. If japonica and indica varieties could only be crossed . . . In 1949 the Food and Agriculture Organization set up the International Rice Commission. Within a few years the IRC had bred several japonica–indica hybrids, and one of them, Mahsuri, was released in 1965 for general use in Malaysia. It was quickly taken up in at least five other major rice-growing countries, and today is still one of the most successful of all rice varieties, particularly in areas where growing conditions are difficult.

Meanwhile, the Rockefeller Foundation had been busy in Mexico, collaborating with the Mexican government to develop local agricultural research facilities, train Mexican scientists and consult Mexican farmers about the crops they knew most

Transplanting by machine: Thailand

about. By the middle 1960s Mexico had not only become self-supporting in wheat, but was growing dwarf high-yielding wheat varieties that did not fall over despite their heavily laden heads.

But there were not enough Rockefellers to energize every national agricultural research institute in Asia, and there was not enough time. In April 1960, therefore, the Ford and Rockefeller Foundations jointly funded the International Rice Research Institute on land shared with the University of the Philippines at Los Baños. Two years later, building work was far enough advanced for research to get under way. Only three years after that, in 1965, IRRI released its first baby – IR8, the result of a cross between Indonesian Peta (productive but rather leggy and apt to flop over or 'lodge') and Taiwanese Dee-Geo-Woo-Gen.

'Dee-geo' means, roughly, 'short legs', and that was the great advantage this parent gave to its IR8 offspring: IR8 responded to chemical fertilizers by growing fast (130 days to maturity), producing many tillers and abundant grain, but remaining firmly upright on its short, stiff stem. It was indifferent to daylength, provided it got plenty of sunshine and warmth, so it could be sown in irrigated fields and harvested at any season.

IR8 produced yields of 8 or 9 tonnes of paddy from a hectare of good land, where previously 4 or 5 tonnes had been considered a bumper harvest. In only four years, IRRI scientists (building on work done in several countries by national institutes and farmers) had produced a winner. The Green Revolution was won. We could all live happily ever after.

It wasn't, of course, to be like that. No one at IRRI ever thought or pretended it would be. IR8 had several snags. It needed plenty of fertilizer, in the right amounts at the right times, and farmers in many areas didn't have the money or the knowhow to apply this. It needed regular supplies of water, and irrigation in many places was still non-existent or unreliable. The impact of new technology, socially and economically, is always very complex and has unexpected effects on the people at the receiving end.

And farmers who embraced the notion of 9 tonnes a hectare with enthusiasm recoiled when they tasted the stuff they'd grown; IR8 is not a rice for the connoisseur (and as far as I know none of it ever reached the supermarkets of the West). In fact, it cooks badly and tastes pretty horrible; strictly for hunger. It also turned out to be highly attractive to a whole range of pests and diseases.

These undesirable characteristics were duly bred out of IR8's successors, and there are now many high-yielding varieties whose milling, cooking and eating qualities are very good. But the impact of new technology on the farmer remains controversial.

Doubt about the Green Revolution's effects was not, however, what dragged it, in the 1980s, if not to a halt at least to a perilous slowdown. Partly, it was a victim of its own success. In several years around 1980 Indonesia, one of the world's perennial rice importers, achieved self-sufficiency and even exported a few hundred thousand

48

tonnes. The international rice market is very volatile, because only a tiny percentage of world production is traded on it. Therefore, rice prices fell sharply, causing severe problems in established exporters such as Thailand and Burma.

Governments soon got the message: rice technology and its support systems were no longer a good investment, particularly when oil revenues were declining and when industrial development claimed more and more of whatever funds were available. And indeed the easy gains had already been made: the infrastructure of distribution systems and milling facilities was in place, and the obvious irrigation projects had been completed. Starvation and civil unrest were no longer immediate threats. It was hardly surprising that in the 1980s yields rose more slowly, then levelled out.

CULT, CULTURE AND MYTH

This is the world we shall lose, in the cultural turbulence of the green revolutions. We cannot regret it, for folklore so often goes with poverty. But those of us who are old enough should be glad that we saw something of the old world at first hand, a world on the wane, retreating now into learned theses and unlearned theme parks. Near Kuala Lumpur there is already a vast new Agricultural Park, where parties of schoolchildren can see eight tiny square rice fields containing rice at eight different stages of growth. In Singapore, we talked to Violet Oon, who founded and runs a weekly newspaper about food. 'What's the attitude of people in Singapore towards farmers?' I asked her. She laughed. 'People in Singapore have no attitude towards farmers!' she said. 'They think rice falls from the sky . . .'

The Gift of Rice

Rice origin myths are much concerned with the sky and the beings who live in it, but they emphasize work as well. Some are Garden-of-Eden stories, which tell how an earthly paradise was spoiled by pride and disobedience. Others regard life as a serious and rather sordid business from the start. The sky itself, according to one of the Malaysian aboriginal peoples, at first lay flat on the earth and was a nuisance to everyone, until the women of the tribe, wielding their long wooden rice-pestles, heaved it upwards and gave us all a chance to breathe and move about. The Bagobo people, who grow rice on Mindanao, between Mount Apo and the sea, tell the story of the hero Lumabat, who was determined to explore the sky but insisted that his sister, Mebuyan, should go with him. Mebuyan absolutely refused, and when her arguments failed to move him she sat firmly inside a rice-mortar. The rice-mortar sank into the earth with Mebuyan still aboard, and as she disappeared from view she scattered handfuls of rice to show that multitudes of souls would follow her. She has stayed underground ever since.

Mebuyan seems to be some sort of Proserpine-figure, the seed that must die. There are countless others. In another Philippines myth, the god Soro has made up his mind to marry a maiden, Bright Jewel. She conceals her love in order to test him. She sends him off to find a food better than any she has ever tasted. He never returns; overcome with remorse, she dies, and the first rice grows from her grave. In central Kalimantan, the Luangan people set special plants in the borders and paths in their dry rice fields. They explain that these plants are the friends of rice and the rice spirit Luing, who is female, and whose blood became the first seeds of rice.

Structuralists can have a lot of fun with rice myths. A Javanese story, some of whose relationships seem to echo those of Soro and Bright Jewel, is that of Tisnawati, the daughter of the supreme god, Batara Guru. She rashly fell in love with a mortal, Jakasudana, when she looked down from heaven and saw him manfully ploughing his

Husking and winnowing rice

50

rice fields. Batara Guru threatened to change her into a rice stalk if he caught her so much as talking to the young man, but he went off to fight some other gods and his daughter materialized in front of Jakasudana, who could hardly believe his good luck. Unfortunately the couple laughed (or, I suspect, giggled) so much that Batara Guru heard them and came back in a hurry. He could not go back on his threat, so Tisnawati became a rice stalk. Poor Jakasudana could only gaze sadly at her, until Batara Guru took pity and changed him into one as well. The Javanese harvest ritual re-enacts their marriage.

There are many versions of the Javanese rice origin myth. Margaret Visser tells a Freudian one in *Much Depends on Dinner*. Significantly, she gives her chapter on rice the subheading 'the tyrant with a soul'. The story starts with Anta, a deformed and shapeless junior god who is depressed by his failure to find any gift for Batara Guru's new temple. He weeps three tears, which turn into eggs. An eagle then swoops down and forces him to break the eggs, but when, reluctantly, he has smashed two of them, the third hatches and releases a beautiful baby girl. She is given to Batara Guru's wife, Uma, to be breast-fed and is named Samyam Sri. Sri grows up so beautiful that Batara Guru, as is the way of gods, lusts after her, but is thwarted by the fact that she has been wet-nursed by his wife and is therefore technically his daughter.

Despite this, he tries several times to rape her, and finally the other gods become so alarmed that they rescue her virtue by killing her and burying her body. From the various parts of it, plants grow, among them sticky rice from her breasts and ordinary rice from her eyes. Batara Guru, remorsefully I hope, but more likely salvaging what he can of his self-respect, gives these to men as food. Sri, elevated to goddess rank as Dewi Sri, becomes the spirit of fertility and increase, protectress of rice fields and those who toil in them, guardian of barns and rice bins, all over the archipelago; and under many other names is worshipped far into the hills of continental South-East Asia.

Other sources produce more complex versions of these myths, and more involved explanations. The Dutch scholar W.H. Rassers sought the earliest surviving Javanese versions of the myths in the shadow-plays, the *wayang kulit*. He summarizes the twists and turns of two of the oldest *wayang* stories, both plainly agricultural. In one, usually played before harvest-time, the princess Sri is sought in marriage by a prince from a neighbouring kingdom; her father wants the marriage to take place, but Sri rejects the prince, saying she will only marry a man who looks like her brother Sedana. She runs away into the forest, where, with the help of a rice farmer and his wife, she sets up a new community and is eventually joined by her brother, who has also said he will not marry unless he can find a woman who exactly resembles his sister.

The Ancestors' Ordeal

Rassers explains this in terms of a pre-Hindu myth of tribal origins, the tribe being split into two halves, one associated with the waxing moon, the other with the moon waning. You were only allowed to marry somebody from the other half of the tribe, a rule of exogamy which helped prevent incest. But since the ancestors were the children of a single supreme god, brother–sister incest is inescapable, a kind of original sin. Therefore each couple must undergo a difficult initiation period and must be transformed and made perfect before they can marry.

Banishment to the forest is one such test; solving difficult riddles, or finding impossible things, are others. The second story that Rassers tells is that of a play often performed at the time when the village and surrounding fields are being tidied and cleaned ready for the next planting, ditches are being cleared and fences mended, both literally and metaphorically.

Batara Guru's status as lord of the universe is threatened by Kanekaputra, who has acquired terrifying power after years of asceticism and meditation on the seabed. Javanese people still practise asceticism for this purpose, though not on this scale. Kanekaputra is grasping in his hand a visible symbol of his power, a bright jewel called Retna Dumilah. Batara Guru tries to grasp it, it shoots out of his hand and falls to the underworld, where it is found by the world-snake, Antaboga, who puts it in a box and hides it. The gods find Antaboga and the box, but they cannot open it, so Batara Guru throws it on the floor and smashes it. A delightful little 3-year-old girl runs out from the wreckage, and at the same time a splendid palace, Marakata, rises in the background. The little girl is given a suitable retinue and is taken to live in the palace. She is also given a name, Tisnawati.

Eleven years pass and little Tisnawati is a beautiful and marriageable young lady of 14. Batara Guru sees her, decides he must have her, and makes her his second wife. (The first, of course, is Uma.) Tisnawati submits to the ceremony but nothing more; she will not go to bed with him unless he first brings her three things. One of them is a food which, once tasted, will satisfy the eater for life. Batara Guru sends one of his servants, Kalagumarang, to search for these impossibilities. Servants in Javanese drama are very like Shakespeare's mechanicals; they behave as clowns, and have the privilege of telling unwelcome truths to their masters. With a roar of mocking laughter, Kalagumarang sets out. The plot thickens until it becomes almost as impenetrable as the jungle into which Tisnawati flees, pursued by her ungainly husband. He attempts to rape her; she dies in his arms; overcome with remorse (or something), he hacks a clearing in the forest for her grave. From her head grows the coconut palm, maize from her teeth, bananas from the palms of her hands, and rice – from her vagina. Meanwhile, Kalagumarang has been turned into a pig and then killed by an arrow. His blood, and his festering body, give birth to all the pests and diseases that attack rice today just as they did in Java fifteen or twenty centuries ago.

Rassers makes the point that these are just two stories among many, and that in most of them, Sri, or Tisnawati, is not a rice goddess but is simply the mother of one half of the tribe of the Javanese, the consort of Vishnu, the ancestress of the 'left' half of the group (and of the figures that occupy the left-hand side of the *wayang kulit* screen), the slightly-older twin, the dark side of human personality, the waxing moon, the eternal female. These stories happen to show her concerned with agriculture, therefore they are popular and potent at seasons when everyone has farm matters very much on their minds.

I can't resist adding one more story which shows the dangers of taking for granted the goddess or her servants. It is one of the best-known Indonesian stories even today; I recently saw its first scene sculpted in a fine relief panel outside a very smart new house in a suburb of Jakarta where the rich and powerful live.

Seven *widadari* – angels, blessed spirits, nymphs, translate them how you will – flew down from heaven one day to a hillside in Java so lovely that no landscape even in heaven could compare with it. In a deep and shady valley there was a pool of clear water where they liked to bathe, and they took off their clothes and splashed about happily. By chance, a poor rice farmer, on his way to his fields, saw them and was, of course, amazed and awestruck. He was not so awestruck, however, as to be unable to think. He quietly picked up the bundle of clothes belonging to the youngest and prettiest of the girls and hid it. Her name, by the way, was Nawang Wulan, which means Clear Moonlight.

When the others came out and flew away to heaven, she was left naked, embarrassed, and no doubt very annoyed. But, to get her clothes back or for some other reason, she agreed to marry him, on condition that he never disobeyed the one absolute order she would give him. He was never to open the lid of the cooking pot when she was cooking rice. With a laugh, he agreed; and they settled down. They lived perfectly happily, with never a cross word, and he noticed that he was rapidly changing from being the poorest man in the village to being the richest. His rice barn was always full; he had plenty to sell in the market, plenty to entertain his friends. How could this be? Curiosity, it is hardly necessary to explain, overcame him. One day he lifted the lid of the cooking pot and peeped in.

There is some doubt as to exactly what he saw there: some say it was a single grain of rice, which would become enough to feed the household, others that it was a tiny girl, crouching in the bottom of the pot. Either way, his wife came in and saw him with the lid in his hand, staring into the pot in amazement. Without a word, she opened the box in which her embroidered cloths were stored, put them on, and flew away into the sky. Soon, he was the poorest man in the village once more.

The Feminine Rice Spirit

It is a fact that the rice spirit is almost always female (though there are exceptions, notably in the Philippines). If you want to connect her with Robert Graves's White Goddess, I don't see why you shouldn't; many stories emphasize the whiteness of her skin, often dusted with rice powder, and the rice plant itself obviously reflects the three ages of woman as maiden, nymph and crone. These stories of randy gods and hasty transformations must, I think, recall Greek myths to the mind of anyone with a classical European education, and I suppose we could trace their very remote ancestry back to the same Hindu or pre-Hindu North Indian beliefs. I wonder, in fact, about the names Sri and Ceres, which sound suspiciously alike; but perhaps this is just another bit of false amateur etymology.

Dewi Sri

Filipino rice spirits, as I said, are often male. One group consisted of four brother gods: Dumangan, the god of good harvests and giver of grains; Kalaskas, who supervised the ripening of the rice grains; Kalasokus, in charge of yellowing and drying the crop ready for harvest; and Damulag, who protected the rice from wind (remember those terrible Philippines typhoons). However, they had a female colleague, Ikapati, who was goddess of cultivated lands and taught agriculture. The Ifugao, in north central Luzon, traditionally regarded Kabunian as supreme god, and Bulul as the god of granaries; they still sell woodcarvings of him to tourists, an alarming figure seated on the ground, arms crossed on his upraised knees, a scowl above his long sharp nose. The Tiruray, over on the west coast of Mindanao, say that their supreme god Minaden used mud to make the world, which was then about as big as a winnowing-tray, and two small people. These little people grew, but could not reproduce. Minaden's brother Meketefu then came and made them man and woman, so they had a child. But there was no food, and the child died. The father asked Meketefu for soil to bury the child, and different food plants sprouted from the parts of the body: rice from the umbilical cord, sweet potatoes from the intestines, taro from the head, bananas from the hands, areca nuts from the nails, corn from the teeth, lime from the brains, cassava from the bones, betel leaf from the ears. So we return to something very like the story of Samyam Sri or Tisnawati.

Curiously, there are also hero-tales from several countries about Promethean figures who invade heaven and snatch the secrets of rice farming from the selfish gods. But rice, like fire, is an irreversible technology: once you have mastered it, you cannot do without it, and to some extent it will master you, so that your existence ever after is a struggle to control the genie you have released. No one is more skilful at dancing on the rim of the technological crater than the Japanese, and their story of how rice was given to mankind is a typically involved one. The goddess of the sun, Amaterasu Omikami, ruler of the Plain of High Heaven, quarrelled with her brother, the storm-god and ruler of the Sea Plain Susanowo-no-Mikoto, because he had broken down the dykes between her rice fields. Amaterasu hid in a cave to sulk, and the world was dark. Other gods and goddesses lured her out by putting a mirror and a jewel in a tree; a goddess then performed an obscene dance, which made all the gods roar with laughter. Amaterasu was first curious, then – when she saw the mirror and the jewel – flattered; she came back out from the cave.

Jewel and mirror, together with a sword later given by Susanowo to his sister, became part of the Japanese imperial regalia. Amaterasu gave her grandson, Ninigi-no-Mikoto, 'God of the Ripened Rice Plant', rice seedlings which she had sown in the fields of heaven, and he planted them on earth; his great-grandson, Jimmu Tenno, was the first earthly Emperor. Japan ever since has been Mizuho-no-Kuni – 'the land of abundant rice'. The Emperor still sows and transplants rice in a sacred field for presentation to the gods at the Shinto temples of Ise, on 15 October and 23 November every year.

In so many stories about rice, laughter – wild, ungoverned, Bacchanalian laughter – seems to be a magic key that unlocks secrets, reveals what someone was trying to hide, or gets the story out of an impasse. The opposite of laughter seems to be not sadness or weeping or reflective silence, but shyness and a feeling that something precious is vulnerable. The story of Amaterasu being lured from the cave and seeing the jewel and the mirror reminds me of all the things farmers do to make sure the rice spirit does not hide herself again. Lucien Hanks, the American anthropologist who lived in a village near Bangkok, describes in *Rice and Man* how Thai farmers of the old school went about this.

They would not start to plough their fields until the King of Thailand, one of whose titles is Lord of the Flatness of the Earth, had ploughed a ceremonial furrow and invoked the appropriate deities: Mae Thorani, goddess of vegetation; Phra Phum, lord of the earth; Nang Megtala, bringer of rain. These acts and prayers alert local sub-deities, who receive the offerings of farmers: food, flowers, incense. When the rice is in bud, like a pregnant woman it must be flattered, but not by a man in case she is overcome by shyness; women take bitter-tasting limes and lemons, perfume and scented powder and mirrors to the fields. When the grains are fully ripe, the farmer finds he cannot offer thanks to the rice mother, Mae Phosop, because the reapers have frightened her away – therefore a woman gleans a handful of stalks, makes a rice doll, and brings it home in a basket under a cloth like a princess in a litter, having called the soul of the rice to inhabit the doll. The doll is ceremonially installed in the granary, to ensure that next season's seed grain will be fertile.

Ceremonies like this are still enacted in many places, remote and not so remote, but of course they are dying and will soon pass out of memory, not because farmers don't believe in Mae Phosop any longer but because they have no more need of her.

Pierre Gourou gives a whole chapter of his book *Riz et civilisation* to rice farmers' rituals. One Ifugao village devoted 191 days each year to them, and sacrificed 467 hens, 76 pigs and 4 buffaloes. The Lamet people, in northern Laos, who grow dry upland rice, say that among all the plants only rice has a soul; they line the roads to the rice fields with altars and flowers so that the soul can find its way there in time for harvest. Or they used to. I like Gourou's story of how people encourage the rain to come if the monsoon is late – he says they do this in several parts of South-East Asia by carrying a cat in a cage round all the houses in the village and throwing water at it. People in Java know a simple way to *prevent* rain (leave some unlaundered underwear on the roof of your house), but rainmaking is much harder magic, and I don't believe throwing water at a cat ever achieved so much as a passing shower.

Japanese rice measure, also used for drinking saké

But of course there may be good scientific observation behind what looks like mumbo-jumbo. The 'friends of rice' planted by the Luangan in borders and paths in their rice fields bear flowers and fruits that ripen a little before the rice does, so they attract monkeys and birds away from the crop. I can just imagine some agricultural extension worker telling the farmers not to bother with such superstitious practices. I have read somewhere that Malaysian farmers plant rice according to the phases of the moon. Whatever Dr Rassers might think of this, they do it to avoid stem-borers which are the larvae of a moth that mates and lays eggs only at full moon. Or, again, they used to. The temptation is always to use pesticide sprays; by the time you realize that these have killed not only the pests but the natural enemies of the pests, as well as the fish in the fields, and are starting to poison the local drinking-water . . . it is very difficult to go back.

56

Green Religion

I can't lament the passing of beliefs which, however charming, often illustrate my own conviction that humans are only happy when they are making life needlessly difficult for themselves. On the other hand, for farmers I can see two positive aspects of blind belief. Making the poor farmer content with his lot is not one of them, but making his life more satisfying intellectually, spiritually, aesthetically, certainly is. For me the classic instance of this is not Bali, where people have by and large always been reasonably prosperous, but India, where desolating poverty prevails today as ever in the past.

Perhaps I am being sentimental in a way I could not be about a country I am more familiar with, but my impression in India is of dense, immensely rich cultural and religious traditions, at all levels of society and regardless of local factions and hostile religious groups. Whatever religion may be in India, it is not an opiate, as is perhaps all too obvious from the newspapers. A small example of its more peaceful side: as we drove along main roads near Delhi, we saw gorgeous peacocks strutting and pecking in the dust of the roadside. 'Peacocks are supposed to be very good to eat,' I said, thinking of medieval European recipes for festive displays. 'And so many people here are hungry – I'm surprised there are any wild peacocks left in India.' The driver looked rather

Mae Phosop

shocked. 'Lord Krishna has a headdress of peacock's feathers,' he said. 'No one here would dream of killing one.'

That's two birds, metaphorically, with one stone: cultural satisfaction *and* ecological awareness. This awareness is the second benefit of belief in unseen supernatural forces; it has constantly reminded the farmer that he is part of a natural system that punishes greed, stupidity, lack of foresight, by disease and infertility. Science of course gets us to the same place in the end; wherever rice is grown, it seems, there are organic farmers and environmentally conscious customers for their produce. These people's attitude deserves respect, not least because it is based on knowledge as well as instinct. But as the world's population continues to rise, we are going to need benign agribusiness and technology as well as good husbandry.

In the Singapore National Museum, where we went after our conversation with Violet Oon, an exhibition about rice had attracted a few visitors. They were mostly parents who had brought their children along, perhaps to educate them. But parents as well as children looked uneasy and bored, gazing at these artefacts from what must have seemed to them an unimaginably distant past. Objects like hoes, rice-pounders, carved storage bins, figures of Dewi Sri and her consort Sedana – these were recognizable at once to anyone who had spent a childhood, fifty years ago, in rural Sumatra and Java. You couldn't expect them to mean anything to people in Singapore today. And there were objects whose uses were even more obscure.

The most charming were the Balinese bird-scarers – little windmills that played a simple gamelan tune and activated figures, cut from tin and painted, of a farmer struggling with a recalcitrant buffalo and his wife pounding rice. But we didn't recall these from trips to Bali in the early 1960s, and we thought they would be better at attracting tourists than scaring birds.

Much more impressive was a splendid woodcarving of a hornbill from Kalimantan, brightly painted with a self-satisfied expression. The Iban tribes regard the hornbill as their sacred ancestor, who, according to some authorities, taught them to plant rice. The Iban know by watching the stars when it is time to start preparing the land for sowing: they watch for the day when the Pleiades rise at the same moment as the sun. Across the border in Sarawak, they say that they are descended from a man called Raja Tindit, who married the youngest of the Pleiades; she taught him the secrets of rice. J. D. Freeman, who wrote *Iban Agriculture* in the 1950s, lists twenty-three Iban names for the rice plant at different stages of growth, including 'like the tail of the rice sparrow'; 'pregnant like a man'; 'pregnant like a woman'; 'newly calling from afar'; and 'ripe lips'.

Freeman asked the farmers why they threshed their padi, not with flails, but by trampling it with their bare feet (which is slower, and sounds painful). Because it would mortally offend the rice spirit to offer it such violence, they said; even treading on the rice, once it was threshed, would be taken as an insult, although if you absolutely couldn't help treading on some, the rice would understand.

The descendants of the hornbill call their ancestor *burung singalung*, and their harvest festival is *gawai burung*, 'the feast of the bird'. In the Singapore museum there was an old photograph of four ancient men celebrating it, and from the delighted grins on their faces you could see they were having a lovely time. They were about to slit the throat of a sacrificial cock, which they would no doubt eat when the gods had had their share. They looked well fed, happy and completely at ease with themselves and the world. They had had a good harvest, they would eat well until the next harvest was due. What more could man ask of the capricious sky?

Sacred hornbill

A BRIEF HISTORY OF RICE

Where did rice cultivation begin? Probably in a thousand places at a thousand different times, within the wide area where wild rices grow. All we can do is make intelligent guesses, and check them against archaeological evidence.

Selection – Unconscious and Conscious

We have seen that the wild, grassy ancestors of rice evolved more than 100 million years ago on the great continent of Gondwana. This broke up, and formed South America, Africa, India and Australia, each fragment bearing its cargo of animal and plant species. India drifted northwards for several million years and eventually coasted into the land mass of Asia with a bump, raising the Himalayas and the mountain chains that extend eastwards towards the South China Sea. It was many millions of years later, in the warm, moist foothills of these mountains, that early men and women first gathered wild rice as food, then realized they could sow it, and then, at first without thinking, started to select and breed varieties that had the characteristics they liked. Somewhat later, people in parts of West Africa did the same, with the rather different species of rice that had evolved there. But of course this long process could not even have started without the invention of something more necessary even than farming – people had taught themselves to cook.

Rice is extraordinarily adaptable, and no doubt wild rices, finding themselves in all sorts of different habitats, developed different characteristics to help them survive. Some learned to tolerate cold nights, others to cope with sudden floods or life in swamps, others to make do with relatively little water. As men and women began to develop the arts of farming, each group cultivated and selected whatever rice grew locally; so the question of which rice came first, wet or dry, need not be asked of rice-farming in general, though it remains very interesting in each locality.

Then, of course, rice itself began to travel. People wanted to grow it in places where wild rice would not naturally grow, because conditions weren't suitable for it. This is when serious breeding began; as rice was 'pulled' north, east and south and west from its natural habitats, it changed and adapted to its new homes. But farmers changed the environment, too. In China, for example, people wanted to grow wet rice but the water supply was uncertain and the soil porous. The first crops must have been disappointing. But the very act of keeping a field under water by building a dyke round it and perhaps diverting a stream into it, and then tilling the soil by digging or trampling the mud, led in a few years to the soil becoming 'puddled': 30–50 centimetres below the surface, a hard, less porous layer of compacted earth built up, which held water better and improved the complex soil chemistry in the layers above it.

Dr T. T. Chang, of the International Rice Research Institute, is perhaps the world's greatest authority on the domestication of rice. He concluded that the evidence – mainly geography and genetics – point to north-eastern India and northern Thailand as the most likely places for the appearance of the first rice farmers, with the major varieties – indica, japonica, javanica – separating from their common stem as rice eaters took them into new areas and new conditions.

Dr Ian Glover, an archaeologist of the University of London, told me that the oldest identifiable rice remains in north Thailand and north Vietnam are not more than about 3,000 years old. In central China, however, far away from rice's 'homeland' and in an area where millet was probably the first staple crop, extensive remains of *Oryza sativa* have been found at Hemudu, south of Shanghai, whose age, measured by the carbon-14 method, is at least 6,000 years. The earliest sites for rice cultivation now known are in the central Yangzi valley; at Pengtoushan, rice was being grown about 8,500 years ago.

Similarly in India and Pakistan: many of the oldest archaeological finds are from areas well away from the mountains, though there are remains of both wild and cultivated rices at Koldihewa, on the edge of the mountain area, which are over 4,000

Old Chinese 'seedling horse'

years old. These remains are often husks, charred grains, or impressions of grains in the clay sides of pots; but they are sufficient for different varieties of rice to be recognized. It is not just the antiquity but the continuity of rice in India that strikes us; the earliest Hindu liturgical texts show rice being used in offerings. 'To Agni, lord of the house, he offers a cake of black rice on eight potsherds . . . to Savitr, a cake of swift-growing rice on twelve potsherds . . . to Brhaspati, lord of speech, an oblation of wild rice . . .' The *Susruta Samhita*, a treatise on medicine and diet written probably before the birth of Gautama Buddha, names dozens of varieties of rice and discusses their effects on the body. Gautama's father, a king of Nepal, was named Suddhodana, 'pure rice', and words for rice occur again and again in placenames and personal names in early Asian history.

In Indonesia, there is some evidence for rice cultivation around 2300 BC in Sulawesi, and across the Malaysian border in Sarawak, but nothing so far of great age in Java, where you would expect rice to have been grown since time immemorial. But all available rice land in Java is so intensively farmed that traces of earlier work could easily have been obliterated. In Kelantan, West Malaysia, which is one of the nation's granaries today, the earliest finds go back only about 900 years. The famous terraces at Banaue in the Philippines are said to be 2000 years old, but, as we have seen, it is not certain how old they really are, or what they were originally intended for. Other South-East Asian peoples terraced and irrigated their hillsides to grow taro, and it is possible that the hill tribes of northern Luzon did what many others have done: started with taro and later switched to rice.

Rice Empires

The first highly organized South-East Asian kingdoms and empires seem to have used rice farmers as their power base, which is not surprising: they were located in the rich delta lands of the Mekong, Menam, Irrawaddy and Red rivers, and a little later in south Sumatra and central Java. Great irrigation works were undertaken, and their remains are still impressive. However, they can be misleading. Growing rice in the flood-plain or delta of a river requires skill not so much in bringing water to the fields as in getting rid of it; drainage and flood relief, not irrigation, is often the purpose of a network of canals. Even storage tanks may be intended for flood control rather than for watering the fields in the dry season. The Khmers' huge waterworks around Angkor may have been for ritual rather than rice. Sri Lanka, on the other hand, still has the huge tanks that once stored monsoon water for the dry-season rice crop.

In areas where the monsoon is reliable, one does not require special irrigation works to grow one crop of rice a year; quite enough water comes from the sky and the local rivers. The reason people started to store water was that they could then grow more than one crop a year. We have to distinguish between 'rainfed' rice (one crop) and 'irrigated' rice (two or three crops). With multiple cropping comes the population explosion, which in turn feeds back new labourers into the system and produces yet more rice from terraces that climb ever higher up the hillsides. Java is a classic example, with a population of about 3 million in 1780 growing to 90 million by 1990; yet Java today is pretty nearly self-supporting in rice, and its society, intensely traditional and conservative in some ways, has managed to adapt itself to the shock of a thirty-fold increase in less than ten generations.

Although rice was obviously a better food than its main rivals – yams, taro, millet – it was a more difficult and riskier crop to grow, and in some places it was seen as the mark of an alien, intrusive culture. The process went on right up into the twentieth century. Even today, a great deal of taro is eaten in west Javanese homes. People in Jakarta who were brought up in parts of eastern Indonesia where rice has never penetrated will send home for supplies of taro or sago, 'proper food', while Javanese migrants to those areas will wrinkle their noses and settle down to teach the locals to embrace rice and civilization.

The expansion of rice, then, was a hand-to-hand affair, a slow pushing-back of a long frontier, a process which may still not be quite complete. But at some point, very far back in time no doubt, people started to load their rice into ships or on to the backs of animals and carry it long distances, either as seed or as a finished food product for export to distant markets.

By about 500 BC rice was being grown over widely scattered areas of India, China, Indo-China, Malaysia, Indonesia and the Philippines. In many of these areas it had been well established for anything up to 4,000 years, perhaps longer; in others it was a more recent arrival, possibly brought by Buddhist monks, who were indefatigable travellers and, one suspects, gourmets. Sometime between 300 BC and about AD 200 it made two significant advances, into the Middle East and Japan. Short grain varieties probably crossed from Korea to the southern tip of Japan, spreading northwards through Kyushu and Honshu, but slowing down as they reached the colder climate of the north. In fact, it was the late eighteenth century before rice reached northern Honshu, and almost a century later before a cold-tolerant variety was bred which would grow on the island of Hokkaido.

In western Asia, new empires and new societies were creating new demands for food, both staples and luxuries. The Assyrians of the seventh century BC had a word for rice, though they did not grow it. Until about 500 BC people in what is now Afghanistan, Iran and Iraq were living mainly on wheat and millet. Then the Parthian Empire attracted trade through the passes of the Hindu Kush from northern India. Bactria, south of the Caspian Sea, became a crossroads of trade routes from the Mediterranean, Persia, India and China. Alexander the Great made his expedition into Asia between 334 and 323 BC. One of his companions, Aristobulus, wrote afterwards that he had seen rice growing in Bactria, Babylon, Susa and Syria (probably the valley of the river Jordan). In other words, Persian influence had 'pulled' rice as far as the valleys of the Tigris and the Euphrates, almost in fact to the threshold of the Roman Empire.

The Greeks and Romans certainly knew about rice. The Greek author Theophrastus mentions it in his writings on India in the fourth century BC – a hundred years before Alexander's time. The Greeks borrowed its name from the previous owners, possibly Indian, possibly Persian, and passed it on to the Romans and eventually to Linnaeus and the botanists: *oryza*. The curious thing is that Greeks and Romans took so little practical interest in rice. They regarded it as a rather exotic and expensive medicine, something for rich faddists to buy at the end of its long journey from India.

Forest regenerating on an upland rice clearing: West Kalimantan

Attitudes to Cooking and Eating

One thing which Asia and the West seem to have shared in those classical times is belief in a system of natural forces which, if you were wise, you went along with, harmonized in yourself if you could, and generally tried to keep in balance. Active and passive, yin and yang, hot and cold, the five Chinese elements, the four humours of Greek doctors – these are by no means forgotten today. The place of rice in this system was not always certain. As a grain, it was usually associated with earth, which was yin, cool. But as one of the two essential components of a meal (the other being the elaborated meat and vegetable dishes) boiled rice was neutral, perfectly balanced between the earth it came from and the fire that cooked it. In *Food in Chinese Culture*, Eugene and Marja Anderson say they found Hokkien Chinese in Malaysia regarded rice as a 'hot', yang food; but this might be because the overseas Chinese felt insecure and needed plenty of heat to strengthen them against hostile surroundings.

On the whole, the coolness of rice seems to be the message China has passed on to the rest of the world. In India, we were told that many people, especially in the north, avoid rice in cold weather because they think it will give them chills, and modern Persians also think of it as cold. Jill Benham, who has an encyclopedic knowledge of Middle Eastern food, has traced the spread of the hot/cold classification of foods from the Far East through Europe and even into South America.

From a different standpoint, one can see three, or perhaps four, quite distinct views of rice developing during its history, and affecting the ways it is cooked and eaten. At one extreme, it is so expensive that a special use has to be found or invented for it – as medicine, for example. But in countries where it has been a major staple food for centuries, it is given semi-divine status and is then normally cooked and eaten separately from other food. I can imagine farmers saying to their wives: 'Look, we toiled, we risked everything, to produce that pure white grain – so when you cook it, don't mess it about.'

Where it has been fairly recently introduced as a crop, and perhaps isn't the most important source of food, people simply regard it as something to be exploited, commercially and gastronomically. Rich men say to their cooks, 'This rice is good stuff, but it gets a bit boring after a while – try cooking it in some sauce, get a bit of flavour into it, can't you?' Or peasants hunt around for wild things they can cook with it, in the single pan that is all they have in the kitchen, so that in the countryside around Valencia (for example) rabbits and snails get tossed into the *paella*.

Peasant societies often start out with grants of land to army veterans. I should like to know how many rice recipes originated round the camp fires of armies on the march – between India and Persia and Iraq, between Egypt and Spain. Rice is just the thing to give the troops: easy to store and carry, because the grain is dry, and easy to cook, because it doesn't need to be ground or baked. If the army settles down to occupy someone else's land for a few months, the men can even grow a crop or two of low-yielding upland rice; it grows faster than wheat and still produces a better yield from the same quantity of seed. Pilaf and biryani, it seems to me, could well have begun as army rations, very basic at first, elaborated in days of peace by men who went misty-eyed at the supper table as they told their wives and children for the hundredth time about the great *nosh* they had (using the old Persian word for 'comforting sustenance') when they crossed the Hindu Kush with Babur.

Chinese traders reported that rice was plentiful in Ferghana, on the trans-Asian route north of the Pamirs, but not in Persia. This probably means that in Persia, as in many parts of South and East Asia, rice-farming was patchy and the few Chinese travellers who came as far as this just happened not to visit rice-growing areas. But it does appear that rice, having made it as far as the Euphrates and possibly the Jordan, then stopped for several hundred years. It was being sold at the Pepper Gate in Alexandria before the Muslim conquest of Egypt, but this was imported rice; as a crop, it did not reach Egypt until the sixth or seventh century AD, by which time the Roman Empire in the West had collapsed.

The word rice does not occur in the Bible, not even in the New Testament, though the parable of the sower, with its references to seed bringing forth fruit sixty or a hundredfold, might well be taken to refer to rice more accurately than to any other grain; I doubt if ancient Palestinian wheat farmers ever got yields anywhere near as high as this. The Talmud mentions rice, however, so it must have reached the Middle East by, at latest, the sixth century AD. Why did it enter Egypt so late? After all, the yearly flooding of the Nile would seem to create ideal conditions for it.

The answer must be that the Egyptians were highly skilled wheat farmers, who saw no reason to change to another crop when they had assured domestic and export markets; if any individuals experimented with rice, they may well have found that the available varieties gave poor yields under local conditions. A harder question is: why, eventually, did Egyptian farmers go to the trouble of finding or breeding varieties that did give good yields? Maybe the demand for rice became strong enough to encourage farmers to overcome the technical problems. The history of Australian rice in the twentieth century suggests that a certain amount of luck still plays its part in these things. Anyway, the Egyptians may have been growing at least a little rice in the century before the event that gave it its next big boost: the explosive growth of Islam.

Not that rice ever became the staple diet of Islam in the West; most Muslims ate wheat, and more ate sorghum than ate rice. But they learnt about rice from the Persians of the Sasanian Empire, whom they defeated in 635, or possibly from the Indian province of Sind, which they conquered in 711. They knew the value of rice in swampy areas, flooded valleys, and places that could be reliably irrigated. At the same time, the rapid growth of their empire, in wealth as well as territory, enormously increased the demand for good food. The early caliphs served huge and opulent feasts, and the habit of ostentatious hospitality spread quickly downwards through the ranks of the aristocracy. Caliph al-Mahdi, in about 780, sent his wazir to India to research new plants and drugs; this man, Yahya ibn Khalid, was also tutor to the young prince Harun-al-Rashid. In the year 945, Caliph Mustakfi gave a splendid feast at which the main topic of conversation was food – how well I know those feasts. The guests discussed 'rare dishes' which included lemons, aubergines, rice and sugar.

As a result of all this, the Arabs extended the area of rice-growing wherever they went, acclimatizing the plants for a few seasons in a particular spot before moving on to somewhere a little cooler or a little drier, selecting (no doubt) the seeds that did best in the new conditions. In his book *Agricultural Innovation in the Early Islamic World*, Professor Andrew Watson points out that rice was about the only crop that could be grown in hot Mediterranean countries in the summer, provided of course there was enough water for irrigation. A geographer of the tenth century, Ibn Hawqal, says that a wealthy emir of Mosul introduced two new crops, cotton and rice, which doubled his income.

Rice was pulled, or pushed, towards the headwaters of Tigris and Euphrates, around the top right-hand corner of the Mediterranean (that is, the coast of southern Turkey), into Turkey itself, along the shores of the Caspian Sea and even up the valley of the river Volga, though this was not strictly Muslim territory. It was taken to southern Morocco, and probably across the Sahara Desert to West Africa, where it was soon competing with the local *O. glaberrima*, though both species are still grown there today. Muslims grew rice in Sicily, whence it was being exported in the late ninth century, and of course Spain, not only around Valencia and Murcia, which has remained a rice-growing area ever since, but also on the island of Majorca, which has not.

By AD 1000, rice was grown more or less throughout the Muslim world, wherever conditions were suitable for it; and from about this time there begins a rich tradition of books on food and cookery, in which rice and rice dishes play a major part. That tradition and its offshoots are among the sources for the rice recipes in this book. However, rice again paused in its onward march for several centuries. Byzantium, the eastern remnant of the Roman Empire, knew about rice, occasionally wrote about it in medical books, but did not grow it; in western Europe, likewise, rice was an expensive and exotic import. In the sixth century AD, Anthimus, a Greek physician at Theodoric's court at Ravenna, advised soft-boiled rice grains in goat's milk as a treatment for stomach upsets. This would certainly have helped courtiers who had overdosed on spiced meats and wine. If returning Crusaders brought anything in the way of food back home with them from *outremer*, their saddlebags certainly did not contain rice. When the Normans took power in Sicily, rice cultivation dwindled and virtually died out.

Rice in the West

For a long time, western Europe regarded rice as another kind of spice. It was certainly reaching England before the middle of the thirteenth century; the *Oxford English Dictionary*'s first citation for the word is from the household accounts of King Henry III in 1234, and we know that between Christmas 1264 and the following Easter the Countess of Leicester's household got through 110 pounds (50 kilos) of rice, costing 1.5 pence a pound, a high price which explained the careful book-keeping and the fact that the rice was locked in the spice cupboard. At about the same time, the accounts of the Duke of Savoy show that rice 'for sweets' cost 13 Imperials a pound, whereas honey was only 8 Imperials. In Milan, rice was heavily taxed as 'spice brought through Greece from Asia'.

The Black Death, which ravaged Italy from 1348 to 1352, and then recurred at irregular intervals as bubonic plague, has been credited with the introduction of rice to the northern Mediterranean. The workforce had been reduced by perhaps one-third, and the low yields of wheat and barley were hardly enough to keep people alive. Rice was a high-yielding, energy-giving crop that required far less labour per sack of grain harvested. Gian Galeazzo Sforza sent a sack of rice to the Duke d'Este of Ferrara in 1475, with a letter telling him that one sack of seed would produce twelve sacks of food grain.

According to present-day Italian writers, however, large tracts of the Piedmont and Lombardy plains had been turned into paddy fields several decades before this famous letter, with the export of seed grain already strictly prohibited as a state secret. The Venetians may have brought rice from Turkey; an early Italian variety was called *Nostrale*, which suggests that this was 'our' rice, as opposed to whatever anyone else might later have imported. According to the Italian historian Aldo de Maddalena, the Milanese governors of Lombardy in the fifteenth century ordered a merchant, who was travelling to South Asia, to bring back a sack of unhusked paddy; this was sown in three places, then transplanted over a large area. Early north Italian rice fields were watered from *fontanili*, little springs whose water was in fact too cold for the rice to bear well. But a particular advantage of rice was that the harvest came much later than the wheat harvest, so there was no shortage of labour. The harvest was also more reliable.

In England, in 1585, rice steeped in cow's milk with white breadcrumbs, powdered fennel seed and a little sugar was thought good for increasing the flow of milk in a nursing mother's breasts. But by the seventeenth century rice was no longer a magical luxury. Dorothy Hartley quotes Gervase Markham, who died in 1637: 'If you will sow rice you may do it, but it is like to prouve a work of curiositie rather than of profit . . .' He explains how to grow rice in an English field, where there is plenty of water but not enough sun to bring it to harvest. Then he discusses it as food. 'If you boyle rice in milk adding thereto sugar and cinnamon, it will provoke unto venerie. Many do think it maketh fat; but seemingly that (according to the physitions) it is not digested in the stomach but verie hardly, it must need nourish but little – How can it possibly make one fat?'

A century or so later, it was being imported to Britain in large enough quantities to be considered quite an ordinary item of diet – usually in milk puddings. Hannah Glasse's *The Art of Cookery Made Plain and Easy* in 1747 contains some twenty rice recipes. Most are puddings, one or two still using almonds as a flavouring as they had been used five hundred years earlier. But the new age is here as well, in a recipe 'to make a Pellow the India way'. Then the availability of cheap rice from new possessions overseas drove this former luxury food further and further down the British market. Nineteenth-century food writers become patronizing about rice. In 1842, the *Domestic Dictionary* says that 'it grows abundantly in the East Indies and in Egypt, and there forms the chief food of the poor . . . There is a deep-rooted belief in England that the frequent and abundant use of rice will bring on blindness; but this opinion is not borne out by experience.' I should think not, indeed.

By this time, rice was being taken to countries very remote from where it grew. Farm workers in nineteenth-century Norway ate a porridge of water and barley on working days, milk and barley on Sundays, but milk and rice for feasts and celebrations. In Finland, rice porridge was served as dessert on Christmas Eve, and Christmas lunch began with the leftover porridge, sliced thick and fried.

Rice across the Atlantic

Columbus's discovery of America, whatever you may think of its broader consequences, did at least help to distribute good food around the world. Chilli peppers and chocolate, as well as the prosaic potato and many other vegetables, were taken from Central America to Asia. In return, America received rice, though it had several false starts there, as in other parts of the world. Some writers suggest that seeds were first taken across on slave ships, and that only slaves had the knowledge of how to grow rice successfully; even that expert rice farmers were sought out in West Africa by traders who had been commissioned to find them. The Spaniards and Portuguese took it to Central and South America, where it has flourished ever since. Filipino rice no doubt came in the galleons from Manila to Acapulco. But in the north, it took rice a long time to get established.

It had been named as a 'desired' crop when several of the earliest colonies were founded. In 1609 it was proposed as a possible crop in Virginia. Unsuccessful trials were made there in the 1620s, and the first settlers in North Carolina experimented with what was probably upland rice, sown in fields that were not flooded. Sir William Berkeley is said to have sowed half a bushel of rice seed in Virginia in 1647 and reaped fifteen bushels. I have not been able to discover what variety of rice this was, but a thirtyfold increase is perfectly credible. Berkeley's success, however, was apparently not followed up. The soil and climate of Virginia were not really suitable; what was needed was a long, warm growing season and plenty of water.

The South Carolina swamps offered both, though they also bred malarial mosquitoes. Here, too, the first settlers had planned to include rice among their produce. The Proprietors of the colony announced in 1677 that they wished to obtain rice seed, and a petition in 1691 mentioned rice as a good crop for the area. Two attempts were made to grow rice from seed brought from Madagascar. In 1694, a brigantine on a voyage from Madagascar is said to have put into Charleston harbour in distress. The master of the ship gave a bag of rice to a local bigwig, who distributed it among his friends. They sowed it, and apparently it did extremely well. A year or two later, a man called du Bois, who was Treasurer of the East India Company, also sent a bag of seed to South Carolina; this supposedly explained the fact that two varieties were grown there. Rice

Old market hall, Georgetown, South Carolina: now a rice museum

eventually got going in South Carolina during the 1690s, grown by slaves on land owned by French Huguenot refugees. Sixty tons was exported to Britain in 1698. Exports climbed steadily until the time of the American Revolution; in 1771 nearly 30,000 tons of rice was shipped out of Charleston on more than 200 ships.

Not all this 'Carolina Gold' went to Britain, despite the Navigation Acts that controlled trade from the colonies. In 1729 the law was modified to allow rice to be shipped direct to any port south of Cape Finisterre, in Brittany. However, when the British occupied Charleston during the Revolution, they allegedly reaped the entire crop and sent the whole lot to England, including next year's seed grain.

Thomas Jefferson Improves the Breed

Carolina rice did well enough as an export commodity to Britain and Europe, but its career was a complicated and somewhat checkered one. Perhaps its most famous benefactor was Thomas Jefferson, who was passionately interested in gardening and agriculture of all kinds and was constantly on the lookout for new plants as well as new export markets for his fledgeling country. When he was sent to Paris as the first Ambassador of the United States of America, he determined to find out why the French preferred Italian rice to American. Was it because American rice had too many broken grains? If so, it must be because the Italians had better machinery for dehusking and polishing the rice.

Jefferson could find no one in Paris who could tell him anything useful, and realized he would have to make the journey to Italy himself, which I suspect he was not at all reluctant to do. He tells the story in his letters and journal. When he returned to Paris, Jefferson wrote to a friend:

> I found their machine exactly such a one as you had described to me in Congress in the year 1775. There was but one conclusion, then, to be drawn, to wit, that the rice was of a different species, and I determined to take enough to put you in seed. They informed me, however, that its exportation in the husk was prohibited, so I could only bring out as much as my coat and surtout pockets would hold. I took measures with a muleteer to run a couple of sacks across the Apennines to Genoa, but have not great dependence on its success.

Jefferson indeed collected rice samples from wherever he could get them: 'mountain rice' from Africa, irrigated rice from Cochin China (probably Laos, Cambodia, or Vietnam). Like-minded friends corresponded excitedly about their acquisitions and sowings, often waiting months for their letters to be answered from across the seas.

71

Benjamin Vaughan writes to Jefferson from London in March 1790 that he has been sent some 'Dry Rice' by the naturalist Sir Joseph Banks. These seeds were brought back from Timor by Captain Bligh after the *Bounty* mutiny; he and his companions had navigated across 800 miles of ocean in an open boat, and the Timor rice seed represented all that Bligh could bring back to London from what had set out as a major botanical expedition. Vaughan enclosed a little packet of the seeds as Jefferson's share of the genetic materials, and Jefferson, now living in New York, sowed them in earthen pots in his house.

But we never learn very much about the results of all these experiments. Probably, like about 99 per cent of agricultural trials with new varieties, they came to nothing. But some of the Italian rough rice reached Charleston, for on 10 November 1787 Jefferson's correspondent Ralph Izard not only sends his comments on the seed but also – which is much more to the point so far as we are concerned – on cooking methods. It was Izard who, seven months earlier, had asked Jefferson to send him 'from one to ten Bushels' of Italian seed rice.

> The Seed which you have sent, and which you say is of the best kind, will bear no comparison with ours; and I am surprized to learn that the price is nearly equal. You say that our Rice dissolves when dressed with Meat. This must be owing to some mismanagement in dressing it. I have

Lunch in the harvest field: near Chiang Mai

examined my Cook on the subject, and find that as Meat requires to be longer on the fire than Rice, they must be dressed separately, until each is nearly done, and then the combination is to be made. The Water must boil before the Rice is put into it, or the grains will not be distinct from each other. The Rice you have sent will be planted. I hope great care will be taken to keep it at a distance from the other Rice Fields; for if the Farina [that is, the pollen] should blow on them, it may be the means of propagating an inferiour species among us. For that reason I should be glad that you would not send any more of it.

Rice growers today would recognize Izard's anxiety about the purity of successful local varieties. The rice culture of South Carolina was to continue for more than half a century after Jefferson's death. It reached its zenith in Georgetown County in the 1840s and 1850s, around the rivers that flow into Winyah Bay. Some of the great plantation houses remain as monuments to their owners, hard-driving men who added acre to acre, 'rounded out' their properties by buying up those of their neighbours, endowed their local churches, and relaxed at the Hot and Hot Fish Club.

It was a privileged but not an easy life; most of the men died in middle age of overwork or disease, and their wives often much younger, of disease or childbearing. And these were the owners, not the slaves. The Civil War, which ended slavery, was the beginning of the end for Carolina rice. By 1900, new rice varieties from Asia were being cultivated in the Mississippi valley by methods that had already revolutionized wheat-farming. The soft earth of the swamps could support neither the new rice nor the new machines. The industry declined. In 1910 a sequence of violent hurricanes battered the dykes and fields so severely that rice-growing was finally abandoned.

I don't suppose it is possible now, or indeed was ever possible, to assess the contribution that Thomas Jefferson and his contemporaries made to the genetic development of rice in North America. A true genealogy of rice would have to trace tens of thousands of accidents and dead ends, careful trials that came to nothing and chance crossings and sowings that turned out fruitful.

This is not to say that rice's family tree is totally hidden from us; geneticists can work back along its branches and make reasonable guesses at how old a particular variety is, where it came from, and why it has colonized a particular environment. Today, Spanish and Italian rices are mainly short grain; long grain types have usually been brought in quite recently to supply a demand. In North America, west coast rice is mostly short grain, having been brought over the Pacific by Japanese immigrants, but the rice of the south-eastern states and the Mississippi is predominantly long grain. Where its ancestors came from we may never know for certain. I like the story about Carolina rice coming originally from Madagascar. All Indonesians know that their ancestors took rice to Madagascar long, long ago.

73

A POSSIBLE FUTURE

In 1990, there were about 5,300 million people on Earth. In that year, the International Rice Research Institute estimated that by 2020 there would be 8,300 million. This figure assumes that, from the year 2000, population growth will start to slow down, mainly because people who live in towns in 'developed' countries tend to have fewer children.

If the forecast is correct, which it may not be, we can see that we have to produce a lot more food than we are doing now. Rice farmers, in particular, have to produce more. If they don't, they will have to grow other staple foods instead. It's true that there is a move away from rice in some Asian countries towards the fashionable Western-style staples, wheat and beef. But these, by and large, use land much less productively than rice does. Wheat is attractive now chiefly because it is cheaper to produce than rice, per tonne, and the world already has (in most years) a large wheat surplus. Much of that surplus, of course, would be eaten now if very poor countries could afford to buy it.

So rice production must increase by 60 per cent. In Asia, I got spot reactions to the challenge from two people. One was a senior IRRI researcher who said darkly, almost glancing over his shoulder as we strolled in the midday sun from office to lab, 'Of course, we could double rice yields in five years, if we could get governments to change their policies.' It was a safe enough comment; IRRI is strictly non-political. I think, though, that the statement was only a mild exaggeration. The other response came from an exporter in a large rice-trading company in Bangkok. He said flatly that he thought a 60 per cent increase in thirty years was impossible. He also implied that it was quite unnecessary.

At least we can probably agree that the world is going to need not only to grow more food but to distribute it better. Farmers, scientists, governments and traders are all going to play big roles; so is that easily overlooked player, the consumer. After all, everyone wants to vary their diet and eat imported foods – everyone who can afford to, anyway. Leaving aside for the moment the question of supply, will the demand for rice really increase that much?

The World Market

The first thing anyone will tell you about the world market for rice is that it is 'thin'. In other words, of all the rice that's grown, only a very small proportion is traded internationally: around 4 per cent. The figure for wheat is about 50 per cent. The market is also extremely lumpy. Some countries are major growers but very minor traders; others just the opposite. As a result of these two factors, the market fluctuates alarmingly. In 1973/4, a crisis year for Asia, world rice production dropped back just 5 per cent from the 1972 figure. On the open market, prices tripled. There is in any case a wide range of prices for different grades of rice; prime Basmati will usually sell for at least three times the price of Thai 'brokens'.

The top rice exporter for many years has been Thailand, which sells up to a third of its crop abroad; this is one reason why Bangkok is the unofficial hub of the rice trade. The USA sells up to half its crop, but it grows only one-third of what Thailand grows, so it is well down in second place as an exporter. Burma was a rival to Thailand before the Second World War, but in its present sad state it has fallen to seventh place, exporting less than 200,000 tonnes a year. Vietnam has recovered well from wartime destruction and is starting to undercut Thai prices, so that it has shot up to third place with exports comfortably above 1 million tonnes.

Other big-league traders are China, India and Pakistan, though China and India buy as much as they sell and Pakistan is not primarily a rice-growing country. Near the far other end of the scale as producers are the Australian rice growers of the Riverina,

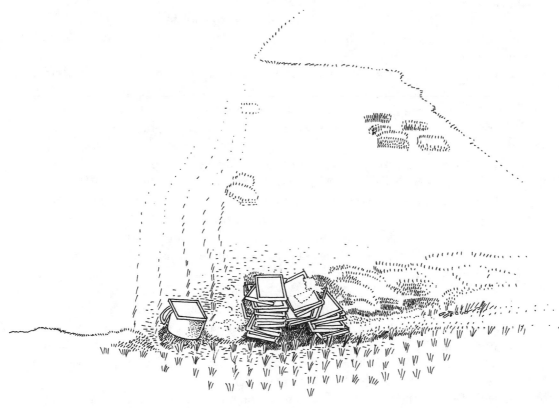

Rice seedlings and seed trays

working manfully to sell three-quarters of their rice abroad. Our Bangkok trader dismissed them with a cheerful wave of his hand: 'They're down under and out of sight and everyone's forgotten them.' This is rather unfair, since an export figure of over 450,000 tonnes puts the 2,400 Australian rice growers in sixth place in the world – more evidence of how weird the rice market is.

So why is it like this? Causes and consequences feed back into each other. Well over half the world's rice is eaten within a few kilometres of where it grew. We obviously have to distinguish between 'local' rice, which still travels in an open cart or on the carrier of someone's bicycle, and 'national' rice, which reaches the city in a truck on a tarmac road. Rice-eating countries are often large and their resources and populations very unevenly distributed. In *Mask of Asia*, George Farwell suggests that self-sufficiency is the politicians' worst fear; control of food prices and imports is an effective lever of power, and they are most reluctant to give it up.

Still, national food distribution is slowly becoming more efficient in almost every country. The distinction between 'local' and 'national' rice is breaking down and will continue to break down as farms become bigger, machines take over the hard labour, and people move into cities and factories. But some countries – Malaysia, for instance – have already said that as a matter of policy they will import up to 40 per cent of their rice, and others – like Indonesia – look as if they will go for industrial growth rather than agricultural. Even in Thailand, rice has fallen from being the top earner of foreign exchange to fourth place, behind textiles, jewellery and computer components. And all these countries want to diversify their farm crops, partly into exportable cash crops like cotton, fruit and spices, partly into new foods for home consumption like dairy products and meat. Singapore and Hong Kong have more farmland than you might expect, but neither grows any rice at all; there's a much higher profit margin on vegetables.

We have already seen that, historically, there were three or perhaps four distinct markets for rice, each with its own attitudes and views as to how rice should be regarded and cooked (page 65). In the last fifty years all these markets have changed, some more than others. The first group – the traditional rice-staple countries – have become less fragmented, less provincial, more national, as transport systems and state control have evened out some of the old imbalances among regions. At the same time the consumption of rice in these countries, per head of population, is going down. Some governments are getting quite worried about this; in Taiwan a semi-private institute is running courses to teach housewives how to make traditional rice dishes, and another organization is inventing rice-based convenience foods. The dominance of plain boiled rice is being challenged. Do-it-yourself microwaved popped rice is on its way. None of these countries is among the top five importers of rice, though some are very dependent on imports to make up their rice deficits.

The second group, those that grow rice as a useful crop but don't regard it as a staple, are diversifying into new types of rice aimed at specific export markets. When the

76

Japanese market eventually opens up to foreign-grown rice, the Australians will be ready with a variety they have custom-bred to Japanese taste. Spanish growers around Valencia are producing un-Spanish long grain rice which they mill and sell to Germany and other EC countries. All rice from outside the EC pays a high import tax, and milled rice pays about three times as much as unmilled, so the Spaniards have a keen competitive edge. Despite these taxes, the EC is the world's biggest importer, at over a million tonnes a year. Brazil comes second; it is Latin America's biggest rice producer, but it cannot grow anything like as much as it needs.

Large amounts of rice are parboiled in India and Thailand, not for local consumption but for export to the Middle East and the Persian Gulf, where parboiled rice is the market leader. In most years, Iran and Saudi Arabia import over half a million tonnes each.

The third group, the regions where rice does not grow, are becoming very diverse and fragmented markets. In Great Britain, the average person eats 3 kilos of rice a year, but this figure conceals the fact that some people eat it three times a day while

Ani-ani: South-East Asian harvesting knife

others hardly ever touch it. During the 1980s, UK rice imports rose by 70 per cent to about 245,000 tonnes (after milling). The increase was all in long grain rice; short grain (most of it for rice puddings) fell slightly. More than a third of the total went to shops and supermarkets, rather less than a third to the catering trade, and about a third to the food industry for breakfast cereals, baking flour, ready-cooked meals, noodles and beer.

Both history and current trends suggest reasons for the unsatisfactory state of the international market in rice. It is a market that in some respects is still stuck in the Middle Ages, despite the impressive technology of a modern rice mill. The quantity traded is just too small for the market ever to have got properly organized; it goes on from season to season on a more or less impromptu basis. There are so many varieties, so many grades and qualities, that every order, every contract is different. Consequently, almost all rice is shipped in bags, from 90-kilo gunny sacks down to 250-gram plastic packets ready for the supermarket shelf. Leonard Hensgens, a former president of the USA Rice Council, told me how he and a colleague went to Jakarta in 1988 and sold the Indonesians two shiploads of bulk rice, the first that that country had ever imported. Local labour was hired to put it in sacks on the dockside, so the price was competitive in the Jakarta marketplace.

On top of the problems of a small, uncertain traded surplus must be piled the

uncertain behaviour of governments. The rice miller we talked to in Amritsar deplored the way the Indian government kept moving the goalposts. The rice trader in Bangkok told us frankly, 'We enjoy the chaos.' The chaos was produced largely by traders trying to guess what the Thai authorities would do next: 'They may suddenly buy a million tonnes and the price will shoot up.' When the new crop is coming in, the government may want to create an artificial demand; they can do this by selling, say, 200,000 tonnes to a neighbouring government at $10 a tonne below the market price. 'But the government doesn't have any rice; they will buy from Thai exporters and pay $10 or $15 higher than today's price. The government can afford to lose.' In other words, Thai farmers are subsidized from public funds, but at rates and times that no one can foresee.

The catch is that no one really knows what the market price is. The market is intensely secretive. It is allegedly controlled by Chinese merchants, 'the six tigers of Bangkok' (though even the number of tigers is in some doubt). Most deals are small, by the standards of the wheat trade, and everything depends on personal contact. The figures that are published every day are supposed to be prices f.o.b. Bangkok, but these are based either on government-to-government sales which intentionally distort the market, or on deals that contain so many concealed discounts and other adjustments that the quoted prices are unreliable. In the wheat market, the USA, with its huge surplus, is the 'supplier of last resort' which fixes the base price for the world. No rice trader has sufficient surplus to claim this uneasy distinction.

Free Trade, Tariffs and Subsidies

We are all supposed to believe in 'market forces' now: unfettered competition, the perfect wisdom of the open market, and what politicians keep calling 'a level playing field'. Chris Black, of the New South Wales Rice Growers, feels that his team is playing uphill and against the wind.

'We are the last free traders of rice in the world,' he told us. 'When the USA and the EC take each other on in a trade subsidy war, we get squeezed in between them like the meat in the sandwich.' Competitors in the rice trade had a score of ways of subsidizing their farmers: low-interest loans, cheap seed and chemicals, free water, guaranteed floor prices for the crop. All the Australians get is a funding programme for rice breeding and research; everything else they pay for, from irrigation to marketing.

The American growers are in a very different situation, though they utter similar complaints of unfair foreign competition. The Murrumbidgee and the Mississippi valleys make an interesting study in similarities and contrasts; both areas have big farms, use similar equipment and methods. Yet some American farmers still grow their own rice, and mill and sell it locally under their own names in a style of rugged independence that would probably not be possible in Australia and may not work in America for much longer. Rice in California is already produced by big corporations. Costs are rising too fast for the small man to keep up, and rice everywhere must be branded, advertised and sold to the widest possible market.

The results can be impressive. The Australians claim to have increased their domestic rice sales by 20 per cent with one brilliantly executed TV campaign. In Louisiana, Leonard Hensgens told us that each American now consumes nearly 21 pounds of rice in a year, and the industry is aiming for 25 pounds in 1995: '25 in '95'. This average hides large regional differences in consumption, and the figure includes rice used in food processing and brewing. Still, it's three times what they were eating twenty years ago.

American rice farmers have the advantage of being concentrated in a few states whose welfare is of particular interest to Washington. They have also been established long enough for rice to have a 'base' – to be included among the crops whose prices are, within a limited acreage, guaranteed by the federal government. The base area can't be extended, so farmers who grow extra rice outside it do so at their own risk. Soya beans don't get as much support per tonne as rice, but they don't require any 'base' acreage because they weren't a major US crop when the foundations of the present agricultural policy were laid in the 1920s. Corn (i.e. maize) does require such a base, but it doesn't have one in Louisiana because people weren't growing it there at the crucial time. So farmers there grow quite a lot of soya beans but not much corn.

Rice-farming in the United States, as in so many other countries, is hard to get into if you weren't born to it. Land and machines are expensive, interest rates are high and cheap loans few. To get anywhere, you usually have to join the local co-operative, which owns the local rice mill; a share in this is expensive. 'New' rice land, if it doesn't qualify for government price support, may produce a crop that sells for less than it costs to produce.

We went to Mer Rouge, in northern Louisiana, to meet Larry Tubbs. He showed us a patch of earth that he was upgrading to make it fit for growing rice. Beside a dried-up creek, three enormous yellow graders were driving in wide loops, scraping up and dropping soil at the direction of a beam of laser light on a central mast. Land which merely looked flat under the huge Louisiana sky was being levelled to make wide terraces as smooth as billiard tables, separated by machine-built levees. At the top of a shallow flight of these terraces we found the feedpipes that would bring ground water for a whole field covering several hectares. The process of levelling and installing irrigation works was expensive, but it would pay in the long run; it made the land worth perhaps three times what it had been worth before.

Larry's son is already a well-established rice grower, so there was no need to ask whether he wanted the family business to be carried on. Larry himself started as a wheat farmer in Missouri but moved south with a small group of like-minded neighbours some years ago, when wheat futures looked unpromising. He did well; most of the others have gone back to Missouri. I asked Larry how he saw the future of rice in America. He shook his head. 'The big will get bigger and the small farmers will disappear,' he said. 'It's a shame, but I don't see how else it can be.' Most of his extensive landholdings are let to tenants on one-year leases; the short lease protects him against a lazy or incompetent farmer, who might in three years do lasting damage to the soil. He himself grows some rice, not covered by any government purchase scheme, which he sells direct to buyers in Latin America, negotiating the deals in person several months ahead of the harvest.

This kind of large-scale, speculative, capital-intensive farming may seem tough, even ruthless, but it is evolving fast in most major rice-growing areas. Environmentally, it is just another way of managing a landscape which ceased to be wilderness a hundred years ago. Socially, it supplies cities with cheap food, though it creates few jobs in the countryside. Economically and politically, it creates problems as well as opportunities. Rice can be sold abroad, which is good for the balance of payments, or gifts and sales can be variously disguised as foreign aid. But to satisfy the conflicting demands of growers, millers, shippers, consumers and – most exigent of all – aid recipients, is a task of huge complexity which few governments would ever dream of leaving to 'market forces'.

Some of the most interventionist governments are the growth leaders of the Far East: South Korea, Taiwan (Republic of China), above all Japan. They are all self-sufficient in rice, and could produce more. None exports or imports much, though a Taiwanese official complained to me that this is because Washington won't allow them to charge an economic price; if Taiwan encroached seriously on Asian markets for US rice, there would be retaliation against Taiwan's electronic goods in America. In Washington, we heard that countries like Taiwan deliberately over-produce and then dump their rice surpluses cheap wherever they can. Likewise in Turkey: the US government has to subsidize its farmers so they can sell rice to Turkey in competition with the unfairly subsidized Italians . . .

But to return to Japan: this is a country where rice still wields its ancient mystical power as something much more than a staple food, something much closer to the soul of the nation. This attitude has transferred itself to contemporary Japanese politics. Rice land pays a tiny fraction of the taxes levied on land that has been built on. Old rural constituencies still send more members to the Diet than mighty cities do. Only about 10 per cent of the Japanese are now farmers, and the average farming family makes only about 15 per cent of its living from the land; but every farmer belongs to the national co-operative federation, and this is a major contributor to the funds of the ruling party.

This set-up has a violently distorting effect on the price of agricultural land in Japan, around US$250,000 a hectare despite the anxiety of many farmers to leave the land, and on the price of rice in the Japanese market, between six and eight times what it costs in most other countries. Imports are forbidden, except of small amounts for industrial use; Australian rice is allowed into Japan on condition it is made into beer and re-exported to Australia. Exports are out of the question, since no other country would be willing to pay Japanese prices.

There are signs that this situation may soon change. The changes will partly reflect and partly cause far-reaching shifts in the complicated web of Japanese attitudes to rice. They have few inhibitions about other foods. Japan is the biggest net importer of food in the world; if fodder for livestock is included, the Japanese buy in just about half of what they eat.

Resources for Farmers

In India, income derived from agriculture is not taxed. This sounds good, but the chief beneficiaries are the wealthy farmers and landowners, who could afford to pay. The vast majority of the very poor have incomes too small to tax anyway.

Not that this has prevented small farmers throughout history and in every part of the world from paying through the nose: to landlords, to moneylenders, to middlemen, to bankers, to colonial powers and imperial officers. A big farmer like Larry Tubbs can afford to sell his rice months before it is harvested, because only a small part of his capital is at risk. Countless peasants and tenant farmers are forced to sell their harvest season by season before it is cut, because they have no capital and this is the only way to pay their debts and ensure that the moneylender will provide them with the means to sow the next crop.

Farmers in this situation cannot save themselves, and they are certainly not going to save the world. Most rice-growing countries in Asia, Africa and Latin America have now completed, or at the very least begun, a programme of land reform. This aims to turn tenants into leaseholders with security of tenure, and to break up big estates. Some governments did this of their own free will; others had it imposed on them. Successes and failures have been plentiful, often in the same country. In the Philippines, the hold of the wealthy landowning families remains firm in many areas. In Indonesia and elsewhere, a rich family can hang on to its estate by re-registering small parcels of it in the names of different family members.

'But,' they might reply, 'why shouldn't we? We're individuals, we have our rights – and if we choose to work together, our land is more efficiently used as one big farm than many small ones. Our problem is not capitalist greed; it's inheritance customs that, whenever anyone dies, try to divide land among all the children.'

Land reform sounds unambiguous: 'land to the tiller' is a slogan whose simple justice we all feel. But a reform programme has to take into account people's attitudes to the land, and the ways in which ownership or use are permitted to change. Inheriting a rice farm in Japan, for example, is no light matter, even if the children, who inherit equal shares, agree on who should stay to farm the land while the rest go to the city. Richard H. Moore, in *Japanese Agriculture*, explains that

> the main problem encountered by rural society is household succession and inheritance. As single heir to the household, the rural farmer bears the responsibility for keeping up the ancestral graves, the household Buddhist altar, co-ordinating the anniversary Buddhist memorial service, sustaining hierarchical or reciprocal social relations with branch or main households in their ancestral line, and finally serving as an important link between rural and urban relatives who at some time past migrated to the city as non-heirs. The annual gift-rice (*zotomai*) sent to urban relatives is a symbolic gesture of this reciprocal relationship.

In many traditional societies, land is sacred, the owner holds it in trust for his or her lifetime and it can only be sold in unusual and very specific circumstances. In Taiwan, as in Japan, to sell the family land is still in some sense to betray one's ancestors. Farmers who think in this way are usually good ecologists, but they effectively 'lock up' land in a system that demands a great deal of labour and offers little scope for capital investment. Are the reformers trying to set up a free market in land, or to use land to express their notion of social justice? Either way, merely confirming the existence of a

IRRI axial-flow thresher

lot of small farms, run by leaseholders instead of tenants, is not by itself going to lead to a reinvigorated, efficient rice-growing industry.

The same sort of argument follows from the demand that small farmers should have access to working capital, usually in the shape of low-interest loans, so that they can buy seed, improve their land or hire machinery. As with land reform, governments have certainly tried. Farmers' banks and farmers' co-operatives seem to be everywhere, and I am sure they do an enormous amount of good. Their organizers do not have an easy life; people in most parts of the world have an instinctive, and in the past often justified, mistrust of banks, while most co-ops demand fixed and regular payments from the farmer in return for benefits which are not fixed and may look very uncertain. A Thai official told me that only about one farmer in four in Thailand belongs to a co-op.

Help for small farmers is excellent in its way and much needed in the short term, but, like subsidies to small farmers in Europe, in the long run it condemns agriculture to remain an undeveloped area of the economy. 'Agribusiness' is often used as a term of abuse for capital-intensive farming practices that overwork and despoil the land. But people grow food either for their own subsistence or to make money; when agriculture ceases to be a business, natural resources go to waste. This is especially serious in a rice-growing area, since rice demands such complex and careful management of resources over an area much larger than that of most individual farms.

What I think we shall see – if things go well – is a fairly rapid transformation of rice-farming communities so that land reform and every other kind of state support for the small farmer will be seen, in retrospect, as parts of a necessary but quite brief transition from 'old rice' to 'new rice'. New rice will be grown by large business units; they may be brigades or communes in China, 'estates' made up of small farms in Malaysia, co-operatives in the Philippines or, in Bali, some sort of organization developed from the irrigation society or *subak*. These businesses may be state-owned or private, but in any case their finance and management will be deeply influenced by government policy. Their capital, even if they are not state-owned, will come largely from public funds, since private investors are unlikely to buy shares in farm produce when they can invest in industry; but the public funds will come from tax revenues that industry generates.

China: Feeding a Billion

One of the most encouraging aspects in this view of the future is the continuing diversity of rice culture. To the casual visitor, the most obvious change in the landscape will be in the flat country along the north coast of Java or in central Thailand: the sweeping curves of field boundaries that now follow the contour lines will be replaced by the straight sides of rectangular fields, levelled by machines in the way we watched Larry Tubbs's field being levelled at Mer Rouge. The contrast between the two types is already a striking one as you fly over rice lands in America and Australia. But the real revolution is going to be in farm management. Rice farming has always required knowledge, experience and judgement. In the future, it will demand highly trained skills and specialization; in return, it will provide a career ladder like any other business enterprise.

This is if things go well. If things go wrong, they could do so in so many different ways that speculation is pointless. As for the international rice trade, I suspect it will go on much as it does now, since 90-odd per cent of rice will still be eaten quite close to where it is grown. But what about the rice itself? Without yet higher yields, it is unlikely that consolidated farm management will be sufficiently skilled, or government policies sufficiently enlightened, to achieve 60 per cent production growth by 2020. Apart from anything else, rice land is being lost – by erosion, flooding, urban and industrial development – at the rate of hundreds of thousands of hectares every year. It will take a good deal of running just to stay where we are.

We have already seen how the first Green Revolution achieved a great increase in world crop yields, not only of rice but of wheat and corn also, just when it was most urgently needed in the 1960s and 1970s. This increase was only partly the result of new 'miracle breeds'; better irrigation, more and better fertilizers and agrochemicals, new machines and more efficient distribution all played their parts, the key to all these being, of course, more money. By the mid-1980s the immediate crisis seemed to be over, the money was needed elsewhere and the yields stopped increasing. Only the flood of controversy showed no sign of abating: had the 'revolution' left the poor of the Third World better or worse off? The weight of evidence on both sides seemed about equal; or, rather, it depended on which area you studied, and how you defined your terms.

My impression, after a year of travelling around talking to people involved with rice, is that most governments are still pretty complacent about the results of the first Green Revolution and the need for a second one. Perhaps one can hardly blame politicians for lacking a sense of urgency about rice shortages if they are currently subsidizing farmers to produce a surplus. But the research institutes, national and international, are still being funded, and there is plenty happening in their laboratories and experimental plots. One of the most interesting places to look at, as we might expect, is China.

China is not the world's biggest rice grower in terms of area. India plants 40 million hectares to China's 33 million. But a Chinese hectare yields more than twice as much as an Indian one, and China is of course by far the top producing country, approaching 180 million tonnes of rough rice a year. Koreans, Japanese, Americans, Australians, all get a larger harvest out of a hectare than the Chinese, but their rice-farming is on a smaller, more intensive scale. Communism may not have enabled China to achieve its maximum potential, but the Chinese have managed to grow an astonishing amount of food.

Rice has been the principal food crop south of the Yangzi for about 1,500 years. Until the Communist Revolution, China followed the traditional pattern of a society of small peasants and tenants, hard-driven by landlords and officials. By 1952, land reform had bulldozed its way across the country and collectivization followed it, too rapidly to be either humane or efficient. Even so, rice production increased. The Great Leap Forward, which started in 1958, replaced collective farms of around 150 hectares with communes about thirty times that size. These were unmanageable, rice harvests dwindled, and by the early 1960s farmers were being organized into a hierarchy of groups: production teams managed the small capital items, like two-wheeled tractors and tillers; brigades managed the larger ones, like threshers and trucks; and the commune was responsible for mills, irrigation systems and other really expensive things. Gradually, many farmers found themselves once again in virtual control of their own affairs. Yields improved. Even the long years of the Cultural Revolution saw a steady increase in production, and when the Gang of Four fell and agriculture returned to more or less private management yields went up again – from 4 tonnes a hectare in 1978 to over 5 tonnes in 1983.

This of course is a country-wide average, hiding a range of failures and successes. Chinese geneticists were starting to breed high-yielding dwarf varieties before the International Rice Research Institute was born or thought of. In the mid-1970s, the latter days of Chairman Mao, the fertile 'fish and rice country' around Suzhou, south of the Yangzi delta, was achieving the Maoist ideal of a rural economy completely dominated by grain production, three harvests a year being won by dint of extreme hard labour and careful watching of the calendar. This meant two rice crops and one of winter grain, an impressive record so far north but not a sufficient reward for the effort that went into it. With Mao's departure, the area devoted to rice actually fell slightly as vegetables crept back into the landscape and farmers were permitted to grow what they wanted and what best suited their soil and weather.

Revolutions need heroes, and Communist China produced plenty. One of them, who really did do some remarkable work, was Chen Yongkang. He was not a highly qualified rice breeder in a government lab, but a farmer born and bred who used his eyes and his intelligence. His family had a small farm in that fish-and-rice country near Lake Taihu, and Chen spent his youth watching the rice grow and observing the various techniques his family and their neighbours used. By 1951 he had bred a new japonica rice variety of his own, which he called *lao lai qing* – 'green when old' – and with this he achieved, on a measured plot of land, a yield equivalent to 10.5 tonnes per hectare. You may say that this was like coddling a giant leek to unnatural size for a flower show; it was still pretty good going in 1951. By the mid-1960s, Chen's techniques were being successfully applied in many parts of China, and in 1978 he scored what must have been a personal best: one barley and two rice crops on a measured plot produced a total crop equal to 24.43 tonnes per hectare.

However, the real achievement of the Chinese has been in growing hybrid rice on a large scale. First-generation (F1) hybrids are famous for what biologists call *heterosis* – the strength and vigour that can result from inheriting widely different genes. The classic example is the mule; but mules are sterile, which suggests that hybrids have problems. One of the problems is that the benefits of 'hybrid vigour' are often lost after the first generation. (This is one reason why you cannot grow a useful apple tree from an apple pip.) Therefore, the farmer who grows hybrid rice cannot keep back the best of this season's crop as seed for the next. It will grow, but it will revert to the ordinariness or even to the vices of its parentage.

In itself, this is not too serious, because almost all modern crop varieties depend on specially grown seed. This is one of the many factors that are drawing the subsistence farmer relentlessly into the world cash economy; he must have money to buy seed, not to mention chemicals, mostly oil-based. Producing good-quality seed for 'ordinary' high-yielding rices is much easier than doing it for F1 hybrids, but is still a specialized job. As generation succeeds generation, the danger is that plants will be accidentally pollinated by other varieties, so that good characteristics are lost and undesirable ones inherited.

Most of our maize is now grown from F1 hybrid seed, and has been for many years. Most rice, however, still is not, because F1 hybrid rice seed is particularly difficult to produce in marketable quantities. Many countries' research institutes are working on it, with greater or lesser inputs of zeal and cash, but only the Chinese, at the time of writing, have cracked it. They started serious work on hybridization in 1964, and achieved their breakthrough in 1973, a remarkably short time. By 1990, more than a quarter of China's rice land was under hybrid rice, and yields were running at up to 13.5 tonnes a hectare. How did they do so much so quickly? One is reminded of Emperor Yang Di's southward extension of the Grand Canal, said to have been completed in a decade around the year AD 600. He did it – or rather, he made other people do it – to bring wheat and rice northward to the less fertile provinces around his new capital.

Hybrid rice certainly cost less suffering and fewer lives than the Grand Canal. But both achievements suggest single-minded determination and obedience, and both made brilliant use of existing natural resources. A crucial stage in the large-scale breeding of hybrid rice was the discovery that a wild variety, found only on the island of Hainan, causes male sterility in the offspring when crossed with cultivated rice. This means that the hybrids cannot pollinate themselves; their ovaries have to receive pollen from a nearby plant. A complicated series of cross-breedings produces first-generation hybrid seeds, their genes stuffed with desirable characteristics, from three or four rows of male-sterile plants alternating with one row of pollinators.

This all sounds very well arranged. Why don't the Chinese make available some of their hybrids, the Americans take over the seed business, and everybody settle down to produce 12 or 14 tonnes to the hectare? That ought to meet any demands made by population increase for at least another forty years. In fact, of course, nothing is that simple. Regardless of politics, there are natural factors ensuring that new rices will always be needed and rice breeding will remain a career with good long-term prospects.

The Vigour of the Breed

First, there is the risk that attends too great reliance on a few varieties of any food crop. The Irish potato famine of the 1840s showed what can happen. As Eugene and Marja Anderson put it, in their paper in *Food in Chinese Culture*,

> In a southern Chinese peasant plot, before the days of miracle grains, chance pollination and natural selection for diversity probably guaranteed that no two plants were genetically identical, or at least that a field would be a marvelous genetic mosaic – allowing resistant strains to develop naturally, heterosis to occur, and microhabitat differences to encourage microdifferentiation in rices.

In the mid-1980s, by contrast, it was estimated that rice IR36 was being sown on 11 million hectares throughout the world: probably the largest one-variety crop ever grown. IR36 can withstand most diseases and pests, and 11 million hectares is less than 8 per cent of the world's rice land, so the risk of trouble is still quite small. But just as flu viruses are constantly mutating to plague us by getting through our bodies' defences, so the enemies of rice can respond fast to any weakness they discover. The more genetic variety there is in the landscape, the better insured we are against a sudden outbreak of disease sweeping through our food supplies.

We need genetic variety, therefore. But where the old farmer's field contained random variation, with many strains that were unproductive and not very good at looking after themselves, we need varieties that are tailored precisely to the places where they are going to grow – this is what the Andersons meant by 'microdifferentiation'. Though IR36 would obviously grow in a wide range of environmental conditions, the trend now is to match the breed as closely as possible to the microhabitat. Habitats, big and small, are always changing, not least because of our activities as farmers; so rice will continue to change as well.

Small habitats we can at least have some control over. The big one – the planet – is another matter. We have already seen some of the ways rice farmers are making their contribution to possible ecological collapse, spraying chemicals on to their fields, chopping down trees. It wouldn't be too difficult to find more; by pumping groundwater, they are lowering water-tables, and by growing wet rice they are releasing large amounts of methane into the atmosphere.

IRRI researchers regard global warming as an unproven hypothesis, but they take it seriously enough to be conducting large-scale experiments on how it may affect rice growers. Rice, as we have seen, was first domesticated near the northern limits of the tropics, and if temperatures near the Equator rise a degree or two it may be necessary to breed new heat-tolerant varieties. It may also become possible, and even advisable, to grow rice in regions that are as yet too cold. I have a kind of regret that I shall probably not live long enough to see the paddy fields of my native Cheshire being irrigated from the waters of the Dee and Mersey. What is alarming is that rising temperatures may raise the sea level and drown much low-lying land. That could include the great river deltas which much of Asia now depends on for its rice.

Somewhere between the local difficulty and the global catastrophe comes the national problem. Some such problems are being tackled very effectively by national research institutes and government ministries – for example, that of distributing rice in countries where people are moving from farms into cities; or, in the Philippines, that of dealing with golden snails. These snails were introduced in 1984 as a new source of protein and a delicacy that farmers could sell to restaurants. They soon broke loose and started a population explosion in the rice fields, eating newly sprouted seedlings. IRRI has designed a counter-weapon, a kitchen strainer and scraper-blade on a long handle, cheaper and greener than anti-snail sprays.

Pests in general, however, are another guarantee of future work for the rice breeder. However pest- and disease-resistant a crop variety may be, within ten or twenty years some bug will have evolved, a result of chance genetic mutation, that can attack it. We have seen that it takes about ten years to get a new variety from the experimental station to the farmer's field, so the geneticist does not sit around waiting for the pest to appear. In the same way, locksmiths and burglars try to stay one step ahead of each other. And in dealing with specific enemies, the scientist has not only a mountain of learned papers to draw on, but the resources of the gene-banks. These are being exploited with an ingenuity matched only by the researchers' patience.

Duncan Vaughan, an English geneticist at IRRI's International Rice Germplasm Center, told me of one such case. 'Grassy stunt virus is a very serious disease of rice in Asia. Pathologists screened the germ plasm in the gene-bank here for resistance to that particular disease, and after going through 20,000 different varieties they could not find anything that was resistant. But fortunately, after testing many different types of wild rice, they found just one population of wild rice that gave a few seedlings that were resistant; in fact it was only three plants out of a batch of thirty seedlings that had the gene that resisted the virus. That gene from those few seedlings was then used by the plant breeder and incorporated into new varieties.' The thirty seeds that produced the three resistant plants had come from wild rice plants of no obvious value, gathered at the side of a jungle path in another country years before.

IRRI no longer breeds new rices for the farmer, but acts as a centre for advanced research and the conservation of germ plasm. Dr Vaughan gave me another example of the value of a germ plasm bank. 'In 1972 and 1973, one of my predecessors was in Cambodia and was able to collect, with people from Cambodia, germ plasm from that country. As we all know, during the 1970s there was trouble in Cambodia and a lot of rice varieties were lost – particularly deepwater traditional varieties. Farmers were not allowed to plant them. Fortunately they were already in the gene-bank here at IRRI.'

So rices which had been developed over centuries to suit local conditions were slowly re-established in their old habitat. But this is just a rather poignant example of the exchanges of genetic material that are constantly going on; 'in fact, last year we distributed about 50,000 different samples of rice worldwide . . .'

Genetic engineering, protoplast fusion, gene transformation, are all being used, or will be used, to improve breeding lines and speed up the process of developing and assessing new rices. Even a relatively simple lab culture technique may cut the development lead time, so its Japanese pioneers told us, from ten years to six or seven. This doesn't just help with the tailoring of standard wet-rice types to local conditions in favoured areas. It makes the improvement of less productive, marginally grown rices economic. These include deepwater rice and, said to be the tastiest of all, upland rice – the *gogo rancah* of the high Indonesian hillsides, sown after the forest has been cleared and burnt, the site abandoned after two seasons for the natural vegetation to recover. There are plenty of hill folk in Asia who live on upland rice, but yields are low and the forest is dwindling; new knowledge may give them more choice in where they live and how they spend their lives.

It would be nice to conclude that this continual effort to assist nature in bringing forth new rices would guarantee the survival of a wide range of flavours and textures on the supermarket shelves of the future. In fact this is unlikely to happen; rice is becoming a standardized product in China and Thailand, just as apples have become in Britain. Breeders do regard flavour and cooking quality as important, and so does the market; virtually all rice now on sale in Western countries is very good, by any standards. Slowly, we are being given a wider choice. But the market wants the next packet of Basmati that you buy to be exactly the same as the last, with no element of chance.

Even in many rice-growing countries, the farmer and his family no longer eat the rice they have grown in their own field. They sell that to the government, and buy their household rice at the village store.

Roger Owen

The Recipes

Introduction

It is my ambition that this book should be useful in practically any part of the world, and should stay useful for many years to come. Fashions and changes in food are now so unpredictable and so sweeping that the second wish may be even harder to make come true than the first. However, I have suggested as many alternative ingredients and cooking methods as I can, in the belief that some way can be found of cooking any dish satisfactorily in any country. I have taken note of new ingredients and new techniques in the hope of making the book time-proof, at least for a while.

Perhaps I should add that it is definitely not my intention to make people eat rice three times a day or with every course of a meal. On the contrary: I know from long experience that rice goes well with any food. I even serve it with a traditional English Christmas dinner, though it was only when I began researching *The Rice Book* that I learned that rice has long been essential to Christmas food in Finland. We are well on the way to living in a world where no food can be regarded any longer as truly 'exotic'; rice certainly is not. It may be fun from time to time to recreate a genuine medieval feast, or to cook a dinner from a classic Arab or Japanese treatise, but in daily life we should not be too much concerned about 'traditional' or 'authentic' cuisine; what matters is that food should be healthy and good to eat.

It follows that no recipe in this book should be considered unalterable, even though I have tested them all and they all work. It is impossible to say how much rice a particular person or family will eat unless you know something of people's backgrounds. The quantities shown here might be too much for Westerners who are not used to rice; they will certainly be too little for hungry Indonesians or Koreans or others who are accustomed to a plate of rice at every meal. Change things, experiment by all means – I would much rather feel that I had encouraged someone to invent a dozen dishes of their own than merely taught them to reproduce one of mine.

The recipes are divided into six sections. The first deals with basic rice cookery and all the various ways of making sure you get perfectly cooked rice every time. This gives you a wide choice of techniques to suit all kitchens. When I am cooking rice at home, whether the quantity is large or small, my own preferred method is always the electric rice cooker. But when I'm away from home, I am perfectly happy to cook rice in a single saucepan. The result is just as good, either way.

The second considers rice simply as an accompaniment to other dishes; even here, there is plenty of variety. The third section is much the longest. It was hard to stop even more recipes slipping into it while I wasn't watching them, and it was impossible to find any satisfactory and helpful way of breaking up the list: one-dish meals, appetizers, soups, first courses are all brought together here because these dishes are so versatile that most of them could come under two or more subheadings.

The main courses, however, were very little problem, and they all fell quite naturally into the divisions of fish and seafood, poultry, meat, and vegetarian and vegan dishes. However, I should not like the general reader to assume that the last of these is aimed only at people who don't eat meat. All the vegetarian and vegan recipes here are included on merit; they contain some of my particular favourites, and they will all stand comparison with any other recipe in the book. Vegetarians and vegans should also note that there are a number of recipes in the third section which they will find acceptable.

To some extent, I have tried to classify dishes by type or group similar dishes together. Like all systems for organizing things, this one throws up some anomalies and leftovers, but on the whole it seems to work quite well. The results show, not surprisingly, that geography and national culture play large parts in deciding how people cook.

The fifth section, on sweet rice cakes and puddings, is made up largely of recipes for the familiar rice pudding in some of the many variations that betray its different origins and checkered history. It makes an excellent dessert, assuming there has not been too much rice in earlier courses of the same meal, but in some forms it is good to have at teatime or even for breakfast, instead of dry rice cereals.

Finally, there is a section on stocks, sauces and relishes, which turn up in several recipes as ingredients, or appear at table with all sorts of dishes.

Most recipe titles are in English, but in many cases a traditional name in the language of the country where the dish originates is given as a subtitle. Often the traditional name will be more familiar to the reader; therefore, both are listed in the Index. If you want to find a list of all the dishes that contain (for example) lamb as a principal ingredient, or all the Indian recipes, then look up 'lamb', 'India', and so on, in the Index.

For the convenience of readers, I have followed the now almost universal practice of giving alternative sets of weights and measures. Liquid quantities are given in litres/pints/US cups; solids in kilograms/pounds, with the exception of raw rice and lentils, which are also given in US cups, as the preference is for measuring these by volume rather than weight. Please bear in mind that a standard American cup holds half a US pint, which is 8 fluid ounces – not 10, as in the UK system.

Tablespoons vary so much in size in Britain that I have used the American spoon, which holds 15 ml/½ fluid ounce, as standard. British readers are strongly advised to find and use a spoon of this size for measuring the quantities given in the recipes.

I want to take this opportunity to record my debts to other writers and cooks. Where

I have drawn on someone else's work, I have mentioned this in the introductory note that accompanies the recipe. But some people have contributed so much that they should be mentioned separately. For Middle Eastern rice dishes, I have been greatly helped by Claudia Roden and Margaret Shaida. Maggie Black and Gillian Riley have given me generous helpings of their knowledge of medieval and renaissance cooking in England and Italy. Helen Saberi has advised me on Afghan food, Anna del Conte on Italian, and Elisabeth Lambert Ortiz on Latin America, Spain and Portugal, and the Caribbean. Their books, and many others that have guided me through the maze, are listed in the Bibliography; but their friendship and hospitality go far beyond the making of lists.

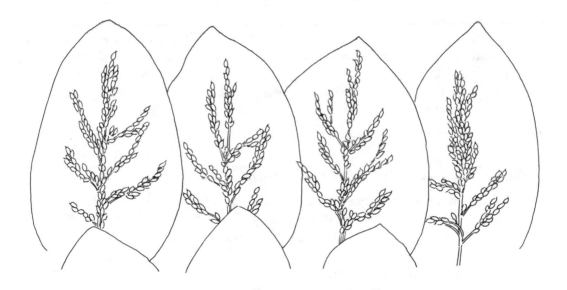

Rice panicles laid on rice flour wafers for a harvest festival: Philippines

PLAIN COOKED RICE

In countries where rice is the staple food, everyone considers himself a connoisseur. To start with, the rice should be the best available. The three types of long grain rice that I normally use in Britain are Thai Fragrant (also known as Jasmine rice), Basmati and long grain American. There are many others, however, which are also very good; and of course the rices I have mentioned are all marketed under various brand names.

Just as important as quality is cooking. Fortunately, cooking rice to perfection is much easier than some people seem to think. If you have an electric rice cooker, good results are pretty well guaranteed, but you can cook rice beautifully in an ordinary saucepan.

This section describes several ways of cooking plain white boiled rice. I also add some more general information about plain-cooking other types – brown, glutinous and parboiled. Recipes later in the book give all necessary instructions for cooking rice with other ingredients.

If you are using good rice, let its flavour speak for itself – don't cook it with salt. Plain white rice, eaten from a separate bowl, is regarded in Asia as a symbol of purity; salt and spices belong in the other dishes on the table. There are, of course, many recipes in which rice and salt are used together with other ingredients.

What should it be like when it's done?

If you go round the world asking what sort of texture perfectly cooked rice should have, you will get different answers everywhere you go. Two obvious extremes are Basmati, which should be light, quite dry, with separate grains, and sushi rice, which must be soft and sticky. Generally speaking, though, people like the mouth-feel of separate grains, tender but not mushy, with just a little bit of bite left in them. Brown rice, of course, is a different matter. The bran coat always remains chewy. Unpolished rice, like the Italian *semilavorato*, remains firm when cooked.

The recipes in this book are from many countries, and they call for quite a lot of different techniques for cooking rice. A great many of them, however, start from the 'absorption' method, in which the rice is put in a pan with just the right amount of water required to cook it.

Most cooking methods allow you to uncover the pan and taste a grain or two of rice to see if it's done. Bite it gently – this will show if the centre is still unacceptably hard. Slightly overcooked rice is not a disaster, but undercooked rice is not very pleasant to eat.

How much to cook?

Quantity is important, of course, but regular rice eaters take it for granted that there is always plenty. Leftovers don't matter because they will become tomorrow's breakfast. If you don't eat rice every day, and don't care for it at breakfast, you will have to try to forecast your needs more accurately. Remember that rice absorbs a lot of water as it cooks: 450 g/1 lb/2 cups of uncooked rice will soak up at least 570 ml/1 pint/2½ cups of water. This would feed my family of four adults. We are moderate rice eaters; the same quantity would barely satisfy two hungry Indonesians, but it might be enough for eight English people who don't eat rice often and therefore find it more filling.

Washing

In most Asian countries, we wash rice several times before cooking. All that's necessary is to put it in the pan, pour on enough cold water to cover it, swirl it around with your fingers, and pour it away, seeing that the water takes with it any bits of husk or discoloured grains that have not been taken out by the miller. (Packeted rice in supermarkets is rigorously screened before it reaches you, so you won't find much.) You can repeat this process once or twice if you wish. The last time, pour away as much of the water as you easily can – there is no need to drain off every last drop.

Many people will say that modern milling, and packaging in sealed plastic packs, make washing unnecessary, and maybe they're right. In Europe, recipes for paella and risotto often tell you quite specifically not to wash the rice.

In some countries, rice is only washed after it has been 'picked over' by hand to clean it. In this, as in so many aspects of rice, different people will tell you quite different things, and they are probably all – so far as their own regions are concerned – perfectly correct. However, I don't use this method of cleaning rice myself and I have never suggested it in any of my recipes.

Soaking

Many of the recipes in this book tell you to soak the rice for periods of time ranging from 30 minutes to overnight. One purpose of soaking is to bleach the rice, so that when it is cooked it will be even whiter. But it also slightly increases the moisture content of the grains, so that the cooking water can penetrate more easily. This means that the grains don't break up in the pan, and therefore don't stick to each other.

The Japanese do not soak their rice, but they wash and drain it about 1 hour before they cook it, so a little moisture is absorbed.

Different dishes require different soaking times; some require more exact timing than others. If the recipe says 'soak', then you will get better results by soaking; if it doesn't, this is because you won't.

Measuring

If you use an electric rice cooker, or the 'absorption' method in a saucepan, it is important to measure the water (or other liquid) accurately.

You can assume you will need, for example, 280 ml/10 fl oz/1¼ cups of water to 225 g/8 oz/1 cup of rice. If your rice is a dry variety, like Basmati, or if you like it rather soft, add a little more water; up to 340 ml/12 fl oz/1½ cups of water to 225 g/8 oz/1 cup of rice. The same quantity of brown rice may require 427 ml/15 fl oz/ nearly 2 cups of water.

But if your rice is to be fried afterwards, don't use any more water than you have to; cooked rice for frying must be fairly dry and fluffy.

Cooking Rice in an Electric Rice Cooker

Electric rice cooker

Put in the rice with the right amount of water (see above, and of course see also the instructions that come with the cooker), and switch on. Do not add any salt. When the rice is done, the cooker will switch off automatically. The rice is ready to serve. You can take the cooker to the table, or transfer the rice to a serving bowl. The cooker automatically switches itself on again at intervals to keep the rice hot. This process is safe (the temperature is high enough to kill bacteria), but after an hour or so continual reheating starts to make the rice rather dry.

The electric cooker also cooks brown rice and glutinous rice correctly; it takes a little longer, but the machine looks after this.

Cooking Rice in a Saucepan: The Absorption Method

450 g/1 lb/2 cups long grain rice, white or brown
570 ml/1 pint/2½ cups water

Put the rice and water in a saucepan, put the saucepan on a moderate heat and bring to the boil. Stir once with a wooden spoon. Let the rice simmer, uncovered, until all the water has been absorbed. This will take about 10 minutes (brown rice, perhaps 15 minutes).

There are four ways to finish cooking – take your pick.

Traditional method

The traditional Oriental way is to keep the rice in the saucepan and put the lid on as tightly as possible. If the lid isn't tight-fitting, you can put a layer of aluminium foil between the lid and the pan. A tea-towel is better still – it stops steam condensing inside the lid and dripping back into the rice. Turn down the heat as low as possible, and leave the rice to cook undisturbed for 10 or 12 minutes. (The time for brown rice is the same as for white.) Don't take off the lid. Take the pan off the heat and set it on a wet tea-towel on your draining board. Leave the rice to rest for 5 minutes, still with the lid on. (The wet cloth will stop the bottom layer of rice sticking to the pan.) Then uncover the pan and put the rice into its serving bowl.

INTIP   With white rice, you will find that there is a layer of rice grains, about ½ cm/¼ inch thick, stuck together on the bottom of the pan like a thin cake. Don't throw this away! In Indonesia, we call this rice cake **intip**. Dry it in the sun, or in the oven as if you were drying bread for breadcrumbs. Then break it into smallish pieces and store in an airtight container. When you have a worthwhile quantity, deep-fry the pieces of intip until they become golden brown. Sprinkle them with a little salt, and you have an unusual and delicious quick snack to serve with drinks. (With brown rice, the intip is so thin and brittle that you can just mix it in with the rest of the boiled rice.)

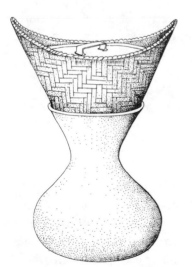

Dandang and *kukusan*: a South-East Asian rice steamer

If you don't want to eat this crusty bottom layer of rice, don't stand your saucepan on a wet cloth while it rests at the end of cooking. The bottom layer will then stick to the pan, and you can soak it off and throw the rice away.

This 'intip' has many other names in different countries. In Spain and Iran, for instance, it is the most prized part of many rice dishes (though not of plain boiled rice). The Iranians call it *tahdeeg*. In Korea and Madagascar the intip is normally left at the bottom of the pan. Water is poured on top of it and boiled, and the resulting liquid is drunk with or after the meal, as if it were tea or coffee. The Koreans call this hot rice water *soong nung* and say that it aids digestion – which I am sure it does.

Note that the other three methods of finishing off boiled rice (see below) do not give any bottom layer.

Steaming

Transfer the rice to a rice-steaming pan with a metal 'basket' to hold the rice, and steam for 10 minutes (brown rice, 15 minutes). The lid should be kept on while the rice is steaming, but it doesn't matter if you take it off to see if the rice is 'done'. The best test for doneness is just to eat a few grains. If the centres are still noticeably hard and resistant to the teeth, give the rice a few minutes longer.

In many parts of South-East Asia, we use a special pan for this process, called in Indonesian a *dandang*. The *dandang* is a metal pot which narrows a little near the top. In this narrow neck rests a basket, called a *kukusan*, woven from strips of bamboo. Steam from the dandang percolates through the woven basketwork and cooks the rice in the *kukusan*.

Oven method

Transfer the rice from the pan to an ovenproof dish. Cover the dish with buttered greaseproof paper, then with aluminium foil. Cook in a preheated oven at 180°C/350°F/Gas Mark 4 for 15–16 minutes (brown rice, 16–20 minutes).

Microwave method

Transfer the rice from the pan to a container which can be microwaved. Cover it with clingfilm/plastic wrap, set the microwave to full power, and cook for 4–5 minutes (brown rice, 6–7 minutes). (This assumes a 650 watt microwave; you may need to experiment a little.)

Other Ways to Cook Plain Rice

In a microwave

It is perfectly possible to cook rice in a microwave without first boiling it in a saucepan. However, you don't save any time by doing so. Some packeted supermarket rices have microwave instructions printed on them, and you must of course follow these. Otherwise, put the rice with the usual quantity of water into a non-metallic container big enough to hold twice as much as you put in (if the container is too small the whole thing will boil over and mess up your microwave). Cover the bowl with clingfilm/plastic wrap or a plate (*not* a metal lid), and cook on full power for 5 minutes. Leave the rice undisturbed and cook on half power for another 15 minutes. (Brown rice takes up to half as long again.) Then fluff with a fork, and the rice is ready to serve.

In salted water (certain recipes only)

Boil the rice in plenty of salted water for 4–10 minutes. The recipe will specify the exact boiling time. This method is usually called for in recipes for biryani, rice salads and some casseroles, and often the rice, usually long grain rice, has to be soaked in cold water for a period of between 1 and 8 hours.

With oil and salt: boiling

If you don't want any **intip** (see above) at the bottom of your saucepan, then put the rice in the pan with the correct amount of water, and add 1 tablespoon of oil and ½ teaspoon of salt. Give the rice a stir with a wooden spoon, cover the pan tightly, and cook on a low heat, undisturbed, for 20 minutes (brown rice, up to 30 minutes). Remove from the heat on to a wet tea-towel and keep the lid firmly on for another 5–6 minutes. Uncover, and carefully fluff the rice with a fork or a wooden spoon while you transfer it into a serving bowl.

Steamer

With oil and salt: steaming

Put the rice, water, oil and salt in a bowl and give them a stir. Put the whole lot into your steamer, with the water down below already boiling, and steam for 18–20 minutes (brown rice, 27–30 minutes).

Cooking Parboiled Rice

As explained on pages 7–8, parboiling is an exceedingly ancient method of processing rice before milling, and it is still big business today. In Europe, the USA and Australia, almost all parboiled rice is sold in packets with full instructions printed on the side. Follow the instructions and you can't go wrong. In some other parts of the world – some regions of India, the Middle East – you may buy loose parboiled rice. The cooking methods are basically the same as those for ordinary rice, but parboiled rice requires more water – usually 850 ml/1½ pints/3¾ cups of water to 450 g/1 lb/2 cups of rice – and cooking takes at least half as long again as it does for ordinary rice: 20–25 minutes instead of 15.

Cooking Easy-Cook, Cook-in-the-Fridge and Other Processed Rices

These are, almost by definition, sold in packets with instructions printed on them. Follow the instructions – different manufacturing processes lead to different products. Easy-cook rice is fine to accompany a meal, but may not be suitable for cooking by the methods required for risotto, paella, pilaf and other elaborated rice dishes.

Cooking Brown Rice

Cook brown rice as you would white rice, but give it more time; suggested cooking times are shown for each method on pages 98–101. Overnight soaking before cooking makes brown rice softer, but does not shorten the cooking time.

Cooking Red Rice and Wild Rice

These have unusually hard grains, and require much longer cooking and more water. Wild rice (which, let me repeat, is not truly rice – it belongs to a different species) is softer if soaked overnight before cooking, but this does not shorten the cooking time. These rices should be cooked by the absorption method (page 98), with 2 cups of water to 1 cup of rice, until the water is fully absorbed. For red rice, this will take about 40 minutes. Wild rice may take 50 minutes or even longer. Test for doneness by biting a grain.

Cooking Glutinous Rice

We have seen on page 10 that glutinous rice is not usually regarded as a staple food or eaten with savoury dishes. In South-East Asian countries, for example, sweetened glutinous rice (see page 342) is served with fresh fruit, such as durian, mango, or jackfruit, as a dessert.

However, there are exceptions to this rule, particularly in the highlands of Laos, Cambodia and Vietnam, where glutinous rice is the main crop and the preferred food. It is steamed and served in a woven bamboo basket like the one shown on page 99. Naturally, you can also steam it in a conventional rice steamer, or cook it in an electric rice cooker.

Glutinous rice (which, let me emphasize once again, does *not* contain any gluten) is easily obtainable in Europe and America, and as a main-course accompaniment I must say I find it extremely good. From it you can also make interesting and rather delicious rice cakes, in the manner of Japan and Korea, which are described on page 105.

As to quantity, 450 g/1 lb/2 cups of uncooked rice will be sufficient for perhaps two hungry Laotians, and will feed varying numbers up to possibly 8–10 English or American people who don't eat rice often. Soak the rice in cold water for 1 hour or longer, then drain it.

In Japan, and many Japanese shops abroad, you can buy cloths to wrap the rice in before you put it in the steamer. These may be aesthetic, or convenient, especially if you are using a woven bamboo steamer where grains of rice can easily get stuck in odd corners, but they are not necessary. In any case, a square of muslin will do the job just as well.

To steam the rice, simply boil the water in the steamer and then put the rice into the pan above it. Steam for 10–15 minutes, testing a grain or two between your teeth to judge when it is done.

If you use an electric rice cooker, put the drained rice into it and add 570 ml/1 pint/2½ cups of water. Switch on the cooker, and it will do the rest.

Whichever method you use, let the rice 'rest', off the heat, for 5 minutes before serving. As a main-course accompaniment, glutinous rice is served and eaten just like any other rice.

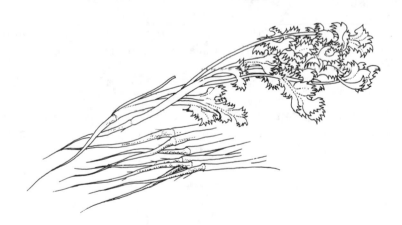

Glutinous Rice Cooked in Coconut Milk

Sailing south from Japan and Korea, we come to where the coconuts grow, and rice and rice cakes are cooked in coconut milk. Although this is often part of the making of sweet cakes, rice cooked in this way is an excellent accompaniment to savoury and main-course dishes. (See also the recipe for Coconut Rice on page 109.) People in these parts – Laos, Thailand, Malaysia, Indonesia – don't make rice cakes by crushing the cooked grains, however; they use rice flour.

Preparation: 2–8 hours soaking
Cooking: 45–50 minutes

450 g/1 lb/2 cups glutinous rice, soaked in cold water for 2–8 hours, then drained
570 ml/1 pint/2½ cups thick coconut milk, heated almost to boiling point
A large pinch of salt

Steam the rice on a high heat for 10 minutes. Then transfer it to a large bowl and pour over it the hot coconut milk with the pinch of salt. Stir well with a wooden spoon. Cover the bowl with a saucepan lid or plate. Leave for 20–30 minutes, by which time the rice will have absorbed the coconut milk. Put the rice back in the steamer and steam for a further 10–15 minutes. Serve hot or warm, with savoury dishes.

If you want to make your rice into a smooth paste, leave it standing in the coconut milk for 50 minutes and steam it, the second time, for 30–40 minutes. You will then have a paste similar to mochi.

Glutinous rice cakes

Several kinds of rice cake can be made from cooked glutinous rice – either freshly cooked, or leftovers. One is a plain, unsweetened cake, called *mochi* in Japan or *ddok* in Korea. Another is crisp-fried and is popular in Java, where it is called *rengginang*.

Plain Rice Cakes
Mochi, Ddok

While the cooked glutinous rice is still hot, pound it in a mortar to make a smooth paste, or blend it in your blender. Another method is to roll the cooked rice with a wet rolling pin. Keep folding the mass of rice over on to itself and rolling again, as if you were making puff pastry, until the grains are well mashed into each other. Keep the rolling pin wet so the rice doesn't stick to it.

You can also make mochi by steaming the rice on a high heat for 10 minutes, then transferring it to a bowl and pouring over it an equal quantity of boiling water. Cover the bowl and let it stand for about 50 minutes, by which time the rice will have absorbed the water. Then put the rice back in the steamer and steam it again for 30–40 minutes.

This rice paste can be shaped as desired. It can be rolled into balls, to be used in soup (page 163), or cubes which can be kebabbed. In Japan, where mochi is an important part of the traditional diet, it is cut into small geometric shapes, sweetened and coloured for use in the tea ceremony.

For storage, roll the paste into cylinders or form it into rectangular blocks and wrap in greaseproof paper and an outer layer of foil. These can be refrigerated for up to 48 hours or frozen for up to 2 months. When you want to use them, let them thaw through completely, then reheat in boiling water for 5 minutes or steam for 5–10 minutes.

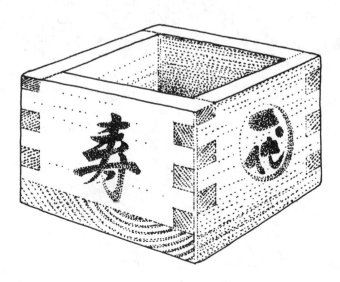

Crisp-Fried Rice Cakes
Rengginang

Some Asian shops in Europe, particularly in Holland, sell these, and of course you can buy them all over Java and in many other parts of Indonesia, ready to fry or ready to eat. They are a little like the rice cakes that are sold in the West as a diet food, but much nicer and, of course, heavier, because the grains have not been puffed. However, they are still quite light and airy.

In Java, most rengginang are sweetened. I much prefer mine unsweetened, and I therefore regard the sugar very much as an option. Rengginang are usually round, 6–7 cm/about 2½ inches across; but you can make them different shapes, or smaller, if you want. Remember that they will become somewhat bigger when you fry them.

Ideally, rengginang should be dried in hot sunshine for at least 5 hours, but they will do very well if you can give them, say, 2 hours in the sun (turning them over occasionally) and then 3 or 4 hours in a warm (not hot) oven. The warmth is to dry them, not cook them. The drying process can be spread over 2 days if need be. The rengginang should then be packed in an airtight container, where they will keep for several months as long as they have not been fried.

Preparation: 2–8 hours soaking
Cooking: 10–15 minutes steaming + time to shape and dry the cakes

Makes about 20–22
rengginang

450g/1 lb/2 cups glutinous rice, soaked in cold water for 2–8 hours, then drained
1 tsp salt
2 tbsp sugar (optional)
Vegetable oil for deep frying

Mix the rice with the salt and sugar, if used, and steam on a high heat for 10–15 minutes. Leave to cool a little, then form the rice into balls and flatten them between the palms of your hands to make round shapes, up to about 1 cm/½ inch thick. Dry these in the sun, as explained above.

When you are ready to use them, deep-fry them for a few minutes so that they become crisp and brittle. If you want to store them, let them cool, then put them in an airtight container. They will stay crisp for up to 2 weeks, provided the container is not too frequently opened.

Compressed Rice/Lontong

One method of cooking rice still remains to be described, and this produces what I will call Compressed Rice. In Indonesia and Malaysia, we call it *lontong*. Rice cooked in this way, and then cut into chunks for serving, is sometimes rather confusingly called 'rice cake', a term which I think should be reserved for the sort of rice cake that has been described in the previous pages.

Compressed rice is always eaten cold, for example with satay; it soaks up the hot satay sauce, and its coolness and soft texture contrast with the hot spices and the meat. In Indonesia and Malaysia, the rice is cooked in a cylinder of banana leaf; or in a little woven packet of coconut fronds, in which case it is called *ketupat* (see illustration page 91).

It is possible to use aluminium foil instead of banana leaf, but much the easiest way of cooking lontong is to use a bag made of muslin (or heatproof perforated paper, if you can get it). Boil-in-the-bag rice ought to be ideal, and the bags themselves are indeed excellent. Unfortunately, almost all boil-in-the-bag rice nowadays is parboiled, and this makes it hopeless for lontong because the grains cannot compress and merge together. If you can find boil-in-the-bag rice that is not parboiled, by all means use it. The cooking instructions will then be exactly as given below.

Preparation: 15 minutes
Cooking: 75 minutes

For 8–10 people

225 g/8 oz/1 cup long grain rice, preferably Basmati or Thai Fragrant, washed and drained
2 bags, about 15 cm/6inches square, made from muslin or heatproof perforated paper
1.7 litres/3 pints/7½ cups hot water, and more later
A pinch of salt

Fill each bag one-third full with rice. Sew up the opening. Boil the water with the pinch of salt. When it's boiling, put in the bags of rice and let the water bubble gently for 75 minutes. Add more boiling water as required during cooking; the bags of rice must always be submerged. When finished, take out the bags, which are now like plump, rather hard cushions, and drain them in a colander. When they are cold, keep them in the fridge until they are to be eaten.

To serve, just cut up the 'cushions' into chunks or slices about 3 cm/1 inch or a little more on a side. Use a large, sharp knife wetted with water. Discard the bags.

Compressed rice is also popular in many other Asian countries. Here is another way of cooking it.

For 8-10 people

225 g/8 oz/1 cup short grain rice
850 ml/1½ pints/3¾ cups water

Boil the rice until it becomes very soft and all the water has been absorbed. It then looks almost like porridge. Transfer it to a flat dish that can fit inside your steamer. Make the top of the rice level with a spoon; the rice should be piled about 3 cm/a little more than 1 inch thick. Cover the rice with foil, put the lid on the steamer, and steam for 20–30 minutes. Leave the rice to cool before cutting it into pieces about 3–4 cm/1½ inches square.

RICE AS ACCOMPANIMENT

Serious rice eaters, who regard it as the staff of life and who feel that, if the meal didn't include a plateful of rice, then they haven't eaten at all – such people would consider that the only proper accompaniment to meat, fish, vegetables and other spicy or even non-spicy dishes is plain cooked rice, of the sort described in the previous section. The Japanese even reserve the honourable word *gohan* for plain white rice. They admit more elaborate rice dishes to their traditional cuisine, such as the sekihan or red rice on page 112, but modern rice products, and all foreign rice dishes, are described by the Japanese-English word *rais-u*.

For this section I have selected twenty ways of cooking rice that can fairly be called traditional and that are clearly meant to be eaten with something else, although several of them, with one or two little additions, quickly turn into one-dish meals. They are simple enough to go well with almost any main-course dish, but because they are cooked with one or two other ingredients (sometimes quite strong-tasting) they will be of special interest to people who like their main dish roasted, grilled, or steamed – that is to say, plainly cooked.

Coconut Rice

This is a very popular way of cooking rice throughout tropical Asia, not quite a celebration dish but certainly a little bit special; it deserves to be made with the best rice you can get.

Preparation: 1 hour soaking
Cooking: about 30 minutes

For 4–6 people

450 g/1 lb/2 cups long grain rice, preferably Basmati or Thai Fragrant or similar, soaked for 1 hour, washed and drained
2 tbsp olive oil or clarified butter
680 ml/24 fl oz/3 cups coconut milk
1 tsp salt
1 pandanus leaf or bay leaf

In a saucepan, stir-fry the rice in the butter or oil for 3 minutes. Add the coconut milk, salt, and the pandanus or bay leaf. Bring to the boil and cook until the rice has absorbed all the liquid.

Then lower the heat, cover the pan tightly, and cook for a further 10–12 minutes undisturbed. Alternatively, the rice can be 'finished' by steaming in a rice steamer, or by cooking in the oven or in a microwave (see plain cooked rice, page 98–100). Discard the leaf, and serve hot.

Street food in Indonesia

Yellow Savoury Rice

Yellow, perhaps because it is the colour of gold, is associated all over South-East Asia with gods, royalty and feasts. Any thanksgiving or celebration party, even if the event celebrated is a very mundane one, is likely to have a large dish of yellow rice at the centre of the table.

Preparation: 1 hour soaking
Cooking: 30 minutes

For 4–6 people

450 g/1 lb/2 cups long grain
   rice: Basmati, Texmati,
   Thai Fragrant, Sunlong,
   etc., soaked for 1 hour,
   washed and drained
2 tbsp vegetable oil
3 shallots or 1 small onion,
   sliced finely
1 tsp ground turmeric
1 tsp ground coriander
½ tsp ground cumin
680 ml/24 fl oz/3 cups
   coconut milk or stock
1 stick of cinnamon
2 cloves
½ tsp salt
1 kaffir lime or bay leaf

Heat the oil in a saucepan. Stir-fry the sliced shallots or onion for 2 minutes. Add the rice, turmeric, coriander, and cumin. Stir-fry for another 2 minutes, then add the coconut milk or stock, then all the other ingredients. Boil the mixture, uncovered, stirring it once or twice with a wooden spoon, until the rice has absorbed all the liquid. Then steam for 10 minutes.

Instead of steaming, you can cover the saucepan tightly, and cook undisturbed on a low heat for 10 minutes; or you can finish off the cooking in the oven or microwave, as described on page 100 for plain cooked rice.

Transfer the rice to a serving dish, discard the cinnamon, cloves, and kaffir lime or bay leaf. Serve hot to accompany meat, fish and vegetables.

Rice with Chestnuts

This mixture of rice with fresh chestnuts is another Japanese inspiration. The texture and flavour of the rice are beautifully complemented and set off by the slight sweetness and chewiness of the chestnuts. Using the simplest and most economical of means, this dish achieves something of the effect of Rice with Lentils (page 123) or even – especially if you serve lamb or a spicy chicken dish with it – of the luxurious sixteenth-century Italian rice dish, with its lamb, veal, chicken and spicy sausage, that is described on page 278. In autumn, when chestnuts are plentiful, you should obviously use fresh ones, but at other times of year dried ones are perfectly good.

Preparation: overnight soaking for dried chestnuts
Cooking: 40 minutes for chestnuts + 35 minutes

For 4–6 people

450 g/1 lb fresh chestnuts, or
  112 g/4 oz/½ cup dried
  chestnuts
450 g/1 lb/2 cups Japanese or
  other short grain rice
½ tsp salt
700 ml/1¼ pints/3 cups
  water

If you are using dried chestnuts, soak them in cold water overnight, drain them, and boil them in slightly salted water for 35–40 minutes. Cut them in halves, or quarters if they are really big. If you use fresh chestnuts, boil them for 15–20 minutes, then peel them and remove the inner skins. Cut them up as described.

Wash the rice and put it into a saucepan with the chopped chestnuts. (See the note below for directions for using an electric rice cooker.) Dissolve the salt in the water, and then pour it into the pan. Boil, over a medium heat, for 10–15 minutes or until all the water has been absorbed. Stir once, cover the pan tightly, turn down the heat as low as possible, and continue cooking for 10 minutes.

Now, without disturbing the lid, place the pan in a deep baking tray or similar vessel. Half-fill the tray with cold water (or put the pan on a folded wet tea-towel; the purpose of this is to stop the rice sticking to the bottom of the pan). Leave the pan for 8–10 minutes undisturbed – do not remove the lid. The dish is then ready to serve, either hot or at room temperature.

Note. If you use an electric rice cooker, put in all the ingredients, switch the cooker on and leave it until it turns itself off. Switch off at the mains (to prevent the thermostat cutting in again) and leave the rice to rest, with the lid undisturbed, for 8–10 minutes before serving.

Rice with Azuki Beans
Sekihan

The Japanese usually serve this dish on special occasions, such as birthdays or weddings. They make it from glutinous rice, and their name for it means simply 'red rice'. For perfect results, glutinous rice must be steamed, not boiled. In Japan, you can buy red rice in the food hall of any big department store; you will see it displayed, still steaming hot, on large trays along with other kinds of cooked rice. The shop assistants will pack it for you in one of the store's pretty lunch boxes, or in a plain box, for you to take away and eat at your workplace or at home – but never, never in the street. Most people eat it at room temperature, but it is perfectly all right to reheat it in a steamer or a microwave. This rice dish is easy to make at home, as long as you remember that it needs 2 nights' soaking time – one night for the beans, one for the rice.

My recipe uses 3 parts short grain (japonica) and 1 part glutinous rice. You can cook these in a rice cooker or a saucepan.

Preparation: 2 nights soaking
Cooking: 25–30 minutes

For 4–6 people

84 gm/3 oz/½ cup azuki beans
250 gm/9 oz/1¼ cups short grain rice
84 gm/3 oz/½ cup glutinous rice
½ tsp salt

Soak the beans overnight, rinse them well, put them in a saucepan and cover them with cold water. Bring the water to the boil, and boil for 6 minutes. Drain the beans in a colander and rinse them again in cold water.

Then start the whole process again – put the beans in a clean pan, cover with cold water, bring to the boil, but boil this time for 10–12 minutes, so that the beans are quite soft and the water has become red. Drain the beans in the colander, but keep the water in a bowl. Keep the beans in the colander to cool. Up to this point, the preparation can be done several hours or up to a day in advance. When the beans are cold, refrigerate them until you are ready to cook them with the rice.

Mix the two kinds of rice together and wash in several changes of cold water. Put the rice in a bowl and add the red water in which the beans were boiled. Leave the rice to soak overnight.

Next day, drain the rice, which has now become pink, but again save the water. Dissolve the salt in the water. (If you are using a bamboo or other steamer, see the note below.) Mix together the rice and the beans and measure them with a cup as you transfer the mixture to an electric rice cooker or a saucepan. Then measure out the same quantity of water and pour it over the mixture. If you are using a rice cooker, all you need do is to switch it on. The mixture will be cooked in the same time as plain rice would be.

If you are using a saucepan, bring the water to the boil, stir the rice and beans once, and then simmer until all the water has been absorbed. Stir once more, lower the heat, cover the saucepan tightly, and leave the rice and beans undisturbed for 10 minutes. Then transfer them into a large bowl, breaking up any lumps with a fork.

Serve hot, or at room temperature.

Note. If you steam the rice and beans in a bamboo steamer (below) or any other kind of steamer (page 101, 188), mix the salt with 5 tablespoons of water and sprinkle this over the rice and beans in the steamer. Steam for 25–30 minutes.

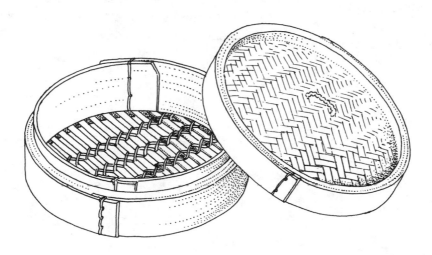

Bamboo steaming basket

Rice with Chickpeas/Garbanzos

This is as typical of Middle Eastern cooking as Rice with Azuki Beans (page 112) is of Japanese. In Japan you may well eat azuki rice with yakatori, which is really a kind of chicken kebab. In the same way, you will find that rice and chickpeas/garbanzos go well with any of the lamb dishes in this book.

Preparation: soak chickpeas/garbanzos overnight
Cooking: 1 hour 5 minutes for the chickpeas/garbanzos + 40 minutes

For 6–8 people

84–112 g/3–4 oz/½ cup dried
   chickpeas/garbanzos,
   soaked overnight
1.1 litres/2 pints/5 cups water
2 tbsp olive oil
1 tbsp butter
2 large onions, chopped
1 tsp ground cumin
Salt and pepper
450 g/1 lb/2 cups long grain
   rice, soaked for 1 hour,
   washed and drained
570 ml/1 pint/2½ cups
   chicken stock or water
1–2 tbsp chopped coriander/
   cilantro leaves or
   flat-leafed parsley for
   garnish

Put the rice to soak. Boil the chickpeas/garbanzos in the water without salt for 1 hour, then add ½ teaspoon salt and continue to simmer for 5 more minutes. Drain, remove and discard the skins, and keep the chickpeas/garbanzos aside.

In another saucepan, heat the oil and butter and stir-fry the onions for 4–5 minutes until they are just slightly coloured. Add the cumin, salt and pepper and the cooked chickpeas/garbanzos. Stir for 1 minute, then add the rice. Continue stirring and cooking for 2 minutes longer. Then pour in the chicken stock or water. Stir again once, bring to the boil, lower the heat and cover the pan. Leave to cook undisturbed for 25 minutes.

Take the pan off the heat and leave it to rest, still covered, for 5 minutes. Serve hot with any meat dish, with salad or cooked vegetables.

Carrot Rice

Like most Persian-style mixed rice dishes, this should produce a thin crusty layer on the bottom of the pan. This crust is on top when the rice is turned out of the pan into its serving dish. After much experimenting, I have concluded that the best way of making carrot rice is in the oven, so that you finish up with both top and bottom deliciously crusty.

For this dish, you need short grain japonica rice. This can be a Californian or Australian Calrose, or a Japanese or Korean type – whichever one you can most easily buy in your neighbourhood.

Preparation: 15 minutes
Cooking: 1 hour

For 4–6 people

340 g/12 oz/1½ cups short grain rice, soaked in plenty of cold water for 1–2 hours
450 g/1 lb/4 cups carrots, peeled and grated
The seeds from 4 or 5 green cardamoms
A large pinch of ground nutmeg
1 tsp salt
570 ml/1 pint/2½ cups milk (full fat or semi-skimmed, as preferred)
28 g/1 oz butter, cut into small pieces

Preheat your oven to 180°C/350°F/Gas Mark 4.

Drain the rice and mix it, in a bowl, with all the other ingredients except the milk and the butter.

Butter or oil a soufflé dish, big enough for the uncooked rice and carrots to half fill it. Put the rice mixture into it and shake it gently or tap it on the table to make sure the rice is evenly spread. Then pour the milk in slowly, disturbing the other ingredients as little as possible, and scatter the little pieces of butter on the surface. Put the dish into the oven and cook for 1 hour, by which time there will be a good golden crust on top.

Serve hot, warm or cold, as an accompaniment to meat or fish.

Jamaican Rice and Peas

In her book *Traditional Jamaican Cooking* Norma Benghiat says that there are many versions of rice and peas in the Caribbean, but nowhere is it such an important part of the national cuisine as it is in Jamaica. It is the centrepiece of most Sunday lunches and festive meals. The 'peas' are usually red kidney beans. 'Rice and peas made with green gungo peas is prepared in the same way, and heralds the Christmas and New Year season.'

Like many other mixed rice dishes, rice and peas should be served with whatever vegetables and meat or fish you choose to make a well-balanced meal.

Preparation: soak beans overnight
Cooking: 1 hour 25 minutes for the beans + 30–35 minutes

For 4–6 people

112 g/4 oz red kidney beans, soaked in cold water overnight

450 g/1 lb/2 cups long grain rice, washed and drained

5 shallots or 1 large onion, chopped

2 or 3 red chillies, de-seeded and chopped

3 cloves garlic, chopped

1 tsp chopped fresh or dried thyme

390 ml/14 fl oz/1¾ cups very thick coconut milk

Salt

2 tbsp chopped spring onions/scallions, green part only

Drain the kidney beans, rinse well, then put them in a saucepan. Cover with cold water and boil for 10 minutes. Drain and rinse again. For the second time, boil the beans in a saucepan on a low heat, with enough water to cover them, for 1 hour.

Add 1 teaspoon of salt and continue to simmer the beans for 15 more minutes. Drain, but this time reserve 285 ml/10 fl oz/1¼ cups of the reddish cooking water.

In another saucepan, heat the oil and fry the shallots or onion, the chillies and garlic, stirring occasionally, for 2 minutes. Add the rice and stir for a few seconds. Then add the beans and the reddish water they were boiled in. Stir again, add the thyme and coconut milk and some salt to taste. Stir once more, cover the pan and cook on a low heat for 20–25 minutes. Remove from heat, spread the chopped spring onion/scallion on top, cover again tightly, and leave the rice and peas to rest for 5 minutes.

Stir the spring onion/scallion into the rice and transfer the whole mixture to a heated serving bowl. Serve hot.

Spicy Coconut Pilaf

Where rice grows, coconuts often grow too. In a rice landscape, the islands of darker green are the crowns of coconut trees which shade the villages beneath. The large number of recipes in this book that use coconut may reflect the importance of coconuts in tropical cuisines, or it may just be nostalgia for the fields and groves I lived among as a child.

However, this is not a Sumatran dish but a pulau from South India – a region, admittedly, that may have influenced Indonesian eating habits in the past. The influence in my case came from Chef T. G. Raman, born and raised in Kerala and now cooking in the Maurya Sheraton Hotel, New Delhi. This pilaf has lovely crunchy textures from the mustard seeds and urad dal/black gram beans. If you want it a bit spicier, add some Gunpowder (page 360) in the final minute of cooking, or serve the Gunpowder in a small bowl and let your guests sprinkle it over the rice for themselves.

Cooking: 25–30 minutes if you need to cook the rice + 5–8 minutes

For 4 people

2–3 tbsp peanut or vegetable oil
¾ tsp mustard seed
1 or 2 small red chillies, chopped
3 tsp urad dal/black gram beans
1 tsp chopped ginger
4–6 heaped tbsp freshly grated coconut
Salt and pepper to taste
600–800 g/1¼–1¾ lb/ 5–7 cups cooked rice
2 tsp Gunpowder (page 360) (optional)

Heat the oil in a wok or large frying pan, and put in the mustard seeds and red chilli. Stir, and add the urad dal/black gram beans. Stir again for a few seconds and add the ginger and grated coconut. Continue stir-frying over a low heat until the coconut is lightly browned. Add salt and pepper, stir once, then add the rice. Stir constantly for 3–4 minutes until the rice is hot. Adjust the seasoning, add the Gunpowder if used, and serve immediately.

Puerto Rican Rice and Beans
Arroz con habichuelas guisadas

A good friend and well-known cookery writer, Alice Wooledge Salmon, gave me this recipe on her return from a trip to Puerto Rico. There, as in Jamaica, rice and peas or rice and beans is a favourite staple, a daily accompaniment to salt cod, fried bananas or plantains, or just a plain fried egg.

If you use annatto seeds, crush them in a little oil in a mortar before combining the mixture with the other ingredients.

Preparation: 8 hours or overnight soaking
Cooking: 1½ hours

For 4–6 people

225 g/8 oz dried pinto or kidney beans, washed, then soaked in water for 8 hours

For the sofrito (the sauce base):

28 g/1 oz/⅛ cup salt pork or green (uncured) bacon, diced
56 g/2 oz/¼ cup lightly smoked ham, diced
1½ tbsp vegetable oil
1 medium onion, finely chopped
2 large cloves garlic, finely chopped
1–2 green sweet/bell peppers/ pimientos, stem and seeds removed, finely chopped
A small handful fresh coriander/cilantro leaves, finely chopped

To make the sofrito, sauté the pork (or bacon) and ham in oil until lightly coloured. Add the onion, garlic, peppers and coriander, then the oregano and annatto or paprika if used. Sauté, uncovered, over a low heat for 10 minutes. Keep aside.

Put the beans in a saucepan and cover them well with cold water. Add the garlic and onion, bring to the boil and skim off any scum that rises to the surface. Cook at a rolling boil for 10 minutes, then reduce the heat and simmer for 40 minutes longer, with the lid ajar. The beans should now be tender. Add the pumpkin flesh and some salt. Continue simmering until the beans and pumpkin cubes are cooked.

Now discard the onion, take out some of the pumpkin cubes with a slotted spoon and mash them with a fork. Stir the mashed pumpkin back into the beans, and add the sofrito mixture, the tomato purée, and a little more water if necessary.

Go on simmering for about 15 minutes more, the lid still ajar. Stir occasionally. Add water if needed, but the sauce should be fairly thick. Taste to check the salt.

Meanwhile, bring 420 ml/¾ pint/1¾ cups of water to the boil, with 2 tablespoons olive oil and ½ teaspoon of salt. Stir the rice into this, lower the heat, and simmer, uncovered, until the water reaches the surface of the rice. Fork the rice, without stirring it,

**A large pinch of dried
  oregano**
**½ tsp annatto, or 1 tsp
  paprika (optional)**

Other ingredients:

2 cloves garlic, peeled
Half a medium onion, peeled
**170 g/6 oz/¾ cup pumpkin
  flesh, cubed**
Salt
**1 tbsp concentrated tomato
  purée**
**340 g/12 oz/1½ cups white
  short grain rice, washed**
Light olive oil

from bottom to top. Cover the pan, turn heat right down and cook undisturbed for 10 minutes, or until grains are tender. Fluff with a fork. Serve immediately, topping the rice with the beans or heaping them side by side. Many people like a little olive oil to dribble over their beans.

Winnowing with fans: Thailand

119

Rice with Fried Coconut and Raisins

I am intrigued by this Colombian recipe from *The Book of Latin American Cooking* by Elisabeth Lambert Ortiz. She says it is typical of coastal Colombia, where coconuts are very much used, and she describes how the fried coconut is made by boiling very thick coconut milk until it becomes oil with a grainy residue. This is how we make coconut oil at home in Indonesia. The grainy, golden residue, which is called *titote* by the Colombians, we call *blondo*; it is used in Java and some other islands for sauces and for cooking meat. I have adapted this recipe a little, leaving out the sugar, since coconut and raisins are already quite sweet.

Cooking: 55–60 minutes

For 4–6 people

170 ml/6 fl oz/¾ cup thick 'first extraction' coconut milk (page 369)
112 g/4 oz/⅔ cups raisins
570 ml/1 pint/2½ cups coconut milk of normal thickness
340 g/12 oz/1½ cups long grain rice, washed and drained
Salt
15 g/½ oz butter (optional)

Pour the thick coconut milk into a heavy saucepan and bring it to the boil on a medium heat. Let this bubble vigorously, stirring from time to time, until the liquid loses its white milky appearance and the oil separates from the grainy residue; this will take about 8–10 minutes. Put in the raisins, stir for 1 minute, then add the thinner coconut milk and simmer for 10 minutes.

Add the rice and ½ teaspoon of salt. Stir it once, and go on simmering for 15 minutes, until all the liquid has been absorbed by the rice. Stir once more, cover the pan, turn down the heat as low as possible and continue cooking for 10–15 minutes more. Uncover, and stir in the butter (if used), mixing it thoroughly. Otherwise, stir the rice well, as if you were frying it, and put in a little more salt if necessary. Transfer it to a serving dish and serve hot, with any spicy meat or fish dish and cooked vegetables or salad.

Soft Savoury Brown Rice

Raw brown rice is simply rice that has not been polished to the whiteness that most people, especially in the East, prefer and expect. It tastes quite nutty and the grains keep a firm texture, even though the cooking time is longer than for white rice.

This savoury brown rice, however, is made with short grain white Japanese or long grain Thai Fragrant rice, so that it has a soft and slightly sticky texture. The brownish colour of the finished dish comes from the spices used in the cooking. Rice cooked this way makes a good accompaniment to grilled meat or fish.

Cooking: 25–30 minutes

For 4–6 people

450 g/1 lb/2 cups Kokuho Rose or Thai Fragrant rice, washed and drained
3 tbsp peanut oil, or melted or clarified butter
4 shallots, finely sliced
1 tsp ground coriander
1 tsp ground cinnamon
4 cloves
4 green cardamom pods
½ tsp freshly ground black pepper
570 ml/1 pint/2½ cups water or stock
½ tsp salt

In a thick-bottomed saucepan, fry the shallots in the oil or butter, stirring all the time, for 2 minutes. Add the ground ingredients and the cloves and cardamom. Stir for 1 minute and add the rice. Stir this around with a wooden spoon for 2 minutes, then add the water or stock, and the salt. Bring the liquid to the boil, stir again and cover the pan. Turn down the heat as low as possible and leave the rice cooking undisturbed for 15 minutes. Then turn the heat off and leave the rice, with the pan still covered, to rest for 5 minutes.

Transfer the rice to a warm serving bowl, discarding the cloves and cardamoms.

Basic Risotto

In her book, *Secrets from an Italian Kitchen*, Anna del Conte reveals that a *risotto in bianco*, a basic risotto, can be made up to an hour or so in advance, moulded in ramekins, and heated when required by being placed for 5 minutes in a bain-marie in the oven.

At this point, you may ask why you have to add the cooking liquid to the rice little by little. And why do Italian restaurants make you wait 25 minutes if you order one? The answer to both questions is in the texture of the rice. You can, as I know by experiment, add the stock all at once, cover the pan tightly, and just leave it to cook. The result is quite nice, but it does not have the smooth, creamy texture of risotto. Conversely, you cannot cook risotto in advance, because the creamy smoothness lasts only a short time. Italian restaurants are therefore right to say you must wait.

These risotto timbales will go very well with Italian beef and veal dishes. I would suggest serving them with the Sirloin Steak Parcels on page 268 – but leave out the rice in the parcels. Vegetarians will enjoy the timbales surrounded by a Hot Mixed Vegetable Salad (page 293).

Preparation: make the stock
Cooking: about 30 minutes

For 4–6 people

56 g/2 oz butter
2 shallots, finely chopped
340 g/12 oz/1½ cups rice,
   Arborio or Vialone Nano
1.2–1.4 litres/2–2½ pints/
   5–6¼ cups stock, kept
   gently simmering
56–84 g/2–3 oz freshly
   grated Parmesan cheese

Heat 28 g/1 oz butter in a wide saucepan, and fry the shallots, stirring constantly with a wooden spoon, for about 2 minutes. Add the rice, and continue stirring until the grains look shiny because they are all well coated with butter.

Pour in a ladleful of stock, give it a stir, then leave it until the liquid has all been absorbed by the rice. Add another ladleful of stock, and proceed as before, stirring occasionally to prevent the rice from sticking to the pan. Go on until the rice is cooked but still slightly *al dente*. It should reach this stage after about 20 minutes. You may not need all the stock.

Add the rest of the butter and half of the Parmesan, and stir vigorously with the wooden spoon. Butter 8 small ramekins or 6 larger ones, and divide the risotto among them, pressing it down quite firmly with the back of a spoon. Cover the ramekins with foil. If you have any leftover risotto, it can be used to make Rice Croquettes (page 132-137).

When you are ready to serve, heat the ramekins as described above. Unmould the risotto on to individual dinner plates as required, and sprinkle them with the remaining Parmesan.

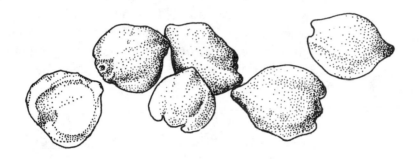

Savoury Rice with Herbs
Nasi ulam

This is a sort of Malaysian version of what the British adapted from India and called kedgeree. Instead of butter, we use thick coconut milk, boiled (with spices) until the milk becomes oil, and the rice turns green from the green and fragrant herbs it has been heated with. In Malaysia, I first ate nasi ulam in a restaurant called Sri Nonya, in Petaling Jaya, just outside Kuala Lumpur. Nonya food is a mingling of traditional Malaysian cuisine with Chinese, and is said to have originated in sixteenth-century Malacca, where Chinese immigrants married local people. The ladies were politely addressed as *Nyonya* or *Nonya*, which means something like 'Madam'. They must have been good cooks, and this particular restaurant does their memory credit. My only criticism of the nasi ulam was that the chef had been a bit too generous with the herbs, so that I could hardly taste the rice. In my version, I have included a list of herbs that you can use, but I would recommend that you select just four or five, whichever are most easily available; the result will be better than if you try to stuff them all in.

123

Preparation: cook the rice and let it cool
Cooking: 15–20 minutes

For 6 people

---

900 g/2 lb/8 cups cooked rice
450 g/1 lb/2 cups cold
  smoked mackerel or
  haddock
4 tbsp freshly grated coconut,
  roasted (optional)
112 ml/4 fl oz/½ cup very
  thick coconut milk
1 tsp Sambal Ulek (page
  350), or 2 green chillies,
  de-seeded and finely
  sliced
2 shallots, finely sliced
1 tsp finely chopped ginger
  root
¼ tsp salt

About 1 tbsp of each of 4 or
5 herbs from the following
list, all very finely sliced or
chopped:

  turmeric leaves, basil,
  mint, watercress, kaffir
  lime leaves, lemon grass
  (use only the soft inner
  part), cashew nut leaves,
  spring onions/scallions,
  wild ginger flowers,
  green chillies, de-seeded

To be added just before
serving:

Juice of 1 lime
More salt to taste

Let the rice cool to room temperature. Remove the skin and bones of the fish and break up the flesh in to fine flakes. Put the rice into a large bowl and mix in the fish and roasted coconut (if used).

Put the coconut milk into a wok or large shallow saucepan, with the Sambal Ulek, shallots, ginger and salt. Bring this to the boil and let it bubble for 8–10 minutes until it becomes oily. Stir, lower the heat, and stir in the rice mixture. Toss and stir this for 3 minutes, until the rice is hot. Add the sliced and chopped herbs, and continue stirring for 1 minute more. Add the lime juice and more salt if needed. Serve hot or warm.

Rice Cooked in Fish Stock
Arroz a banda

This wonderfully golden, aromatic dish is from the region of Valencia. We had spent much of a morning talking to Ali Zamani Valian, the Commercial Director of the Ibérica de Arroces rice mill, and he was kind enough to invite us to join a small party who were to have lunch at a private club in nearby Oliva. It was a most splendid meal, which, to my surprise, followed an almost Japanese pattern. We started with several fish hors d'oeuvres and a delicious garlicky salad with olives, a succession of small courses that left us feeling already quite satisfied. Then came in this golden arroz a banda, in the big paella pan straight from the kitchen. Our host scored two lines across it with his fork to divide it into quarters, and the four of us set off, each eating his own portion straight from the big dish. I scraped and crunched the crusty layer of rice at the bottom with enthusiasm.

The following is a good recipe, but the result may not be quite as fine as the dish I ate that day; a simple homemade fish stock cannot compete with one made professionally, from a large variety of freshly caught fish. Nor does a gas or electric stove distribute heat quite as evenly as an expertly managed wood fire under a paella pan. But this version will not disappoint you.

If you have a friendly fishmonger nearby, you may be able to buy good fish heads for the stock cheaply, plus bones of fish that have been filleted. Best of all are the heads and bones of turbot. Otherwise, make Fish Stock as described on page 346.

Use a paella pan if you have one, otherwise a casserole or large frying pan. You will need a lid big enough to cover the pan while the rice is 'resting' at the end. If you have no saffron, use turmeric in preference to any other colouring.

Preparation: make the fish stock
Cooking: 25–30 minutes

For 4–6 people

450 g/1 lb/2 cups short grain rice, ideally Spanish rice, such as Bomba or Calasparra, from the Valencia region; or Italian risotto rice

In a paella pan, casserole or large frying pan, heat the oil and fry the crushed garlic, stirring all the time, for 1 minute. Add the powdered ingredients, briefly stir these, and pour in the fish stock. Let this simmer for a few minutes before adding the rice, a little at a time, over a period of about 3 minutes. stirring constantly.

Add the tomatoes and continue simmering, stirring occasionally, for 10–12 minutes. Adjust the seasoning and add the chopped parsley (if used). Stir again and

1.1 litres/2 pints/5 cups fish
  stock (page 346)
2 tbsp olive oil
6–8 cloves garlic, crushed
2 large tomatoes, peeled,
  de-seeded and chopped
½ tsp chilli powder
½ tsp paprika
½ tsp saffron powder or
  turmeric
1–2 tsp finely chopped
  flat-leaf parsley (optional)
Salt to taste

level the surface of the rice gently with the back of the
spoon. Turn off the heat and cover the pan; leave the
rice to rest for 8–10 minutes. Serve hot, as described
above.

Fried Rice
Nasi goreng

Not only every rice-growing country, but every region, one may say every family, has
its repertoire of savoury fried rice recipes. Yet there is a great difference between a
badly made fried rice and one that has been cooked in accordance with a few basic but
important and practical guidelines.

The rice should be cooked about 2–3 hours before it is to be fried, so that it has time
to get cold. Freshly cooked, still-hot rice will go soggy and oily if you fry it. The cold
rice must be mixed in with the other ingredients when those ingredients are already
cooked and still hot. From then on, the mixing and stir-frying must be done on a low
heat and must continue until the rice is hot but not burnt.

If you are going to use seafood or meat, it is best to stir-fry this separately. You can
use the same spice mixture as is given here for the fried rice, if you wish. Then mix the
meat or seafood into the rice in the final 2 minutes before serving; or simply spread it
on top of the rice on the serving dish.

Preparation: cook the rice and cool for at least 2 hours
Cooking: 10 minutes

For 4–6 people

---

340 g/12 oz/1½ cups long
grain rice, cooked by any
of the methods described
on pages 98–100, and
allowed to cool
2 tbsp vegetable oil
1 tbsp butter
3 shallots or 1 small onion,
sliced finely
2 cloves garlic, sliced finely
(optional)
2 red chillies, de-seeded and
chopped finely; or ½ tsp
chilli powder
1 tbsp light soy sauce
1 tsp paprika
2 tsp tomato purée or tomato
ketchup
112 g/4 oz/1 cup button
mushrooms, wiped and
thinly sliced
3 medium-size carrots, diced
very small
Salt to taste

Heat the oil and butter in a wok or large frying pan. Stir-fry the shallots and garlic for about 1 minute, then add the other ingredients, except the rice, and go on stir-frying for 5–6 minutes or until the vegetables are cooked. Add the rice, and mix it thoroughly with the vegetables so that it becomes hot and takes on the reddish tinge of the paprika and tomato. Serve hot, on a heated serving dish, either by itself as an accompaniment to the main course; or garnished with sliced cucumber, sliced tomatoes, watercress and Crisp-Fried Onion (see page 358); or topped with seafood or meat as described above.

This basic fried rice can also be frozen for up to 2 months; thaw completely before reheating in the oven at 180°C/350°F/Gas Mark 4 for 15–20 minutes, or in the microwave. Cover the rice with aluminium foil to prevent it from drying in the oven.

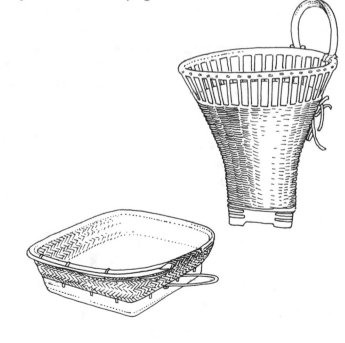

Rice baskets: Thailand

Mexican Rice and Refried Beans

This dish will be found on most Tex-Mex menus, though I must admit I have never eaten it in a restaurant. A friend in Mexico City cooked the refried beans for me when I visited her many years ago, and I thought then how well they would go with rice, particularly if the beans and the rice were mixed together.

It is obviously a good vegetarian and vegan dish, but it is also a worthy accompaniment to fish and meat. My friend in Mexico served the refried beans, *frijoles refritos*, with tortillas. Here, however, I suggest you mould the rice and beans in individual ramekins.

I have always soaked beans overnight, but Elisabeth Lambert Ortiz, in *The Complete Book of Mexican Cooking*, says that this is not necessary. This will save me the distress of waking up in the morning and realizing that I forgot to put the beans to soak before I went to bed. Remember, though, not to put any salt into the pan when cooking begins; salt at this stage prevents the beans from becoming tender.

Preparation: soak the beans (if you do); cook the rice
Cooking: about 2½ hours

For 6–8 people

450 g/1 lb/2 cups pinto beans or red kidney beans

6 shallots or 2 large onions, finely chopped

3 cloves garlic, finely chopped

2–6 small red or green chillies, or serrano chillies, or dried red chillies, chopped (and de-seeded, if you want them less hot)

1 bay leaf

Salt and pepper

155 g/5½ oz/1½ cups cooked short grain rice

1 or 2 tomatoes, skinned, chopped and de-seeded

5 or 6 tbsp olive oil or peanut oil

Whether the beans have been soaked or not, wash them and put them in a large saucepan. Cover with cold water and add half of the chopped shallots or onions and garlic, all the chillies and the bay leaf. Bring to the boil and simmer for 1 hour, skimming off the scum frequently.

Now add 1 tablespoon of the oil and more hot water if needed, and continue cooking for 30–45 minutes or until the beans are soft. Add the salt, stir the whole thing, and continue cooking for another 30 minutes. By this time there should be very little liquid remaining. Add the cooked rice and mix all well together.

In a large frying pan, heat another 2 tablespoons of the oil and fry the remaining shallots (or onions) and garlic until they are just starting to change colour. Add the chopped tomatoes and continue stirring for a minute or two. Add half of the rice and beans. Stir the mixture with a wooden spoon while mashing the beans so that the whole thing becomes a heavy paste. Put this back into the saucepan with the rest of the rice and beans and mix everything well together. Adjust the seasoning and simmer for a few minutes to heat through.

The dish is now ready to serve. Up to this point, however, it can be prepared some hours in advance and chilled, already moulded in individual ramekins if you like.

If it has been stored the mixture must be refried before serving. Heat 2 or 3 tablespoons of oil in a frying pan or skillet. Unmould the mixture, if it has been moulded. Fry the mixture for 3 or 4 minutes on each side, turning over once only. If it has not been moulded, mash it, as before, while frying. Serve as suggested above.

Masks made from rice baskets: Thailand

Grilled Sticky Rice Rolls
Pulut panggang

Preparation: 2–4 hours soaking
Cooking: 1 hour 50 minutes

To make 12–16 rolls

450 g/1 lb/2 cups glutinous
   rice, soaked for 2–4 hours
900 ml/just over
   1½ pints/4 cups coconut
   milk
¼ tsp salt
Banana leaf (for wrapping) or
   aluminium foil

For the filling:

112 g/4 oz/½ cup, firmly
   packed freshly grated
   coconut (peel off the
   brown skin before grating)
4–5 shallots, sliced
2 dried red chillies, soaked in
   hot water until soft
56 g/2 oz dried shrimps,
   soaked in hot water for 10
   minutes, then drained
1 tsp ground coriander
5-cm/2-inch stem of lemon
   grass, outer leaves
   discarded, chopped
1 tsp sugar
½ tsp salt
2 tbsp peanut oil

Put all the ingredients for the filling, except the grated coconut, into a blender and blend until smooth. Transfer this paste into a non-stick frying pan and cook it, stirring all the time, for 4 minutes. Remove it from the heat and mix in the grated coconut. Adjust the seasoning and leave to cool.

Steam the rice for 10 minutes, then put it into a bowl and stir in the coconut milk. Cover the bowl and leave the rice to soak up the coconut milk for 10 minutes. Put the rice back into the steamer and steam again for 10 minutes. Then leave it to cool until it is cool enough to handle.

Now divide the rice into 12–16 portions and put each portion on a piece of banana leaf or aluminium foil about 20 cm/8 inches square. Press the rice flat with your hand to make a little oblong, about 2 × 4 cm/1 × 1½ inches. Put a portion of filling on top of each rice oblong, then roll it up, using the banana leaf or foil to help you. If you are using banana leaf, fold it to close each end of the roll and pin the ends shut with cocktail sticks. With foil, all you need do is give the ends a twist. Go on making rolls until the rice and filling are used up.

Up to this point the rolls can be prepared in advance, in which case they should be stored in the fridge until 30 minutes before they are to be grilled. Ideally, grill them on charcoal. If they are wrapped in banana leaf, leave this in place until it chars; if in aluminium foil, remove this before grilling. If you don't have a charcoal stove, a gas or electric grill is very nearly as good. Grill for about 5 minutes each side, turning them over once only. Serve warm or hot.

Rice with Lentils
Addas palow

I am indebted to Margaret Shaida, author of *The Legendary Cuisine of Persia*, for this recipe. It makes an excellent accompaniment to any lamb or goat dish.

Preparation: 4–8 hours soaking
Cooking: 20 minutes + 35–70 minutes or longer

For 6–8 people

450 g/1 lb/2 cups long grain rice, preferably Basmati, soaked in salted cold water for 4–8 hours, then washed and drained
3 tsp salt
2.3 litres/4 pints/10 cups water
84 ml/3 fl oz/¼ cup olive oil
56 g/2 oz clarified unsalted butter
112 g/4 oz/½ cup green lentils, cleaned and washed in several changes of water
56 g/2 oz/⅓ cup sultanas, cleaned and soaked in warm water for 20 minutes, then drained
112 g/4 oz/⅔ cup stoned dates, halved and fried briefly in oil, then drained

For the garnish:

1 large onion, sliced and fried in oil until golden brown, then drained on absorbent paper

In a large saucepan, bring the water to the boil with 3 teaspoons of salt. When it boils, put in the rice and keep it at a rolling boil for 3–4 minutes. Drain the rice in a colander and rinse for a few seconds under the cold tap.

Cook the lentils in a smaller saucepan, using just enough boiling water to cover them, for 5–8 minutes. In the last minute of cooking, add ½ teaspoon of salt. Drain.

Pour about 84 ml/3 fl oz of the best olive oil you have into a wide, shallow pan or casserole. Heat this and spread one-third of the rice over the bottom of the pan, then all the lentils on top of the rice. Spread another one-third of the rice on top of these, then the sultanas, then the remaining rice, finally the dates. Pour the clarified butter evenly over everything.

Wrap the lid of the pan or casserole in a damp tea-towel and cover the pan tightly. Cook on a low heat for 30 minutes. Take off the tea-towel, replace the lid, and put the pan into a preheated low oven at 120°C/250°F/Gas Mark ½. It can stay there until you are ready to serve the rice, 30 minutes or even 1 hour later. When you take the pan out of the oven, put it on a wet cloth or a tray of cold water for 5–8 minutes so that the crust of rice at the bottom of the pan will come out easily.

Arrange the rice on a heated serving platter. Garnish with the fried onion, and put pieces of the rice crust around the edge. Serve immediately.

SOUPS, APPETIZERS, FIRST COURSES, ONE-DISH MEALS

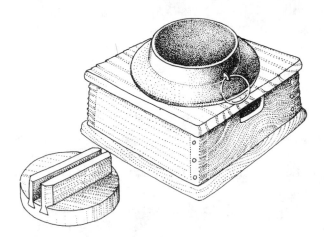

Traditional Japanese iron *kama*

This is by far the largest recipe section, and its boundaries still seem rather uncertain. More and more dishes have slipped into it, and it was often a question whether the newest addition should settle here or be sent on its way to one of the other parts of the book. But that's how it is with rice; whatever you make with it is so versatile that it can do duty at many different times of day and at various points in a meal.

I have tried, at least, to organize this motley collection into the subdivisions mentioned in the title. But in amongst them you will find several breakfasts, snacks for elevenses and teatime, a lot of canapés for your drinks party, a refreshing chilled soup, lots of picnic food and some splendidly ethnic dishes from several picturesque parts of the world.

Rice croquettes

Rice croquettes are very much a Western concept. I don't recall coming across anything similar in Asia – at least, not until very recently. In Indonesia, certainly, our croquettes, rissoles, or fritters might be made of potatoes, sweet potatoes, wheat flour, sweet corn, lentils or other pulses, but not rice.

These are a good way to use leftover boiled or steamed rice, but there is no need to wait for leftovers before you make them. They are excellent as a snack, a canapé with drinks, or a first course. A few of them with a green salad make a simple but very attractive lunch or supper.

Risotto or other short grain rice is particularly good for making these. The croquettes are best when deep-fried in a deep-fryer or a wok. They are a little high in calories, perhaps, but delicious.

132

Rice and Fish Croquettes

There are of course, in different countries, many variations on the theme of fish croquettes, and I dare say many of them originated as this one did, by chance. I found one day that, for some reason, I had a lot of leftover sushi with raw cod. It is simply not done in Japan to serve yesterday's sushi, and as an Indonesian I can never bring myself to throw away rice. So I made these croquettes, which are just as good, in a different way, as those made from leftover risotto.

As you may not have any leftover sushi, the recipe below starts with the uncooked rice. You can use any locally obtainable white fish instead of the cod.

Preparation: 50 minutes to assemble
Cooking: 15–20 minutes to fry

Makes 18–30 croquettes,
depending on size

340 g/12 oz/2 cups cod fillet,
   sliced thin
1 tbsp salt

For the marinade:

56 ml/2 fl oz/¼ cup rice
   vinegar
1 tsp salt
56 ml/2 fl oz/¼ cup water

Other ingredients:

112 g/4 oz/½ cup Japanese
   or other short grain rice,
   washed and drained
225 ml/8 fl oz/1 cup water
5 tbsp rice vinegar
2 tsp sugar
1 tsp salt
3 eggs
2 tbsp finely chopped spring
   onions/scallions
112 g/4 oz/⅔ cup
   breadcrumbs
Vegetable oil for deep-frying

Sprinkle the 1 tablespoon of salt over the fish and leave it to stand for 30 minutes, then rinse thoroughly in cold water. Mix the ingredients for the marinade. Marinate the fish for 5 minutes. Then drain it, chop it, and keep aside.

Put the rice and water in a small saucepan and cook on a medium heat until all the water has been absorbed. Lower the heat, cover the pan, and leave undisturbed for 5 minutes. Remove from the heat and leave the lid tightly on. In another pan boil the rice vinegar, sugar and 1 teaspoon of salt for 2 minutes. Stir to dissolve the sugar and salt, and leave to cool.

Transfer the rice to a wooden or glass bowl and, with a wooden spoon, stir in the cooled vinegar. Leave the rice to cool also. When it is cold, put in the chopped fish. Break 1 egg into the mixture, add the spring onions/scallions, and mix well with your hand. Form the rice mixture into croquettes, and, if you are not ready to fry them, store them in the fridge.

To fry the croquettes, start by breaking 2 eggs into a small bowl and beating them. Spread the breadcrumbs on a tray. Heat the oil in a deep-fryer or wok to 190°C/375°F (at this temperature, a cube of bread dropped into the oil browns in 1 minute). Dip each croquette in the egg, then roll it in the breadcrumbs. Fry the croquettes in batches until golden brown. Drain on absorbent paper and serve hot or warm.

Rice Croquettes with Bananas and Prawns/Shrimps

On many tropical islands there are bananas that are suitable for cooking and abundant and cheap prawns, so banana and prawn fritters are popular. By including rice you create a satisfying snack or starter. Choose the best cooking bananas you can buy in your neighbourhood. If you live in a country where bananas come from supermarkets, an alternative is ripe plantains, which you will be able to find in street markets and ethnic shops in large towns.

If you use frozen prawns/shrimps, make sure they are well and truly thawed out before you cook them.

Preparation: cook the rice; 10 minutes to assemble
Cooking: 20–25 minutes to deep-fry

Makes 10–12 croquettes

310 g/11 oz/3 cups cooked
    short grain rice or cold
    Basic Risotto (page 122)
2 eggs, beaten
2 or 3 large ripe bananas or
    ripe plantains, peeled and
    cut into (altogether) 20–24
    round slices
10–12 prawns/shrimps,
    cooked or uncooked,
    peeled and de-veined
Salt and black pepper, or salt
    and cayenne pepper to taste
About 5–6 tbsp fine
    breadcrumbs
570 ml/1 pint/2½ cups or
    more corn oil or sunflower
    oil for deep-frying

Put the cold rice or risotto into a bowl and add the beaten egg with a little salt and pepper. Mix well with your hands, cover the bowl and set aside in a cool place.

Season the prawns/shrimps with salt and pepper or cayenne pepper. Put a large spoonful of cooked rice or risotto on to a sheet of greaseproof paper. Pat it flat, put a slice of banana in the middle, then a prawn on the banana and another slice of banana on top of the prawn. Carefully lift the edges of the rice so that they cover the banana slices and the prawn, and roll the croquettes into a ball by rotating it with your palm on the greaseproof paper. Repeat this process until you have made all the croquettes.

Heat the oil in a deep-fryer or a wok to 190°C/375°F, or until a cube of bread dropped into the oil turns brown within 1 minute. Roll 3 croquettes in the breadcrumbs and deep-fry for 4–5 minutes or until they are golden brown. Take them out with a slotted spoon and drain on absorbent paper. Continue frying 3 at a time until all the croquettes are fried. Serve hot or warm.

Curried Egg and Rice Croquettes

The Mild Curry Sauce described on page 355 gives its flavour to these croquettes, and is also served with them. With watercress or slices of cucumber, these make an attractive first course.

Preparation: cook the rice; make the sauce; assemble and chill, 40 minutes
Cooking: 10 minutes

Makes 8–10 croquettes

570 ml/1 pint Mild Curry
  Sauce (page 355)
5 hard-boiled eggs, peeled
4 tbsp plain/all-purpose flour
310 g/11 oz/3 cups cooked
  short grain rice or
  glutinous rice
2 raw eggs
3 tbsp plain/all-purpose flour
170–225 g/6–8 oz/
  1–1⅓ cups breadcrumbs
Vegetable oil for deep-frying

For the garnish:

Cucumber slices or a few
  sprigs of watercress

Heat half the curry sauce in a saucepan, and when it boils sift in the 4 tablespoons of flour. Stir vigorously with a wooden spoon until the sauce becomes quite thick. Add the cooked rice, still stirring vigorously. Chop the hard-boiled eggs roughly and mix them into the sauce also. The mixture should now be thick enough to form into croquettes; when you have made them, chill them for at least 30 minutes. Up to this point they can be made up to 24 hours in advance.

Just before you serve the croquettes, beat the raw egg in a bowl and spread the flour on a small plate, the breadcrumbs on a larger, flat one. Heat the oil in a wok or deep-fryer. Dip each croquette in the beaten egg, coat it with flour and roll it in breadcrumbs. Deep-fry the croquettes for 3–4 minutes, turning them over once. Drain on absorbent paper and serve immediately, garnished with the cucumber or watercress. Heat the remaining sauce and serve it in a bowl or sauceboat for guests to help themselves.

Note: The croquettes can, if you prefer, be shallow-fried in a non-stick frying pan using about 6 tablespoons of olive oil. Fry them for about 4 minutes each side, turning them over once.

Wild Rice Croquettes with Ham

These are equally good with black glutinous rice, so choose whichever you are most familiar with or comes easiest to hand. You can if you wish substitute salt beef, pastrami, or ox tongue for ham. The croquettes can be deep-frozen for up to a month before they are fried. If you are planning a big drinks party, you can freeze them in one large pack; otherwise, pack them in small batches so you will only have to thaw out what you need.

Preparation: 40 minutes
Cooking: 70–80 minutes

Makes 50–55 small
croquettes

---

170 g/6 oz/¾ cup wild rice
  or black glutinous rice
700 ml/1¼ pints/3 cups
  water
112 g/4 oz butter
8 tbsp rice flour or plain/
  all-purpose flour
570 ml/1 pint/3 cups milk or
  coconut milk
4 shallots or 1 onion,
  chopped
1 egg, lightly beaten
112 g/4 oz/½ cup ham or
  other meat, diced (see
  above)
¼ tsp cayenne pepper or
  chilli powder
¼ tsp ground or grated
  nutmeg
½ tsp salt
1–2 tbsp chopped parsley or
  coriander/cilantro leaves

Put the rice and water in a saucepan. Bring to the boil, stir the rice once, and cover the pan. If using black glutinous rice, cook for 30 minutes; if using wild rice, cook for at least 30 minutes, possibly longer. Then leave the rice to cool.

Meanwhile, melt half the butter in a small saucepan and add the flour. Stir with a wooden spoon for 1 minute. Then add the milk, a little at a time, stirring continuously, until you get a smooth, thick sauce. Leave to cool a little, then add the lightly beaten egg and mix well.

Heat the rest of the butter in a wok or frying pan and stir-fry the shallots or onion until soft. Then add the cool rice, with the pepper or chilli powder, nutmeg, salt, and parsley or coriander/cilantro leaves. Stir and mix these for 2 minutes, then add the white sauce and ham, and continue stirring and mixing for another 2 minutes. Transfer the mix to a bowl and leave it to get cold.

When it is cold, put a tablespoonful on to a piece of greaseproof paper or foil and roll it into a croquette shape. Go on until all the mixture is used up. Alternatively, roll the mix into a roll about 2.5 cm/1 inch in diameter, and cut from it croquettes about 5 cm/2 inches long. Pack them in layers, with greaseproof paper or clingfilm between the layers. Then freeze them for at least 1 hour, or until they are needed.

To coat the croquettes:

8 tbsp rice flour or plain/
    all-purpose flour
3 large eggs, beaten
285–340 g/10–12 oz/
    1⅔–2 cups fresh
    breadcrumbs
Sunflower oil or corn oil for
    deep-frying

Before you fry them, take the croquettes from the freezer and immediately coat each one with flour and dip it in the beaten egg. Then heat the oil in a wok or deep-fryer to 190°C/375°F; at this temperature, a cube of bread dropped into the oil browns in 1 minute. Now roll 4 or 5 croquettes in breadcrumbs, and deep-fry them for 4–5 minutes or until they are golden brown. Take them out with a slotted spoon or wire scoop, and drain them in a colander lined with absorbent paper. Carry on like this till they are all done, and serve hot or warm.

Seller of krupuk (prawn crackers): Java

Spinach and Rice Balls

These make delicious canapés, and are best of all when they are deep-fried, but if you are averse to fried food you can bake them in the oven. You need a soft rice – a short grain or a soft long grain like Thai Fragrant; not Basmati or parboiled rice.

Preparation: cook the rice; 40 minutes + refrigeration
Cooking: 20 minutes

Makes about 20

675–900 g/1½–2 lb young spinach
310 g/11 oz/3 cups cooked rice
2 tbsp olive oil
6 shallots, sliced
4 cloves garlic, finely chopped
2 slices of lean bacon, diced very small
Salt and freshly ground black pepper
2 eggs, separated
84–112 g/3–4 oz/½–⅔ cup homemade breadcrumbs
¼ tsp ground nutmeg
Oil for deep-frying

Remove the spinach stalks and wash the leaves thoroughly. Then put the spinach into lightly salted boiling water for 2 minutes. Drain it in a colander and rinse with cold water. Squeeze out the excess water and spread the leaves on a chopping board. Chop the spinach with a knife and set aside.

Fry the shallots, garlic and bacon in the olive oil for 3–4 minutes. Take them out and drain them on absorbent paper. When they are cool enough to handle, mix them in a bowl with the cold cooked rice. Season with salt and pepper, and mix the spinach into the rice also. Then do the same with the egg yolks, mixing everything together by hand. Keep on until you feel the rice and spinach are sticking together ready to be formed into balls about the size of a walnut.

Put a little oil on the palm of each hand, and roll each ball firmly. Line a small tray with clingfilm and place the spinach balls on this, in one layer. Refrigerate for at least 30 minutes so that they set firmer still. If you intend to bake them, preheat the oven to 200°C/400°F/Gas Mark 6.

Beat the egg white lightly with a fork in a bowl. Season the breadcrumbs with salt, pepper and nutmeg, then spread the crumbs on a small tray.

When the oven reaches the correct temperature, bring the spinach balls from the fridge and roll each of them first in the egg white, then in the breadcrumbs. Oil a baking tray and arrange the balls on it. Bake for 20 minutes, turning them over after 10 minutes. Alternatively, deep-fry them in batches for 5–6 minutes until slightly browned. Serve hot or warm.

Javanese Stuffed Rice Rolls
Lemper

These are the best things of their kind that I have eaten anywhere. The stuffing, of shredded chicken very mildly spiced, perfectly complements the glutinous rice cooked in coconut milk. Traditionally these rolls are cooked in banana leaves, but in London I make them in a Swiss roll tin.

Use the same-sized cup to measure the rice and the coconut milk. You will need a Swiss roll tin about 22.5 × 32.5 cm/19 × 13 inches, and some greaseproof paper.

Preparation and cooking: about 1-1½ hours altogether

Makes at least 10–12 slices, more if slices are thinner

450 g/1 lb/2 cups glutinous rice, soaked in cold water for 40–60 minutes, and drained
570 ml/1 pint/2½ cups coconut milk
¼ tsp salt

For the stuffing:

2 chicken breasts
4 shallots, chopped
3 cloves garlic, chopped
3 candle nuts or macadamia nuts or blanched almonds
1 tsp ground coriander
½ tsp ground cumin
½ tsp brown sugar
1 kaffir lime leaf (optional)
½ tsp salt
¼ tsp ground white pepper
2 tbsp peanut oil or olive oil
140 ml/5 fl oz thick coconut milk

Boil the rice in the coconut milk with ¼ teaspoon salt until all the liquid has been absorbed by the rice. Transfer the rice to a steamer and steam it for 15 minutes. Turn off the heat, but leave the rice in the steamer until you are ready with the stuffing.

Boil the chicken breasts in water with a large pinch of salt for about 10 minutes. Take them out, and let them cool on a plate. When they are cool, shred them finely.

Blend the rest of the ingredients for the stuffing with half of the coconut milk until smooth. Put the liquid into a small saucepan, bring it to the boil and simmer for 8 minutes. Add the shredded chicken meat and the rest of the coconut milk and continue simmering until all the coconut milk has been absorbed but the mixture is still moist. Adjust the seasoning, and leave to cool.

Line the Swiss roll tin with a sheet of greaseproof paper and spread the rice on this, pressing it down (with another piece of greaseproof paper) to fill the tin evenly. Spread the cool spiced chicken evenly over the rice. Then roll it up as if you were making a Swiss roll. Cut it into slices with a large knife that has been wetted in hot water. Serve warm or cold as a teatime snack, or with drinks.

A variation, still traditionally Javanese, is to wrap the rice roll in a plain omelette. Or you can wrap it in Japanese nori (page 375) to make a kind of Japanese-Javanese sushi.

139

Stuffed Vine Leaves
Dolmas

You can buy ready-made dolmas (or dolmades), but they are usually mass-produced and not very good. Making your own takes time and a little patience, but the results justify the trouble, especially if you enjoy jobs that give you time to think or to sit down and talk with a friend. Once you have started, go on and make plenty. Freeze some, so you can astonish people at your next party by offering them these delicious canapés even after a busy week at the office.

The very best dolmas are made with your own fresh vine leaves from the garden, but leaves preserved in brine are perfectly good. As for the stuffing, I have tried many combinations of ingredients, with and without meat, and I give here two of my favourites, both vegetarian. The first is sweet and sour, the second hot and sour with a little Oriental spice.

Preparation: 1 hour
Cooking: 60–90 minutes

Quantities in each stuffing recipe are sufficient for 24–26 dolmas

112 g/4 oz/½ cup short grain rice, washed, soaked in cold water for 30 minutes, and drained

28 g/1 oz/scant ¼ cup raisins, chopped

4 dried apricots, soaked in hot water for 10 minutes, drained and chopped

56 g/2 oz/⅓ cup walnuts, chopped

1 tsp cinnamon powder

2 tbsp chopped spring onions/ scallions or chives

2 tbsp chopped parsley

2 tbsp chopped mint

1 tsp salt

If you are using fresh vine leaves, blanch them first in boiling water for 1 minute, then refresh in cold water and drain. Leaves preserved in brine are salty, so wash them in hot water, then blanch them for 2 minutes, refresh in cold water, and finally wash again in cold water to get rid of the salt. With preserved leaves, don't put any salt into the cooking water.

Mix together all the stuffing ingredients in a bowl. Then stuff the leaves as shown in the illustration on the next page.

A wide pan (with a tight-fitting lid) is best, so all the stuffed leaves can be fitted close together in a single layer or at most 2 layers. Use any leftover or torn fragments of leaves to line the pan. Spread half the chopped onions and half the chopped tomatoes on the bottom of the pan and sprinkle them with pepper (and, if fresh vine leaves are used, with salt also). Then arrange the stuffed vine leaves on top – quite tightly so that they don't unwrap during cooking. Spread the rest of the chopped tomatoes and onions over the leaves. Mix the water, oil and lemon juice in a bowl and pour these over the contents of the pan.

1 tbsp lemon juice
2 tbsp olive oil

Hot and Sour Stuffing:

112 g/4 oz/½ cup short grain
   rice, washed, soaked in
   cold water for 30 minutes,
   and drained
56 g/2 oz/⅓ cup chopped
   walnuts or pine nuts
3 tbsp chopped spring onions/
   scallions or chives
3 tbsp chopped coriander/
   cilantro leaves
1 tsp ground coriander
½ tsp ground cumin
1 tsp chilli powder
1 tbsp lemon or lime juice
2 tbsp olive or peanut oil
1 tsp salt

Other ingredients:

30–35 vine leaves, fresh or
   preserved
2 large onions, chopped
4 tomatoes, chopped
Salt and pepper to taste
1 tbsp lemon juice
2 tbsp olive or peanut oil
8 tbsp hot water

Cover everything with a plate, so that the stuffed leaves have some weight on top of them, and put the lid on tightly. Simmer very gently for 1 hour. Uncover, and taste. If you think the dolmas are not quite done, add another 8 tablespoons or so of hot water and continue simmering, still tightly covered, for another 20 minutes or longer. Make sure the pan does not become completely dry; as a rule, the onions and tomatoes will help to keep the stuffed leaves moist.

Serve the dolmas cold. If you freeze them, take care to thaw them completely, steam them for 4–5 minutes, and cool to room temperature before serving.

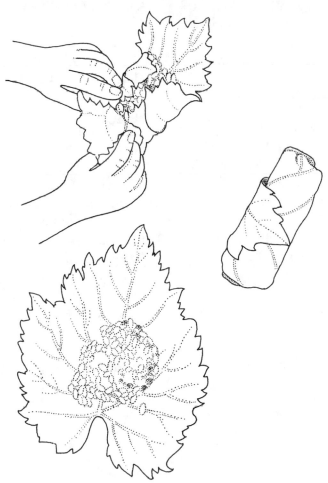

Filling and rolling a vine leaf

141

Blini with Rice Flour
with Spiced Aubergine/Eggplant Purée

People in Indonesia make pancakes called *serabi*, and eat them for breakfast with sugar syrup flavoured with ginger or vanilla, or else with sweetened coconut milk. If this reminds you of American breakfast pancakes eaten with maple syrup, that is not surprising, for they are very similar. A Russian *blin* is the same sort of thing again. The blini described here are made, like serabi, of wheat flour mixed with some rice flour. They are very good for breakfast, but I suggest using little ones as bases for savoury fish or – as here – for a spiced aubergine/eggplant purée. They make an excellent appetizer with a drink before dinner.

Preparation: 10 minutes + 30–50 minutes resting
Cooking: 18–20 minutes

Makes 35–40 blini

For the blini:

112 g/4 oz/⅔ cup **plain
    wheat flour**
56 g/2 oz/⅔ cup **rice flour**
1 tsp baking powder
¼ tsp salt
1 egg
390 ml/14 fl oz/1¾ cups
    **milk or coconut milk,
    slightly heated**
Butter

Mix the two kinds of flour together in a bowl with the baking powder and salt, then sift this mixture into another bowl. Make a well in the middle and break the egg into it. With a wooden spoon, turn the egg in a circular movement, mixing it gradually into the flour. Continue this movement as you add the warm milk, a little at a time, so that you get a smooth batter. Leave to rest for 30–50 minutes. Stir again before cooking.

Slowly heat a cast-iron blini pan or griddle and brush it with butter. Pour the batter into the holes in the blini pan, or, with a griddle, use a tablespoon to pour spoonfuls of batter on to it so that they make more or less circular shapes. Cook gently for about 2 minutes, then turn the pancakes with a palette knife and cook them on the other side for a further 2 minutes. Serve them straight away if possible; if you keep them warm in the oven, limit this to a few minutes. Blini can be frozen for a couple of weeks or so; let them thaw out completely, and warm them for a minute or two over a moderate heat before serving.

For the aubergine/eggplant
purée:

3 medium-size aubergines/
  eggplants
1 red sweet/bell pepper
2–3 tbsp virgin olive oil
5 shallots, finely chopped
2 cloves garlic, finely
  chopped
1 tsp finely chopped ginger
  root
¼ tsp chilli powder or ground
  white pepper
½ tsp ground cumin
Salt
1 tbsp chopped coriander/
  cilantro leaves or chives
2 tsp lemon or lime juice

Brush some oil on the aubergines/eggplants and pepper and roast them on a baking tray in the oven at 180°C/350°F/Gas Mark 4 for 30–35 minutes, or longer for the aubergines/eggplants. Take them out as soon as their skins are charred all over. Leave them to cool a little, then peel them and remove the pepper seeds. Set the pepper and aubergines/eggplants aside in a glass bowl.

In a small frying pan, fry the shallots and garlic in the olive oil until quite soft. Add the ginger, chilli powder and cumin, and stir for 1 minute. Season with salt. Combine this mixture with the aubergines/eggplants and pepper, mashing them all together until smooth. This can be done in a food processor, but the machine must run for only a few seconds; the rough texture that comes from mashing with a wooden spoon tastes nicer.

Stir in the coriander/cilantro leaves or chives, and the lemon or lime juice. Spread or dollop the purée on top of the hot or warm blini, and serve.

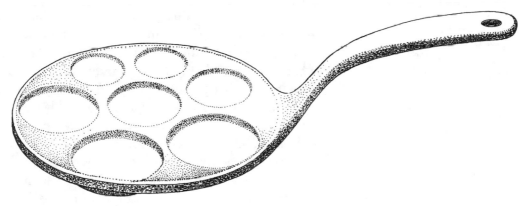

Blini pan

143

Rice Flour Crisps with Mung/Green Gram Beans
Rempeyek

I don't think you can find a more delicious crisp anywhere than these Indonesian rempeyek. You may have to practise for a few minutes to get the frying of them just right, but there is nothing difficult about them. You do, however, need to go to an Oriental shop to get really fine rice powder; the rice flour sold in most supermarkets is not fine enough.

Instead of mung/green gram beans, you can also use peanuts, which many people think are even nicer but which involve more work – you have to cut each peanut in half. Once that is done, the procedure is exactly as described here.

Preparation and cooking: about 1½ hours altogether

Makes 50–60 savoury crisps

112 g/4 oz/⅔ cup mung/
    green gram beans, soaked
    overnight
2 candle nuts
1 clove garlic
2 tsp ground coriander
1 tsp salt
112 g/4 oz/⅔ cup rice
    powder
225 ml/8 fl oz/1 cup cold
    water
Peanut oil or sunflower oil
    for frying

Drain the mung/green gram beans. Pound the candle nuts and garlic together, or put them in a blender with 56 ml/2 fl oz/¼ cup of the allocated water and blend until smooth. Transfer to a bowl, then add the coriander and salt. Mix in the rice powder, and add the remaining water, a little at a time, stirring and mixing thoroughly. Add the mung/green gram beans to this batter.

To fry rempeyek, you need a non-stick frying pan and a wok. Heat some oil in the pan, and enough in the wok to deep-fry the rempeyek. Take 1 tablespoon of batter, with some beans in it, and pour it into the frying pan so that it forms a single flat shape. Go on until the frying pan is full – you will probably be able to fry 6 or 7 at a time. When they have been frying for between 1 and 2 minutes, transfer them to the hot oil in the wok. Deep-fry them until crisp and golden – this will take a few minutes. Then put them to drain and cool on absorbent paper. Continue until the batter and beans are used up.

Leave to get cold before storing in an airtight container. In the container, rempeyek will stay crisp for up to 2 weeks.

144

Courgettes/Zucchini Stuffed with Spicy Rice

If the courgettes/zucchini are to be served with drinks, the rice stuffing needs to be bound with egg before they are baked or steamed. If you serve them as an accompaniment to a meat or fish main course, then the egg binding is optional. Choose good, plump courgettes/zucchini, as near the same length and girth as you can find.

Preparation: 30 minutes
Cooking: 25–30 minutes in the oven or 8–10 minutes steaming

For 4–6 people as an accompaniment to a main course; 10–12 as a snack with drinks

6 courgettes/zucchini, weighing 450–500 g/ 16–18 oz, washed
1.7 litres/3 pints/7½ cups water
½ tsp salt

For the stuffing:

112 g/4 oz/½ cup uncooked Basmati or Patna rice, washed and drained
3 tbsp olive or peanut oil
2 cloves garlic, finely sliced
4 shallots, finely sliced
½ tsp chilli powder
½ tsp paprika
½ tsp ground coriander
½ tsp ground cumin
The chopped-up flesh of the courgettes/zucchini
1 egg (optional)
Salt to taste

Heat the 7½ cups water in a saucepan with ½ teaspoon salt. When it boils, put in the courgettes/zucchini whole, and boil for 3 minutes. Remove them with a slotted spoon into a colander. Bring the water to the boil again and put in the drained rice. Keep it at a rolling boil for 8–10 minutes. Drain the rice into a colander.

Cut the courgettes/zucchini in half lengthways and with a small spoon scoop out some of the flesh. Chop this finely and reserve it for use later.

Heat the oil in a frying pan and fry the garlic and shallots, stirring all the time, for 2 minutes. Add the powdered ingredients and the courgettes/zucchini flesh and continue stirring for 2 more minutes. Add the cooked rice and mix well. Turn off the heat and let the rice cool to room temperature. Adjust the seasoning and add the egg (if used), mixing everything well together.

Arrange the hollowed courgettes/zucchini halves in an oiled ovenproof dish and spoon the rice filling into them. Cover the dish with aluminium foil and bake in the oven at 180°C/350°F/Gas Mark 4 for 25–30 minutes. Alternatively, if you prefer, steam them for 8–10 minutes.

When they are cooked, transfer the courgettes/zucchini to a serving dish. If they are to be served as a snack or with drinks, cut them into small pieces with a sharp knife. Otherwise, serve them as they are, hot, warm, or cold, as a main-course vegetable.

Variation. This stuffing, if you leave out the chopped courgettes/zucchini, is very good for filling sweet peppers or pimientos. The quantities shown here will be sufficient for two large red or green peppers. Cut the peppers lengthways, remove the seeds, and blanch in boiling water for 2 minutes. Refresh in cold water, dry them with kitchen paper, then fill them and bake them as for the courgettes/zucchini above.

Kibbeh of Ground Rice with Almond Sauce

I am always on the lookout for good savoury dishes that use rice flour. Kibbeh is a delicious mixture of minced lamb with either rice flour or bulgur, formed into small balls or croquettes and then baked or deep-fried. I have adapted this recipe from Claudia Roden's *New Book of Middle Eastern Food*, with the author's permission.

The fried kibbeh, by themselves, make good finger-food or canapés with drinks. Claudia Roden also gives an excellent recipe for almond sauce to serve with the kibbeh as a main course.

Preparation: 40 minutes
Cooking: 40–45 minutes

Makes 20–25 kibbeh

For the filling:

140 g/5 oz/⅔ cup minced lamb
2 tbsp finely chopped parsley
A pinch of ground allspice
Salt and pepper to taste

For the kibbeh shells:

285g/10 oz/1⅓ cup minced lamb
170 g/6 oz/1 cup ground rice

Mix all the ingredients for the filling in a glass bowl. Then blend the finely minced lamb and the ground rice thoroughly in a food processor. Season with salt and pepper and add 3–4 tablespoons of cold water. The result should be a smooth paste that can be formed into small balls, about as big as a walnut. Put a little oil on to the palms of your hands to stop the mixture sticking to them.

Make a hollow in each ball with your finger, and fill it with a teaspoon of the filling. Pinch the sides of the hole together to close it firmly. Roll it once between the palms of your hands to make a nice shape – something like a miniature rugby football. Deep-fry the filled kibbeh, a few at a time, for 4–5 minutes or until they are golden brown.

146

2 shallots, finely sliced
Salt and pepper to taste
3–4 tbsp cold water
Oil for deep-frying

For the almond sauce:

56 g/2 oz/½ cup ground
   almonds
850 ml/1½ pints/3¾ cups
   lamb or chicken stock
Salt and pepper to taste
1 clove garlic, crushed
2 tbsp finely chopped parsley
2 tbsp lemon juice, or more to
   taste

For the garnish:

1 tbsp chopped parsley
2 tbsp roasted pine nuts

Now (assuming you are going to serve the kibbeh as part of a meal) make the sauce. Mix the almonds and cold stock together in a saucepan. Bring to the boil, season to taste, and add all the other ingredients except the garnish. Simmer gently, stirring from time to time, for 20 minutes. Just before serving, add the fried kibbeh, stir, and transfer to a heated serving bowl. Garnish with parsley and pine nuts. Serve the kibbeh hot, with boiled or steamed rice and accompanied by a salad or cooked vegetables; or cold, without sauce, as a snack.

Moulds for *kratong thong* (golden cups): see page 148

Golden Cups
Kratong thong

This is a Thai recipe, but very similar things are found in other parts of South-East Asia: little crisp-fried cups formed by coating the *outside* of the mould with the batter. They are easy to make, though there is a knack, which you rediscover each time; I invariably have to throw away the first ten or a dozen cups. But then you get the hang of it, and in an hour or two you can turn out hundreds – they cost very little, and in a thoroughly airtight container will keep crisp for up to a week. You can fill them with all kinds of things; here, I suggest a meat and a vegetarian filling. You fill them, of course, just before serving them.

All rice flour recipes turn out better if you use the finest rice powder that you can get. The moulds can be bought from most good Thai shops, with two or four mounted on one handle (see illustration, page 147). The four-cup model is, of course, more productive, but it takes more practice to use efficiently. You don't want batter to get inside the mould.

Preparation and cooking: about 2–2½ hours

Makes 150–160 cups

For the cups:

84 g/3 oz/scant ½ cup plain/ all-purpose flour
84 g/3 oz/scant ½ cup rice powder
390 ml/14 fl oz/1¾ cups cold water
A tiny pinch of salt
Vegetable oil for deep-frying

Put the flour in a bowl, add the other ingredients and mix them well with a wooden spoon to make a smooth batter.

The best way to cook these cups is to use a deep-fryer with a thermostat; the oil temperature should be kept between 180° and 200°C/350° and 400°F. But a wok or saucepan will do; you will just have to adjust the heat from time to time, using your own judgement.

Heat the oil, and heat the mould initially by putting it in the oil for 4 minutes so that it gets really hot. Dip the hot mould up to the brim in batter and hold it there for 8–10 seconds. Don't let batter overflow into the mould. A layer of batter will start to cook and will stick to the mould when you lift it away. Plunge the mould and batter into the hot oil. Hold it there for 10 seconds, then shake the batter cups off the mould and into the oil. (You may need to give them a shove with a chopstick or a fork to free them.) Let them deep-fry a few more seconds so they really are golden, then lift them out with a slotted spoon and put them to drain

For the meat filling:

3 tbsp peanut oil
4 cloves garlic, finely
   chopped
4 large red chillies, de-seeded
   and finely chopped
450 g/1 lb fillet of pork, or
   chicken breast without
   skin, minced
2 tsp finely chopped
   coriander/cilantro leaves
2 tsp whole green or black
   peppercorns, coarsely
   ground
3 kaffir lime leaves, finely
   shredded
2 tsp finely chopped basil
   leaves
1 tsp sugar
2 tbsp fish sauce or light soy
   sauce

For the vegetarian filling:

112 ml/4 fl oz/½ cup peanut
   oil
112 g/4 oz/1 cup tempeh,
   diced, or waxy potatoes,
   diced
3 carrots, peeled and diced
2 parsnips, peeled and diced
1 large onion (about 225 g/
   8 oz/2 cups), finely
   chopped
2 cloves garlic, finely
   chopped
1 tsp chilli powder or paprika
1 tsp ground coriander
½ tsp ground cumin
½ tsp salt
3 tbsp water
1 tbsp chopped parsley or
   coriander/cilantro leaves

on a tray lined with kitchen paper. Continue doing this till all the batter has been used up.

Stir-fry the garlic and chillies in a wok or frying pan for 1 minute. Then add the minced meat. Stir-fry for 2–3 minutes, and add the rest of the ingredients. Continue stir-frying for another 2–3 minutes or until the meat is almost dry. Adjust the seasoning. Leave to cool to room temperature. Fill the cups just before serving.

Stir-fry the tempeh or potatoes in a wok or frying pan for about 4 minutes or until golden brown. Remove with a slotted spoon and drain on kitchen paper. Discard the oil from the wok, except about 2 tablespoons. In this, stir-fry the onion and garlic for 1 minute. Add the carrots and parsnips and continue stir-frying for about 2 minutes more. Add all the ground ingredients and salt. Stir again and add the water.

Cover the pan and simmer for 2–3 minutes, stirring once or twice. Add the tempeh or potatoes and adjust the seasoning. Stir for 1 more minute, then remove from the heat. Leave the mixture to cool to room temperature. Fill the cups just before serving, with the chopped parsley or coriander/cilantro leaves sprinkled on top.

Burmese Fish Soup with Rice Vermicelli
Mohinga

This soup can be served as a party dish or a one-dish meal, with all the accompaniments displayed on a large plate and the soup itself in a big bowl, kept piping hot on a hotplate. The guests help themselves as they please.

One thing that is still not to be had in the West is banana trunk, a traditional ingredient of mohinga. This can be replaced by banana flowers, which are sold fresh in quite a lot of Asian shops, or canned palm hearts, which you can get in most delicatessens. In Burma they use powdered roasted rice to thicken the sauce, but this is unnecessary; the noodles soak up the runny soup very effectively.

I have cooked mohinga in London with various kinds of fish, and my conclusion is that conger eels and monkfish are best. The conger eel bones take a little trouble to extract, but monkfish is ideal; if you just buy the tail, the flesh is easily filleted and the thick bones go into the stock pot.

Preparation and cooking: about 1½ hours altogether

For 6–8 people, or more as part of a buffet

450 g/1 lb monkfish tails, filleted

For the fish stock:

675 g/1½ lb conger eel
The bones of the monkfish tails
1.1 litres/2 pints/5 cups water
3 fresh or dried red chillies, cut in halves
¼ tsp ground turmeric
2 stems lemon grass
1 tbsp fish sauce

First make the stock. Put all the ingredients in a large saucepan and bring to the boil. Simmer for 5 minutes, then take out the conger eel and leave it to cool on a plate while the stock continues to simmer. When the eel is cool enough to handle, separate the flesh from the bones and skin. Keep the flesh aside and put the rest back in the stock. Continue to simmer for another 30 minutes, then strain the stock and discard the solids. Meanwhile, prepare the accompaniments of the dish – these do not need to be served hot, but the soup must be.

If you are using banana flower, boil it whole in slightly salted water for 6–8 minutes. Drain and quarter it, then cut it into fairly thick slices. If using palm hearts, drain and rinse them before you slice them. Put the flower or palm hearts on one side of a large serving dish. Put the rice noodles in a large bowl, pour very hot water over them to cover them, and leave them to soak for 4–5 minutes. Then drain them, and put them on the dish also. Arrange the other accompaniments on the same dish, with the chilli sauce in a small bowl in the centre.

For the accompaniments:

1 banana flower, the 2 outer
  layers of leaves discarded,
  or 450 g/1 lb/2 cups
  canned palm hearts, cut
  into rounds 1 cm/½ inch
  thick
450 g/1 lb rice stick noodles
Chilli sauce for the soup
Crisp-Fried Onion (page 358)
4 hard-boiled duck or hen
  eggs, peeled and quartered,
  or 12 quail eggs
Lentil Fritters (page 152) .
2–3 tbsp chopped flat-leaf
  parsley

To finish the fish soup:

2 tbsp peanut oil
3 shallots, finely sliced
3 cloves garlic, finely sliced
1 large red chilli, de-seeded
  and finely sliced
1 tsp finely chopped ginger
  root
5-cm/2-inch piece of lemon
  grass, outer leaves
  discarded, the soft inner
  part finely chopped
850 ml/1½ pints/3¾ cups
  coconut milk
The boneless flesh of the
  conger eel
The monkfish fillets, cut into
  bite-sized pieces
Salt and pepper to taste

Now for the soup. Heat the oil in a largish sauce-pan, and stir-fry all the sliced and chopped ingredients for 2 minutes. Put in the coconut milk, bring this to the boil, and add the fish. Simmer for 4 minutes. Add some of the strained fish stock: use your own judgement as to how much you will need for the people who will be eating it. Adjust the seasoning.

To serve, put some of the noodles and the other accompaniments into individual soup bowls, and ladle the hot fish soup on top of them. (The Lentil Fritters can be eaten by hand, as if they were bread rolls.) Guests should be encouraged to help themselves and to keep on doing so.

Lentil Fritters

Preparation: 25 minutes
Cooking: 20 minutes

Makes 30–32 fritters

2 tbsp sesame or peanut oil
1 onion, finely chopped
1 tsp ground coriander
1 tsp salt
225 g/8 oz/1 cup red lentils,
  washed and soaked in cold
  water for 10–15 minutes,
  then drained
140 ml/5 fl oz/⅔ cup cold
  water

To be added later:

4 tbsp chopped spring onions/
  scallions or Chinese chives
5 tbsp plain/all-purpose flour
  or rice powder
1 tbsp cornflour/cornstarch
1 egg, beaten
¼ tsp ground white pepper
200 ml/7 fl oz/⅞ cup
  vegetable oil for frying

Heat the sesame or peanut oil in a wok or frying pan and stir-fry the onion for 2 minutes, then add the ground coriander, salt and lentils. Stir-fry these for 2 minutes, then add the water. Simmer, stirring often, for 5 minutes or until the lentils have absorbed all the water. Leave to cool.

When cool, add the rest of the ingredients. Mix well, and adjust the seasoning. Heat the oil in a frying pan, and drop in the batter, a heaped teaspoonful at a time. Fry 7 or 8 teaspoonfuls in each batch, for 1–1½ minutes a side, turning the fritters over once. Take them out with a slotted spoon and drain on absorbent paper. Serve hot, warm, or cold, as an accompaniment to Burmese Fish Soup (mohinga, the previous recipe), or by themselves as a snack.

Machine building the levee between two rice fields: USA

South Indian Rice Soup
Rasam

This hot and sour soup is somewhat similar to the famous Thai tom yam gung soup, which of course is made with prawns/shrimp, and to the sinigang of the Philippines, which can be made with fish, prawns/shrimp or pork. Rasam, however, is entirely vegetarian, and the rice, even if only a little of it, is always put into the soup. It reminds me very much of my Indonesian sayur asam, except that that has boiled peanuts in it and we eat it with the rice served in a separate dish.

The rasam broth is made with lentils and tamarind, so the result is cloudy, not clear. But with the rice and vegetables in it – carrots, mooli/white radish – it looks appetizing and tastes refreshing.

Preparation and cooking: about 1¼ hours altogether, not including cooking the rice

For 4–6 people

For the broth:

1.7 litres/3 pints/7½ cups water
28 g/1 oz/¼ cup tamarind pulp
56 g/2 oz/¼ cup red lentils, washed and drained
1 large tomato, quartered
1–2 green chillies, chopped
¼ tsp asafoetida/hing (optional)
Salt

Other ingredients:

4 small carrots, peeled and cut into thin rounds
½–1 small mooli/white radish, peeled, cut in half lengthways, then sliced thin
80 g/2½–3 oz/⅔ cup cooked rice
112 g/4 oz/1 cup water spinach or watercress, trimmed and well washed

Combine all the ingredients for the broth in a large saucepan. Bring this to the boil and simmer for 40–50 minutes. Pass it through a sieve into another saucepan. Bring it back to simmering point and add the carrots and mooli/white radish. Simmer for 5–8 minutes, then add the rice and water spinach or watercress. Continue to simmer for about 3 more minutes. Adjust the seasoning and serve hot.

Thai Chicken and Galingale Soup with Rice Vermicelli
Kai tom ka

Like mohinga, the Burmese fish soup, this is an excellent one-dish meal or a soup, depending on how much of it you serve. The vegetable accompaniments are usually cooked together with the chicken, and the dish is served very hot so that the cold rice vermicelli that was put in the bottom of each guest's bowl quickly heats up. Thai people usually add some nam prik and crisp-fried onions in small bowls for guests to help themselves.

It is worth the trouble of finding small round white aubergines/eggplants (see illustration on page 362) and baby sweet corn, not to mention canned bamboo shoots that have been cut into pretty shapes. These are all available in Thai and other Asian food shops.

Preparation: 1¼ hours
Cooking: 20–25 minutes

For 6–8 people

The chicken and the stock:

- **1 large free-range chicken, cleaned and cut into 4 pieces**
- **2.3 litres/4 pints/10 cups water**
- **5-cm/2-inch piece of fresh galingale, washed and sliced, or 3–4 small pieces of dried galingale**
- **3 stems of lemon grass, washed, each cut into 3 pieces**
- **4 kaffir lime leaves**
- **2–4 small dried red chillies**
- **1 onion, sliced**
- **1 tsp salt**

Put all the ingredients for the stock into a large saucepan. Bring to the boil and simmer for 25–30 minutes. Take out the chicken and remove the meat from the bones. Cut it into fairly large pieces and keep aside. Put the bones and skin back into the pot and continue simmering on a very low heat for another 20–30 minutes.

Strain the stock through a fine sieve into another saucepan. You should have almost 1.2 litres, about 2 pints/5 cups; if necessary, add hot water to make up this quantity. Bring this stock back to the boil and add the bamboo shoots, aubergines/eggplants and baby sweet corn. Simmer for 8 minutes, then add the chicken meat. Simmer for 5 more minutes and add the coconut milk or creamed coconut, the fish sauce and the lime or lemon juice. Continue cooking on a low heat for 5–8 minutes more. Adjust the seasoning, add the basil leaves, and serve hot. Put a helping of rice vermicelli in each individual bowl and ladle the hot soup on to it.

Other ingredients:

450 g/1 lb canned bamboo
   shoots, preferably already
   stamped into shapes,
   otherwise sliced; drained
   and rinsed
225–285 g/8–10 oz small
   round aubergines/
   eggplants, cut in halves
225–285 g/8–10 oz baby
   sweet corn, cut in halves
170 ml/6 fl oz/¾ cup very
   thick coconut milk, or
   112 g/4 oz/½ cup creamed
   coconut, chopped into
   small pieces
1 tbsp fish sauce
4 tbsp lime or lemon juice

10–16 basil leaves
Salt if needed
225–340 g/8–12 oz
   (more if this is served
   as a one-dish meal) rice
   vermicelli, soaked in
   hot water for 5
   minutes, then drained

Philippines Sour Soup with Prawns/Shrimp
Sinigang na hipon

In the Philippines, *sinigang* is a stew but with a lot of liquid, predominantly sour liquid. It can be made with pork, fish, or (as here) with prawns/shrimp. It is always served with rice; the meat or fish, vegetables and rice are put on a plate, so that people can help themselves, and the sauce or soup is ladled into individual bowls to be consumed, with a spoon, all through the meal.

In fact, this is a one-dish meal that follows the usual pattern of meals in South-East Asia. Everything is put on the table together, and to follow you have simply some fresh fruit.

Preparation: 30 minutes
Cooking: 20–25 minutes

For 4–6 people

1.1 litres/2 pints/5 cups fish
  stock or water
3 shallots, finely sliced
2 cloves garlic, crushed
1 tsp chopped ginger root
½ tsp chilli powder
170 g/6 oz/1½ cups runner
  or French beans, cut into
  2-cm/¾-inch lengths
225–285 g/8–10 oz/
  2–2½ cups mooli/white
  radish, peeled and sliced
  into thin rounds
8–10 small round white
  aubergines/eggplants, cut in
  halves, or 1 medium purple
  aubergine/eggplant, cubed
112–170 g/4–6 oz water
  spinach or watercress,
  trimmed and washed
3 tbsp fish sauce (patis or
  nam pla)
225 ml/8 fl oz/1 cup
  tamarind water
450–675 g/1–1½ lb large
  prawns/shrimp, 4 to 6 of
  them with heads and shells
  on for garnish, washed
  thoroughly, legs removed;
  the rest peeled and
  de-veined

Put about 112 ml/4 fl oz/½ cup of the fish stock in a saucepan with the shallots, garlic, ginger and chilli powder. Bring to the boil and simmer for 3–4 minutes. Then add the rest of the stock. Bring to the boil again, and when boiling add the vegetables, except the water spinach or watercress. Lower the heat and simmer for 4 minutes.

Add the water spinach or watercress, fish sauce and tamarind water. Continue simmering for 2 more minutes. Adjust the seasoning, bring back to the boil and add the prawns/shrimp. Cook for 4–5 minutes, then remove the pan from the heat. Add the calamansi or lime juice and chopped coriander/cilantro. Serve straight away, with 1 whole prawn/shrimp (with head) as garnish for each portion. Serve the rice and Chilli Sauce (if used) in separate plates or bowls.

Other ingredients and
accompaniments:

340 g/12 oz/1½ cups long
  grain rice: cook by
  absorption method and
  then steam (page 98)
1 tbsp calamansi juice or lime
  juice
1 tbsp chopped coriander/
  cilantro leaves
Any Chilli Sauce (page 350–1)
  (optional)

Chilled Rice Soup with Papaya

I ought to explain at once that this is not really a soup. It is a combination of soft-cooked rice with freshly made coconut milk and small slices of sweet papaya. When I was a child, I used to eat this almost every day for breakfast. It is delicious and – so I was led to believe – very good for you. Here I recommend it as a cool refresher for a hot summer day.

Preparation: about 15–20 minutes

For 4 people

1 ripe papaya, peeled, cut in
  half lengthways, the seeds
  removed
850 ml/1½ pints/3¾ cups
  coconut milk
¼ tsp salt
A pinch of chilli powder or
  white pepper (optional)
155 g/5½ oz/1¼ cup cooked
  soft rice

Cut each half of the papaya crossways into 3, then cut these pieces into small, thin slices. Put the coconut milk in a bowl and add the salt, and chilli or pepper if used. Stir well, and add the cooked rice and the papaya slices. Chill.

Just before serving, stir the soup again and serve straight away in bowls or glasses. Eat with a spoon.

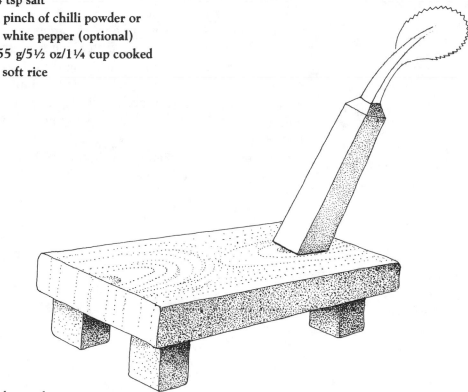

Kukuran: for grating coconut

Minestrone with Rice

This is very much a Mediterranean soup, with its garnish of Parmesan cheese, but with rice instead of pasta.

Preparation: soak beans 8 hours or overnight + boil for 40 minutes
Cooking: 1½ hours

For 8–10 people

2.3 litres/4 pints/10 cups water, and more later
340 g/12 oz/2 cups dried haricot beans, soaked for 8 hours or overnight
340 g/12 oz/2 cups dried cannellini or pinto beans, soaked for 8 hours or overnight
170 g/6 oz/¾ cup short grain Italian or Japanese rice
2 tbsp olive oil
340 g/12 oz/3 cups leeks, trimmed and well washed, cut into thin rounds
2 cloves garlic, finely chopped
340 g/12 oz/2 cups ripe tomatoes, peeled, de-seeded and chopped
5 medium carrots, peeled and diced
450 g/1 lb/4 cups courgettes/ zucchini, diced
450 g/1 lb/4 cups baby green beans, topped and tailed
Salt and pepper
112 g/4 oz grated Parmesan cheese
4 tbsp chopped flat-leaf parsley

Boil the beans, each kind separately, in plenty of water, without salt, for 40 minutes. Drain them all into one colander and refresh with cold water.

Put 2.3 litres/4 pints/10 cups of water into a large pan with all the beans. Bring it to the boil and let the beans simmer for 25 minutes. Add the rice and continue to boil for another 15 minutes. Discard any froth or scum that comes to the surface.

While the beans and rice are boiling, heat the oil in a small pan and sauté the leeks and garlic for 1 minute or so, then add the tomatoes. Season with salt and pepper and continue to simmer for 3–4 minutes.

When the rice has simmered for 15 minutes, add the leek and tomato mixture to it, including the oil. Add the carrots and continue to simmer for 6 minutes. Then add the courgettes/zucchini and green beans. Continue cooking for 5–6 minutes, until all the vegetables are tender.

Adjust the seasoning, and serve hot, garnished with Parmesan and chopped parsley.

Green Rice Soup

The green colour of this soup may come from sorrel, which is my own favourite, or spinach, lettuce leaves, or watercress. Each of them, of course, will give its characteristic flavour. About 80 g/2½–3 oz of cooked white rice will be sufficient. However, as you may not have any cooked rice left over, the recipe also shows how to make this soup using uncooked rice.

Preparation (excluding making the stock): 10 minutes
Cooking: 15 minutes

For 4–6 people

1.1 litres/2 pints/5 cups
    water
A pinch of salt
56 g/2 oz/¼ cup white rice,
    washed
2 tbsp olive or peanut oil, or
    ghee/clarified butter
3 shallots or 1 onion,
    chopped
1 clove garlic, chopped
¼ tsp ground or grated
    nutmeg
¼ tsp ground white pepper
1.1 litres/2 pints/5 cups meat
    or vegetable stock
112–170 g/4–6 oz/
    1–1½ cups sorrel (or
    spinach, lettuce leaves, or
    watercress), shredded
More salt and pepper to taste

Heat the water with a pinch of salt. When it is boiling, put in the rice, bring it back to a rolling boil and cook for 6 minutes. Drain the rice and save the cooking water to add to the stock, if it is needed, or to add to the soup if it turns out too thick for your liking.

Heat the oil or butter in a large saucepan and sweat the onion and garlic in it. Add the nutmeg and pepper, stir, and pour in the stock. Bring this to the boil and add the rice. Simmer for 10 minutes, then add the shredded sorrel or other greens. Continue simmering for 4 more minutes.

Put everything into a liquidizer and blend until smooth. Transfer back to the saucepan. Adjust the seasoning and the consistency: if the soup is too thick, add some of the rice cooking water, but if it is too thin, cook it a few minutes longer, stirring frequently, until you get the desired creaminess. Serve hot, warm, or cold.

Chicken and Hot Sausage Gumbo

Gumbo can be served as soup, with just a little rice in it, or it can become a substantial dish if you start by putting plenty of rice on your plate and then ladling the gumbo on to it.

The word *gumbo* really means okra/ladies' fingers, and perhaps the first gumbo was simply a way of cooking these. Having given their name to the dish, the okra then became just an optional ingredient – at any rate in Louisiana, which is the place most people associate with gumbo. This chicken gumbo does not include okra at all, but uses filé powder instead (page 371). I give an alternative recipe without filé powder for those who don't wish to go hunting for it or don't like sassafras.

Preparation: cook the rice; 40 minutes
Cooking: about 70 minutes

For 4 as a lunch or supper dish, or 8–10 as a soup

---

1 medium-sized chicken
2–3 tbsp rice flour
1 tsp salt
½ tsp cayenne pepper or chilli powder
140 ml/5 fl oz/⅔ cup vegetable oil
2 onions, chopped
2 celery stalks, chopped
4 cloves garlic, chopped
1 large sweet pepper/bell pepper, de-seeded and diced
1 tsp chopped fresh or dried thyme
2 tsp filé powder
½ tsp cayenne pepper or chilli powder
225 g/8 oz/1 cup chaurice or other hot pork sausages (page 287)

Take all the chicken meat from the bones and cut it into small cubes, about 1 cm/½ inch square. Use the bones and skin to make the stock. Put the chicken meat into a bowl with the rice flour, 1 teaspoon of salt and ½ teaspoon of cayenne pepper or chilli powder. Mix these well together and leave them in a cool place while you prepare the rest of the ingredients.

Cut the sausage into small pieces. Heat the oil in a thick-bottomed pan, and fry the chicken pieces, now seasoned and well coated in flour, in three batches; they should be just slightly browned. Take them out with a slotted spoon and drain on kitchen paper. Remove some of the oil from the pan, leaving about 3 tablespoons and the flour sediment at the bottom. In this, fry the onions, celery, garlic and diced pepper, stirring all the time, for 3 minutes. Add the thyme, filé powder, and cayenne pepper or chilli powder while continuing to stir for 1 more minute.

Now put in the sausages and chopped tomatoes, and the chicken meat. Stir again, cover the pan, and simmer for 5 minutes. Add half of the stock and continue to simmer, covered, for 50–60 minutes. Add the rest of the stock, adjust the seasoning and continue to cook until the gumbo has the consistency you want; this can be as soupy or as thick as you choose.

2 red tomatoes, skinned and
chopped
Salt and pepper to taste
1.4–1.7 litres/2½–3 pints/
6¼–7½ cups chicken
stock
155–310 g/5½–11 oz/
1½–3 cups cooked rice
2 tbsp chopped spring
onion/scallion
2 tbsp chopped parsley

Divide the rice among however many plates are
required, and serve the gumbo hot, ladled over the
rice. Garnish with chopped spring onions/scallions
and parsley.

Pounding rice by hand: Northern Luzon

Chicken and Okra Gumbo

This is my adaptation of a Creole gumbo for those who don't eat pork. Chicken or turkey sausages are available in large supermarkets in many parts of the world. If you don't find them hot enough, add more cayenne pepper or chilli to the gumbo, or make your own Chicken and Rice Sausage as described on page 225. The red peppers are to be roasted in the oven until the skins are charred – this gives the gumbo a nice smoky flavour.

Preparation: cook the rice; 40 minutes
Cooking: about 70 minutes

For 4 or 8 people

1 medium-sized chicken
1 tsp salt
½ tsp chilli powder
140 ml/5 fl oz/⅔ cup
    vegetable oil
2 onions, chopped
2 stalks of celery, chopped
4 cloves garlic, chopped
2 large red sweet/bell peppers,
    roasted, skinned,
    de-seeded, and diced
1 tsp chopped fresh thyme
112 g/4 oz/1 cup okra,
    chopped

225 g/8 oz/1 cup chicken
    or turkey sausage, cut
    up small
½–1 tsp chilli powder
1 tbsp tomato purée, or 2
    red tomatoes, skinned
    and chopped
Salt and pepper to taste
1.4–1.7 litres/
    2½–3 pints/
    6¾–7½ cups chicken
    stock
155–310 g/5½–11 oz/
    1½ cups cooked rice
2 tbsp chopped spring
    onions/scallions
2 tbsp chopped parsley

When you have assembled all the ingredients, follow the method described for Chicken and Hot Sausage Gumbo on page 160.

Miso Soup with Bean Curd and Rice Cake

This is not an authentic Japanese soup, but one that I made up for vegan readers. It becomes a substantial one-dish meal with any of the rice cakes described in this book – mochi or ddok (Japanese or Korean – page 105), or Indonesian lontong (page 107), or the Mooli/White Radish Steamed Cake on page 298.

You can make the vegetable stock to your own favourite recipe, or follow the one on page 345. If you prefer to use ready-made dried mochi from a Japanese shop, remember to soak the little cakes in hot water for 5–10 minutes to make them soft, then cut them into 2.5-cm/1-inch squares. Alternatively, the hard, dried cakes can be boiled vigorously for 2 minutes, then refreshed under the cold tap.

Preparation: 30 minutes
Cooking: 25 minutes

For 4–6 people

2 tbsp peanut or olive oil
2 shallots, finely sliced
1 tsp finely sliced ginger root
2 tbsp white miso
1 tbsp light soy sauce
390–450 g/14–16 oz/
    3½–4 cups tofu, cut into
    2.5-cm/1-inch cubes
850 ml/1½ pints/3¾ cups
    vegetable stock
28 g/1 oz/¼ cup dried
    shiitake mushrooms,
    soaked in hot water for 20
    minutes, then sliced
112 g/4 oz/1 cup mooli/white
    radish, peeled and diced
3 medium carrots, peeled and
    diced
170 g/6 oz/1½ cups fresh
    young spinach, washed
    thoroughly and roughly
    shredded
225–340 g/8–12 oz/
    2–3 cups lontong,
    mochi, ddok or Mooli/
    White Radish Steamed
    Cake, cut into 2.5-cm/
    1-inch cubes
Salt and pepper
2 tbsp chopped parsley

Heat the oil in a saucepan and fry the shallots and ginger for 1 minute. Add the miso and soy sauce, stir, and mash the miso with a wooden spoon. Add about 4 tablespoonfuls of the stock. Now add the tofu and simmer for 3–4 minutes, then pour in the remainder of the stock. Bring it to the boil and simmer for about 8 minutes.

Add the mushrooms, mooli/white radish and carrots, and continue simmering for 8 minutes. Add the spinach and rice cakes, adjust the seasoning, and simmer for 2–3 minutes longer. Then serve hot, sprinkled with chopped parsley.

Pumpkin Risotto

This rich golden risotto should be made with a good flavoursome stock, such as the meat stock on page 344, or the vegetable stock in the same section for a vegetarian risotto.

Preparation: 30 minutes
Cooking: 25–30 minutes

For 4–6 people

2 tbsp olive oil
1 stick celery, finely sliced
285 g/10 oz/1⅓ cups Italian rice: Arborio, Vialone Nano, etc.
2 or 3 bay leaves
A pinch of saffron or turmeric
225 g/8 oz/2 cups pumpkin or butternut squash, peeled and cubed
1.7 litres/3 pints/7½ cups stock
Salt and pepper
4–5 tbsp grated Parmesan cheese

Heat the stock in a saucepan and let it simmer while you are cooking the risotto.

Heat the oil in another saucepan, sauté the celery for 1–2 minutes, and then add the rice. Stir this around for 2–3 more minutes. Pour in a ladleful of stock, add the bay leaves, stir the rice again and leave undisturbed for 1 minute. Then stir again until all the liquid has been absorbed by the rice. Add a second ladleful of stock and proceed as before; then a third ladleful, and do the same again. Then, the fourth time round, put in 3 ladlefuls of stock and the pumpkin or squash cubes. Stir once, and cover the pan for 2 minutes so that the pumpkin or squash will cook.

Then uncover the pan and continue to stir the risotto. Add more stock, with the saffron or turmeric, and salt and pepper. Keep on stirring. Adjust the seasoning and taste the rice and squash to make sure they are cooked. The rice should ideally still be al dente, not quite soft. The whole process takes about 20–25 minutes. You may not need all the stock – once the rice is cooked it will not absorb any more. As soon as the rice is done, take the pan off the heat, stir in the grated Parmesan, and then keep the lid tightly on the pan for 2–3 minutes while the risotto rests. Then remove the bay leaves and serve at once.

Risotto with White Truffles
Risotto con tartufi

For this recipe, I am indebted to Franco Taruschio, of the Walnut Tree Inn at Llandewi Skirrid. I can't, this time, claim to have watched him cook it, but I have eaten it, and I think it is hardly necessary to say that it is absolutely delicious. However, I include it here as a Western rice dish that will take some time to become a family meal in any Eastern country where rice is a staple. It is not just that the truffles, if they were obtainable in the East, would be priced far beyond everyone's reach; the creamy consistency of a risotto would be entirely foreign. People in Asia only cook rice to this texture with milk or coconut milk if it is to be liberally dosed with sugar and made into a sweet dish, such as Indian kheer (see page 340).

The truffles, of course, make this something really special. If you can't get them, for whatever reason, this is still a real, complete, and extremely good risotto.

Preparation: 10 minutes
Cooking: 25–30 minutes

For 6 people

½ onion, finely chopped
675 g/1½ lb/3 cups risotto rice
2.3 litres/4 pints/10 cups chicken stock
A glass of white wine
84 g/3 oz butter
1 tbsp oil
84 g/3 oz Parmesan cheese, grated
White truffles

Melt half the butter with the oil in a large heavy saucepan and sauté the onion gently until transparent and light gold in colour.

Add the rice and stir it in, thoroughly but gently, so that it absorbs all the butter and oil. Stir for 5 minutes, then add the glass of wine and reduce.

Add 1 cup of boiling stock and cook, stirring, until it is absorbed, then add another cup of boiling stock and continue the process until all the stock has been used up and absorbed by the rice. This takes about 20 minutes. Turn off the heat.

Add the remainder of the butter and the Parmesan cheese and gently but thoroughly stir them in.

Cover the pan and let the risotto settle for 2 minutes. Serve with white truffle shaved on top, and extra Parmesan.

Risotto with Wild Mushrooms

In *Secrets from an Italian Kitchen*, Anna del Conte has a recipe for risotto with asparagus. If that is an early spring treat, then here, following her method, is one for the autumn. My preference is for morels, and I would even stuff some as a garnish. But by all means use other mushrooms, especially if you have just been mushroom hunting, either in the woods and fields or in the market. If you use dried morels you will need only half the quantity of fresh ones.

Preparation: 40 minutes
Cooking: 25–30 minutes

For 4 people

1.7 litres/3 pints/7½ cups
   Vegetable or Beef and
   Chicken Stock (page
   344–345)
70 g/2½ oz unsalted butter
3 shallots, finely sliced
Salt
285 g/10 oz/1⅓ cups
   Arborio or Vialone Nano
   rice
450 g/1 lb/4 cups fresh
   morels or other
   mushrooms, or 225 g/8 oz/
   2 cups dried ones
56 g/2 oz freshly grated
   Parmesan cheese
Freshly milled black pepper

For the stuffing:

4 tbsp ricotta cheese
1 tsp freshly chopped oregano
1 clove garlic, very finely
   chopped
Salt and pepper

Wash the fresh morels thoroughly to get rid of all the dirt and sand in their little crevices, and cut off their stems. The same applies to dried morels, which then need to be soaked in hot water for 40–45 minutes. Keep the stems and soaking water to use in stock.

Reserve 8 well-shaped morels to be stuffed as a garnish. Slice the rest thinly and keep aside. Start cooking the risotto about 15 minutes before you start cooking the stuffed morels, so everything is ready at about the same time.

To Cook the Stuffed Morels. Mix the ricotta with oregano and garlic, and season with salt and pepper. Stuff the morels with this mixture. Heat the milk in a small pan, put in the stuffed morels, and cook them on a low heat for 5–8 minutes, turning the morels over several times. Add the parsley and Parmesan cheese just before serving.

Mushrooms that cannot be stuffed can still be cooked in the same way as morels, and used as garnish. In that case, omit the ricotta cheese, and add the oregano to the milk.

To Cook the Risotto. Heat the stock and keep it simmering gently as you cook the rice. Heat 40 g/1½ oz butter in a heavy saucepan, and add a little salt. Sauté the shallots and sliced morels, stirring constantly with a wooden spoon, for about 4 minutes. Add the rice and continue stirring until all the grains are coated and glossy with butter.

112 ml/4 fl oz/½ cup milk
1 tbsp chopped parsley
2 tbsp freshly grated
   Parmesan cheese

Put in a ladleful of stock and let the rice absorb it as you stir it a few times. Then add another ladleful, stir a little as the rice absorbs it; then another ladle, and so on until the rice is al dente. This requires about 18–22 minutes from the time you start adding the stock. You may not need all the stock.

Remove the pan from the heat, add the remaining butter and half the Parmesan, and cover the pan for 2 minutes. Uncover, and give the risotto a good quick stir. Serve straight away, with the remaining Parmesan sprinkled on top and the stuffed morels shared out equally. Give each serving a few turns of the pepper mill.

A Variation. If you have plenty of time and want to impress your guests, mould the risotto in ramekins. Unmould each helping on to one of your best dinner plates and arrange the stuffed morels at the side of the risotto – not on top. Sprinkle Parmesan cheese, chopped parsley and freshly milled black pepper over it all.

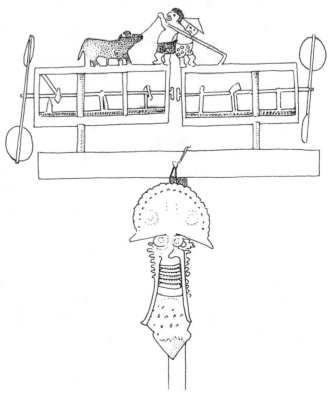

Bird scarer: Bali

167

Spicy Minced Duck
Laab

Laab is a speciality of northern Thailand: a spicy ground meat, usually made with beef. I recently had Laab made with duck, however, at the Blue Elephant in Fulham, London, where it was served on crisp lettuce leaves and tasted extremely good. When I make it myself, I serve it this way as a first course, or I put it on a plate of freshly cooked Thai Fragrant rice for lunch or supper, or for a buffet party I pile it on a platter lined with various kinds of lettuce leaves.

One of the principal ingredients is roasted rice which has been ground to a coarse powder. To roast rice, simply heat it in a frying pan without any oil, stirring it continuously with a wooden spoon for about 4 minutes, so that every grain is nicely browned. You can grind it in a mortar, or put it in a blender or coffee-grinder, but don't grind it fine.

The recipe below works equally well with either duck or beef. If you don't like your food too chilli-hot, use the minimum amount of chilli, but do use some.

Preparation: 50 minutes
Cooking: 10–12 minutes

For 6–8 people as a first course,
4 as a one-dish lunch or supper,
or 8–10 as part of a buffet

2 tbsp peanut oil
3 shallots, finely chopped
2–4 small chillies, chopped
6 duck breast fillets, skin removed, minced
6-cm/2½-inch stem of lemon grass, outer leaves discarded, the soft inner part finely chopped
56 ml/2 fl oz/¼ cup chicken stock
3 tbsp lemon juice
2 tbsp fish sauce

2 kaffir lime leaves, finely sliced
4 tbsp Thai Fragrant rice, roasted until lightly browned, then coarsely ground (see above)
2 tbsp finely chopped spring onions/scallions
Salt if required
12–16 coriander/cilantro leaves, the stems removed, for garnish

Stir-fry the shallots and chillies in the oil for 1–2 minutes. Add the ground meat and continue stir-frying for 2 more minutes. Add the rest of the ingredients except the ground rice, spring onions/scallions and coriander/cilantro leaves. Increase the heat and continue cooking on a high heat until all liquid has been absorbed. Stir, and adjust the seasoning. Remember that the fish sauce is very salty, so don't add salt unless you find it is needed.

Add the ground rice and spring onions/scallions. Stir for 2 more minutes. Serve as suggested above, garnished with the coriander/cilantro leaves.

Rice and Aubergine/Eggplant Turban

Rice and aubergines/eggplants are cooked together in many Middle and Far Eastern cuisines, and in many different ways. Aubergines/eggplants are notorious for soaking up a great deal of oil when fried, so a recipe like this is a way to get the goodness and flavour of the aubergine/eggplant without the oil. It is a moulded dish, with aubergine/eggplant slices containing the rice. If you make it in a ring mould, when it is turned out for serving the result looks something like a turban – I suppose this, with the Middle Eastern associations of the main ingredients, explains the name. But you can of course cook it in individual ramekins, like the Rice and Spinach Timbales on page 171.

If you make this as a starter, serve it with tomatoes or Red Pepper and Tomato Sauce (page 349). As a main course, it will go well with any meat, or simply with cooked vegetables for a vegetarian meal, and some plain boiled rice if you wish.

Preparation: cook the rice; 40–50 minutes
Cooking: 45–50 minutes

For 4 as a main course, or
6–8 as a starter

___

For the aubergine/eggplant
lining:

**3–4 large aubergines/
eggplants, cut lengthwise
into slices about 5 mm/
¼ inch thick (any
leftovers can be diced and
mixed with the rice)**
1 tbsp olive or vegetable oil
2–3 eggs, lightly beaten
Salt and pepper
¼ tsp chilli powder
¼ tsp ground coriander

For the rice:

**1 large aubergine/eggplant,
plus the leftovers from the
lining**
2 tbsp olive oil
2 cloves garlic, chopped
**1 large red chilli, de-seeded
and chopped**
**3 tbsp chopped spring onions/
scallions**
**3 tbsp chopped flat-leaf
parsley**
½ tsp salt
**350–500 g/1–1½ lb/
4–6 cups cooked rice**
2 hard-boiled eggs, chopped

Boil the aubergine/eggplant for the rice, whole, in slightly salted water for 8–10 minutes. Then dice it and leave to drain in a colander.

In a saucepan, fry the chopped garlic and chilli in 1 tablespoon of olive oil, stirring all the time, for 1–2 minutes. Add the spring onions/scallions and stir for another minute. Then add all the remaining ingredients for the rice, stirring everything together, gently, with a wooden spoon. Adjust the seasoning, and set the mixture aside while you prepare the aubergine/eggplant for the mould.

Brush a little oil on to the surface of a non-stick frying pan. Heat the pan and when it is hot drop in several of the lengthwise slices of aubergine/eggplant. Brown one side for about 2 minutes, then turn over for 2 more minutes on the other side. Transfer the slices to a tray lined with absorbent paper. Continue until all the slices are roasted.

Turn on the oven to 180°C/350°F/Gas Mark 4. Season the beaten eggs on a plate with salt and pepper, chilli and coriander. Dip the aubergine/eggplant slices into this spiced egg before arranging them in the mould. Remember to leave some overhang all round, which you will fold over on top of the rice later. Any odds and ends of aubergine/eggplant should be diced and mixed with the rice, together with any leftover beaten egg.

Spoon the rice mixture into the mould, pressing it down gently with the back of the spoon. Fold the overhanging aubergines/eggplants over on top of the rice, so that the rice is entirely wrapped. Cover the mould with aluminium foil. Bake in a preheated oven at 180°C/350°F/Gas Mark 4 for 35–40 minutes.

Remove the mould from the oven and leave to rest for 5–6 minutes. Then take off the foil and run a knife round the edge of the mould. Put a large plate upside down over the mould and turn the whole thing over to unmould the 'turban'. Cut it into however many pieces you require; and serve hot or warm.

Rice and Spinach Timbales

Rice and spinach often go together in the cooking of Afghanistan, India and other Eastern countries. Several examples will be found among the pilafs in the Main-Course Dishes section of this book. Here is a rice-and-spinach dish for a first course or a light lunch. You will need 8 ramekins – the 112 ml/4 fl oz/½ cup size.

Preparation: cook the rice; 35–45 minutes
Cooking: 15–20 minutes

For 8 people as a first course, or 4 as a light lunch

Mild Curry Sauce (page 355)
675 g/1½ lb fresh spinach
1 onion or 1 leek, weighing about 112 g/4 oz
15 g/½ oz dried prawn/ shrimp, soaked in hot water for 10 minutes, drained and chopped; or 4 anchovy fillets, soaked in milk for 10 minutes, drained and chopped
2 cloves garlic, finely chopped
1 green chilli, de-seeded and finely chopped
2 tbsp olive oil
Salt and pepper
230–310 g/8–11 oz/2–3 cups cooked rice
2 eggs

Remove the stalks from the spinach and wash thoroughly. Reserve about 16 large leaves to line the ramekins. Blanch these leaves in boiling water for 30 seconds. Remove them with a slotted spoon and plunge them into very cold water to stop them cooking. Spread these leaves on kitchen paper. Then use 2 leaves to line each ramekin, letting them hang over the rim. Shred the rest of the spinach and keep aside. Chop the onion finely, or if you are using a leek, wash it first, then chop.

Heat the olive oil in a wok or saucepan. Fry the onion or leek(s) for 2–3 minutes, add the garlic, green chilli and dried shrimps or anchovies. Stir again for 1 minute, and add the shredded spinach. Stir-fry for 3–4 minutes, until the spinach is cooked. Season with salt and pepper, and add the rice. Continue to stir-fry until there is hardly any liquid left. Remove the wok from the heat and leave to cool.

Stir the eggs into the mixture. Adjust the seasoning, and spoon the mixture into the lined ramekins. Fold the overhanging leaves over to cover it. Cover each mould with aluminium foil. Put them in a large saucepan, and pour hot water into the pan around them until it comes halfway up the sides of the ramekins. Bring this water to the boil, cover the pan, and simmer for about 15 minutes.

Reheat the Mild Curry Sauce. Run a knife around each timbale to separate it from the ramekin, then unmould the timbales on to individual small plates. Serve the sauce in a sauce-boat or jug, to be poured over or around the timbales.

Rice Moulds with Blue Cheese

These make an excellent first course, with the risotto rice moulded in small ramekins.

Preparation: 5–8 minutes
Cooking: 30–35 minutes

For 4 people

56 g/2 oz/¼ cup butter
170 g/6 oz/¾ cup **Arborio or
other Italian risotto rice**
200 ml/7 fl oz/⅞ cup milk
200 ml/7 fl oz/⅞ cup hot
water
¼ tsp ground or grated
nutmeg
¼ tsp salt
1 egg yolk
112 g/4 oz/½ cup
**Gorgonzola, Danish Blue,
or other blue-veined
cheese, crumbled**

For the garnish:

2 large tomatoes
Salt and pepper
3 tsp finely chopped chives or
basil

Melt the butter in a saucepan and add the rice. In another pan, mix the milk and the hot water. Stir the rice with a wooden spoon, add a ladleful of warm milk-and-water, stir again. When the liquid has been absorbed by the rice, add another ladleful. Repeat this process until the milk-and-water is used up and the rice is cooked. This will take 18–20 minutes. Add the nutmeg and salt, and mix well.

Heat the oven to 220°C/425°F/Gas Mark 7. Leave the rice to get cool. When it is at room temperature, beat in the egg yolk. Line 4 ramekins with clingfilm and fill them with the rice, pressing it down into each one quite firmly.

Put the ramekins upside-down on a well-greased baking tray or Pyrex dish. Lift off the moulds carefully, and the clingfilm. Scatter the crumbled blue cheese on top of each rice mould, and press gently with a fork. Put the tray in the heated oven and cook for 7–8 minutes, until the cheese bubbles.

While the rice moulds are in the oven, prepare the garnish. Put the tomatoes in a small bowl and pour over boiling water to cover them. Leave for 1 minute, drain, and pour cold water over them; they can now be easily skinned. Cut each skinned tomato into quarters, then each quarter into 2. Spoon out and discard the seeds. Sprinkle the tomatoes with salt and pepper and chives or basil.

Arrange equal portions of tomatoes on 4 small plates. When the rice moulds are ready, put one on each plate and serve immediately.

Rice for sushi

Making sushi at home is a wonderfully presumptuous thing to do, but who cares? You can have a lot of fun and give a lot of pleasure, and maybe get some insight into the professional skills that a top chef must have in a famous Tokyo sushi bar.

But this is the very top end of the sushi market, and for the average person eating sushi is a more prosaic experience. Two Japanese friends invited me to their local, which they described alluringly as 'automatic sushi bar'. Were robots replacing chefs as they had replaced car workers? In fact, the staff were reassuringly human. The automatic bit was the ingenious horizontal moving platform, like a miniature baggage carousel in an airport, which carried an endless train of sushi portions, each enough for a couple of mouthfuls, on coloured saucers ceaselessly past the customers. You had only a second or two to judge by eye which portions were freshest and which had already done a dozen or two revolutions of the carousel. You helped yourself to whatever you fancied, and as you ate a little stack of saucers grew beside you. When you had had enough, you took your stack to the cashier, who calculated your bill according to the colours of the saucers.

Sushi is exquisitely simple, so simple that I have not the confidence to attempt more than four sushi recipes in this book. I think each of them is well worth making, however, and they should be made at home, to be eaten the moment they are ready.

First of all, here is how you prepare the rice with vinegar ready to be used in sushi.

450–675 g/1–1½ lb/2–3 cups short grain rice, such as Kokuho Rose or Calrose, washed and left to drain for 30–60 minutes

For the dressing:

112 ml/4 fl oz/½ cup rice vinegar
4 tbsp granulated or castor sugar
2 tbsp hot water
1½–2 tsp salt

Cook the rice in a saucepan, using the absorption method described on page 98–100, or in an automatic rice cooker. Mix the dressing well in a small glass bowl, and keep it in a cool place until needed.

Transfer the hot rice to a large bowl. A wooden one is best, but a glass bowl or a glazed earthenware mixing bowl will do. Leave it to cool for a few minutes, then pour in the vinegar dressing a little at a time while you gently lift the rice and move it from side to side with a wooden spoon. Don't stir it vigorously; the action is more like the gentle tossing of a salad. Taste the rice from time to time as you pour on the vinegar – you may not want all of it.

Cover the bowl with a damp tea-towel/dishcloth and keep it in a cool place until you are ready with the topping.

Rice Salad Japanese Style

Sushi toppings are usually raw fish or shellfish, but there are one or two types that use cooked ingredients – for example, this 'scattered sushi'. I regard this as a very good rice salad, made to resemble quite closely the dish that in Japanese is called *bara-zushi*.

There are two ingredients of the traditional dish that I do not use here because they are very expensive and, outside Japan, difficult to get. They are kelp or konbu, and gourd ribbon. Dashi, or Bonito Stock, is quite simple to make, even without konbu (recipe on page 347). But by using a basic fish stock such as that described on page 346, you will produce a very good dish, even though it is not really bara-zushi. Feel free to substitute some other kind of mushroom for the shiitake if you wish.

The quantities given here will be sufficient to go with the amount of sushi rice described on page 173 – that is, 450–675 g/1–1½ lb/4–6 cups.

Preparation and cooking: about 1 hour altogether

For 4-6 people

4–6 eggs, made into a plain
  omelette which is then cut
  into strips
56 g/2 oz/½ cup dried
  shiitake, or 112 g/4 oz
  fresh shiitake or other
  mushrooms, sliced or
  quartered
56 g/2 oz/½ cup mangetout/
  sugar peas, cut diagonally
  across into two, or left
  whole if they are very
  small
8 large uncooked prawns/
  shrimp, without heads,
  peeled and de-veined
28 g/1 oz dried shrimp
112 ml/4 fl oz/½ cup fish
  stock or the water in which
  the shiitake were soaked
1 tbsp mirin (see page 374)
1 tbsp light soy sauce

Soak the dried shrimps in a bowl of hot water for 10 minutes or longer, until they expand and become soft. Drain, and keep aside.

At the same time, if you are using dried shiitake, soak them in hot water (and of course in a different bowl) for 30 minutes. Drain them, reserving the soaking water for use instead of fish stock (or, if you are using fish stock anyway, just put the soaking water and the stems of the shiitake into the stock pot).

Heat the fish stock or soaking water in a saucepan, and add the mirin and soy sauce. Let this liquid come to the boil, then add the drained and dried shrimps and the tofu. Simmer for 3 minutes, then strain the remaining liquid into a frying pan, keeping the shrimps and tofu aside.

Turn the heat up high under the frying pan and put in the fresh prawns/shrimp. Stir them around for 2 minutes, then add the shiitake and mangetout/sugar peas. Continue stirring for another 2 minutes. By this time the liquid will have evaporated. At this point you can if you wish pour in the oil, to give the prawns/shrimp, shiitake and mangetout/sugar peas an attractive glaze.

112 g/4 oz/1 cup fried tofu
   (page 382), quartered
1 tbsp peanut oil, for glazing
   the prawns/shrimp, etc.
   (optional)

Now put the sushi rice on to a serving platter. Add the mixture of dried shrimp and tofu, and toss carefully to mix them into the rice. Lastly, arrange the omelette strips, fresh prawns/shrimp (cut across into halves), shiitake and mangetout over the surface of the rice. Serve warm or cold.

Sushi Rolled with Smoked Salmon

This is another sushi which will appeal to everyone. Think of it as a salmon and cucumber sandwich, but round instead of flat, with rice instead of bread, and with the salmon on the outside.

To roll the sushi, you need a Japanese bamboo mat (see the illustration below). Alternatively, you can use a Swiss roll tin.

The ingredients listed here will combine with only half the quantity of sushi rice given on page 173. You can either double these quantities, or make a different sushi with the remaining rice.

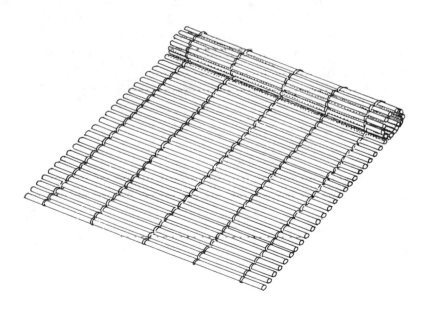

Bamboo mat for rolling sushi

Preparation and cooking: about 45 minutes altogether

Makes 4 rolls, each of which can be sliced into 4–6 small canapés; for 3–4 people as a light lunch accompanied by a salad

---

225–285 g/8–10 oz sliced smoked salmon
1 long cucumber, cut into 4 lengthwise, the seeds removed

The object is to make 4 rolls or cylinders of rice, with a strip of cucumber running lengthwise down the middle of each, and salmon covering the outside.

Divide the rice into 4 portions. Line the bamboo mat or Swiss roll tin with clingfilm/plastic wrap. Arrange a quarter of the smoked salmon to cover almost the full width of the mat or tin, but only about half its length. (If you line the whole length you will end up with a very thick roll.) Moisten your hand in water, then carefully spread one portion of the rice on top of the salmon slices, making sure it is spread evenly. Put one cucumber strip on top of the rice – it need not be perfectly central.

If you are using a bamboo mat, roll it carefully away from you to make a compact roll. Take care not to allow the plastic wrapping to get rolled into the centre. Remove the mat, and keep aside the roll, still wrapped in its plastic. Repeat the process for the other 3 portions.

If you use a Swiss roll tin, the flat tin can only act as a guide. Roll each portion by picking up the edge of the plastic wrap nearest you, and move it up and away from you and then down to form the roll. Make it as compact as you can without being too heavy-handed or squashing it.

Refrigerate the rolls in their plastic wraps for 10 minutes or so. Then unwrap them and slice each one across into 4–6 slices. Serve immediately.

Sushi and Salmon Terrine

You may think at first this looks a little contrived. In fact, it is the easiest way to present sushi rice with raw fish. As it is done Western-style, it should be eaten with knife and fork, not chopsticks. I suggest serving slices of the terrine on mixed salad leaves, dressed with mayonnaise or a vinaigrette. By all means add a little finely chopped fresh or pickled ginger root to the salad dressing if you wish. For the best results, you need to prepare and assemble this dish not too long in advance.

As a variation, make your terrines in ramekins. Depending on their size, you can serve one to each person or cut them in halves.

Preparation: 2–4 hours marinating
Cooking: 30–40 minutes

For 8–10 people as a first course or 4–6 for lunch

310–390 g/11–14 oz/
   3–3½ cups sushi rice
   (page 173)
675–900 g/1½–2 lb fresh
   salmon fillet, sliced thinly

For the marinade:

3 tbsp best olive oil
½ tsp rice vinegar or lemon
   juice
½ tsp salt
1 tsp ginger juice
A pinch of ground white
   pepper
1 tsp mirin or ½ tsp caster
   sugar (optional)
1 tbsp finely chopped spring
   onions/scallions or shallots

Mix all the ingredients for the marinade in a glass bowl and marinate the salmon slices for 2–4 hours. Drain just before you assemble the sushi terrine.

Line the terrine mould, first with clingfilm/plastic wrap, then with slices of salmon. Then fill the mould with sushi rice to a depth of about 2.5–3.5 cm/1–1½ inches. Gently press the rice down and level it with the back of a spoon. Lay more salmon on the rice, then more rice, finally a top layer of salmon. Cover with clingfilm/plastic wrap or greaseproof paper and refrigerate for 30 minutes.

Unmould the terrine onto a flat plate. With a large sharp knife, wetted with hot water, slice it and serve as suggested above.

Sushi with Scallops Rolled in Nori

Here are some ingredients which will enable you to create something quite different with the other half of your sushi rice.

Nori are paper-thin sheets of prepared seaweed, which can be bought, in various sizes, in Japanese or Oriental shops in most large towns in Europe, America and elsewhere. For this recipe you will need several small packets of nori strips, up to 24 of them, about 2 cm/¾ inch wide or a bit less (see page 375). As with the smoked salmon sushi, the idea is to make 4 rolls, each of which is then sliced into 4–6 little canapés. Alternatively, the quantity will be enough for 3 or 4 people for a light lunch, with some salad.

It is essential that the scallops are very fresh.

Preparation: 45–50 minutes

Makes 16–24 canapés; or sufficient for 3–4 people, as described

---

8 scallops, with or without their corals, well washed and cut crossways into halves (but with the corals left whole)
2 tbsp lemon juice
¼ tsp salt

Dissolve the salt in the lemon juice. Put the washed scallops in a glass bowl and pour the juice over them. Move the scallops around so that every surface is well coated in the juice. Then leave them in a cool place for 5 minutes and drain.

When you are ready to roll the sushi, divide the rice into 4 portions. Cover your bamboo mat, or line your Swiss roll tin, with clingfilm/plastic wrap. Spread the first portion of rice as described in the smoked salmon sushi recipe, but directly on to the plastic. Then lay 4 scallop halves, and 2 of the corals if you have them, in a row across the middle of the rice; when you roll everything up, the scallops will of course be the 'core' of the sushi.

Roll the rice into a compact roll or cylinder as described on page 176, and repeat for the remaining portions. Refrigerate the rolls, still wrapped in plastic, for 10–15 minutes.

To serve the sushi, unwrap each roll from its plastic cover and cut into 4–6 slices, their thickness more or less matching the width of the nori strips. (It doesn't matter if the strips don't cover the full thickness of the sushi.) Wrap a strip of nori round each piece; the rice is quite sticky enough to hold it in place. Serve at once, before the nori has time to lose its crispness.

Rice Salad with Curried Eggs

Make the rice salad as described on page 302 (Rice Salad with Asparagus) but without the asparagus – in other words, cook the rice in slightly salted water. This is how to make the curried eggs.

Preparation: 30–35 minutes

For 6 people as a starter, or
4 as a light lunch

12 small hen eggs, boiled for
  6 minutes
140 ml/5 fl oz/⅝ cup hot
  water
3–4 tbsp plain yogurt
2 tbsp raisins

For the curry paste:

2 shallots, chopped
2 cloves garlic, chopped
1 tsp chopped ginger root
2 candle nuts or 4 blanched
  almonds
1 small red chilli
1 tsp ground coriander
½ tsp ground cumin
1 tsp ground turmeric
¼ tsp ground cinnamon
½ tsp salt
2 tbsp water
2 tbsp olive or peanut oil

For the garnish:

Parsley, coriander/cilantro
  leaves, or watercress

Cool the eggs in cold water to room temperature before peeling them.

Blend all the ingredients for the paste until smooth. Cook the paste in a saucepan for 4 minutes, stirring often. Add the hot water and simmer for 5 minutes, then add the yogurt. Stir, and add the eggs and the raisins. Simmer for 3 minutes. Adjust the seasoning. Leave the curried eggs to cool a little, then cut each one into halves.

To serve, divide the rice salad among 6 plates, and arrange 4 halves of eggs on each, like the petals of a flower, the whites uppermost. Pour the curry sauce equally on each serving, and decorate with parsley, coriander/cilantro leaf, or watercress.

A Japanese Rice Casserole
Kama-meshi

This is a well-established example of Japanese fast food, popular at railway stations, one of which – Yokokawa, on the line from Niigata to Tokyo – is particularly famous for it. It has much in common with donburi (page 277) but is cooked in a traditional rice pot called a *kama* (see illustrations on page 132 and 181).

The meat in kama-meshi may be either chicken or beef, or both. For me, the secret of getting this rice casserole to taste really good is the stock (page 344). This recipe reproduces pretty accurately the kama-meshi I bought on the platform at Yokokawa Station. It makes an excellent one-dish meal, and I wouldn't want to add any other flavours to those that are here already.

Preparation: 15 minutes + making the stock
Cooking: 28–30 minutes

For 4–6 people

340 g/12 oz/1½ cups
    Japanese short grain rice,
    or Californian or
    Australian Calrose or
    similar, washed and
    drained about 1 hour
    before cooking starts
450 g/1 lb/2 cups skinned
    and boned chicken breast
112 g/4 oz/1 cup boiled beef,
    sliced thinly and cut into
    small pieces (this should be
    taken from the beef joint
    used for the basic Beef and
    Chicken Stock described
    on page 344)
1 tbsp dark soy sauce
2 tbsp saké
570 ml/1 pint/2½ cups Beef
    and Chicken Stock (page
    344)

Cut the chicken breast in half lengthways, then slice each half diagonally into thin pieces. Put these slices into a glass bowl, pour over them the dark soy sauce and 2 tablespoons of saké, and mix these with your hand so that the meat is well coated with the liquid.

If you are using dried shiitake mushrooms, rinse them well in cold water and then soak in hot water for at least 10 minutes or up to 30 minutes. Put the water they have been soaked in, and the mushroom stems, into your stockpot. Slice the mushrooms thinly. Fresh shiitake should be washed and sliced in the same way (but not soaked); the stems go into the stock pot.

Put 112 ml/4 fl oz/½ cup of the stock into a small saucepan. Bring to the boil and add the marinated chicken slices, the beef, bamboo shoots and mushrooms. Stir and mix well, lower the heat, cover the pan and simmer for 3 minutes.

Put the rice with the remaining stock and a large pinch of salt into a larger saucepan or a casserole with a lid. Stir, and bring this to the boil. When it is boiling, add the light soy sauce and 1 tablespoon of saké, and give the mixture another stir. Then add the chicken and beef mixture from the other pan. Don't stir it vigorously, but move the pieces around gently

112 g/4 oz/⅔ cup thinly
  sliced bamboo shoots
56 g/2 oz/½ cup fresh or
  112 g/4 oz/1 cup dried
  shiitake mushrooms
1 tbsp light soy sauce
1 tbsp saké
3 tbsp chopped spring onions/
  scallions

with a wooden spoon so that the meat, bamboo shoots and mushrooms sit on top of the rice. The stock should be sufficient to cover the meat. Cover the pan or casserole tightly, and leave to cook undisturbed on a medium heat for 20 minutes. Then take it off the heat, uncover briefly, and put in the chopped spring onions/ scallions. Cover again, and leave the casserole to rest for 5–6 minutes. Serve straight away, piping hot.

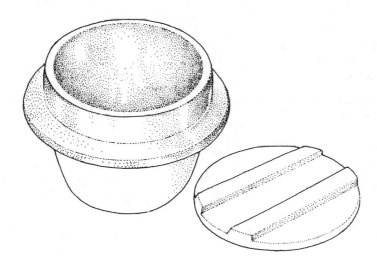

Earthenware *kama*: Japan

Rice Salad with Avocado and Smoked Salmon

Whoever first served avocado and smoked salmon together was certainly inspired. When I was a child, I doubt if there was any smoked salmon within a thousand miles of us; but there was a prolific avocado tree in my parents' front garden. Indonesians usually regard avocados as dessert, and we made ours into a sweet, milky mousse, from which, many years later, I developed a rather delicious ice-cream. Today, in big Indonesian cities and the tourist hotels, people are learning to enjoy guacamole and prawn and avocado salads, but the full potential of the avocado has yet to be appreciated.

This rice salad can of course be made with large fresh prawns/shrimp, if you can get them. But if frozen cocktail prawns/shrimp are all that's available, then smoked salmon is much, much better.

Preparation: 10 minutes
Cooking: 10 minutes to cook the rice + time for it to cool

For 4 people

285 g/10 oz/1⅓ cups rice, preferably Thai Fragrant or Basmati, washed and drained
Assorted salad leaves to garnish
2 ripe avocados
225–340 g/8–12 oz smoked salmon

For the dressing:

1 tbsp chopped chives or onions
1 tbsp chopped coriander/cilantro leaves
½ tsp sugar
½ tsp chilli powder
1 tsp soy sauce
3 tbsp olive oil
2 tbsp rice vinegar or wine vinegar
2 tbsp warm water

Cook the rice in boiling salted water for 6–8 minutes. Drain, and transfer to a large bowl.

Mix all the ingredients for the dressing in a glass bowl. Use half of this to dress the rice while it is still warm.

Peel the avocados, then slice them and put the slices immediately into the remaining dressing. Make sure they are well coated with the dressing, so that they do not discolour. Cut the smoked salmon into strips.

When the rice is cold, transfer it to a platter and arrange the lettuce leaves on top. Arrange the smoked salmon strips between the leaves, then the avocado slices on top of them, with the dressing. At this point, the salad can be refrigerated for up to 1 hour; after that time, the avocado will start to discolour. Serve at room temperature, not too chilled.

Note. If you buy avocados still quite hard, they may take many days to ripen. To ripen them in 48 hours or less, wrap each avocado in a plastic bag and bury it completely under loose rice grains in your store cupboard.

Kedgeree

When I first came to England, I remember being very surprised to find kedgeree on the breakfast menu of the hotel we stayed in – rice for breakfast I was used to, but not with toast and butter. After thirty years, my English husband will still only eat rice at breakfast if there is really nothing else; but his generation did not spend their working lives 'up country' in India or Malaya.

Oriental dishes which became popular in eighteenth- or nineteenth-century Europe were usually, and quite understandably, very different from their originals. *Khichri* was recorded by an English writer in the 1660s as 'Beans pounded, and Rice, which they boile together . . . Then they put thereto a little Butter melted.' Madhur Jaffrey, in *Eastern Vegetarian Cooking*, points out that there are 'wet' khichri, which are really rice porridges similar to those that are found in all rice-growing countries, and 'dry' ones. Europeans in the East took to khichri for breakfast and supper, because, like the local people, they found it digestible and soothing, good for invalids or those with hangovers. The French chef Charles Francatelli, writing in the 1870s, included in his book a recipe for kedgeree which he called *Riz à la Soeur Nightingale*. Whether he had Florence Nightingale's permission to use her name in this way, I don't know.

Fish is not an ingredient of khichri but in India often comes to table with it; the English regard kedgeree as basically a fish-and-rice dish. This is fine, as long as kedgeree does not become an excuse for serving up any old tired leftover fish. I give here my favourite kedgeree, which I like to eat at lunchtime rather than breakfast – I would certainly dispense with the toast and butter. I have chosen smoked mackerel with coarsely ground black peppers, which you can buy ready-prepared from supermarkets, but you can of course use whatever fish you like best.

Preparation: 10 minutes
Cooking: 20 minutes

For 4–6 people

340 g/12 oz/1½ cups long grain rice (Basmati, Texmati, Sunlong, etc.), soaked in cold water for 30 minutes, then drained
2–2.5 litres/3–4 pints/ 7½–10 cups water

Heat the water with ¼ teaspoon of salt in a large saucepan. When it boils, put in the rice and stir so that the rice will not stick to the bottom. Bring the water back to the boil and cook for 6–8 minutes, so that the rice is tender but not soft. Drain the rice in a colander. Leave it to cool for a few minutes.

Put the rice in a large bowl and carefully mix it with the flaked fish and chopped eggs. Season with a little salt, and some chilli if you like it hot. Melt the butter in a wok or saucepan and stir the kedgeree into it.

340 g/12 oz/1½ cups smoked
  peppered mackerel, or
  smoked haddock, skinned,
  the bones removed, and
  finely flaked
56 g/2 oz butter
2–3 hard-boiled eggs, finely
  chopped
½ tsp chilli powder, or 1
  chilli, de-seeded and finely
  chopped (optional)
Salt
1 tbsp flat-leaf parsley
1–2 tbsp Crisp-Fried Onions
  (page 358)

Keep tossing and stirring for about 3 minutes, until it is heated through. Serve straight away, on well-heated plates, with the Crisp-Fried Onions and parsley sprinkled over it.

Provençal Salad of Stuffed Squid

Silvija Davidson, a friend who is also an excellent cook, developed this recipe for me after a visit to the Camargue, the wetlands near the mouth of the Rhône where rice has long been grown as a marginal crop but is now becoming a major industry.

This is a sophisticated and delicious first course, or a complete lunch accompanied by a newly baked baguette and some more salad on the side. If you cannot buy red rice locally, use wild rice instead. The dried sea lettuce can be replaced by young spinach leaves. But the squid must be very fresh.

Preparation: about 1½ hours, including cooking the rice

For 6–8 people as a first
course or 4–6 as a cold main
course with extra salad

---

24 small-size squid, the
  pouches about 10 cm/
  4 inches long, weight
  before cleaning about
  1.5 kg/3 lb/8 cups

Clean the squid in the usual way, removing head, body, quill and purplish skin (fins and tentacles are not used in this recipe). Wash the pouches thoroughly and drain well.

Heat the olive oil until just hot in a wide sauté pan. Add the shallots and garlic and cook very gently until these are translucent and soft. Place the squid pouches in a single layer in the pan (you may need to do this in batches) and cook them gently for a minute or two.

6 tbsp good olive oil

6 shallots, peeled and finely
diced

3 cloves garlic, peeled and
crushed

600 ml/¾ bottle Provençal
rosé wine or any good, dry
white or rosé

For the stuffing:

170 g/6 oz/¾ cup red rice or
wild rice

½ tsp dried fennel seeds

½ tsp sea salt

3 yellow sweet/bell peppers

84 g/3 oz/1 cup oil-cured
black olives, stoned and
diced

For the dressing:

1½ tsp Provençal-style
mustard or Dijon mustard

3 tbsp lemon juice

6 tbsp extra virgin Provençal
olive oil

3 tbsp juices from grilled
peppers (see below)

1 tsp Pernod, ouzo, or other
aniseed-flavoured liquor
(optional)

Sea salt and freshly milled
pepper to taste

For the garnish:

1 tsp crushed mixed
peppercorns

84 g/3 oz/1 cup dried sea
lettuce (page 379), soaked
in warm water for 15
minutes and drained

Turn them over and cook them for 2–3 minutes longer, until the squid are just opaque. Return the earlier batches to the pan, add the wine, bring it all gently to the boil and simmer for a further 2 or 3 minutes, until the squid are just tender to the touch. Remove the squid from the pan with a slotted spoon, put them into a bowl and cover them with a plate. Keep them aside to soften further while you prepare the filling. Keep the cooking liquid.

Measure the volume of rice, then put the rice in a saucepan with the fennel seeds and salt. Then measure double that volume of the reserved cooking liquid, pour this into the pan with the rice and bring it to the boil. Stir once, then cover the pan and simmer it very gently for about 40 minutes, until the grains are no longer crunchy but are still resilient.

All the liquid should by now have been absorbed, but if the rice is soft and some liquid remains, drain this off before transferring the rice to a mixing bowl.

While the rice is cooking, grill the peppers under a high heat until their skin blackens and blisters all over. Place them in a covered bowl until cool enough to handle. Then strip off the skin and remove the stem, core and seeds, sieving the juices into a bowl. Dice the peppers finely.

Arrange the squid pouches on kitchen paper to drain. Whisk or blend together the dressing ingredients. Add the peppers, olives, and two-thirds of the dressing to the rice in the mixing bowl, mix well, and adjust the seasoning. Carefully stuff the squid pouches with the mixture, using a tiny spoon or your fingers; push the mixture in firmly, but take care not to tear open the pouches.

When the squid are stuffed, arrange some sea lettuce fronds on a platter, place the squid on top, and sprinkle with the remaining dressing and the crushed peppercorns. Serve at room temperature or chilled. This salad may be made 24 hours in advance, but must be kept well covered in the refrigerator.

Rice and Liver Pudding

This is my adaptation of a Finnish recipe given to me by Jaakko Rahola, who writes about food in Finland. He says that rice was first imported into that country in the seventeenth century, but that until the nineteenth century only the wealthy could afford it. Rice was a luxury that most people ate only on Christmas Day, usually as porridge.

This liver pudding intrigues me. The original version suggests that it should be served with a lot of butter and lingonberry jam. If you can't get this jam, I would forget about the butter as well and serve the pudding as a light lunch, with a salad and a spicy Indian fruit chutney. It would be equally good as a pâté for a first course, accompanied by bread or toast if you wish.

The mixture described here can also be cooked as a sausage. If you do it this way, leave out the milk, so that the mixture is thicker. Proceed in the same way as for other sausages in this book (e.g. page 225) and serve cold or hot.

Jaakko describes this dish as a liver casserole. He says it is similar to the Swedish korvkake or sausage cake and to the Scottish haggis, except that it uses rice instead of oats.

Preparation: 35 minutes
Cooking: 70–90 minutes

For 4 or 8 people

225 g/8 oz/1 cup short grain
  or Thai Fragrant rice,
  washed and drained
670 ml/24 fl oz/3 cups water
2 tsp salt
505 ml/18 fl oz/2¼ cups
  milk
2 eggs
56 g/2 oz butter
1 onion, chopped
450 g/1 lb liver: chicken,
  calf, or pig, minced, or
  blended until smooth

112 g/4 oz/⅔ cup raisins
  or dried apricots,
  chopped (optional)
2 tsp treacle or honey
  (optional)
1 tsp finely chopped
  ginger root
1 tsp finely chopped
  marjoram
1 tsp salt

Boil the rice in the salted water, uncovered, for 10–15 minutes. Remove from the heat and stir in the cold milk, mixing it well. Keep aside. Preheat the oven to 160°C/320°F/Gas Mark 3.

In a frying pan, fry the onion in the butter until slightly browned. Cool this a little, then mix it, with all the other ingredients, into the rice. The mixture must be well seasoned, sweetish, and thin, because it thickens as it bakes.

Butter an ovenproof dish and pour the mixture into it. Dot some more butter on top, and bake for 70–90 minutes. Serve hot, as suggested above.

Moulded Rice with Crabmeat

This is equally good as a one-dish lunch, with a salad, or as a first course. The only difference is in the size of the ramekins that you mould the rice in. You have a wide selection of possible sauces from pages 347–57 or whatever takes your fancy. Instead of the yellow rice described here, you can use sushi rice (page 173).

Preparation: 20 minutes
Cooking: 25 minutes

For 2 people as a complete lunch, or 4 as a first course

For the rice:

112 g/4 oz/½ cup short grain or Thai Fragrant rice, washed and drained
1 tbsp olive or peanut oil or clarified butter
½ tsp ground turmeric
285 ml/10 fl oz/1¼ cups fish stock or chicken stock
A pinch of salt

Heat the oil or clarified butter in a saucepan and add the drained rice. Stir continuously for 2 minutes, then add the turmeric. Stir for 2 more minutes – by that time the rice will be a uniform pale yellow. Add the stock and the salt. Give the rice another stir, bring the stock to the boil, cover the pan and lower the heat. Let the rice simmer for 20 minutes, undisturbed. Take the pan off the heat and stand it, still covered, on a wet tea-towel for 5 minutes.

Ten minutes before the rice is ready, heat the butter or oil for the crabmeat in a frying pan and fry the shallots until soft. Add the crabmeat and spring onions/scallions or chives, and stir gently to mingle these together. Cook on a moderate heat for 2 minutes. Season with salt and pepper and continue cooking for 1 more minute, turning the mixture over gently.

For the crabmeat:

2 shallots, finely sliced
2 tbsp butter or oil
225 g/8 oz/1 cup fresh
   crabmeat (white meat only)
   or the best quality canned
   or frozen crabmeat
Salt and pepper to taste

For the garnish (if served as a
first course):

1 cucumber, washed, peeled,
   and sliced into thin rounds

Butter 2 large or 4 smaller ramekins and line their bottoms with greaseproof or bakewell paper. Divide the crabmeat among the moulds and press it down into each with the back of a spoon. Put the rice on top of the crabmeat, also pressing it down so that it is level with the rim.

To unmould, run a knife around the inside of each ramekin, and turn it over on to a plate. Tap the bottom of the ramekin lightly and lift it off. Discard the paper from the top of the crabmeat. Garnish with cucumber slices arranged round the moulded rice. Serve warm or cold, with sauce if you wish, as suggested above.

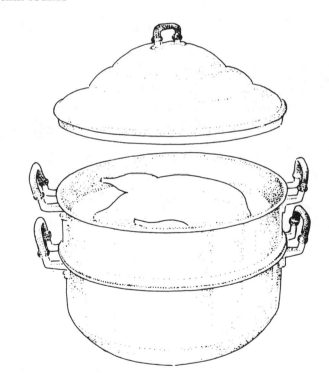

Beef and Rice Omelette

My Sumatran grandmother used to construct massive omelettes out of duck eggs, grated potatoes, a little grated coconut and a lot of crushed chillies. Many years later, I realize how similar these were, on the surface at any rate, to Spanish omelettes, which are also quite thick, well-browned and crusty on the outside and soft inside. This variation is made with beef and rice. With a salad, it makes a very tasty light lunch.

On page 357 I have suggested that beef used in making Rhubarb Khoresh can go into this omelette, but you can use any boiled beef, leftover roast beef, or salt beef from the local delicatessen.

Preparation (assuming you already have some cooked beef and rice): 10 minutes
Cooking: 12–14 minutes

For 4–6 people

- 3 tbsp olive or peanut oil
- 5 shallots or 1 large onion, finely chopped
- 2 cloves garlic, finely chopped
- ½–1 tsp chilli powder
- ½ tsp salt
- 112 g/4 oz/½ cup cooked beef, thinly sliced and cut into small pieces
- 60 g/2 oz/½ cup cooked rice
- 1 tbsp freshly grated coconut or desiccated coconut (optional)
- 5 duck eggs or 7 hen eggs

Stir-fry the shallots and garlic for 3–4 minutes in 2 tablespoons of oil in a frying pan, preferably non-stick. Add the other ingredients, except the eggs. Stir and mix for 2 minutes.

Beat the eggs in a large bowl. Transfer the mixture from the frying pan to the bowl with the beaten eggs, and mix everything well together. Adjust the seasoning. Brush the pan with the remaining oil and set it on a low heat. When the pan is hot, pour the mixture into it and cook, shaking the pan from time to time, for 3–4 minutes or until the top is set but not quite cooked.

Now put a large plate upside-down over the pan and turn the pan and plate over together so that the half-cooked omelette comes out on the plate. Put the frying pan back on the stove and slide the omelette back into it, cooked side now uppermost. Continue cooking for a further 2 minutes, then cover the pan and leave the omelette to rest for 2 minutes. Uncover, cut the omelette into 4 or 6 pieces, and serve straight away.

Rice with Calf Liver, Chicken and Caramelized Shallots

In all the testing and tasting that I have done for this book, I am glad to say that I have never become tired of rice. On the contrary, I have enjoyed inventing new dishes, in the hope that readers will cook them often. This is one of them. Savour it by itself, then follow it with plenty of salad in a piquant dressing to balance the meal. If shallots are not obtainable, use small pickling onions or small red Oriental onions (not the big red ones from supermarkets).

Although it is possible to cook everything except the liver a little ahead of time, this is really a last-moment dish. Think of it as a kind of risotto; provided you have all the ingredients prepared in advance, you will be absent from your guests only for 20 minutes, starting from the moment you begin heating the oil.

Preparation: 20 minutes
Cooking: 20–25 minutes

For 4–6 people

340 g/12 oz/1½ cups long
   grain rice, preferably Thai
   Fragrant or Sunlong; at
   any rate a rice which
   becomes soft when cooked;
   not Basmati
670 ml/24 fl oz/3 cups water
½ tsp salt

For the meat and liver:

2 chicken breast fillets,
   without skin, sliced thinly
   into bite-sized pieces
450 g/1 lb calf's liver, sliced
   like the chicken
2 tbsp light soy sauce
2 tbsp mirin or dry sherry
1 tbsp lemon juice
½–1 tsp ground black pepper

Preheat the oven to 180°C/350°F/Gas Mark 4. Put a flameproof serving platter or casserole with a lid into the oven to get very hot.

Put the chicken and calf's liver in separate bowls, and rub the pieces with a mixture of the light soy sauce, mirin or dry sherry, lemon juice and black pepper.

Wash the rice and drain it. Put the water and ½ teaspoon of salt in a saucepan. Add the drained rice and cook on a low heat, with the lid on, undisturbed, for 20 minutes (starting from the time you put the rice into the cold water). Then remove the pan from the heat but keep the lid on for 5 minutes longer.

About 7 minutes after you put the rice on the stove to cook, heat the oil in a large frying pan. Add the shallots or onions and stir continuously for 5 minutes. Add the sugar, salt and chilli powder (if used). Stir again for 2 minutes, then pour in the wine or stock. Increase the heat and let this bubble for 4–5 minutes. Add the chicken pieces. Cover the pan for 2 minutes. Then uncover and turn the chicken pieces over. Cover again for 1 minute. Adjust the seasoning, stir and mix well. This caramelized mixture will be ready

For the caramelized mixture:

- 2–3 tbsp olive oil or peanut oil
- 8 shallots or pickling onions or small red onions, peeled and quartered
- 8 cloves of garlic, halved lengthwise
- A pinch of chilli powder or a few drops of Tabasco (optional)
- 2 tsp sugar
- ¼ tsp salt
- 112 ml/4 fl oz/½ cup white wine or chicken stock
- 112 g/4 oz Cheddar or other mild hard cheese, grated (optional)

at about the time the rice is ready.

Transfer the rice into the platter or casserole which has been heating in the oven. Keep the oven on, and work as fast as you comfortably can. Spread the grated cheese (if used) evenly on top of the rice and arrange the chicken pieces on top of the cheese. Put the full platter or casserole back in the oven.

Reheat the frying pan with the caramelized mixture, and put in the calf's liver. Stir-fry for 1 minute only. Now turn off the oven, take out the platter or casserole, and spread the calf's liver pieces with the shallots on top of the chicken. If you are using a casserole, put the lid on it. Take it at once to the table and serve immediately, preferably on to hot dinner plates.

Ploughing rice fields: Lombok

Tian de Sardines

When I saw this recipe in the April 1992 issue of *House & Garden*, I at once wanted to cook it. Alice Wooledge Salmon, who was formerly a chef at one of London's best hotels and is now among Britain's leading cookery writers, has given her permission for its appearance here. She quotes Elizabeth David's *Mediterranean Food*: 'Up in the [Provençal] hills they do not despise the addition of salt cod, [while] on the coast this is replaced with fresh sardines or anchovies.' I suggest this dish should be served with a green salad, as a first course or a light lunch. If you can persuade your fishmonger to clean and prepare the sardines for you, so much the better; cleaning them at home is rather a long job.

Preparation: 90 minutes (including cleaning the sardines)
Cooking: 30 minutes + 20 minutes cooling

For 4 people as a main course, 6–8 as a starter

675 g/1½ lb fresh sardines
500 g/1 lb 2 oz fresh young spinach
1.1 kg/2½ lb fresh young Swiss chard
Olive oil
3 cloves garlic, finely chopped
Salt and black pepper
56 g/2 oz/¼ cup white long grain rice
2 large eggs
100 g/3½ oz grated Parmesan cheese
Some fairly coarse homemade breadcrumbs

Scale and gut the sardines, discarding the heads, tails and all bones. Rinse the fillets and set aside.

Remove the stalks from the spinach, wash the leaves thoroughly, shred roughly and drain. Remove the green chard leaves from the white ribs, wash the leaves and leave them to drain. The white ribs can be put into a vegetable stock pot.

Put the spinach and chard leaves in separate heavy-bottomed saucepans with a clove of garlic, chopped, and 1 tablespoon of olive oil in each. Cover and cook on a low heat for 2 minutes. Uncover, and continue cooking until all the liquid has evaporated. Season with salt and pepper.

Meanwhile, wash the rice and put it into boiling salted water. Let it boil for 6 minutes, then drain and refresh under cold running water. Leave to drain in a colander.

Beat the 2 eggs in a large bowl. Add the spinach, chard, rice, 75 g/2½ oz of the grated Parmesan cheese, and the remaining chopped garlic. Mix these well.

Lightly oil a gratin dish or a large, heavy terrine of about 1.7 litres/3 pints/7½ cups capacity. Spread two-thirds of the rice and spinach mixture over the bottom of this. Cut each of the sardine fillets across into 2 or 3 pieces and season them. Arrange them in an even layer on top of the rice and spinach. Dribble some olive oil over them, then spread the rest of the rice and spinach on top, dribble more olive oil and sprinkle the remaining Parmesan cheese and a handful of breadcrumbs over everything.

Bake in a preheated oven at 220°C/425°F/Gas Mark 7 for 20 minutes. Then turn the oven up to 240°C/475°F/ Gas Mark 9 and continue cooking for a further 10 minutes to brown the top. Take the tian out of the oven and leave it to cool for about 20 minutes, then serve.

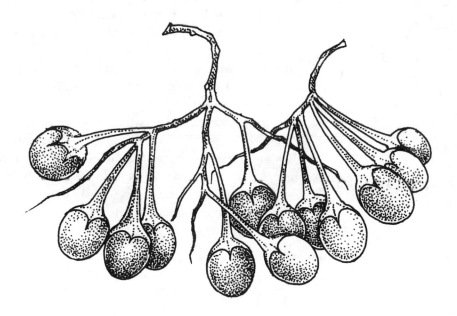

Chinese Spicy Rice Sausage

Like the other sausages described in this book, these are rolled and wrapped in clingfilm or banana-leaf squares (page 225).

Preparation: 6–8 hours soaking + 30 minutes
Cooking: 35–40 minutes

For 4 people as a light lunch with salad, or 8–10 as a first course with other sausages

450 g/1 lb/2 cups glutinous rice, soaked in cold water for 6–8 hours, washed and drained
28 g/1 oz dried shrimp, soaked in hot water for 10 minutes, drained and chopped
3 tbsp peanut oil
4 shallots or 1 onion, chopped
1 tsp chilli powder or roughly ground black pepper
1 tsp five-spice powder (optional)
1 tsp sesame oil
1 tbsp light soy sauce
1 tsp salt
1.5 litres/2½ pints/6¼ cups water for boiling

Put the rice in a steamer and steam for 10 minutes.

In a wok or frying pan, heat the peanut oil and stir-fry the shallots or onion for 3 minutes. Then add the chopped shrimp, chilli powder or pepper, five-spice powder (if used), sesame oil, soy sauce and salt. Stir, and add the steamed rice. Continue stirring and mixing everything well together. Then take the pan off the heat and let the mixture cool for a few minutes.

When it has cooled sufficiently, knead the mixture with your hands a little. Then make it into 10 or 12 sausages and wrap these in clingfilm/plastic wrap, but don't wrap them too tightly; the rice grains will swell a little when the sausages are boiled.

Bring the water to the boil in a large saucepan and boil the sausages for 20–25 minutes. You can then unwrap and serve them straight away, or refrigerate them for up to 3 days. If you do keep them in the fridge, reheat and brown them slightly in a little oil or butter just before you serve them.

MAIN-COURSE DISHES

Rice with Fish and Seafood

Where there is rice, there is usually plenty of water, and therefore fish. Rice and fish together provide a pretty well-balanced diet, and that is no doubt why they are so closely linked in the mind of anyone who grew up in rice country. And the link goes deeper than the conscious mind: rice and fish provide symbols for the imagination to play with. Rice is fixed, law-abiding, dependable, like the land it grows in. Water is its opposite. Rice makes people settle and live ordered lives, but fishing sends them back to their origin as hunters. In a subsistence economy, rice is always costly, in labour and risk if not in cash; fish, with luck, are free.

For you and me, alas, fish are now rather expensive, and our choice is usually limited to what the supermarket can offer. This is good as far as it goes, but if you have a really good independent fishmonger within travelling distance then the journey to his shop is well worth making; as witnesses, I offer the queue of Japanese sashimi-fanciers that regularly assembles outside the doors of a certain fish shop in south-west London. You can go one better, and order your fish to be rushed to you from Cornwall

Sampan

(or wherever) as soon as it is landed. I have done this occasionally, but the occasions have to be very special. The reward is fish so fresh that their eyes sparkle and their flesh requires only the briefest cooking, or even no cooking at all.

A real fish market, the kind where anyone can go and buy in any quantity, is an astonishing place: the everyday world of invoices and van drivers comes face to face with the scarcely imagined creatures of the deep. I am glad to have seen the old Billingsgate before it moved downriver, and the fish market on the Rialto in Venice (I hope it is still there), and the market on Sydney waterfront. I'm surprised people haven't written more about the world's great food markets, and even gastronomic tours seem to spend far more time in restaurants than in the places where the chefs go to buy the food. But a restaurant, like a rice field, is a symbol of order, whereas a market is always full of unknown forces, like the sea.

Spiced Rice and Squid

I have purposely kept the spices in two separate groups: the sweet ones for the rice, the hot ones for the squid. So the two parts of the dish have their own distinct flavours, which combine harmoniously together at the end.

Preparation: 30 minutes + 10–15 minutes marinating
Cooking: 20–25 minutes

For 4–6 people

450–550 g/1-1¼ lb squid, thoroughly cleaned and cut into rings or bite-sized pieces

For the marinade:

2 tbsp lime juice
1 tsp finely chopped lemon grass
1 tsp finely chopped chillies, red or green

Mix all the ingredients for the marinade in a glass bowl and marinate the squid for 10–15 minutes.

Heat the olive oil in a saucepan, and fry all the ingredients for the rice, except the rice itself and the stock or water, stirring all the time, for 3 minutes. Add the stock or water, and bring to the boil. When it is boiling, put the rice in, stir, and lower the heat. Simmer for 10–15 minutes, until all the liquid has been absorbed by the rice. Cover the pan tightly and leave it on a very low heat for 10 minutes.

Drain the squid and spread them on top of the rice. Again tightly cover the pan and leave it on a medium heat for just 1 minute. Then put the pan, still tightly covered, on to a wet folded tea-towel/dishcloth, and leave it undisturbed for 2 minutes.

1 tsp finely chopped parsley
2 cloves garlic, crushed
2 tbsp light soy sauce or fish
   sauce
1 tsp sugar
1 tbsp olive oil or peanut oil

For the rice:

340 g/12 oz/1½ cups Thai
   Fragrant or other long
   grain rice, washed and
   drained
2 tbsp olive oil or peanut oil
2 shallots, finely sliced
2 cloves
5-cm/2-inch cinnamon stick
2 green cardamoms
½ tsp salt
505 ml/18 fl oz/2¼ cups fish
   stock or water

Other ingredients:

28 g/1 oz butter (optional)
1 tbsp chopped coriander/
   cilantro leaves

Take off the lid, adjust the seasoning, and stir the rice and squid well together, picking out all the spice solids – cloves, cinnamon stick and cardamoms if you can find them. At the same time, add the butter (if used) and coriander/cilantro leaves. Serve hot, accompanied by cooked vegetables or a green salad.

Steamed Tuna with Rice

This is an excellent one-dish meal, preferably cooked in a ceramic or enamel pot with a tight-fitting lid that can come direct from stove to table. For me, the chillies are an important ingredient, but of course you can put in fewer chillies or none at all if you prefer. If you soak the rice and prepare the other ingredients in the morning, you can count on the food being ready to serve 30 minutes after the pot goes on the stove.

Preparation: 2 hours soaking + 40 minutes
Cooking and resting: 30 minutes

For 4 people

340 g/12 oz/1½ cups long grain rice, preferably Basmati, soaked in cold water for at least 2 hours

4 tuna steaks, each weighing 140–200 g/5–7 oz

½ tsp salt

½ tsp chilli powder

1 tbsp lemon juice

3 tbsp olive or peanut oil

2 onions, finely chopped

450 g/1 lb button mushrooms, cleaned and sliced

2–6 large red chillies, de-seeded and chopped (optional)

1 tsp finely chopped ginger root

2 large tomatoes, skinned and chopped

Salt and pepper

450 g/1 lb spinach or cos lettuce, washed and coarsely shredded

390 ml/14 fl oz/1¾ cups fish stock or water

Rub the tuna steaks with salt, chilli powder and lemon juice, and refrigerate.

Fry the onions in the oil for 2 minutes and add the mushrooms. Continue to stir-fry for 1 minute, then add the chillies (if used), ginger and tomatoes. Season with salt and pepper and simmer for 4 minutes. Keep aside in a cool place, or refrigerate if there are still several hours to go before final cooking.

When you are ready to start cooking, drain the rice and take everything you will need out of the fridge. Put the rice and the fish stock, or water, into the cooking pot and bring to the boil. When it boils, turn the heat down and simmer for 10 minutes, uncovered.

Spread half of the spinach or cos lettuce evenly on top of the rice, and half of the onion-tomato-and-mushroom mixture on top of that. Then arrange the tuna steaks, side by side, and on top of them the remaining spinach or lettuce, and finally the remaining onions, etc.

Cover the pot tightly, increase the heat a little, and continue cooking for 15 minutes. Remove from heat, put the pot on a wet tea-towel/dishcloth, and leave to rest for 5 minutes. Then uncover the pot and bring it immediately to the table.

Hot and Sweet Prawns/Shrimp with Fried Rice

I first ate these prawns/shrimp in the Cooking School of the Oriental Hotel in Bangkok, and since then I have written about them several times and talked a great deal. At the School, the prawns/shrimp were small and very fresh, cooked in their shells, so we ate them, shell and all, as an appetizer.

Here I use medium-sized prawns/shrimp, more mature and as likely as not frozen, therefore with tough shells. These should be removed in the kitchen to save messing about at table. Allow five or six prawns/shrimp per person for a main course dish with Fried Rice (page 126) and salad.

Preparation: 15 minutes
Cooking: 8–10 minutes

For 4–6 people

25–30 medium-size uncooked prawns/shrimp without heads, peeled, de-veined, and washed
84–112 ml/3–4 fl oz/½ cup water
3–4 tbsp grated palm sugar or dark brown soft sugar
1–2 small red chillies, chopped, or 8–10 whole black peppers, crushed in a mortar
3 tbsp fish sauce
2 tbsp chopped coriander/ cilantro roots or leaves

Drain the prawns/shrimp in a colander and pat dry with kitchen paper. Sprinkle them with a little salt and keep aside in the fridge.

Heat the water in a wide shallow saucepan. Add the sugar, chillies or peppers, and fish sauce. Bring to the boil and stir to melt the sugar. Simmer for 3–6 minutes, stirring often, or until the liquid starts to thicken. Add the coriander/cilantro roots or leaves. Stir again, then add the prawns/shrimp. Keep stirring for 3–4 minutes, until they are glazed in the caramel- ized sauce. Serve straight away, as suggested above.

Portuguese Salt Cod with Rice and Potatoes

This is a combination of two recipes: bacalhau a bras (salt cod cooked with potatoes and egg) and arroz de bacalhau (rice with salt cod). All Indonesians are familiar with salted fish, because until very recently this has been the only way to preserve fish on their journey from where they are caught to where they are cooked; even today it is usually more practical to salt fish in bulk than to freeze them. Naturally a lot of rice is eaten, just to absorb or mask the salty taste of the fish, and potatoes are a usual accompaniment, cooked with other vegetables in highly spiced coconut milk. A combination of salt fish, rice and potatoes, made richer still with (in this case) eggs, is certainly one of the most satisfying, not to say filling, one-pot meals, especially for a large and hungry family. You just need a little green salad to serve with it.

Salt cod, alas, is no longer a cheap fish, but there is no reason why you should not use less costly alternatives: smoked fish like haddock or mackerel are good, or indeed almost any locally procured fish, depending on what part of the world you live in, that has been dried and salted or smoked. Choose free-swimming fish with plenty of meat; flatfish and bottom-dwellers are not suitable for this dish. Salted fish needs to be soaked in water for several hours or overnight, then drained and washed well under the cold tap. Dry the fish with a tea-towel or kitchen paper before removing all the skin and bones and flaking the flesh ready for cooking.

I give two methods for making this Portuguese dish, both good: one uses very little oil because the potatoes and rice are boiled together. The other is much richer because the potatoes are fried and the eggs are then scrambled in among them.

Preparation: 20–25 minutes (excluding soaking the salt cod)
Cooking: 32–35 minutes

For 6–8 people

450 g/1 lb/2 cups short grain
  Spanish or Italian rice, or a
  soft long grain such as
  Thai Fragrant or Sunlong
450 g/1 lb/4 cups waxy
  potatoes, peeled and cut
  into julienne strips
2 medium onions, chopped

Method 1 In a medium-size, heavy-bottomed sauce-pan or casserole with lid, heat the olive oil and fry the onions until soft and transparent. Add the julienne potatoes and continue cooking for 3 minutes, stirring often. Add the flaked fish, tomatoes and bay leaves. Stir and simmer for 1 or 2 minutes, then pour in the rice and stir continuously for a further 2 minutes. Add the water, bring it to the boil, lower the heat and cover the pan. Cook undisturbed for 20 minutes.

Beat the eggs, and season with pepper but very little salt. Uncover the pan, and pour the beaten eggs in, stirring them into the rice and other ingredients. Put the lid back on and let the whole thing rest for 5

4 red tomatoes, skinned and
  chopped (the seeds can also
  be removed, if preferred)
340–450 g/12–16 oz salt cod
  or other salted or smoked
  fish (see above)
680 ml/24 fl oz/3 cups water
8 eggs
2 tbsp olive oil (or 113 ml/
  4 fl oz/½ cup vegetable oil
  if the potatoes are to be
  fried)
2 bay leaves
2 tbsp chopped parsley or
  coriander/cilantro leaves
Salt and pepper to taste
56 g/2 oz/½ cup black olives,
  pitted and halved, to
  garnish (optional)

minutes. Serve straight away, sprinkled with the chopped parsley or coriander/cilantro leaves and the olives if used.

Method 2 Cook the rice exactly as for Method 1, but without adding the potatoes. While the rice is cooking, heat the vegetable oil in a large frying pan, preferably non-stick, and fry the potatoes until they are cooked but not coloured. This will take 7–8 minutes, possibly a little longer, so give yourself enough time to have the potatoes cooked at the same time as the rice is ready.

When the potatoes are done, pour away as much of the oil as possible but keep the potatoes in the pan on a low heat. Season them with salt and pepper. Beat the eggs and pour them over the potatoes. Stir the mixture gently – the eggs must not become an omelette, but should just be lightly scrambled. Pour the potato-and-egg on to the rice-and-fish, sprinkle the parsley or coriander/cilantro leaves and olives (if used) over everything, and serve immediately.

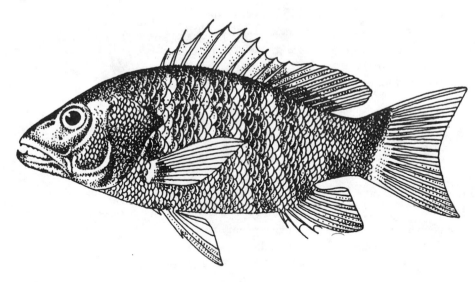

Red snapper

Paella with Seafood

For home cooking, I find I get best results by cooking the rice and seafood separately and combining them together just before I serve them. Doing it this way, however, you need a really good fish stock for the rice. You should still use your paella pan, if you have one, to cook the rice; otherwise, a casserole will do perfectly well.

Preparation: 1 hour
Cooking: 18–20 minutes

For 4–6 people

For the rice:

2 tbsp olive oil
1 onion, finely sliced
2 cloves garlic, finely sliced
½ tsp cayenne pepper or chilli powder
2 large tomatoes, skinned and chopped, or 2 tbsp tomato purée
112 g/4 oz/1 cup fresh or reconstituted butter beans, or fresh broad beans/fava beans
170–225 g/6–8 oz/1 cup flat green beans or runner beans, cut into 5-cm/2-inch pieces
A large pinch of saffron strands, crushed in a mortar, or ½ tsp ground turmeric
710 ml/1¼ pints/3 cups hot fish stock
Salt and pepper to taste
450 g/1 lb/2 cups Spanish or Italian short grain rice

For the seafood:

450 g/1 lb/4 cups cod fillet, cut into cubes about 3 cm/1¼ inches square
225 g/8 oz/2 cups squid, cleaned and cut into small pieces
450 g/1 lb/2½ cups uncooked king prawns/jumbo shrimps, with or without heads, cleaned but not shelled
225 g/8 oz/2 cups mussels, cleaned
2 tbsp olive oil
1 onion, finely sliced
3 cloves garlic, finely sliced
½ tsp cayenne pepper or chilli powder
3 large tomatoes, skinned and chopped
A large pinch of saffron strands, crushed in a mortar (optional)
Salt and pepper
420 ml/¾ pint/2 cups hot fish stock or water

Start with the rice. Heat the oil in the paella pan or casserole and fry the shallots and garlic, stirring all the time, for 2–3 minutes. Add the rest of the rice ingredients, except the rice itself and the fish stock. Stir, and simmer for 3 minutes. Add the stock and simmer for 2 minutes, then bring the liquid fully to the boil and add the rice. Stir everything well together and spread the rice evenly over the bottom of the pan. Lower the heat, partially cover the pan, and continue to simmer for 10–15 minutes.

While the rice is cooking, cook the seafood. Fry the onion and garlic in the oil in a large casserole or frying pan for 1 minute. Add the cod cubes and fry them, top and bottom, for 2 minutes in all. Then add the tomatoes and all the ground ingredients, with the salt and pepper and the stock or hot water. Bring the whole thing to the boil and add the mussels. Let them cook for 2 minutes, then add the rest of the seafood. Stir everything carefully together and cover the pan. Turn up the heat and leave the seafood to cook for 3 minutes *only*.

Uncover, adjust the seasoning of the seafood, and arrange it all on top of the cooked rice in the paella pan or casserole. Serve immediately.

Seafood Hotpot

This is an adaptation of a Japanese dish. I enjoy eating it in the Japanese way, using chopsticks to pick up the seafood and vegetables and rice, and then lifting the bowl with both hands and drinking the broth directly from it. But you can just as well use a spoon and fork.

If you serve this hotpot as the main course, I recommend serving plain cooked rice with it in a separate bowl. If you serve it as a soup, you will probably want to forget about the rice – especially if the main course that follows is itself rice-based. Otherwise, put a spoonful of rice in each helping of soup. Everything for the hotpot can be prepared well in advance and refrigerated until you are ready to start cooking.

Preparation: 50–60 minutes
Cooking: 4–5 minutes

For 4 people as a main
course or 8 as a soup

1.1 litres/2 pints/5 cups
  Bonito Stock (page 347);
  or 570 ml/1 pint/2½ cups
  Fish Stock (page 346)
  combined with the same
  quantity of chicken stock
3 tbsp light soy sauce
3 tbsp mirin
1 tbsp ginger juice
¼ tsp (or more) chilli oil
Salt (if necessary)
2 tbsp lemon juice (optional)
8 king prawns/jumbo shrimp,
  shelled and de-veined
340 g/12 oz fillet of sea bass
  or salmon
340 g/12 oz monkfish tail,
  cut into thin slices
8 live hard-shell clams,
  brushed clean and kept in
  salted water
8 fresh scallops, cleaned and
  cut in halves, the corals
  left whole
8 fresh shiitake or button
  mushrooms, cleaned and
  sliced or quartered

Other ingredients:

340 g/12 oz/3 cups firm,
  fresh tofu, soaked in
  hot water for 10
  minutes, drained, and
  cut into 16 cubes
2 Chinese cabbage leaves,
  coarsely shredded
112 g/4 oz/1 cup
  mangetout/sugar peas,
  topped and tailed
56 g/2 oz/½ cup spring
  onions/scallions,
  cleaned and cut into
  thin rounds

Blanch the mangetout/sugar peas and Chinese cabbage. Start cooking the rice, assuming you are serving
the hotpot with rice.

   Pour the stock into a pan, and heat until it starts to
simmer. Add the soy sauce, mirin, ginger juice and
chilli oil. Bring to the boil and add the prawns/shrimp,
sea bass or salmon, and monkfish. Go on simmering
for 2 minutes only. Then add the clams, scallops and
mushrooms. Continue to simmer for 2–3 minutes –
not more. Adjust the seasoning, and add the lemon
juice, if used.

   Divide the other ingredients among the soup bowls
and ladle over them the hot broth with the seafood.
Serve at once.

Crayfish/Crawfish Etouffee

This is one of the recipes I brought back from a trip to New Orleans. *Etouffee* is a stew of crayfish/crawfish, prawns, or shrimps, made with the Cajun 'trinity' of onion, celery and green sweet/bell peppers and served on rice. In Louisiana, the crawfish season is from November to mid-June; many of the crawfish actually come from the rice fields.

In Britain, if you have a good fishmonger, you will sometimes be able to get Scandinavian crayfish, but failing these use large uncooked prawns/jumbo shrimp. For myself, I like to make this stew with dry white wine and cayenne pepper instead of black pepper.

Preparation: 25 minutes
Cooking: about 15 minutes

For 4–6 people

900 g/2 lb crayfish/crawfish
    tails or large prawns/jumbo
    shrimp, washed, then
    boiled for 3–4 minutes
28 g/1 oz butter and 1 tbsp
    olive oil
1 large onion, finely chopped
1 stalk celery, finely chopped
2 green sweet/bell peppers,
    de-seeded and finely
    chopped
2 cloves garlic, finely
    chopped
1 tbsp plain/all-purpose flour
    (optional)
2 tbsp chopped parsley
2 tbsp chopped spring onions/
    scallions
1 tsp cayenne pepper or black
    pepper
225 ml/8 fl oz/1 cup dry
    white wine or water
Salt to taste

Peel the crayfish/crawfish or prawns/shrimp and set aside. Heat the butter and oil in a wok or saucepan and fry the onions, celery and green pepper for 5–6 minutes, stirring most of the time. Add the garlic, cayenne pepper, flour (if used) and salt. Stir for 3 minutes, then add the wine or water. Bring to the boil and simmer for 4 minutes.

Adjust the seasoning and add the peeled crayfish/crawfish tails or prawns/shrimp. Simmer for 3 more minutes, then add the parsley and spring onions/scallions, stir for just a few seconds more, and serve straight away with plenty of rice.

Dover Sole Stuffed with Mushrooms and Rice

Preparation: 1 hour
Cooking: 30–40 minutes

For 4 people

For the fish:

**4 medium-size Dover soles,
    cleaned**
3 tbsp olive oil
½ tsp salt
½ tsp chilli powder
1 tsp lemon juice

For the rice:

2 tbsp olive oil
1 small onion, chopped
2 cloves garlic, chopped
1 red chilli, de-seeded
1 green chilli, de-seeded
**84 g/3 oz/¾ cup button
    mushrooms, cleaned and
    chopped**
**170 g/6 oz/¾ cup Basmati
    rice, washed and drained**
**285 ml/½ pint/1¼ cups fish
    stock or water**
Salt
**10 black olives, pitted and
    chopped**
**2 tomatoes, skinned,
    de-seeded and chopped**
**2 tbsp chopped coriander/
    cilantro leaves**

For the garnish:

**2 tbsp toasted pine kernels,
    or toasted slivered
    almonds, or croûtons**

Using a very sharp knife, cut the fish along the backbone and cut the flesh away from the bones. Then, with a pair of scissors, cut the backbone at both ends. Ease out the small bones from the flesh. You can now quite easily take out the whole skeleton. Pull out carefully any small bones that are still embedded.

Skin the fish carefully, and fold the top fillets back so that the fish becomes a container for the stuffing. When all 4 fish have been prepared like this, brush them all over with the mixture of oil, salt, chilli powder and lemon juice. Then put them aside in a cool place while you make the stuffing.

Stir-fry the shallots, garlic and chopped chillies in a saucepan for 2 minutes. Add the mushrooms and continue stir-frying for another 1 minute. Add the rice, and stir it until all the grains are coated in oil. Pour in the stock or water and season well with salt. Bring the water to the boil, cover the pan tightly, and simmer for 12–15 minutes. Then transfer the rice at once to a bowl, at the same time stirring into it the olives, tomatoes and coriander/cilantro leaves.

Up to this point, everything can be prepared up to 24 hours in advance and the rice and fish stored separately in the fridge.

If you are ready to serve the meal, preheat the oven to 180°C/350°F/Gas Mark 4. Lay the fish side by side on a well-oiled baking tray and spoon the rice into them, dividing it equally among them. Dribble some more olive oil over the rice. Cook in the oven, uncovered, for 12–15 minutes, and serve immediately.

A Fish Pilaf
Fish plov

This is a recipe from Lesley Chamberlain's *The Food and Cooking of Russia*. According to her, *plov* is one of the dishes that Russia borrowed from Central Asia, and it is traditionally made with bream from the Caspian Sea, though she suggests carp or pike as good substitutes; failing those, catfish, brill, monkfish, John Dory, or halibut will do.

Preparation: 15–20 minutes
Cooking: 20–25 minutes

For 4–6 people

Salt to taste
2 bay leaves
1 parsley root or ½ parsnip
A few black peppercorns
4 onions
450 g–675 g/1–1½ lb/4 cups filleted fish, cut into smallish pieces
2 tsp ground black pepper
3 tbsp fresh parsley
2 tbsp fresh dill
1 tsp crushed fennel seeds
2 pinches saffron or turmeric
140 ml/5 fl oz/1 cup sour cream
2–3 carrots
7 tbsp olive or other vegetable oil
390 g/14 oz/1¾ cups Italian rice, washed and soaked in hot water for 30 minutes
juice of ½ lemon

Bring just under 1 litre/1½ pints/3¾ cups of water to the boil and add salt, the bay leaves, half the parsley root or parsnip, a few crushed peppercorns and half an onion. Add the fish, and simmer for 10 minutes. Then transfer the fish to a heatproof serving dish, and cover with 2 finely chopped onions, the remaining grated parsley root or parsnip, half the black pepper, the parsley, dill, fennel seeds and half the saffron or turmeric. Sprinkle with salt and pour the sour cream over all. Set this to cook very slowly, either on the stove or in a steamer for about 10–15 minutes.

In another pan, soften the remaining onion and the carrot, both finely chopped, in the oil. Strain the fish bouillon into the pan, bring it to the boil and add the rice. Let it come back to the boil on a medium heat. Add the remaining pepper and saffron, stir, cover, and cook on a very low heat for 8–10 minutes. Remove from heat and leave the rice to rest, still covered, for 5 minutes.

Serve the rice, sprinkled with lemon juice, in a bowl, and the fish on the dish on which it was cooked.

Prawns/Shrimp in Rich Coconut Sauce
Sambal goreng udang

Prawns/shrimp cooked this way are popular all over Indonesia and Malaysia, and are of course always eaten with rice; flavours, textures and colours of the rice and prawns complement each other precisely. Like Rendang (page 269), this is one of the fundamental South-East Asian dishes, and I therefore include it in all my books.

In London, I make this with frozen king prawns/jumbo shrimp from the supermarket, peeled, de-veined, partly pre-cooked. This cuts out a lot of preparation, and the prawns/shrimp are excellent provided they are cooked for 4 minutes only and are not reheated thereafter.

Preparation: about 15 minutes
Cooking: 20 minutes

For 6–8 people

420 ml/15 fl oz/2 cups hot water
5-cm/2-inch piece of fresh lemon grass
2 kaffir lime leaves, or lemon or bay leaves
2 ripe tomatoes, peeled and chopped
112 g/4 oz/1 cup creamed coconut, chopped
1 kg/2 lb frozen king prawns/ jumbo shrimp, thawed completely

For the paste:
3 shallots or 1 small onion, chopped
2 cloves garlic
5-cm/2-inch piece of fresh ginger root, peeled and sliced
3 large red chillies, de-seeded and chopped
1 tsp shrimp paste (optional)
2 candle nuts or macadamia nuts or blanched almonds chopped (optional)
1 tsp ground coriander
1 tsp paprika
½ tsp salt, or more to taste
1 tbsp tamarind water or lemon juice
2 tbsp olive or peanut oil
2 tbsp cold water

Blend all the ingredients for the paste until smooth. In a saucepan, bring this paste to the boil and cook it for 4 minutes, stirring continuously. Add the hot water, lemon grass, and kaffir lime, lemon or bay leaves. Bring the mixture back to the boil and simmer gently for 20 minutes. Add the tomatoes and the creamed coconut; stir to dissolve the coconut. Simmer and stir for 2 more minutes. Adjust the seasoning. Up to this point, the sauce can be made up to 24 hours in advance and kept in the fridge (but it cannot be frozen).

When you are ready to serve the prawns/shrimp, bring the sauce to a rolling boil, stir it, and put in the prawns/shrimp (which must be totally thawed, otherwise harmful bacteria may survive the brief cooking). Simmer the prawns/shrimp for 4 minutes only – any longer and they will become tough and tasteless. Discard the lemon grass and leaves. Serve hot with rice, accompanied by stir-fried vegetables or a salad.

Twelfth-century Chinese pump

Stuffed Trout, Armenian Style

I have to thank Lesley Chamberlain for letting me reproduce this recipe from her excellent book, *The Food and Cooking of Russia*. She gives two stuffings for the trout; both are delicious, one has rice in it. She suggests that whichever one you choose the fish should be served either with rice (I think white or brown rice would be equally suitable) or with bulgur.

A refinement, if you feel like doing it or can persuade your fishmonger to do it, is to bone the trout before you stuff it. First, snip off the fins and cut off the head. Slit the back open with a sharp knife, keeping the knife immediately above the backbone. Open up the fish so that it lies flat on a firm surface. With the knife, start lifting the bone at the head end and gently prise it upwards all the way to the tail.

Preparation and cooking: about 1 hour altogether

For 2–4 people

2 large trout, weighing altogether 675–900 g/ 1½–2 lb, heads removed, cleaned and if possible boned, seasoned inside and out with salt and pepper

Stuffing No. 1:

6 prunes or dried apricots, soaked in warm water for 2–3 hours, then chopped; or fresh damsons, or fresh sour apricots, peeled and chopped
1 pomegranate, or 1 eating apple plus 1 tsp lemon juice
2 large onions, finely chopped
1 tsp dried basil
2 tbsp butter
Salt and pepper

Stuffing No. 2:

70 g/2½ oz/⅓ cup short grain rice, or Thai Fragrant, cooked at a rolling boil in salted water for 6 minutes, then drained
84 g/3 oz butter
3 tbsp chopped parsley
1 tsp finely chopped ginger root
56 g/2 oz/⅓ cup raisins, soaked in warm water for 2 hours
Salt and pepper

Other ingredients:

140 ml/5 fl oz white wine, or 84 ml/3 fl oz olive oil plus 2 tbsp butter for frying

Prepare and mix the chosen stuffing. For Stuffing No. 1, cut the pomegranate in half and carefully take out the seeds, discarding the rest; if you use an apple, peel and dice it and rub the lemon juice all over the pieces to prevent discoloration. Fry the onions in butter until soft; let them cool before mixing them with the fruit. Season well with salt and pepper. For Stuffing No. 2, mix everything while the rice is still hot, but let it cool before you stuff the fish.

After you have stuffed the fish, there is no need to sew them up or close the opening in any way, but remember to lift them carefully in and out of the pan.

To cook, lay the stuffed fish in a non-stick pan, pour the wine over them, cover the pan and simmer for 8–10 minutes. Alternatively, without the wine, fry them in the oil and butter for the same length of time, turning them over once.

A third method is to bake them in a preheated oven at 180°C/350°F/Gas Mark 4 for 30–35 minutes. Lay them in a buttered ovenproof dish, pour the wine over them, season with salt and pepper, and then pour some extra melted butter on top – about 2 or 3 tablespoons.

In all cases, serve hot.

Hot Curry of Fish

I used to make this curry with salmon – but salmon was cheaper in those days, and now I think this sauce is just a bit too strong for such a delicate fish. So cod or monkfish has taken its place, though I still like to poach a salmon fillet in the Mild Curry Sauce on page 355. This hot curry should be eaten with plenty of white rice or compressed rice (page 107).

Preparation: about 1 hour, including making the coconut milk
Cooking: about 30 minutes

For 4–6 people

450–675 g/1–1½ lb cod
   steaks or monkfish fillet,
   cut into largish cubes and
   rubbed all over with salt
   and pepper
84 ml/3 fl oz/⅓ cup olive oil
1.1 litres/2 pints/5 cups
   coconut milk made from
   170 g/6 oz desiccated
   coconut (page 368)
450 g/1 lb small new potatoes,
   scrubbed and washed

For the curry paste:

4 shallots or 1 onion,
   chopped
3 cloves garlic, chopped
5-cm/2-inch piece of lemon
   grass, outer leaves
   discarded, chopped
2.5-cm/1-inch piece of
   fresh galingale, peeled
   and chopped
2 kaffir lime leaves,
   shredded
1 tsp ground pepper
4–5 red chillies, de-seeded
   and chopped
1 tbsp roasted coriander
   seeds
1 tbsp roasted cumin seeds
½ tsp ground nutmeg
½ tsp ground turmeric
1 tbsp fish sauce
2 tbsp tamarind water or
   lemon juice
2 tbsp peanut oil
1 tsp salt

Make the coconut milk and keep this aside. Brown the fish lightly in the oil, and keep this aside also.

Put all the ingredients for the paste in a blender, with 3 tablespoons of coconut milk, and blend them until smooth. Transfer this paste to a saucepan. Bring it to the boil and simmer for 5–6 minutes, stirring often. Add the rest of the coconut milk and bring it almost to boiling point; put in the potatoes, and simmer, uncovered, for 15–20 minutes. Adjust the seasoning and taste the potatoes – they should be almost cooked but not quite.

Add the fish cubes and continue to simmer for 8–10 minutes. Don't thicken the sauce – it should be like soup. To serve, simply ladle fish and potatoes and piping hot sauce directly into a plateful of rice or lontong.

Salmon Pudding with Rice

This is adapted from a Swedish recipe in Alan Davidson's *North Atlantic Seafood*. The original version uses salted salmon instead of fresh.

Preparation: 15–20 minutes
Cooking: 1 hour

For 3–4 people as a main course, or 6 as a starter

---

170 g/6 oz/¾ cup rice: Thai Fragrant, Calrose, Japanese, or a risotto rice such as Arborio or Vialone Nano
340 g/12 oz/2 cups salmon fillet, cut into small cubes
285 ml/½ pint/1¼ cups milk
56 g/2 oz butter
2 eggs, separated
½ tsp salt
¼ tsp ground white pepper
1 tsp sugar
3–4 tbsp breadcrumbs

Wash the rice in several changes of water, and drain. Beat the egg yolks in a bowl for 1–2 minutes. Beat the whites until stiff.

Heat the milk in a saucepan until it almost boils. Put in the rice, stir once, and leave it to simmer until all the milk has been absorbed by the rice (this takes about 15 minutes). Take the pan off the heat, stir in the butter, and set aside to cool.

When the rice is cool, stir in the beaten egg yolks, the salmon, salt, pepper and sugar. Finally, fold in the stiffly beaten egg whites, and adjust the seasoning.

Butter a 1-litre/1¾ pint/4½ cup pie or soufflé dish, sprinkle 2 tablespoons of breadcrumbs over the bottom, and pour in the rice and salmon mixture. Spread the remaining breadcrumbs on top of this, and bake in a preheated oven at 180°C/350°F/Gas Mark 4 for 40–45 minutes, so that it is lightly browned.

Remove the dish from the oven, let it rest for 3 or 4 minutes, then run a knife around the edge and turn the pudding out on to a plate. Cut into portions with a sharp knife wetted in warm water. Serve immediately, with melted butter if you like.

Rice and Salmon Parcels

This is a westernized version of *pais ikan*, a West Javanese way of cooking fish and spices in a banana-leaf packet. Here, the fish is wrapped in filo pastry. You can make either one big parcel, which is suitable for a buffet, or smaller individual ones. Whichever you choose, cut the parcel just before serving to reveal the colour of the salmon inside and to release the delicious vapours that have been trapped inside during cooking.

As a contrast to the pink salmon, either green or white vegetables are effective – white ones can include stir-fried beansprouts, or mooli/white radish julienne. I would probably serve this with a Mild Curry Sauce (page 355), but Almond Sauce (page 354) would be equally good, or indeed no sauce at all, in which case a salad is the best thing to go with it. These parcels are also ideal for picnics.

Preparation: 1 hour
Cooking: 35–40 minutes

For 6–8 people

390 g/14 oz/1¾ cups short
    grain rice, preferably
    Japanese, washed and
    drained about 1 hour
    before cooking
2 sheets of filo pastry (to
    make one large parcel; 1
    sheet each for individual
    parcels)
675 g/1½ lb salmon fillet,
    whole or already cut into 6
    or 8 pieces, rubbed all over
    with salt and pepper
450 g/1 lb/4 cups courgettes/
    zucchini or cucumber,
    sliced into thin rounds
1 tsp salt

Cook the rice some time in advance, either in an electric rice cooker or by the absorption method and steaming (page 98–100). Leave to get cold. Put the courgettes/zucchini or cucumber in a colander, sprinkle with salt, and leave to stand for 10 minutes. Rinse them well and pat dry with kitchen paper. Stir-fry the courgettes/zucchini or cucumber in the clarified butter or oil for 2 minutes. Leave to cool.

Brush one side of the filo pastry with butter or oil, and lay the sheets one on top of the other, oiled side uppermost. Lay the cold rice in the middle of the pastry, leaving sufficient margin to fold the pastry over the top, and shaping the rice so that the edges are straight and the surface level. Lay the fish on top of the rice, spread the ginger and caper mixture over the fish, and finally the slices of courgettes/zucchini or cucumber on top of that.

Fold the pastry over everything to make an oblong parcel. Brush the top and sides of the parcel with butter or oil and place it on a greased baking tray. Bake in a preheated oven at 190°C/375°F/Gas Mark 5 for 35–40 minutes. Cut the parcel into 6 or 8 slices and

3 tbsp clarified butter or olive oil

To be mixed together:

1 tsp finely chopped ginger root

1 tsp finely chopped lemon grass, the inner soft part only (optional)

1 clove garlic, finely chopped

2 tsp capers, chopped

1 green chilli, de-seeded and finely chopped, or ¼ tsp chilli powder

1 tbsp creamed coconut, dissolved in 2 tbsp hot water (optional)

2 tbsp unsalted butter, melted

12–16 fresh green peppercorns, lightly crushed (optional)

¼ tsp salt or more to taste

1 tsp sugar

serve hot or cold. If you are serving a sauce also, this should be served separately.

Note. To make individual parcels, you will need 1 sheet of pastry for each. Fold it to make a square, brush it with butter or oil, then proceed as above, dividing rice, fish, mixture and courgettes/zucchini equally among the parcels. Wrap the parcels as if you were making envelopes, folding each corner into the middle and tucking the last one under the others to seal the packet. Bake as described above.

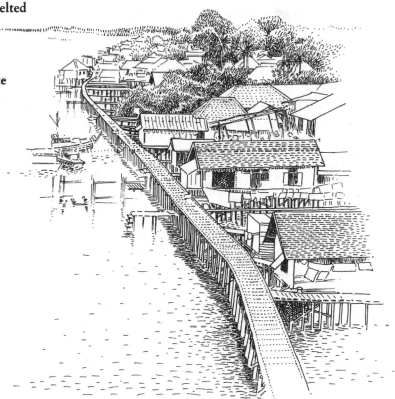

Riverside houses: Pontianak, West Kalimantan

215

Rice and Salmon Pie
Koulebiaka

This internationally renowned Russian pie has, traditionally, a wide range of fillings. Salmon with rice has proved to be the most popular, particularly in Finland, where this is a national dish. Every household has its own version. This is the personal favourite of Silvija Davidson, who gave me the recipe.

Preparation: cook the rice; 1½ hours
Cooking: 45–60 minutes

For 4–6 people

For the yeast dough:

450 g/1 lb/2 cups strong
   unbleached flour
1 tbsp fast-action dried yeast,
   or 28 g/1 oz fresh yeast
1 tsp salt
170 g/6 oz unsalted butter
140 ml/5 fl oz/¾ cup milk
140 ml/5 fl oz/¾ cup crème
   fraîche or soured cream
2 eggs, free range
2 egg yolks, free range

For the filling:

675 g/1½ lb salmon fillets
   without skin, in one piece
   or several pieces
225 g/8 oz/2 cups onion,
   peeled and diced
225 g/8 oz/2 cups wild or flat
   mushrooms, wiped and
   sliced
84 g/3 oz unsalted butter
Juice of 1 lemon

Sift the flour, dried yeast and salt into a bowl and make a well in the centre. (If using fresh yeast, mix this with a little warm milk and a pinch of sugar and set it aside for 10 minutes until it becomes active and frothing.) Scald the milk and butter, then let them cool to blood temperature. Pour them into the well with the soured cream, whole eggs and egg yolks, beaten together. With a wooden spoon, gradually incorporate the liquid into the flour. Knead vigorously for 10 minutes until the dough is elastic. Put it in a greased bowl, cover it, and set it aside to rise to double the original volume (about 1½ hours). When it has risen, punch it down, knead it briefly, divide the dough into two roughly equal pieces, wrap them, and chill them in the fridge until you are ready to assemble the pie.

Cook the salmon in 56 g/2 oz butter for 2 minutes on one side, then turn it over and cook it for 2 more minutes. Set it aside, season it, and sprinkle it with half the lemon juice. Cook the onion in the remaining butter until it becomes translucent. Add the mushrooms and a pinch of salt. Cover the pan, and cook the vegetables until the juices run. Remove the lid, turn up the heat and drive off the juices. Place the onion and mushroom in a mixing bowl with the remaining lemon juice, cooked rice, raw egg, herbs, spices and seasoning, and mix everything together well.

216

310 g/11 oz/1⅓ cups long grain rice, brown or white
1 raw egg, free range, beaten
1 tbsp finely chopped flat-leaf parsley
1 tbsp finely chopped fresh dill
½ tsp freshly grated nutmeg, or to taste
3 hard-boiled eggs, free range, sliced
Salt and pepper to taste

Other ingredients:

2 tbsp soured cream
56 g/2 oz unsalted butter

On a floured board, roll out one piece of the chilled dough to an oblong about 1 cm/⅓ inch thick, which will fit your baking sheet. Place this on the baking sheet, and spoon on to it half the rice mixture, leaving a rim about 4 cm/1½ inches wide. Arrange the salmon on top of the rice, and slices of egg on top of the salmon. Cover with the remaining rice mixture. Dampen the edges of the dough with water. Roll out the second piece of dough to the same size as the first, and place over the filling. Press the edges together firmly, turn them up, then press them together again with the tines of a fork. Make a small hole in the top centre of the pie, and, if you have a few scraps of dough left over, form these into decorative leaves or plaits/braids, dampen them and press them into place on the pie.

Brush the pie all over with soured cream and bake it in a preheated oven at 200°C/400°F/Gas Mark 6 for 45–60 minutes, until the pastry is golden brown. Place the pie on a serving platter, melt the butter and pour it through the hole into the pie. Serve hot, with (for example) a green salad dressed with soured cream and sprinkled with fresh dill.

Prawn/Shrimp Risotto

Although I have placed the other risotto dishes elsewhere in the book, this one makes such a good main course that I feel it belongs here. It can be followed by a separate course of green vegetables or salad. It is as beautifully pink as the Pumpkin Risotto on page 164 is golden.

Since a risotto can be easily moulded and turned out on to the plate, I suggest moulding this in individual ramekins. For a main course, you need fairly large ones: I use ramekins 9 cm/3½ inches in diameter and 6 cm/2¼ inches deep.

You can of course use lobster instead of prawns/shrimp if you wish. In either case, buy uncooked shellfish, because you need the shells for the stock.

Preparation: 45 minutes
Cooking: 20–25 minutes + 5–8 minutes heating in the oven

For 4–6 people

1.1–1.4 kg/2½–3 lb
  uncooked king prawns/
  jumbo shrimp, in their
  shells and with heads
8 shallots or 2 onions, finely
  chopped
4 cloves garlic, crushed
1 tbsp olive oil
1 tsp paprika
1 bay leaf
1.7 litres/3 pints/7½ cups
  cold water
285 ml/10 fl oz/1¼ cups
  good dry white or rosé
  wine
56 g/2 oz butter
340 g/12 oz/1½ cups
  Arborio or Vialone Nano
  rice
1.1 litres/2 pints/5 cups
  prawn stock (see below)

Peel the prawns/shrimp and remove their heads. Wash the heads and shells thoroughly and keep aside. De-vein the prawns/shrimp by making a deep cut down their backs, then removing the black vein. The deep cut will also make them curl up as they cook. Wash the prawns/shrimp under the cold tap, drain them in a colander and dry with kitchen paper. Rub them with the crushed garlic and about ½ tsp salt. Refrigerate.

Now make the stock. Heat 1 tablespoon of olive oil in a saucepan and fry half the shallots or onions for 1 minute. Then add the prawns/shrimp shells and heads. Continue stirring for a minute or two, and add the paprika and bayleaf. Stir again, and add the water. Bring to the boil, and simmer gently for 20–25 minutes. Strain the stock through a sieve lined with muslin into another saucepan. Up to this point, everything can be done up to 24 hours in advance, in which case allow the stock to cool and store it in the fridge.

You should aim to start cooking the risotto about an hour before your guests are due to arrive. Take the prawns/shrimp from the fridge so that they are at room temperature when cooked. Bring the stock back to the boil and simmer very gently, so that it stays hot as the risotto is being made. Season the stock with salt and

Salt and cayenne pepper to
    taste
2 tbsp freshly grated
    Parmesan cheese
4 tbsp cream (optional)
3 tbsp chopped flat-leaf
    parsley

cayenne pepper, and pour the wine into it while continuing to simmer.

Heat half the butter in a wide saucepan and sauté the remaining shallots or onions until soft. Add the rice and stir continuously for 2–3 minutes so that the grains are well coated with the butter. Now proceed as usual in making risotto: add a ladleful of hot stock to the rice, stir the rice occasionally, and add the next ladleful only when the rice has absorbed the previous one. The rice will be cooked in 20–22 minutes from the moment the first ladleful of stock was put into it. You will not need all the stock for the rice – what is left over will be used for cooking the prawns/shrimp.

Butter the ramekins and line their bottoms with greaseproof paper. Put the remaining butter and the Parmesan into the risotto and stir vigorously for a minute or so. Then divide the risotto among the ramekins, pressing it down hard with a spoon. Cover each ramekin with aluminium foil.

About 30 minutes before you are going to serve the dish, preheat the oven to 180°C/350°F/Gas Mark 4. When it is hot, heat the ramekins and the risotto in the oven in a bain-marie (a baking tray half-filled with hot water) while you cook the prawns/shrimp.

Heat 420 ml/15 fl oz/2 cups of the remaining stock in a saucepan. When it is boiling, put in the prawns/shrimp. Cook them for 3 minutes only, and adjust the seasoning. Then, if you are using cream, lower the heat, add the cream, and stir the prawns/shrimp around. Remove from heat and sprinkle parsley on top. Transfer the prawns/shrimp, with the clear or creamy sauce, on to a heated serving platter. Unmould the risotto on to heated serving plates and serve at once, offering the prawns/shrimp around to the guests so that they can help themselves.

Rice with Poultry

Keeping chickens is a universal human experience. That is an exaggeration, I am sure, but most of us have helped to feed somebody's hens at some time in our lives. In urban Asia, people who may hardly ever see a rice field still have fowls free-ranging in their backyards. When I lived in Surrey, half my neighbours seemed to be building chicken runs, though their wire netting was usually not proof against the local foxes.

The human race as a group eats more poultry than it does red meat, and in the world there must be a vast number of chicken recipes. Many are variations on a few basic themes. Chicken soup is made all over the world, and with rice or barley is well known to be a powerful food for growing children, invalids, and everyone else in a properly conducted household. In this book, however, I am only trying to gather a few representative recipes from rice-growing or rice-eating countries. Rice is an essential part of some of these dishes, while others are normally served with rice.

Not all are chicken recipes, though most are. Chicken is, I have to say, rather bland, especially the factory-farmed birds that are increasingly difficult to avoid nowadays. Chicken is therefore good with spices, whether these are applied in a marinade or a stuffing or with the accompanying rice. Rice itself, of course, is a perfect foil for chicken because it absorbs and carries moisture and flavour without disintegrating into mush. This has led me to include some very good recipes for stuffings in this section, for use not only in hens but in ducks and turkeys. The 'exotic stuffing' of the duck on page 251 is equally good inside a turkey – or a large chicken.

Now that supermarkets sell packeted portions of birds, we can buy a boned turkey leg or chicken thigh and fill it with a delicately spiced stuffing. The boneless duck breast is especially useful, because one breast is a good single portion, whereas one cannot be quite sure in advance how much meat one is going to get off a whole duck. With a chicken, on the other hand, there is much more to be said in favour of buying the whole bird; when you have taken from it all the meat you require, the carcass will make good stock for risottos and sauces, or you can make real chicken soup.

Chicken Biryani

Most biryanis take time to prepare and cook, but the result is well worth the little extra trouble. My biryanis are not, I must add, authentically Indian; they have been influenced by Indonesian attitudes and techniques. This chicken biryani is a quick version, but delicious for all that. If you gather together all the ground ingredients in a single bowl before you actually settle down to cook, you will feel you are halfway there already.

Preparation: 10–15 minutes
Cooking: 15–18 minutes + 5 minutes waiting

For 4 people

4 boneless, skinned chicken breast fillets, sliced diagonally into very thin slices
2 tbsp olive oil
2 shallots, chopped
2 cloves garlic, chopped
1 tsp finely chopped ginger root
½ tsp chilli powder
½ tsp ground cumin
1 tsp ground coriander
A pinch of ground nutmeg
¼ tsp ground cinnamon
¼ tsp ground turmeric
170 ml/6 fl oz/¾ cup natural yogurt
1 tsp sugar
3 tbsp raisins or sultanas (optional)
Salt and pepper
225–285 g/8–10 oz/ 1–1¼ cups rice: Basmati, Texmati, or Australian long grain

1.7 litres/3 pints/7½ cups water
½ tsp salt

For the garnish:
1 tbsp fried shallots
2 tbsp ground almonds

Wash the rice and drain. Boil the water in a large saucepan. When it boils, put in ½ teaspoon of salt and the rice, a little at a time so that the water stays on the boil. Stir the rice once and keep the water at a rolling boil for 8 minutes. Drain the rice in a colander and set aside.

In another large saucepan, or a casserole with a tight-fitting lid, heat the oil, and fry the shallots, garlic and ginger root for 2 minutes, stirring all the time. Put in the chicken slices. Increase the heat and stir-fry the chicken for 3 minutes. Now add all the ground ingredients, stir again for a few seconds only, add the yogurt, and continue stirring for 1 minute. Add the sugar and raisins or sultanas (if used), stir again once, adjust the seasoning. Then pile the rice on top of the chicken and sauce.

Cover the saucepan or casserole with aluminium foil or a tea-towel/dishcloth and put the lid on tightly. Lower the heat and leave it to cook undisturbed for 10 minutes. Remove from the heat and let it rest, undisturbed and with the cover still tightly on, for 5 more minutes. Then uncover, sprinkle the garnishes over the dish, and bring it to the table, if possible in the pan or casserole in which it was cooked. Serve straight away, with freshly cooked beans or okra.

Vinegared Chicken and Rice Casserole

This is no ordinary casserole, but a direct descendant of a modern Japanese dish: chicken cooked in vinegar and served as part of a succession of dainty cuts of fish, seafood, poultry and meat in an expensive restaurant or saké bar. In the saké bar, this exquisite food and the rice wine complement each other; you do not *eat* rice until the very end of the meal, when a small bowl of the whitest rice is served to each guest, to be eaten with chopsticks down to the very last grain.

If you prefer to serve the vinegared chicken by itself in the Japanese way, then you don't need to make it into a casserole at all. However, I think this is one of the best chicken-and-rice casseroles that I have developed. If you are cooking this outside Japan, the rice to go for is Kokuho Rose or another Californian Japanese rice, or Californian or Australian Calrose.

Preparation: 50 minutes + overnight marinating – you need to prepare and cook the chicken the day before you cook the casserole, as well as make the stock
Cooking: 20 minutes + 5 minutes resting

For 4–6 people

3 chicken breast fillets, with skin, cut into cubes
6 chicken thighs, boned and cut into cubes
2 tbsp plain/all-purpose flour or rice flour
A pinch of salt
Vegetable oil for frying

For the marinade:

1 tbsp sesame oil
1 tbsp peanut or vegetable oil
1 onion, finely sliced
4 spring onions/scallions, cut into 2.5-cm/1-inch lengths
3 whole dried red chillies

First, prepare the marinade. Heat the two kinds of oil in a wok or frying pan and fry the onion and spring onions/scallions for 2 minutes. Add the rest of the ingredients and boil for 5 minutes. Transfer to a glass bowl and leave to cool.

Mix the flour and salt and coat the chicken pieces with them. Heat the oil in a non-stick frying pan or wok and fry the chicken cubes in batches for 4–5 minutes each batch. Put all the fried chicken, while still hot, into the cold marinade. Leave to cool again, and then cover the bowl and refrigerate overnight.

Take the chicken and marinade out of the fridge a few hours before cooking the casserole. Take out the chillies and keep them aside.

Now, the final cooking. Combine the chicken and the marinade with the rice, the stock and 1 tablespoon of soy sauce in a casserole or saucepan. Stir it all once, bring it to the boil and then cover the casserole (or pan). Lower the heat and simmer for 20 minutes. Place the casserole on a wet tea-towel/dishcloth and leave to rest, still tightly covered, for 5 minutes.

112 ml/4 fl oz/½ cup rice
  vinegar or raspberry
  vinegar
112 ml/4 fl oz/½ cup Bonito
  Stock (page 347) or
  chicken stock
1 tbsp light soy sauce
1 tbsp dark soy sauce
1 tbsp mirin or 1 tsp sugar

For the rice:

450 g/1 lb/2 cups short grain
  rice (see introduction
  above), washed and drained
570 ml/1 pint/2½ cups
  Bonito Stock or chicken
  stock
1 tbsp light soy sauce

De-seed the chillies, and cut them into small pieces. Serve the rice and chicken in the casserole they were cooked in, or transfer them from the saucepan to a serving platter. Sprinkle the cut-up chillies over the top, and serve straight away.

Boy with ducks

223

Donburi with Chicken and Mushrooms

This is my own favourite way of making donburi (see page 277). I use only the thigh meat of the chicken, without the skin, and fresh as well as dried shiitake; also plenty of spring onions/scallions, cut into julienne strips, butter rather than oil, and half a glass of dry white wine in the stock. It may not be authentically Japanese, but it is quite irresistible even so. You can of course omit the wine, or use mirin instead, but remember that mirin is much sweeter.

Preparation: 30–35 minutes + 1 hour to make the stock
Cooking: 10 minutes

For 4 people

450 g/1 lb/2 cups short grain
   or soft long grain rice (e.g.
   Thai Fragrant or Calrose)
700 ml/1¼ pints/3 cups
   water

Other ingredients:

340–450 g/12–16 oz/
   3–4 cups chicken thigh
   meat, the skin removed,
   cut into thin strips
112 g/4 oz/2 cups fresh
   shiitake mushrooms
28 g/1 oz/¼ cup dried
   shiitake, rinsed and soaked
   in hot water for 30 minutes,
   then drained (but save the
   water for the stock)
56 g/2 oz butter
3 cloves garlic, sliced into
   very thin strips
2.5-cm/1-inch piece of ginger
   root, peeled and sliced into
   very thin strips

You can cook the rice in advance by the usual method (page 98–100), but it should, if possible, be still warm when you finish cooking the chicken and mushrooms. However, as with any donburi, the meat-vegetable-and-sauce component can be stored in the fridge, *separately* from the rice, for up to 48 hours. Rice and meat can then be brought together just before serving, and reheated in a microwave. Give it 2–3 minutes for each portion, on full power.

Make the chicken stock. Put the bones and skin from the thighs into the saucepan, add the mushroom stalks and the water you soaked the dried shiitake in, plus 850 ml/1½ pints/3¾ cups of cold water. Simmer for about 1 hour. Then strain the stock, measure the amount you need and keep it aside.

Slice the mushrooms thinly. In a wok or large frying pan, melt the butter and stir-fry the garlic, ginger and green chilli for 1–2 minutes. Add the chicken strips and stir-fry for 3 minutes. Then put the mushrooms in and go on stir-frying for another 1 minute. Pour in the wine, or mirin, if you are using it, and the soy sauce. Increase the heat and let this bubble for 2 minutes.

Reduce the heat a little and add the stock. Simmer for 2–3 minutes. Adjust the seasoning. Divide the rice among 4 large serving bowls, then serve out the chicken and mushrooms equally, and finally the sauce. Serve at once, very hot.

1 green chilli, de-seeded
    and sliced like the ginger
    root
5 spring onions/scallions,
    trimmed and washed,
    then cut into julienne
    strips
2 tbsp light soy sauce
112 ml/4 fl oz/½ cup dry
    white wine or 2 tbsp
    mirin (optional)
340 ml/12 fl oz/1½ cups
    chicken stock, made as
    described below
Salt and pepper to taste

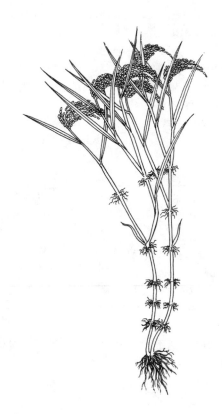

Deepwater rice plant

Chicken and Rice Sausage

Cooked rice or rice flour are good for binding homemade sausages; if you are accustomed to using breadcrumbs, you may like to experiment with rice in your own favourite sausage recipe. This Louisiana *boudin* (which I suppose is the same word as 'pudding') doesn't actually use very much rice; for a real spicy Chinese rice sausage, see page 194. But if you make both, and serve them as a first course, sliced, with your own apple sauce, the combination is delicious.

Nowadays, in London at any rate, the decline of the old-fashioned family butcher has made it difficult to buy sausage skins in small quantities. In cooking all the sausages for this book, therefore, I have used clingfilm/plastic wrap. This enables you to make fresh sausages even for just one or two people. Of course, you can also use the traditional banana leaf wrapping if you are lucky enough to live in a place where banana trees outnumber supermarkets.

Preparation: cook the rice, if used; 30 minutes + 30–60 minutes chilling
Cooking: 8–15 minutes

For 2–4 people as a starter with salad, or for 8 when served with, for example, Chinese Spicy Sausage (page 194) and Hot Pork Sausage (page 287).

---

4 chicken breast fillets,
    without skin
56 g/2 oz/½ cup cooked rice,
    preferably short grain, or 2
    tbsp rice flour
1 large onion, finely chopped
3 cloves garlic, chopped
2 tbsp olive or peanut oil
½ tsp cayenne pepper or
    chilli powder
2 tbsp spring onions/scallions,
    chopped
½ tsp dried thyme
A large pinch of grated
    nutmeg
Salt and pepper to taste
Oil or butter for last-minute
    frying

Cut the chicken breast fillets into small pieces, then put them into a blender or food processor. Blend until smooth.

Fry the onion and garlic in 2 tablespoons of oil until slightly coloured. Take off the heat and leave to cool. When cold, put these and the other ingredients (except the oil or butter for final frying) into the blender. Blend for a few seconds. Remove the mixture from the machine and refrigerate for 30–60 minutes so that it becomes firmer and easier to handle. Divide the mixture into 4 portions. Put each portion on to a strip of clingfilm/plastic wrap large enough to roll round the sausage and to let you twist-seal the ends. Banana-leaf casings can be pinned at the ends with cocktail sticks.

Half-fill a saucepan with water, bring it to simmering point, and put in the wrapped sausages to cook for 6–8 minutes. Then take them out, let them cool, and unwrap them from the clingfilm/plastic wrap or banana leaf casings. The sausages can be refrigerated for up to 48 hours, in which case they must be allowed to return to room temperature right through before they are fried.

To serve the sausages, fry them in oil or butter, turning them often, until they are nicely browned all over. They can be eaten hot or warm, sliced and accompanied by a green salad with a vinaigrette dressing, or as described in the introduction to this recipe.

Philippines Chicken Adobo with Rice

For people who live in rice-growing countries, and especially for those who eat rice three times a day by choice, the best rice of all is plain boiled rice. If you proceed to cook it further in the oven, as you will do if you are influenced by foreign recipes (including many in this book), then for these purists you are overcooking it. The recipe that follows is worthy in its own right of inclusion here, but it is respectfully dedicated to the purists, for here the boiled rice is served in a separate bowl and everyone can help themselves and mix it with their Chicken Adobo, or *Adobong Manok*, as they call it in the Philippines. I suggest you boil the rice while the chicken dish is cooking.

Preparation time: 15–20 minutes
Cooking: 40–45 minutes

For 4–6 people

450 g/1 lb/2 cups long grain rice, plain boiled (page 98-100)

1.1–1.4 kg/2½–3 lb chicken, cut into serving pieces, the fat and skin discarded

6–8 cloves garlic, finely chopped

112 ml/4 fl oz/ ½ cup white vinegar or rice vinegar

1.1 litres/2 pints/5 cups water

1 or 2 kaffir lime leaves or bay leaves

1 tsp salt

½–1 tsp coarsely-ground black pepper or chopped chillies

½ tsp ground turmeric

½ tsp paprika

2 tbsp fish sauce or light soy sauce

2 tbsp peanut oil

140 ml/5 fl oz/⅔ cup very thick coconut milk

Put the chicken pieces into a large saucepan, add the garlic, vinegar, water, kaffir lime or bay leaves, pepper or chilli, and salt. Bring to the boil, cover the pan, reduce the heat, and simmer for 20 minutes.

With a slotted spoon, transfer the chicken pieces to a colander. Turn the heat up under the saucepan and boil the stock until it has reduced to half its original quantity. This will take about 20—25 minutes.

Heat the oil in another saucepan and add the turmeric and paprika. Stir, and add about 6 table-spoons of the coconut milk. Stir once, and put in the chicken pieces. Stir these until every piece is coated in the orange-coloured sauce. Pour in the reduced stock and the rest of the coconut milk. Bring the liquid to the boil and let it bubble gently, stirring often, for 10–15 minutes. Add the fish sauce or soy sauce. Adjust the seasoning, and serve hot, with the plain boiled rice. Any lightly-cooked or stir-fried vegetable will make a suitable accompaniment.

Jambalaya with Chicken

There is no ham here, and if you use chicken or turkey sausage you can avoid pork altogether. On the other hand, if you use spicy chaurice and smoked andouille, or their European alternatives – I am thinking of German or Spanish sausages that are smoked or highly spiced – then of course you will get that much closer to the authentic Louisiana flavour. I have to say that my cooking instructor in New Orleans did not take kindly to my suggestion of hot Italian sausage, with fennel seeds, but I am unrepentant. I admit, though, that this might more strictly be called a rice casserole.

Buy a whole chicken to make this dish. Then you can use the carcass, skin and giblets for the stock. For the best results, allow the slices of chicken to marinate for at least 2 hours, or overnight.

Preparation: 1 hour, including making the stock, + 2 hours (or overnight) marinating
Cooking: 25–30 minutes

For 6–8 people

For the chicken marinade:

3 tbsp warm water or dry
　　white wine or sherry
1 tsp fresh or dried thyme
2 cloves garlic, crushed
½ tsp ground white pepper
1 tbsp tomato ketchup
½ tsp salt

Other ingredients:

900 g/2 lb/4 cups chicken
　　meat, the skin removed,
　　sliced
3 tbsp olive or peanut oil
1 large onion, chopped
2 stalks celery, chopped
1 large green or red sweet/bell
　　pepper, de-seeded and diced

Mix all the ingredients for the marinade in a bowl, and marinate the chicken slices for 2 hours or overnight in the fridge.

Strain and measure the stock, and keep it hot on the stove till you are ready to use it. In a large heavy-bottomed saucepan or casserole, with a lid, heat the oil and stir-fry the onion, celery and diced pepper for 2 minutes. Then put in the marinated chicken and the sausages. Stir, and cover the pan for 4 minutes. Uncover, and continue stirring for 2 minutes, then add the rice. Stir the rice until every grain has a shiny coating of oil. Pour in the hot stock, and add the tomatoes, cayenne or chilli powder, and garlic. Bring all this to the boil, stir once, and put the lid on the pan. Lower the heat and cook for 20–25 minutes, undisturbed.

Take the pan off the heat, uncover it, adjust the seasoning, and add the chopped spring onions/scallions and parsley. Put the lid on tightly and let it rest for 5–8 minutes. If you are still not quite ready to eat, put the pan or casserole, with the lid still tightly on, into a warm oven. Serve hot.

450 g/1 lb/2 cups spicy pork
    sausage, or chicken or
    turkey sausage, diced
½ tsp chopped fresh or dried
    thyme
2 bay leaves
½ tsp cayenne pepper or
    chilli powder
3 cloves garlic, finely
    chopped
390 g/14 oz/2⅓ cups
    chopped fresh or canned
    tomatoes
450 g/1 lb/2 cups long or
    medium grain rice
700 ml/1¼ pints/3 cups hot
    chicken stock
4 tbsp chopped spring onions/
    scallions
4 tbsp chopped parsley
Salt and pepper to taste
Tabasco or other chilli paste
    or sauce, to taste

Paella Valenciana

In July 1991 I had lunch at El Delfin, a restaurant facing the sea at Malva Rosa, just outside Valencia. You eat in a large, white room, with black furniture and a stone floor, a bar at the end near the kitchen door, a breeze just lifting the corners of the white tablecloths; when a particularly fine dish comes to table, other patrons are likely to walk across and comment on it appreciatively, praising the cook, Señora Cesar. It is, of course, a family business. I was allowed into the kitchen to watch the Señora prepare this dish in the traditional way, in a shallow iron pan – a *paella* – over a wood fire. The fire heats the bottom of the pan evenly, so that the bottom layer of rice is nice and crunchy but not actually burnt. I bought a *paella* in a Valencia department store and have used it many times on my gas stove, with good results; but of course the gas ring does not distribute the heat evenly and my first paellas were a little burnt in

229

the middle. The hotplate of an electric stove is not big enough for these very wide pans, so the answer is, with gas or electricity, to cook your paella in a shallow saucepan, about the same diameter as the heat source, and with a lid.

I give here the original ingredients that I saw Señora Cesar use, and I have also suggested some alternatives which I have tested and which produce practically the same result, though the people of Valencia, who are rightly proud of their cuisine, might not like you to call it a Paella Valenciana. In particular they would not permit saffron to be replaced by turmeric, which I do not hesitate to do, considering that saffron is an astronomic price and that I grew up among people who use turmeric every day. I entirely agree, however, that you must not mix meat and seafood here. Paella Valenciana was originally a dish of the inland rice farmers, who kept chickens, snared rabbits and picked up edible snails wherever they could, but who were too far from the coast to eat fresh fish. A seafood paella (page 202) is a different thing altogether.

The Valencia way to eat this dish, among family or friends, is just to put the *paella* in the middle of the table and let each person eat his or her way from the edge towards the centre. I'm told that 10 or 12 people, or more, can eat this way at a big round table, and after seeing some of the gigantic old *paellas* that are still in use there, I can well believe it.

The best rice to use is of course the short grain rice that has been grown around Valencia and Murcia since the time of the Moors, who built the irrigation canals that are still the basis of rice farming in the region today. In Calasparra, in the hills above Murcia, they grow rice which is stamped *Denominación de Origen* as if it were a fine wine; and a few farmers still grow a low-yield traditional variety called Bomba, the seed for which (so I was told by the commercial director of a big local rice mill) is delivered to the growers by taxi. Bomba rice is packed by hand in cotton bags, sealed with a lead seal and sold in Valencia for the equivalent of about £3/US$5 a kilo. Spain exports rice to several European countries; limited amounts are available in a few shops in Britain and the United States.

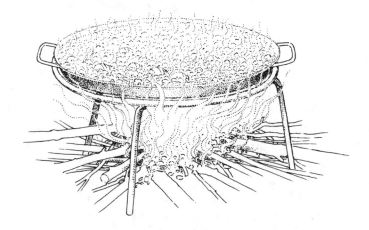

Paella

If you are not able to get Spanish rice, use the best short grain you can find: Japanese or Korean, or Italian Arborio. If you use dried butter beans, soak them overnight first.

Preparation: 20 minutes
Cooking: 40 minutes

For 4–6 people

3 tbsp olive oil
2 chicken breast portions and 2 chicken thighs, cut into small chunks with the bones and skin
225–340 g/8–12 oz/ 1–1½ cups rabbit meat, cut into small chunks
1 small onion, finely sliced
4 cloves garlic, finely sliced
1 tsp cayenne pepper
2 large tomatoes, skinned and chopped, or 2 tbsp tomato purée
112 g/4 oz/1 cup fresh butter beans, or reconstituted dried butter beans, or fresh broad beans
170–225 g/6–8 oz/¾–1 cup flat green beans or runner beans, cut into 5-cm/2-inch pieces
2 pinches saffron strands, crushed in a mortar, or ½ tsp turmeric
16–20 snails, cleaned (optional)
1.1 litres/2 pints/5 cups hot chicken stock or hot water
Salt and pepper to taste
450 g/1 lb/2 cups short grain rice

Heat the oil in the pan, and when it is hot add the chicken and rabbit pieces and fry them, turning often, for 3 minutes. Add the onion, garlic, cayenne pepper and tomatoes or tomato purée. Stir all together for 1 minute. Add the beans and saffron, and stir again. Cover the pan for 2 minutes. Uncover, and add the snails (if used), and stir; then put in the hot chicken stock, water, and salt and pepper. Cover the pan again and let this simmer for 18–19 minutes. Up to this point, the dish can be prepared several hours in advance.

By now the liquid should just be enough to cook the rice. If you are doubtful about this, transfer the solids to another container; then measure the liquid – it should be just about 850 ml/1½ pints/3¾ cups. If necessary, add some more hot water. Bring the liquid back to the boil and put in all the solids and the rice. Stir the whole thing well, adjust the seasoning and cover the pan. Lower the heat and leave it all to cook undisturbed for 15 minutes.

Turn off the heat and let the pan rest for 5 minutes. Serve hot from the pan, or transfer to a warm serving dish. Scrape the thin crust from the bottom of the pan and scatter it over the top so that everyone gets a fair share.

Chicken with Rice
Arroz con pollo

In *The Book of Latin American Cookery*, Elisabeth Lambert Ortiz proposes that this should be called 'Pollo con Arroz', because that is how it always gets translated: Chicken with Rice. In Eastern countries, rice and chicken dishes are so many and various that they have to have long and detailed names just so that people can tell them apart. In translation they become longer still, so on menus and in cookbooks they come to be lumped together under the catch-all title of Chicken Rice.

Readers of my other books will be acquainted with my paternal grandmother, some of whose recipes I have included here. Elisabeth's husband, Cesar Ortiz, also had the good fortune to grow up with a grandmother who was a superb cook, and this arroz con pollo is the recipe of Doña Carmen Sarabia de Tinoco.

Preparation: 20 minutes
Cooking: 55–60 minutes + 5–6 minutes waiting

For 4–6 people

1 chicken, about 1.5 kg/ 3–3½ lb, cut into 10–12 pieces and seasoned with salt and pepper
1–1.2 litres/1¾–2 pints/ 4½–5 cups chicken stock or water
3 tbsp olive oil
1 onion, finely chopped
2 cloves garlic, finely chopped
1 or 2 chillies, de-seeded and chopped (use jalapeño chillies if available)
1 tsp ground cumin
⅛ tsp ground saffron
340 g/12 oz/1½ cups long grain rice
4 tomatoes, peeled, de-seeded and chopped

Wash the rice and drain. Heat the oil in a large saucepan and brown the chicken pieces a little in the oil, then set them aside. In the same oil stir-fry the onion, garlic and chillies for 1–2 minutes. Add the cumin and saffron, stir, then put the chicken pieces back into the saucepan. Pour in the chicken stock or water and add ¼ teaspoon of salt. Cover the pan, bring to the boil and simmer for 30 minutes.

Put 1 tablespoon of oil in a flameproof casserole that has a lid. Stir the drained rice into this, making sure the rice grains are well coated in the oil. Add ¼ teaspoon of salt. Transfer the chicken pieces from the saucepan to the rice casserole, using a slotted spoon. Strain the stock into a bowl and put the solids into the casserole.

Measure 700 ml/1¼ pints/3 cups of stock. If you don't have quite enough, make up the amount with water. Pour this into the casserole and add the chopped tomatoes. Stir the whole lot together once, put the lid on the casserole, lower the heat and leave it to cook undisturbed for 20 minutes. Then remove it from the heat and take the lid off just long enough to pour in the sherry (if used) and add the red pepper

½ tsp salt
56 ml/2 fl oz dry sherry
  (optional)

For the garnish:

1 large red pepper, de-seeded
  and cut into strips

garnish. Cover again tightly, and leave to rest for 5–6 minutes.

Bring the casserole to the table and serve hot, accompanied by cooked vegetables or a mixed salad.

Drying rice sheaves: West Java

Philippines Glutinous Rice Paella
Bringhe

Doreen Fernandez, who is a leading food writer in Manila as well as a professor at one of the Philippines' top universities, tells me that this dish is popular in the provinces of Bulacan and Pampanga, north of the capital. It is thought to be a Filipino version of paella, because it uses Spanish chorizo.

The recipe that Doreen sent me is very mild indeed, with hardly any spices. For me, any dish that has an ingredient as pungent as *patis*, the Filipino fish sauce, needs some chilli or cayenne pepper to balance it. In my version, I have used Thai *nam pla* because it is more likely to be obtainable in the West, but you could also use the strong shrimp paste that Indonesians call *terasi*, and Malaysians *balachan*.

Preparation: 20 minutes
Cooking: 30–35 minutes

For 6–8 people

2 tbsp lard or peanut oil
1 onion, finely chopped
2 cloves garlic, finely chopped
2 green chillies, de-seeded and chopped
1 medium-size chicken, cut into serving pieces
450 g/1 lb/2 cups chorizo, sliced
3 tbsp ginger juice
225 g/8 oz/1 cup glutinous rice, washed and drained
225 g/8 oz/1 cup long grain rice, washed and drained
½ tsp cayenne pepper
3 tsp fish sauce or 1 tsp crumbled shrimp paste
1.1 litres/2 pints/5 cups thin coconut milk
1 bay leaf
Salt if needed
1–2 red sweet/bell peppers, roasted and skinned, then cut into strips, or 340 g/12 oz/ 1½ cups canned pimientos
2–3 hard-boiled eggs, quartered
banana leaves (or aluminium foil)

Heat the lard or oil in a large wok or wide shallow
saucepan, and stir-fry the onion, garlic and chillies for
2 minutes. Add the chicken pieces, turning them over
until they are browned on all sides. Add the chorizo
slices and the ginger juice. Continue stir-frying for 1
minute, then add both kinds of rice and the cayenne
pepper. Stir these around again for a minute or so,
then add the fish sauce followed by the coconut milk.
Bring to the boil, add the bay leaf, and give the whole
thing another stir. Lower the heat, cover with banana
leaves or foil, then put the lid on the pan tightly, and
simmer for 20–25 minutes.

Uncover, and adjust the seasoning. Lay the peppers
on top, replace the cover and let the dish rest for 5
minutes. Then serve hot, garnished with the hard-
boiled eggs.

Chickens for sale: Banaue

235

Caramelized Poussins/Rock Cornish Game Hens with Rice and Raisins

This is a Moroccan chicken recipe which I have somewhat adapted to make it into a most attractive and delicious party dish. Allow one bird per person if you are serving it with a simple accompaniment such as lightly cooked vegetables or a salad. Alternatively, cut the chickens in half and serve them with more rice on the side, spicy stir-fried mixed vegetables, or a vegetable gratin. For a three-course dinner party, you could start with a fish first course, such as a fish kebab, and finish with a chilled dessert or fresh fruit to make a well-balanced menu.

For the centrepiece of an Oriental-style party or a summer garden party, arrange the birds, whole or halved, on a bed of white or yellow rice in a large serving dish, and garnish with parsley and almonds.

Preparation: 30 minutes
Cooking: about 2 hours altogether

For 4 or 8 people

225 g/8 oz/1 cup **Basmati or Patna rice**, washed in 2 changes of water and drained

1.1 litres/2 pints/5 cups water

½ tsp salt

140 g/5 oz butter

1 tsp chopped ginger root

4 tbsp chopped spring onions/scallions (optional)

3 tbsp sugar

1 tsp powdered cinnamon

¼ tsp ground cumin

A pinch of ground cloves

1 tsp ground coriander

¼ tsp cayenne pepper or chilli powder

¼ tsp ground allspice (optional)

First of all boil the water with ½ teaspoon of salt. When it is boiling, add the drained rice and continue boiling for 3 minutes. Tip everything into a colander in the sink and leave the rice to drain and to cool.

While it is cooling, gather together all the ground and powdered spices and put all of them, except the saffron or turmeric, together in a bowl.

In a largish saucepan, heat 28 g/1 oz of butter and fry the chopped ginger root and spring onions/scallions (if used), stirring, for 1 minute; then add the spices from the bowl. Stir the mixture around for 1 minute and add the raisins and almonds. Stir for 1 more minute before turning off the heat. Put the rice into the saucepan, mix it well with the other contents, and leave to cool.

Melt 56 g/2 oz butter in a small saucepan and stir in the saffron or turmeric. When this mixture is cool enough to handle, smear it over the outsides of the poussins/game hens. Then stuff the birds with the cold rice mixture and close the openings with wooden cocktail sticks, or sew them up with strong thread.

Arrange the poussins/game hens in a saucepan which is large enough to hold them in one layer, quite

½ tsp ground black pepper

2 pinches pulverized saffron
   or ¼ teaspoon turmeric

112 g/4 oz/⅔ cup raisins

56 g/2 oz/½ cup sliced
   almonds

4 poussins/Rock Cornish
   Game Hens, about
   450–500 g/16–18 oz each,
   cleaned, and rubbed inside
   and out with salt

1.1 litres/2 pints/5 cups
   chicken stock

tightly. Pour in the hot water or stock and add the 3 tablespoonfuls of sugar. Cover the pan and simmer for 1½ hours, basting the birds from time to time with the liquid. At the end of this time the cooking liquid will have been considerably reduced and will be starting to caramelize on the bottom of the pan. Remove the birds into a large roasting tin and add the remaining 56 g/2 oz of butter to the saucepan. Continue heating the sauce in the pan, while stirring rapidly with a wooden spoon, for 1–2 minutes. Then spoon this caramelized sauce over the poussins/game hens and rub it evenly all over them.

Up to this point the whole dish can be prepared several hours in advance. If you want to make the sauce described below, don't wash the large saucepan.

To make the sauce (which is optional), put 112 ml/ 4 fl oz/½ cup of stock or yogurt into the saucepan in which the poussins/game hens were cooked. Adjust the seasoning, and heat before serving.

Twenty-five minutes before serving the meal, put the roasting tin into a preheated oven at 180°C/350°F/ Gas Mark 4. To serve, take the birds out of the oven and remove to a warm serving dish. Serve them straight away, with or without sauce.

Steamed Chicken with Glutinous Rice

Kuala Lumpur, like many of Asia's fast-growing cities, is now well filled with huge shopping malls and plazas, some very glitzy indeed, others full of quite modest little shops. It is almost a tradition now that the food shops and restaurants are in the basement, and for anyone interested in food a couple of hours browsing (literally or not) in one of these places is more instructive than a day in the museums. In the basement of a rather grand shopping plaza I found a 'food court', a large open space with chairs and tables in the middle and open counters around the sides. Each of these counters is a separate business, offering maybe half-a-dozen specialities, which are illustrated by large coloured pictures. You walk around, decide what you want to eat, and pay for it at the counter where it is sold; the cashier who handles the money does not handle the food. The cooking is done very quickly, usually in front of you, and you carry your meal away and look for somewhere to sit down and eat it. Everything is brightly lit, spotlessly clean, efficient and friendly, and the food is almost always excellent and remarkably cheap.

For the dish described here, the cook assembles the necessary ingredients in a glossy black iron pot: a ladleful of stock from the bubbling stock pan, then the chicken, the mushrooms and the steamed rice. The pot is tightly covered, he turns up the gas flame, and while everything is cooking together he makes up a tray of sambals and pickles and lays beside them a pair of chopsticks wrapped in a paper napkin; finally a wooden tripod, on which with a flourish he places the iron pot. I had plenty of time to make my notes on the recipe as I sat at my table, waiting for the rice to cool a little so I didn't burn my tongue.

At home, I make this in a large casserole with a lid.

Preparation: 2 hours or overnight marinating + 30 minutes
Cooking: 90–105 minutes

For 6 people, served as a one-course lunch or supper

675 g/1½ lb/3 cups chicken breast and thigh meat, cut into small bite-size pieces

For the marinade:

3 tbsp oyster sauce

Mix the ingredients for the marinade well in a glass bowl and marinate the chicken pieces, in a refrigerator, for 2 hours or overnight.

Steam the glutinous rice for 45 minutes. While it is steaming, heat the oil in a wok or frying pan and fry the mushrooms, stirring all the time, for 2 minutes. Take them out with a slotted spoon and drain on absorbent paper.

In the same oil, stir-fry the chicken pieces with the marinade for 3–4 minutes. Take them out and keep aside, with the mushrooms. There will be some juice

1 tbsp mirin or Shaohsing
    wine
1 tsp dark soy sauce
1 tsp light soy sauce
1 tsp finely chopped ginger
1 tsp sesame oil
1 tsp sugar
1 tsp corn or potato flour

For the rice:

450 g/1 lb/2 cups white
    glutinous rice, washed and
    drained
3 tbsp peanut oil, and more
    later
84 g/3 oz/¾ cup dried
    Chinese mushrooms,
    soaked in hot water for 20
    minutes, then sliced thinly;
    the soaking water and
    mushroom stems should be
    kept for the stock pot
6 shallots, sliced finely
1 tsp salt
1 tsp dark soy sauce
1 tsp five-spice powder
    (optional)
700 ml/1¼ pints/3 cups
    water or stock

For the garnish:

2 red chillies, de-seeded and
    finely sliced
3 spring onions/scallions,
    cleaned and finely sliced
2 tbsp roughly chopped
    coriander/cilantro leaves

left in the wok. Add to it 1 tablespoon more oil, heat, and fry the shallots for 2 minutes. Then add the steamed glutinous rice, along with the dark soy sauce, the five-spice powder (if used), and a little salt. Toss and stir for 1 minute, then put in the water or stock. Cover the wok and simmer for 8–10 minutes; in this time, the liquid will be absorbed by the rice. Turn off the heat. Adjust the seasoning.

Butter or oil the casserole and spread the mushrooms and chicken pieces on the bottom. Then add the rice, making sure the casserole is only three-quarters full. Press the rice down gently with a spoon. Cook on a very low heat on the stove, tightly covered, for 30 minutes, or in a preheated oven at 160°C/320°F/ Gas Mark 3 for 40–45 minutes. Serve hot, with the garnish sprinkled on top.

Hainanese Chicken Rice

This dish, which is one of a vast number of chicken-and-rice dishes from many different countries, must have originated on the island of Hainan in the South China Sea, but today it is better known in Singapore, Malaysia and Taiwan. It has become a restaurant speciality, for presentation to Western customers and guests. I had a particularly good one at the Kuala Lumpur Hilton; it is not really very difficult to make, but like a lot of Oriental food it has a lot of fiddly bits, small accompaniments to make the elements of the dish more elaborate and eye-catching. There are three dips – soy sauce, chilli sauce and ginger sauce – as well as garnishes for the chicken broth; these details are what give Hainanese chicken its individuality.

Preparation: 1 hour 10 minutes
Cooking: 35–40 minutes

For 4–6 people

450 g/1 lb/2 cups rice: Thai Fragrant (Jasmine) or other long grain rice, or Japanese

For the chicken and the broth:

1 chicken, about
   1.5–1.75 kg/3½ lb
1.7 litres/3 pints/7½ cups
   water, and more later
1 onion, chopped
1 carrot, peeled and halved
10 whole black peppers
½ tsp salt

Cut the chicken in halves, trim off fat and gristle, and wash the inside of the chicken thoroughly. Put the chicken, water, and all the ingredients for the broth into a large saucepan. Bring to the boil and simmer, covered, for 30 minutes from the time the water starts to boil.

Take out the chicken and when it is cool enough to handle carefully cut the meat, with the skin intact, from the bones. Set aside the meat in another saucepan, with the lid on.

Put the bones back in the pan where the chicken was cooked, add more water if necessary, and bring back to the boil. Simmer gently for 1 hour to make a good chicken broth. Strain the broth through muslin and discard the bones and other solids.

While the chicken and the broth are boiling, prepare the sauces and the garnish.

For the chilli sauce:

3 large red chillies, boiled for 3 minutes
1 tbsp peanut oil
2 cloves garlic, crushed
2 tbsp lime juice
1 tsp sugar

For the soy sauce:

2 tbsp light soy sauce
1 tbsp Shaohsing wine or dry sherry
1 tsp sesame oil

For the ginger sauce:

2 tsp grated ginger root
2 tbsp hot water

For the garnish:

2 tbsp chopped spring onions/ scallions
2 tbsp Crisp-Fried Onions (page 358)
Slices of cucumber, lettuce leaves

Chop the boiled chillies and fry them in the peanut oil for 1–2 minutes, then add the rest of the ingredients. Mix well, and keep this chilli sauce in a small bowl or ramekin. Mix the soy sauce with the wine or sherry and the sesame oil, and put this in another bowl. Mix the grated ginger and water, and keep the ginger sauce likewise in a small bowl.

Plain-boil the rice (page 98–100), or cook it in a rice cooker. If you have plenty of stock, you can boil the rice in stock instead of water.

At the same time, put 1.4 litres/2½ pints/6¼ cups of the broth into the saucepan with the chicken meat, bring to the boil and simmer for the same length of time as it takes the rice to cook. When the rice is ready, take the chicken out with a fork and slice the meat, fairly thinly, into strips about 2.5 cm/1 inch wide. As far as possible, cut diagonally across the grain of the meat, leaving the skin on one edge of each slice.

Arrange lettuce leaves and cucumber slices on 4 or 6 dinner plates and distribute the slices of chicken among the plates, laying them on top of the lettuce and cucumber. Adjust the seasoning of the broth and serve in individual soup bowls, garnished with chopped spring onions/scallions and Crisp-Fried Onions. The rice should be served to each person in another individual bowl, and the three sauces placed where everyone can help themselves. I personally would put a little ginger sauce into the broth, some chilli sauce with my rice, and the soy sauce on the chicken.

This dish is best eaten with either chopsticks and a soup spoon, or a spoon and fork.

Qabili Pilaf

According to Helen Saberi, who gave me this recipe from her book about Afghan food, *Noshe Djan*, this is probably the best-known and most popular pilau in Afghanistan. You can make it with lamb or chicken, with or without raisins, but it must have carrots.

Preparation: 30 minutes + 2 hours soaking + 50 minutes to prepare and cook the meat
Cooking: 40–45 minutes

For 4–6 people

450 g/1 lb/2 cups long grain
  rice, preferably Basmati
3–4 tbsp olive oil or vegetable
  oil
1 large onion, grated or very
  finely chopped
700–800 g/about 1¾ lb
  lamb, or 1 chicken, cut
  into 8 or 10 pieces
850 ml/1½ pints/3¾ cups
  water, and some more later
2–3 large carrots, cut into
  matchsticks or coarsely
  grated
112 g/4 oz/⅔ cup raisins
  (optional)
2 tsp ground cumin
¼ tsp saffron (optional)
Salt and pepper

Rinse the rice in several changes of water. Then soak in cold water for at least 30 minutes or up to 2 hours.

Heat the oil in an ovenproof saucepan and fry the onion, stirring all the time, for 3 minutes. Add the lamb or chicken pieces, stir them around for 2–3 minutes, then add 850 ml/1½ pints/3¾ cups of water and some salt and pepper. Bring to the boil, then cover the pan and simmer for 35–40 minutes, until the meat is tender.

Transfer the stock into a measuring jug but leave the meat in the pan. You will need 700 ml/1¼ pints/ 3 cups of liquid to cook the rice, so you will have to add some water to the stock to make up this amount.

Spread the raisins (if used) and carrots on top of the meat in the saucepan, then sprinkle over this the cumin and saffron (if used). Drain the rice that has been soaking and put the rice on top of the carrots. Now pour in the 700 ml/1¼ pints/3 cups of stock plus water, and add some more salt and pepper. Cover the pan, bring the contents back to the boil and simmer for 15–20 minutes, until all the liquid has been absorbed by the rice.

Keep the lid very tightly on the pan, and continue cooking on the lowest possible heat for another 25–30 minutes. Alternatively, put the saucepan into a pre-heated oven at 150°C/300°F/Gas Mark 2 for 30–40 minutes. (It can safely stay in the oven for longer, if you are not ready for it and want to keep it hot.)

To serve this dish Afghan-style, transfer the rice, carrots and raisins to a bowl, and the meat to a well-warmed serving platter. Mix the rice, carrots and raisins and heap them on top of the meat, so that the meat is hidden by them. Alternatively, serve the meat on one dish, put the rice separately into a bowl, and arrange the carrots and raisins as a garnish on top of the rice. If you consider both these methods to be unnecessarily fiddly, just stir the whole lot well together in the saucepan and pile it all on the serving platter. It will still look and smell very appetizing.

Old Japanese saké barrels

Savoury Rice with Crisp-Fried Chicken
Nasi kebuli

This Indonesian rice and chicken dish must have been a Middle Eastern pilaf in its previous incarnation. Some Indonesians may tell you that dishes of this sort can be made with lamb or goat's meat, and that is certainly true of the Qabili Pilaf on page 242; but not of this. It was a favourite family dish when I was very small, and for my sisters and me the great attraction was, precisely, the crisp-fried chicken.

Preparation: 1 hour soaking the rice + 15 minutes
Cooking: 1¼ hours

For 4–6 people

450 g/1 lb/2 cups long grain
   rice, soaked in cold water
   for 1 hour, then washed
   and drained
450 ml/16 fl oz/2 cups
   vegetable oil

For the stock:

1.5–1.7 kg/3¼–4 lb roasting
   chicken, cut into 8 or 10
   pieces
4 shallots or 1 onion,
   chopped
2 tsp ground coriander
1 tsp ground cumin
A pinch of ground galingale
   (optional)
5-cm/2-inch piece of fresh
   lemon grass
A small stick of cinnamon
A pinch of grated nutmeg
2 cloves
1½ tsp salt
1.4 litres/2½ pints/6¼ cups
   cold water

For the garnish:

1 tbsp Crisp-Fried Onions
   (page 358)
A few leaves of fresh parsley
2 tsp chopped fresh chives
Sliced cucumber

Put the chicken and all the ingredients for the stock into a saucepan and pour in the cold water. Bring to the boil and cook until the chicken is tender, which will take about 30–45 minutes. Start preparing the next stage about 10 minutes before the chicken is ready.

Stir-fry the rice in a saucepan with 2 tablespoons of oil for 5 minutes. Then strain off the stock from the chicken and add it to the rice. You need 570 ml/ 1 pint/2½ cups of stock to cook the rice; if you find you are short of stock, add water to make up the quantity. Boil the rice in this until it has absorbed all the liquid – this takes only a few minutes. Then steam the rice for 10 minutes, or 'finish' it as described for plain cooked rice on page 99–100.

While the rice is cooking, deep-fry the chicken in the remaining oil. When everything is ready, serve on a single large dish: pile the rice up in the centre, surround it with the chicken portions, and garnish it with Crisp-Fried Onions, chives, parsley and cucumber.

Peruvian Duck with Rice

I have several interesting Peruvian recipes, given to me by a friend who used to live in Peru and who has also translated them for me. This is one of them, called in Spanish *arroz con pato*. I took to it at once because I love duck and I also love green chillies, of which the original recipe calls for no fewer than 15 – as many as my grandmother used to put in her West Sumatran green duck stew. There are differences, however, the main one being that my grandmother would not have dreamt of putting beer or lager into her food, nor would she have cooked the rice together with the duck.

For my version of this recipe, I have reduced the quantities of chilli and lager, and I use only the breast meat, not the entire bird. Duck breast fillets can be bought in packs of two in most supermarkets. The rice is cooked in the stew.

Preparation: 10 minutes
Cooking: 30–35 minutes + 5 minutes resting

For 4 people

2 large onions, chopped
4 large green chillies, de-seeded and chopped
1 green sweet/bell pepper, de-seeded and chopped
8 cloves garlic, chopped
1 tsp ground cumin
Salt
2 tbsp chopped coriander/cilantro leaves
1 tbsp olive oil or vegetable oil
4 duck breast fillets
390 g/14 oz/1¾ cups Basmati rice, washed and drained
420 ml/¾ pint/ just under 2 cups chicken stock
285 ml/½ pint/1¼ cups lager
112 g/4 oz/1 cup cooked green peas
1 red sweet/bell pepper, de-seeded and cut into triangles or diamonds

Heat the oil in a frying pan and put in the duck breast fillets, skin side down first. Leave to brown for 3 minutes. Turn over, and again leave to brown for 3 minutes. Transfer the duck breast fillets on to a chopping board, cut each fillet diagonally into 4 pieces, and put them into a casserole with a lid.

In the same frying pan, stir-fry all the chopped ingredients, except the coriander/cilantro, for 2 minutes. Then transfer these to the casserole. Add the cumin and coriander/cilantro leaves, some salt, and the chicken stock. Put the lid on the casserole and simmer for 15 minutes. Add the rice, stir, and pour in the lager. Stir again, and adjust the seasoning. Put the lid back on tightly, lower the heat, and simmer for 20 minutes.

Remove the casserole from the heat, and uncover just long enough to add the cooked peas and red peppers. Cover again, and leave to rest for 5–6 minutes. Bring the casserole to table and serve immediately, accompanied by more cooked vegetables.

Tea-Smoked Duck with Fried Rice

This is a Chinese recipe, adapted from Yan-Kit So's 'Smoked Duck, Sichuan Style' in her *Classic Chinese Cookbook*. She cooks the whole duck, but here I use only the duck breast fillets, which are easier to handle and which are conveniently packaged and sold in pairs in most supermarkets. It is still a dish that needs a little advance planning, but the taste and texture of the smoked duck more than repay the little extra trouble.

You can use a smoke box (page 247), or a large thick-bottomed saucepan with a tight-fitting lid, or a wok with a domed lid. Keep the kitchen well ventilated, as some smoke will inevitably escape. The advantage of a smoke box with spirit burners is of course that you can do the whole job out of doors.

You can make the Fried Rice while the duck is steaming; the recipe is on page 127. To go with it, any stir-fried vegetable is good.

Preparation: overnight in the fridge + 30 minutes
Cooking: about 80 minutes

For 4 or 6 people

4 or 6 duck breast portions, with skin
1½ tsp salt
170 g/6 oz/¾ cup plain/all-purpose flour
112 g/4 oz/⅔ cup brown sugar
4 tbsp black tea leaves
2.5-cm/1-inch piece of ginger root, peeled and thinly sliced
2 large spring onions/scallions, trimmed and washed, then cut into rounds
1 whole star anise
1 tsp Sichuan peppercorns

Rub the duck breast portions with the salt and keep them in the fridge overnight. Next day, rinse well and dry each fillet with kitchen paper. The duck is now ready for smoking. Whatever vessel you use, line the bottom part of it with a double layer of aluminium foil. On this, spread the tea leaves, flour and brown sugar. Put a wire rack over these and lay the duck pieces side by side on the rack.

Cover the vessel tightly and put it on a medium heat for 10 minutes; then open the pan, turn the pieces over, and continue smoking for another 10 minutes.

Transfer the duck pieces to a heatproof dish that will fit inside your steamer. Alternatively, you can steam them in a wok – see illustration on page 387. Mix the ginger, spring onion, star anise, Sichuan pepper, wine or sherry, soy sauce and sesame oil in a bowl, then pour this mixture over the duck, turning the pieces so that all sides are well coated with it. Then steam the duck pieces for 1 hour.

**2 tbsp Shaohsing wine or dry
sherry**
1 tbsp light soy sauce
1 tbsp sesame oil
**Peanut oil or corn oil for
deep-frying**

Remove the duck pieces from their cooking juices and dry them with kitchen paper, then leave them to get cold. (The juice, which is mostly fat, should be discarded.) Up to this point, everything can be prepared well in advance, though it is better to fry the rice shortly before it is to be served.

When the fried rice is ready and you are ready to serve the meal, deep-fry the duck breast portions in oil for 6–8 minutes or until the skins are quite crisp. Don't let the meat become too dry, however, as this will make it stringy and chewy. Serve immediately.

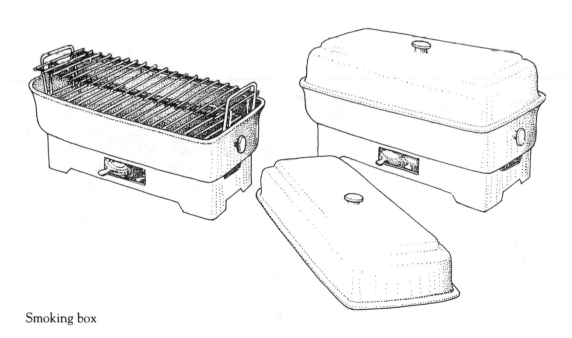

Smoking box

Larry Tubbs's Smoked Duck Stuffed with Rice

Larry Tubbs is a big rice grower near Mer Rouge, Louisiana. He loves to hunt duck, and to cook; we talked about rice, and ducks, and ways of cooking them, for more than an hour in his comfortable office, where pictures of ducks in flight cover the walls. He didn't give me this recipe in detail, but he described so vividly how he smoked and stuffed his ducks that I had no difficulty in making the dish myself when I came back to my own kitchen. The combination of spices and herbs can be varied to suit your own taste.

Larry will cook 16 or 20 duck breasts at one go. As I have to get mine from the supermarket, I limit myself to 8. The process of smoking and cooking is quite lengthy, but it is not difficult and the result is so unusual and delicious that it is well worth the trouble. You can use a smoke box (page 247) with wood smoking powder, if you already have this equipment, or you can smoke the meat with tea, sugar and flour in an ordinary saucepan with a tight-fitting lid, or in a wok with a domed lid.

Preparation: overnight marinating and prepare the stuffing; cook the rice; 1 hour (including smoking)
Cooking: 1 hour

For 8 people

8 duck breast fillets, with skin

For the marinade:

6 cloves garlic, chopped
2 or 4 small fresh or dried chillies
2 tsp chopped ginger root
1 tsp chopped thyme or lemon grass
½ tsp ground cinnamon
¼ tsp grated nutmeg
1 tsp salt
2 tbsp lemon juice
2 tbsp water
2 tbsp olive oil or peanut oil

Blend all the ingredients for the marinade until smooth. Transfer the mixture to a glass bowl, and marinate the duck breast fillets overnight in the refrigerator.

The stuffing also needs to be prepared several hours before smoking starts. Fry the shallots and garlic until soft. Add the ground ingredients and salt. Stir these well together over a low heat for 1 minute. Leave them to cool, then transfer them to a bowl and stir in the minced pork, liver and rice. Add the chopped parsley (or coriander/cilantro leaves) and mix well in. Refrigerate.

When you are ready to smoke the duck, divide the stuffing into 4 portions and put each portion between 2 duck breast fillets, with the skin on the outside. Tie the 2 fillets and the filling with string in 3 places to hold the package together. Then wrap each of your 4 packages in muslin or banana leaves, making them as compact as possible. Tie the ends of the muslin with string, or pin the banana leaves with cocktail sticks.

For the stuffing:

225 g/8 oz/1 cup lean pork, minced
2 duck livers, minced
112 g/4 oz/1 cup soft cooked rice
2 tbsp olive oil or peanut oil
3 shallots, chopped
2 cloves garlic, chopped
1 tsp ground coriander
1 tsp ground cumin
½ tsp cayenne pepper
2 tbsp chopped parsley or coriander/cilantro leaves
Salt

For the smoke (if not using a smoker with smoking powder):

3 tbsp tea leaves (Lapsang Souchong, Earl Grey, or Darjeeling)
3 tbsp plain/all-purpose flour or rice flour
3 tbsp brown sugar

Line a thick-bottomed saucepan or a wok with a double layer of aluminium foil. On this, spread the tea leaves, flour and brown sugar. Put a wire rack over this and lay the packages of stuffed duck on the rack. Don't pack them too closely together – smoke must be able to circulate all round each package. Cover the pan or wok tightly and put it on a medium heat for 35–45 minutes. Open the pan and turn the packages over once during this time. Some smoke will escape throughout the process, and more when you open the pan, so keep the kitchen well ventilated.

Turn the heat off but leave the pan or wok covered for a further 15–20 minutes. Then unwrap the duck, but leave the breast fillets and stuffing tied together. Roast in a preheated oven at 160°C/320°F/Gas Mark 3 for 50–60 minutes.

Leave the duck to cool for 5 minutes before you untie the pieces and cut the meat and stuffing into thick slices. Serve with plenty of salad and a piquant dressing.

Laser-controlled land levelling

Roast Duck Stuffed with Rice, Pistachios and Raisins
Ordek dolmasi

All over the East there is an infinite variety of ways of stuffing a duck with rice. The Chinese and Laotians like to use glutinous rice, but on the other side of Asia the Turks prefer Basmati or at any rate a long-grain variety. This recipe is adapted from one in Ayla Algar's book, *Classical Turkish Cooking*, with her permission.

If you allow half a duck per person, you will not need to serve anything more as a main course except some salad.

Preparation: 2–4 hours soaking + 35–40 minutes
Cooking: 1¼–1½ hours cooking

For 4 people, or 8 as part of a buffet

2 ducks, about 1.5–1.8 kg/ 3½–4 lbs each, prepared ready for roasting

For the stuffing:

340 g/12 oz/1½ cups long grain rice, preferably Basmati, soaked in cold water for 2–4 hours, then drained
3–4 tbsp melted unsalted butter
2 large onions, finely chopped
1 tsp salt
56 g/2 oz/⅓ cup raisins
4 tbsp chopped fresh mint
½ tsp ground allspice
½ tsp ground cloves
½ tsp ground cinnamon
½ tsp freshly ground black pepper

Heat the butter in a saucepan and fry the onions for 3–4 minutes, stirring all the time. Add the rice and continue stirring until all the grains are coated with the butter. Then add all the other ingredients, except the stock and the pistachios. Continue stirring for 2 more minutes; then add the stock.

Stir once more, cover the pan, and simmer for 15 minutes. Then remove the pan from the heat but leave it covered for another 15 minutes. Then uncover and mix in the chopped pistachios. Adjust the seasoning, and leave the rice stuffing to get really cold.

As you prepare to cook the ducks, preheat the oven to 240°C/475°F/ Gas Mark 9. Divide the cold rice stuffing equally between the ducks, stuff them and sew the flaps shut or close them with wooden cocktail sticks. Rub the ducks with salt and pepper and put them on a rack in the roasting tray, then into the oven. After 40 minutes, turn the temperature down to 180°C/350°F/Gas Mark 4. Leave the ducks to roast for another 35–50 minutes, making 1¼–1½ hours altogether.

When you take the ducks out of the oven, put them on a large serving platter and let them rest there for 5 minutes. Then cut each duck lengthways into halves, and serve immediately.

450 ml/16 fl oz/2 cups duck
   or chicken stock
84 g/3 oz/⅔ cup shelled
   pistachio nuts, boiled for 2
   minutes, then skinned and
   coarsely chopped
Salt and pepper

Duck with Exotic Stuffing

As I have already suggested in the introduction to the Poultry section, this recipe works just as well with turkey. For a bird weighing up to 4.5 or 5.5 kilograms/10 or 12 pounds, you will need double quantities of all the ingredients shown below, and you will need another stuffing for the neck cavity; chestnut, or the traditional sage and onion. But the quantities given here will be ample to stuff 4–6 turkey drumsticks or thighs. You will need to bone them first, and when they are stuffed tie them well with string. Then steam them, as described below for the duck, before you roast them. If you are doing a whole turkey, you obviously cannot steam it first; therefore, steam the stuffing by itself in a bowl for 10–15 minutes before putting it into the turkey.

Preparation: 35–40 minutes
Cooking: 2–2¼ hours

For 4–6 people

2 kg/4½ lb oven-ready
   Aylesbury duck, rubbed
   inside and out with 1 tsp
   salt

For the stuffing:

2–3 red chillies, de-seeded
4 shallots, peeled
2 cloves garlic
5 tbsp chopped creamed
   coconut, diluted in 6 tbsp
   hot water

The duck liver, chopped
   (optional)
112 g/4 oz/1 cup fresh
   shiitake mushrooms,
   thinly sliced
112 g/4 oz/½ cup pork
   tenderloin, minced
2 tbsp chopped coriander/
   cilantro leaves

2 tbsp finely chopped
   spring onions/scallions
1 tbsp fish sauce
½ tsp salt
¾ tsp ground white
   pepper
4 tbsp glutinous rice,
   washed and drained

Blend the chillies, shallots, garlic and coconut milk together until smooth. Mix with the other stuffing ingredients in a bowl, and fry a small ball of this stuffing to taste the seasoning. Add more salt if necessary. Then stuff the mixture into the body cavity of the duck, and sew up the skin or pin it with wooden cocktail sticks.

Place the duck on a plate or bowl, and steam for 80–90 minutes, adding some water about halfway through. When the duck is steamed, transfer it to a flat ovenproof dish. Everything up to this point can be done well in advance.

When you are ready to serve the duck, place it in a preheated oven at 200°C/400°F/Gas Mark 6 for 30 minutes. Finish it under the grill for 5 minutes to brown it well. Put the cooking juices in a small pan and leave them for a few minutes so that the oil separates and comes to the top. Discard the oil and heat the remaining juices to be used as a pouring sauce. The duck can be eaten hot, warm, or cold.

Pigeons with Three Herbs on a Bed of Rice

This recipe is taken from Geraldene Holt's *Recipes from a French Herb Garden*. Her version uses brown rice; I cooked the same dish with what was for me a novelty, red rice from the Camargue. There is more about this red rice on pages 6 and 184.

Preparation: 10–15 minutes
Cooking: 1½–2 hours

For 2 or 3 people

2 plump oven-ready wood
   pigeons
3 sprigs each of thyme,
   rosemary and marjoram
56 g/2 oz butter
1 thick slice of smoked
   streaky bacon
1 shallot, finely chopped
Salt
Freshly milled pepper
225 g/8 oz/1 cup red
   Camarguais rice
570 ml/1 pint/2½ cups game
   or chicken stock, or water

Make sure the pigeons are clean and have no down or feathers on them. Tuck a sprig of each herb into the body cavity of each bird.

Melt the butter in a cast-iron casserole and cook the bacon and shallot for 2 minutes. Add the pigeons, and turn them over in the butter until they are browned all over. Transfer them to a plate and season with salt and pepper.

Stir the rice into the butter in the casserole, pour in the stock, and bring to the boil. Place the pigeons on top of the rice and tuck the remaining herbs around them.

Cover the casserole and cook in a moderate oven (160°C/320°F/Gas Mark 3) for 1½–2 hours until the pigeons are tender and the rice has absorbed all the liquid and is cooked.

Quails Cooked in Wine with Red Rice

This red rice is grown in the Camargue, in southern France, and it is exported in small quantities at least as far as Germany and London. It has a nice nutty flavour, rather reminiscent of the 'pecan rice' that I bought in New Orleans. You could certainly use pecan rice for this quail recipe.

Like brown rice, red rice needs to be cooked with twice its own volume of liquid, so the wine is eked out with stock or water.

Preparation: 20 minutes
Cooking: 60–70 minutes

For 4 people

4 quails, cleaned and dressed
   ready to cook
1 tsp salt
1 tbsp lemon juice
4 tbsp olive oil
6 shallots, finely sliced
2 cloves garlic
170 g/6 oz/1½ cups button
   mushrooms, thinly sliced
1 tsp chopped oregano or
   marjoram
1 tsp fennel seeds
1 tsp paprika
340 g/12 oz/1½ cups rice:
   red Camarguais, pecan, or
   brown
225 ml/8 fl oz/1 cup dry
   white wine
340 ml/12 fl oz/1½ cups
   chicken stock or hot water
Salt and freshly milled pepper

Clean inside the quails by wiping them with kitchen paper, then rub them inside and outside with salt and lemon juice. Set the quails aside while you prepare the other ingredients.

Preheat the oven to 160°C/320°F/Gas Mark 3. Heat the oil in a casserole with a lid, and brown the quails for 2–3 minutes. Add the shallots, garlic, mushrooms and fennel seeds. Stir them around while, at the same time, turning the quails around. Add the oregano or marjoram, paprika, wine, and some salt and pepper. Stir, and cover the casserole. Simmer for 5 minutes.

Uncover, and add the rice, stirring everything round in the casserole while you heat the stock in another saucepan. When the stock is hot, pour it (or hot water, if you are not using stock) into the casserole. Bring it to the boil. Adjust the seasoning and cover the casserole. Put it in the preheated oven and leave it there for 1–1¼ hours. Serve piping hot, with lots of salad.

Rice with Meat

In the introductory part of this book you will have read about how eating habits are changing: prosperous Asians want to eat less rice and more meat and bread, so they can be more like Americans, while Westerners want to eat less cholesterol and more fibre. There is something good in both these trends. To see the Far East more comfortably off, and the West leaner and fitter, must be encouraging. Even the news that there are now 3 million vegetarians in Britain is, in a way, pleasing, though perhaps this is not the right place to quote it.

With meat, of course, we come to people's strongest likes and dislikes, not to mention prescription and taboo. The goat curry on page 260 may not appeal to everyone, but in London I always make it with lamb anyway. Some north Europeans seem not to like lamb; I think we would all agree that it needs strong, assertive flavours to go with it, like garlic or mint or – there are plenty of others in the pages that follow.

We start with lamb, go on to beef, and finish with pork. Not surprisingly, perhaps, there is a Middle Eastern flavour in the lamb dishes, stretching from Greece all the way to northern India. With beef, we move abruptly to the Far East, and then to the Americas. Rogan Josh, from India, is usually made with lamb, but this is my beef version. The two South-East Asian recipes were originally for buffalo meat, which explains why they take so long to cook – an old buffalo that has spent its life ploughing rice fields is tough. Of course, beef cooked in this way is beautifully succulent and tender.

Perhaps the most striking recipe in this section is the sixteenth-century Italian *minestra di riso con diverse carni* on page 278; I assure you that this is not put in as a historical curiosity, it really is delicious. The pork dishes are relatively few, but come from many parts of the world. Everyone eats pork, unless their religion specifically forbids them to.

People with small appetites may find the quantities given in these recipes rather generous. This is partly a matter of upbringing – in Asia, at least for guests, there must always be abundance of food – and partly of temperament. But I think you should keep to the quantities shown. A lot of these dishes are fairly time-consuming to make, and they will all, as leftovers, keep quite happily in the fridge for at least 24 hours. Many of them actually improve with keeping, as the sauces and spices sink deeper into the texture of the meat. So, after a hard day's work for a dinner party, I count on at least a day, often two days, free of cooking as we eat up the remains.

Rice and Lamb Casserole with Potatoes

This simple family supper dish can be cooked from raw meat, such as lamb or goat, or made with leftover roast lamb. You can serve it with gravy, or a spicy sauce such as Mild Curry Sauce (page 355) or Piri-Piri Sauce (page 351), or with any sweet fruit chutney.

Preparation: 15 minutes
Cooking: 30–40 minutes

For 4–6 people

3 tbsp olive or peanut oil
450 g/1 lb/2 cups lamb, raw
  or roasted, sliced or diced
1 onion, finely chopped
2 cloves garlic, finely
  chopped
225 g/8 oz/1⅓ cups fresh or
  canned tomatoes, skinned
  and chopped
340 g/12 oz/3 cups small new
  potatoes, boiled then cut in
  halves
450 g/1 lb/2 cups medium or
  long grain rice, washed and
  drained
700 ml/1¼ pints/3 cups lamb
  stock
Salt and pepper to taste

Preheat the oven to 180°C/350°F/Gas Mark 4. Heat the oil in a saucepan and stir-fry the meat for 3 minutes. Add the onion and garlic, stir once and cover the pan. Leave to cook on a low heat for 4 minutes. Uncover the pan and put in the tomatoes. Season with salt and pepper, and continue to simmer, covered, for 15 minutes.

At the same time, in another saucepan, bring the stock to the boil and when it is boiling add the rice. Stir once, and add salt and pepper if the stock is not already seasoned. Cook the rice on a medium heat, uncovered, for 15 minutes. Then add the halved potatoes and stir them in with the rice. Cover the pan, lower the heat, and leave to cook for 10 minutes more.

Now transfer the rice and potatoes into a well-buttered casserole. Adjust the seasoning of the lamb-and-tomato mixture and pour this on top of the rice and potatoes. Cover the casserole with a lid or with aluminium foil, and put it in the preheated oven for 10–15 minutes. Serve hot, accompanied by any green salad.

Baked Lamb Cutlets with Rice and Courgettes/Zucchini

This is one of many East-meets-West one-dish meals that are good for a family dinner or as part of a large buffet. In many countries, of course, goats are more commonly kept than sheep, so throughout this book you should read 'goat' for 'lamb' when appropriate. And in this recipe, you can use goat's milk instead of milk from cows or coconuts.

If you are serving this as a one-dish meal, or a main course more or less complete in itself, you should allow 2 cutlets per person; as part of a buffet, 1 per person will be enough. You need a large baking dish that can accommodate all the cutlets in one layer.

Preparation: 30–35 minutes
Cooking: 80–90 minutes

For 6 or 12 people

12 lamb cutlets from the best
  end of the neck, trimmed
  of excess fat and seasoned
  with salt and pepper
560 g/1¼ lb/2½ cups
  Basmati or other long grain
  rice, washed and drained
2 tbsp olive oil or peanut oil
2 large onions, chopped
2 tsp grated ginger root
¼ tsp chilli powder
450 g/1 lb/4 cups courgettes/
  zucchini, sliced into thin
  rounds
4 tbsp plain/all-purpose flour
  or rice flour
5 eggs
1.1 litres/2 pints/5 cups
  milk: cow's, goat's, or
  coconut
Salt and pepper to taste

Boil the rice in slightly salted water, keeping it at a rolling boil for 8 minutes. Drain. Turn the oven on to 190°C/375°F/Gas Mark 5.

Fry the onions in the oil until soft, then add the ginger, chilli powder and courgettes/zucchini. Stir-fry for 2 minutes, then set aside to cool.

Put the flour in a bowl and break all the eggs into it. Whisk the flour and eggs well together, then add the milk a little at a time, continuing to whisk until you have a smooth batter. Season the batter with salt and pepper and leave it to stand for 30 minutes.

Butter or oil the baking dish. Spread the rice on the bottom, then the onion and courgettes/zucchini mixture on top of it. Arrange the cutlets on top of this, and pour the batter over all. Bake for 20 minutes, then lower the heat to 160°C/320°F/Gas Mark 3 and continue cooking for a further 1 hour. Serve immediately.

Rice with Lamb, Couscous Style

I love Moroccan couscous, but I find that the grain is much harder to handle than rice. So here is a well-known pumpkin couscous adapted for use with rice. If you use shoulder of lamb, ask your butcher to cut it into chunks.

You can cook this in a couscoussière, but two ordinary saucepans will do the job very well. This recipe specifies chickpeas/garbanzos, but if they are not available you can substitute fresh broad beans for them, or any other locally grown beans, or indeed any dried beans, for example, borlotti or pinto beans.

Preparation: 30–60 minutes soaking the rice + 1 hour
Cooking: 45–50 minutes

For 4–6 people as a
one-dish meal, or 8–10 as
part of a buffet party meal

450 g/1 lb/2 cups white or
  brown Basmati, soaked in
  cold water for 30–60
  minutes, washed and
  drained
84–112 g/3–4 oz/½ cup
  dried chickpeas/garbanzos
  (or substitutes: see above),
  soaked overnight
2 tbsp olive oil
1 kg/2 lb 3 oz lamb on the
  bone, preferably neck or
  shoulder, cut into chunky
  pieces
1.7 litres/3 pints/7½ cups
  water, and more later
4 medium-sized onions,
  chopped
1 tsp chopped ginger root
4 carrots, peeled and each
  one cut into 4 or 5 pieces

Cook the chickpeas/garbanzos or beans in plenty of water for 1 hour. Add some salt just 5 minutes before the hour is up. At the end of the hour, drain the beans and keep them aside. If you use chickpeas/garbanzos, skin them by putting them in cold water and rubbing them gently between your fingers. The skins will rub off and float to the surface. You will need to repeat the process 2 or 3 times to get rid of the skins altogether.

Put the chunky pieces of lamb into a large saucepan or the bottom part of your couscoussière. Add 2 tablespoons of olive oil and heat the pan, keeping the lid on, for 2 or 3 minutes. Uncover, and stir the meat so the pieces are browned all over. Then add the onion, ginger, turmeric, Harissa, paprika and some salt. Stir the mixture once or twice, and pour the water over it. Bring this to the boil, cover the pan again and simmer for 40 minutes.

Uncover the pan, and skim off the froth that has come to the surface. Using a ladle and a measuring jug, transfer 700 ml/1¼ pints/3 cups of this stock to another pan. Replace the liquid by putting enough hot water into the first pan to just cover the meat.

Bring the stock in the second pan to the boil, and put in the rice. Stir, bring the stock back to the boil, cover the pan and simmer for 15 minutes. Then take the pan off the heat but keep it tightly covered.

225–285 g/8–10 oz/
  2–2½ cups turnips, peeled
  and cut into largish cubes
450 g/1 lb/4 cups pumpkin,
  peeled and cut into largish
  cubes
1 tsp turmeric
4 tomatoes, skinned and
  chopped
½ tsp Harissa (page 350)
1 tsp paprika
Salt to taste

Meanwhile, transfer the pieces of meat from the first pan to a chopping board, and separate the meat from the bones. Discard the bones, and cut the meat into smaller pieces. Put these back in the pan, and add the chickpeas/garbanzos or beans, carrots, turnip, pumpkin and tomatoes. Cover the pan and simmer for 10 minutes. Adjust the seasoning. If you are using a couscoussière, you can now put the rice in the top basket and continue cooking for 5–8 minutes more. This will heat the rice through again, but it is not essential, since the rice is already completely cooked.

Transfer the rice to a serving platter. Pour over it 2 ladlefuls of the hot cooking liquid from the meat and vegetables. Keep aside the remainder of the cooking liquid in a bowl and serve it as a sauce. Arrange the meat and vegetables on top of the rice. Serve, with a small bowl of Harissa so that people at the table can help themselves.

House with rice storage bin: Burma

A Sumatran Goat Curry

All Oriental meat dishes are intended to be served with rice, usually plain cooked rice. This one (which in Indonesia is called *gulai bagar*) is no exception. My West Sumatran grandmother used to make it with a whole young goat, cut up into large joints. The meat was then sliced from the joints and put back into the sauce to keep hot until the meal was ready to serve. Indonesians do not like their meat rare, and any kind of curry needs lots of time to allow the meat to absorb the spices it is cooked in.

Preparation: 50–60 minutes
Cooking: 1–1½ hours

For 6–8 people

1 leg or shoulder of goat or
  lamb, cut with the bone
  into 4 or 5 pieces
28 g/1 oz/⅓ cup, firmly
  packed freshly grated
  coconut or desiccated
  coconut
2 tsp coriander seeds
5 candle nuts or blanched
  almonds
8 shallots or 2 large onions,
  thinly sliced
4 cloves garlic, thinly sliced
5 red chillies, de-seeded and
  sliced
4 cloves
A pinch of grated nutmeg
2 tsp chopped ginger
1 tsp turmeric
1 stick cinnamon
4 cardamoms
½ tsp ground cumin
1 tbsp chopped lemon
  grass

In a wok or frying pan, roast the 28 g/1 oz fresh or desiccated coconut until golden brown (this takes only a few minutes). Then roast the coriander seed in the same way, stirring continuously, for 2–3 minutes. Blend these roasted ingredients with the candle nuts or almonds, or pound them together in a mortar.

Heat the oil in a large saucepan and stir-fry the shallots or onions, garlic and chillies for 2 minutes. Add the meat and cover the pan for 2–3 minutes. Add the candle nut and coconut mixture, stir, cover the pan again and continue cooking for another 2–3 minutes. Add all the remaining ingredients *except* the tamarind water, salt, aubergines/eggplants and 285 ml/½ pint/1¼ cups of the coconut milk.

Simmer for 50 minutes. Add the rest of the coconut milk, the tamarind water and salt to taste. Go on cooking for 20–30 minutes or until the sauce is beginning to thicken. Add the aubergines/eggplants. Continue to simmer until these are cooked – this should not take longer than 5–6 minutes.

To serve the dish, take out the chunks of meat and slice or carve them as you please. Arrange the meat in an ovenproof casserole, and the aubergines/eggplants on top of the meat. Remove excess oil from the surface of the sauce with a ladle or by pouring it away. Discard all unwanted solids: cloves, cardamoms, cinnamon and leaves. Pour the sauce over the meat. Keep the

3 kaffir lime leaves or bay leaves

850 ml/1½ pints/3¾ cups coconut milk made from one fresh coconut or 340 g/12 oz/4 cups firmly packed desiccated coconut

Salt

2 tbsp tamarind water (page 381)

3 tbsp oil

2 aubergines/eggplants, each cut into 6 or 8 thick slices, or 8–10 small round aubergines/eggplants (illustration on page 362)

dish hot over a low flame or in a moderate oven until the moment comes to serve it; it should arrive at the table very hot.

Cooking rice or meat in green bamboo

Rice Casserole with Lamb

This is really a kind of mutated biryani, or more properly an Indonesian biryani, cooked in coconut milk instead of yogurt. In India, biryani is a party dish, meant for a big celebration with a good many people present. On such occasions it is served with a whole convoy of vegetable and meat dishes, the biryani being, as it were, the flagship of the feast. However, it makes a rich and satisfying meal on its own. Here, the Indonesian ingredients are listed, with the corresponding Indian ones shown as alternatives.

Preparation: 2–4 hours soaking + 35–45 minutes
Cooking: 40 minutes

For 6–8 people

For the rice:

675 g/1½ lb/3 cups Basmati, Texmati, or other long grain rice
2.3 litres/4 pints/10 cups water
1 tsp salt

For the meat:

1.5 kg/3 lb 4 oz/6¼ cups lamb: lean meat from the leg or shoulder, cut into cubes
570 ml/1 pint/2½ cups coconut milk, or 140 ml/ 5 fl oz/⅔ cup plain yogurt and 450 ml/16 fl oz/2 cups water
Salt to taste

For the paste:

2 red chillies, seeds removed, or 1 tsp chilli powder

Soak the rice in slightly salted cold water for at least 2 hours, preferably 4 hours or longer.

Put all the ingredients for the paste in a blender (except the saffron strands, if used) and blend them until smooth. In a saucepan, bring this paste to the boil and simmer for 4–5 minutes, stirring often. Add the meat cubes, stir, cover the pan and cook for 5 minutes. Uncover, add a little salt and the coconut milk or yogurt. Stir and go on cooking for 3–4 minutes; if you are using yogurt, stir continuously during this time, gradually adding 450 ml/16 fl oz/ 2 cups water. Then simmer for 30–35 minutes, stirring often. If you are using coconut milk, put it all in at once; you may need to simmer a little longer, so that the sauce becomes quite thick.

While the meat is cooking, heat the water for the rice in a large pan with 1 teaspoonful of salt. As soon as it boils, drain the rice and discard the water it was soaked in. Add the rice to the boiling water a little at a time, so that it continues at a rolling boil. Leave the rice to boil for 6 minutes, then drain.

When the meat is cooked, transfer it to a deep casserole. Pile the rice on top of the meat. (If you are using saffron strands, stir them into a bowl containing 3 tablespoonfuls of warm milk or water, and dribble this over the rice.) Cover the casserole very tightly,

3 shallots, sliced

4 cloves garlic, chopped

1 tsp chopped ginger root

4 candle nuts or macadamia
 nuts, or 6 blanched
 almonds

1 tbsp whole coriander seeds

1 tsp whole cumin seeds

¼ tsp grated nutmeg

½ tsp whole peppercorns

3 cloves

2 green cardamoms

2.5-cm/1-inch piece of
 cinnamon

1 tsp turmeric, or a large
 pinch of saffron strands

2 tbsp peanut oil or olive oil

3 tbsp coconut milk or water

For the garnish:

2 large onions, sliced

3 tbsp raisins or sultanas

3 tbsp slivered almonds

4 tbsp olive oil for frying

and put it into a preheated oven at 180°C/350°F/Gas Mark 4 for 35–40 minutes.

While the casserole is in the oven, prepare the garnish. Heat 4 tablespoonfuls of oil in a frying pan and fry the slivered almonds for 1–2 minutes, until they are slightly coloured. Take them out with a slotted spoon and drain on absorbent paper. In the same oil, fry the raisins or sultanas for 1–2 minutes, and take them out. Last, fry the sliced onions, stirring almost all the time, for 8–10 minutes so that they are brown and slightly caramelized.

When the rice and lamb are cooked, stir the raisins or sultanas and the onions into the rice and meat, and sprinkle the almonds on top. Serve immediately.

Moussaka with Rice

I have often enjoyed moussaka made in the classic way with potatoes and aubergines/ eggplants and topped with Mornay sauce and grated Gruyère or Parmesan cheese. It tastes delicious; but of course it is very rich, because the aubergines/eggplants and potatoes have been fried and the Mornay sauce has been made with lots of butter. This version, with rice, is intended as a light lunch or supper dish. You can make it in elegant individual dishes or in one big casserole for 4. Serve it hot, with a green salad.

Preparation: 40 minutes soaking + 1 hour
Cooking: 35–40 minutes

For 4 people

For the meat:

2 tbsp olive oil
4 shallots or 1 large onion,
    finely sliced
4 cloves garlic, finely sliced
225–340 g/8–12 oz/
    1–1½ cups cooked lamb
    (roasted or boiled), cut into
    small bite-sized slices
¼ tsp cayenne pepper
2 tbsp light soy sauce

For the rice:

112 g/4 oz/½ cup long grain
    rice, washed, soaked in
    cold water for 40 minutes,
    then drained
1.7 litres/3 pints/7½ cups
    water
½ tsp salt

For the aubergines/eggplants:

2 medium-size aubergines/
    eggplants, boiled whole in
    slightly salted water for 6
    minutes
4 tbsp chopped tomatoes

For the sauce:
1 tbsp ghee or clarified
    butter
1 tbsp plain/all-purpose
    flour
2–4 cloves garlic, crushed

1 tsp ground coriander
140 ml/5 fl oz/⅔ cup
    plain yogurt,
    preferably low fat
1 egg yolk
4 tbsp grated cheese
    (optional)

Heat the oil and stir-fry the shallots and garlic for 2 minutes. Add the meat slices and stir them about for 1 minute, then add the seasoning. Stir for another minute and divide the slices among 4 individual dishes or simply transfer them to a casserole.

In a large saucepan, bring the water to a rolling boil. Add the salt and the rice. Stir, and bring the water back to the boil. Cook the rice for 8 minutes and drain it in a large colander. When it is well drained, arrange the rice on top of the meat.

Slice the aubergines/eggplants and arrange them to cover the rice. Spread the chopped tomatoes over the aubergines/eggplants, and season with salt and pepper.

Preheat the oven to 180°C/350°F/Gas Mark 4. Heat the clarified butter. Put in the garlic and the flour, and stir vigorously with a wooden spoon. Add the ground coriander. Continue stirring while you add the yogurt, a spoonful at a time. If the sauce is still lumpy, beat it with an egg beater until it is smooth. Add the egg yolk and mix well. If you are using grated cheese, you can either mix the cheese into the sauce and spread the mixture over the aubergines/eggplants, or you can pour the sauce over the aubergines/eggplants and sprinkle the cheese on top.

Cover the casserole or individual dishes with lid(s) or foil and cook in the preheated oven for 35–40 minutes. Serve immediately.

Lamb Stuffed with Rice

Boned shoulder or leg of lamb will be quite suitable for this. For a better presentation, you may prefer best end of neck tied into a crown shape. Your butcher will prepare this for you, and it has the advantage of making a deep cavity for the rice stuffing. This stuffing is delicious, but there won't be enough rice in it for 6 hungry people; you can serve plain boiled potatoes as an accompaniment, or plain steamed or boiled rice, along with some cooked vegetables and Mild Curry Sauce (with mint, page 355). If you use a boned shoulder or a leg of lamb, roll the stuffing inside the meat and tie the meat with string.

Preparation: 45–50 minutes
Cooking: 60–70 minutes

For 6 people

1 shoulder, or leg, of lamb
  weighing about 2 kg/4½ lbs,
  boned; or double best end of
  neck, giving 12–14 cutlets,
  trimmed and tied in the
  shape of a crown

For the stuffing:

112 g/4 oz/½ cup Basmati or
  other long grain rice,
  washed and drained
3 tbsp olive oil or peanut oil
2 large onions, chopped
6 cloves garlic, chopped
1 tsp chopped ginger root
½ tsp chilli powder
2 tbsp ground almonds
  (optional)
2 tsp ground coriander
2 tbsp chopped dried apricots
  or raisins
2 tbsp chopped parsley or
  coriander/cilantro leaves
Salt and pepper to taste

Rub the meat with some salt and pepper. Cook the drained rice in plenty of slightly salted boiling water for 8 minutes. Drain and leave to cool.

Stir-fry the onions in a wok or frying pan for 5 minutes. Add the rest of the ingredients, except the rice and the parsley (or coriander/cilantro leaves). Continue stirring for 2–3 minutes. Then add the rice, and stir everything well together. Finally add the parsley or coriander/cilantro leaves, salt and pepper, and stir again for 2 minutes. Adjust the seasoning and set aside to cool.

When the stuffing is cold, put it into the cavity of the crown, or if you are using leg or shoulder roll the meat with the stuffing inside it and tie the meat with string in 3 places.

Roast the stuffed joint on a well-oiled baking tray in a preheated oven for 50–60 minutes at 180°C/350°F/ Gas Mark 4. Then let the meat rest for 10 minutes before carving. Serve hot, with the accompaniments and sauce suggested in the introduction above.

Rice with Lamb and Yogurt
Tah chin

An Iranian friend in Oxford, Soraya Tremaine, gave me this recipe. It can also be made with chicken, but kid – young goat's meat – is especially delicious. My choice would be the cutlets taken from the best end of neck of goat or lamb, or the whole leg of a lamb or kid. The leg needs to be scored deeply before it is marinated in yogurt, then roasted for 40–45 minutes in the oven at 180°C/350°F/Gas Mark 4, then sliced before the final cooking with the rice. With cutlets, the preparation is much simpler.

Preparation: overnight marinating
Cooking: about 1½ hours

For 4–6 people

For the marinade:

3 cloves garlic, finely chopped
A large pinch of saffron strands
2 shallots, finely chopped
½ tsp ground cinnamon
1 tsp salt
½ tsp cayenne or white pepper
225 ml/8 fl oz/1 cup plain yogurt
1 tsp sugar (optional)

Other ingredients:

12 cutlets, some of the fat discarded
450 g/1 lb/2 cups long grain rice, preferably Basmati, soaked in salted cold water for 4–8 hours, then rinsed and drained
84 ml/3 fl oz/⅓ cup olive oil

Using a pestle and mortar, crush the garlic, saffron and shallots to a yellowish paste. Transfer this to a glass bowl and mix in the remaining ingredients for the marinade. Marinate the cutlets overnight.

Cook the drained rice in salted boiling water for 6–8 minutes, keeping the water at a brisk rolling boil all the time. Drain in a colander, then briefly hold the rice under the cold tap and drain it again.

When you are ready to assemble and cook the tah chin, shake off the marinade from the cutlets and brown them in the olive oil for about 2 minutes on each side, turning them over once. Keep them aside.

Put the butter in a wide, shallow pan. In a bowl, mix about 230 g/8 oz of the cooked rice with the marinade. Heat the butter, and when the pan is hot spread this rice and marinade mixture over the bottom. Lower the heat, arrange the cutlets on top of the rice, and spread the remaining rice over them. Wrap the lid of the pan in a damp tea-towel/dishcloth and cover the pan with it. Continue cooking on this low heat for 20 minutes.

While it cooks, warm the milk in a small saucepan and dissolve in it the other large pinch of saffron by stirring vigorously with a wooden spoon. Pour the milk and saffron mixture over the rice, and remove the tea-towel/dishcloth, put the lid back on the pan and

56 g/2 oz butter
A large pinch of saffron
    strands
3 tbsp milk
Fried onion to garnish

put the pan into a preheated oven at 180°C/350°F/Gas Mark 4 for 45–60 minutes.

When the rice and lamb are cooked, take the pan from the oven and set it on a wet cloth or a tray of cold water. Leave it to rest for 5–8 minutes. To serve, arrange the rice and meat on a heated serving platter. The rice crust from the bottom of the pan, which is called *tah-deeg* in Persian, can be laid whole on top of the rice, or broken into large pieces and set around the edge of the dish. Scatter the fried onion garnish over everything.

Beef in Sesame Seeds, Chilli and Garlic

This is my version of the famous Korean beef dish, bulgogi. Bulgogi is always served with rice, either plain or as a Bibimbab (page 310). You can now buy, in many places, a special gadget for grilling the bulgogi, but I find it easier simply to fry the beef on a griddle with a very small amount of oil; that way, the meat is more juicy and succulent.

Preparation: 20 minutes + overnight marinating
Cooking: 5–8 minutes

For 4–6 people

675 g/1½ lb sirloin or rump
    steak, very thinly sliced
    across the grain
3–4 tbsp olive oil or peanut
    oil

For the marinade:
2 tbsp white or brown
    sesame seeds
2 shallots, chopped
3 cloves garlic
2–4 small dried red
    chillies
1–2 tsp finely chopped
    ginger root

1 tbsp mirin
¼ tsp salt
1 tbsp light soy sauce
2 tbsp olive oil or peanut
    oil
1 tsp sesame oil
    (optional)

Blend all the ingredients for the marinade until smooth. Pour the marinade into a glass bowl and mix the slices of beef well into it. Cover the bowl with clingfilm/plastic wrap and refrigerate overnight.

Heat the oil in the griddle and fry the beef in 2 batches for only 2 minutes each batch, turning the slices over once. Serve straight away accompanied by plain boiled rice and cooked vegetables, or by Bibimbab (page 310).

A Parcel of Sirloin Steak with Rice, etc.

This is another one-dish meal, just for 2. As soon as you discover how easy these parcels are to make, however, you can throw a party and make lots of them to impress your guests. The 'etc.' is another challenge. Design your own parcel filling – but I suggest you try mine first. It consists of shiitake mushrooms, black olives, peppers, and plenty of shallots and garlic.

For best results, last-minute cooking is necessary, with no reheating. The preparation, of course, can be done in advance. You need two sheets of greaseproof paper or aluminium foil, each 25 × 38 cm/10 × 15 inches. Fold each sheet in half across its width and cut the folded sheet into a half-circle, so that it makes a full circle, or oval, when you open it again. Brush one side with butter or oil, and keep aside till you are ready to make up your parcels.

Preparation: 2–4 hours marinading (or overnight) + 25–30 minutes
Cooking: 5–8 minutes

For 2 people

2 sirloin steaks, weighing about 140–170 g/5–6 oz each
112–170 g/4–6 oz/½ – ⅔ cup Thai Fragrant or Basmati rice, washed and drained

For the marinade:

1 tbsp light soy sauce
1 tbsp mirin or dry sherry (optional)
1 clove garlic, crushed
1 tsp ginger juice
A large pinch of chilli powder

Other ingredients:

3 tbsp olive oil or peanut oil
4 shallots, finely sliced

Mix all the ingredients for the marinade in a bowl and rub the mixture well into the steaks. Leave these in a cool place for 2–4 hours, or overnight in the fridge.

Cook the rice in slightly salted water at a rolling boil for 6–8 minutes. Drain and leave to cool.

When you are ready to finish cooking the parcels, turn on the oven to 190°C/375°F/Gas Mark 5. Heat the oil in a frying pan and brown both sides of the steaks very quickly in the hot oil. Put the steaks on a plate. In the same oil, fry the shallots and garlic, stirring continuously, for 2–3 minutes. Add the diced peppers, olives and mushrooms, together with the remains of the marinade. Stir-fry for 2 more minutes, and season with salt and pepper.

Lay the circular sheets of paper flat on the table, oiled side up, and place half the rice on one half of each sheet. Put the steak on top of the rice. Divide the pepper-and-mushroom mixture equally and put it on top of the steaks. Sprinkle the parsley or coriander/cilantro leaves on top of everything. Fold the paper over and seal the parcels by folding the edges of the paper tightly together.

2 cloves garlic, finely sliced

1 green or red sweet/bell
pepper, de-seeded, then
blanched and diced

10–12 black olives, pitted
and chopped

56 g/2 oz/½ cup fresh
shiitake mushrooms, stalks
removed, sliced

2 tbsp chopped flat-leaf
parsley or coriander/
cilantro leaves

Salt and pepper

Put the parcels on a baking tray and bake in the oven for 5–8 minutes. Serve immediately, with the parcels still done up; one of the pleasures of this dish is to open your parcel and smell the wonderfully aromatic vapour that ascends from it.

If you don't want to eat off paper or foil, carefully tear off part of the wrapping and with a large fork ease the contents of the parcel on to the plate, pulling the remains of the wrapping away. You may prefer to do this in the kitchen, so you have a chance to tidy up the presentation on each plate.

Rendang

This classic dish from West Sumatra may be said to represent Indonesian cooking at its best and most original. The recipe appears in all my books and I make no apology for including it here. Rendang is invariably eaten with rice, which is the perfect complement to the richness and succulence of the meat; either Thai Fragrant or other long grain rice, or steamed glutinous rice.

In Western countries, rendang is sometimes described, quite wrongly, as a curry. Although the name is sometimes applied in Malaysia to curried meat dishes, an authentic rendang is nothing like a curry, as you will see. When it is cooked, the meat should be dark brown, almost black, chunky and dry, with the dryness of meat that has absorbed the medium it was cooked in over a period of several hours.

Vegetarians can make excellent rendang, as people in Sumatra often do, with jackfruit instead of meat. By ending cooking while there is still some sauce left in the pan, you have a traditional variant called *kalio*.

Another good scheme is to add red kidney beans in the last hour of cooking. This is what we used to do to eke out the meat when times were hard, but it tastes extremely good. If you use dried red kidney beans, soak them overnight first, then boil them in plenty of water for 30–45 minutes before draining them and adding them to the rendang about an hour before you expect it to be ready. (The precise timing of this gets easier with experience; you want the beans to be tender inside and crunchy outside. If they are fried too long in the rendang oil, they become hard and chewy.)

At home, I would use more chilli, and all the spices would of course be fresh.

Preparation: 25–30 minutes
Cooking: 3 hours

For 6–8 people

1.35 kg/3 lb/6 cups buffalo
    meat or beef: preferably
    brisket, otherwise topside
    or silverside, cut into cubes
    about 2-cm/¾-inch square
6 shallots
4 cloves garlic
3-cm/1¼-inch piece of ginger
    root, peeled
1 tsp turmeric powder
6 red chillies, de-seeded, or 3
    tsp chilli powder
½ tsp galingale powder
2.3 litres/4 pints/10 cups
    coconut milk
1 bay leaf
1 fresh turmeric leaf
    (optional)
2 tsp salt

Peel and slice the shallots finely, and roughly chop the chillies and ginger. Put them in a blender with 4 tablespoons of the coconut milk, and blend until smooth. Put all these ingredients, with the coconut milk, into a large wok or saucepan. (It is generally more convenient to start in a pan, and transfer to a wok later.) Put the meat into the pan also, making sure that there is enough coconut milk to cover it.

Stir the contents of the pan, and start cooking, on a medium heat, uncovered. Let the pan bubble gently for 1½ hours, stirring from time to time. The coconut milk will by then be quite thick, and of course much reduced.

If you started in a large saucepan, transfer everything to a wok and continue cooking in the same way for another 30 minutes, stirring occasionally. By now the coconut milk is beginning to reduce to oil, and the meat, which has so far been boiling, will soon be frying. From now on, the rendang needs to be stirred frequently. Taste, and add salt if necessary. When the coconut oil becomes thick and brown, stir continuously for about 15 minutes, until the oil has been more or less completely absorbed by the meat. Serve hot with lots of rice.

Picadillo

This is a well-known Mexican dish, and very easy to cook. It is a special favourite of mine, partly because it was the very first 'foreign' food I experimented with when I was newly married in Java; an American friend gave me the recipe. If it had turned out badly, who knows what would have become of my career as a cook? In fact it was so good that in thirty years I have only added two of my own ingredients: ginger, and chopped hard-boiled eggs as a garnish. A true picadillo, as described by Elisabeth Lambert Ortiz in *The Complete Book of Mexican Cooking*, is garnished with fried almonds and uses chopped apples instead of gherkins, and of course has no ginger – but I like ginger.

Preparation: 30 minutes
Cooking: 25–30 minutes

For 4–6 people

_____

450 g/1 lb/2 cups long grain
  rice, washed and drained
3 tbsp olive oil
4 shallots or 1 large onion,
  chopped
3 cloves garlic, chopped
1 tsp finely chopped ginger
  root or oregano (optional)
2 or 3 green chillies or
  jalapeño chillies, seeds
  removed, finely chopped
450 g/1 lb/2 cups lean beef,
  minced
1 green sweet/bell pepper,
  de-seeded and cut into
  small cubes
450 g/1 lb ripe tomatoes,
  skinned, de-seeded and
  chopped; or a 390 g/14 oz
  can of chopped tomatoes
Salt and pepper to taste
56 g/2 oz/⅓ cup raisins
56 g/2 oz/½ cup black or
  green olives, pitted and
  halved, or pimiento-stuffed
  olives, halved
2 tbsp chopped gherkins
2 hard-boiled eggs, chopped
  (optional)
2 tbsp chopped parsley

Cook the rice by any of the methods described on pages 98–100. Time it so that it is ready at about the same time as the minced-meat mixture.

Heat the oil in a wok or large saucepan. Fry the shallots (or onion), garlic, ginger (if used) and chillies, stirring all the time, for 3 minutes. Add the minced beef, and stir and turn it well for 3–4 minutes to mix it with the other ingredients as it cooks. Add the sweet/bell pepper and tomatoes. Stir again, and simmer for 15 minutes, stirring occasionally.

Adjust the seasoning and add the rest of the ingredients, except the chopped eggs and parsley. Stir everything together and continue to simmer for 2 more minutes.

The best way to present the picadillo is to mix about one-third of the meat mixture with the hot rice in a large bowl. Then transfer this to a serving platter. Pile the rest of the meat on top, and garnish with the chopped eggs and parsley. Serve hot, for lunch or supper, with a green salad.

Hamburger Steak with Rice

A homemade hamburger is something special, not just for the family but guests as well. Quite apart from flavour, it has a special appeal for anyone who is not especially fond, or perhaps capable, of chewing their way through a great hunk of steak.

I find the best cut of beef for hamburgers is rump steak, minced at home with a small mincing machine or a sharp knife or cleaver. A food processor may save time, but you still need to chop the meat to the right texture with a knife. However, if you prefer to buy the beef ready-minced, choose the leanest you can find.

Rice is used in this recipe to give bulk. If you also use rice to stuff the hamburger, it will absorb the juices from the meat, which are delicious. So this dish makes a good lunch or supper, accompanied only by steamed vegetables or a green salad.

Don't forget to fry the onions or shallots first. Even if the hamburger itself is very lightly done, the cooked onions will give it a sweetness and aroma it otherwise wouldn't have had.

Preparation: 40 minutes
Cooking: 6–8 minutes *or* 18–20 minutes

For 4 people

112 g/4 oz/½ cup rice, glutinous or Thai Fragrant, soaked in cold water for 1 hour, then drained

450–675 g/1–1½ lb/3 cups rump steak, minced

3 tbsp olive oil or peanut oil

8 shallots or 1 large onion, finely sliced

2 cloves garlic, finely sliced

½ tsp cayenne pepper, or chilli powder, or freshly ground black pepper

1 tsp ground coriander

½ tsp salt

2 tsp light soy sauce

½ tsp ginger juice

2 tbsp chopped spring onions/ scallions, or chives, or dill

Steam the glutinous rice for 15 minutes, or, if using Thai Fragrant rice, cook it by the absorption method (page 98).

Stir-fry the shallots or onion and the garlic in oil for 5–6 minutes. Leave them to cool. In a bowl, and preferably using your hands, mix all the ingredients *except* half the rice. Do not knead the mixture, just mingle everything lightly together.

Divide the remaining rice into 8 portions. Divide the meat mixture also into 8. Roll each of the meaty portions into a ball between your hands, make a good-sized hollow in it with your thumb, and place a portion of rice therein. Then form the mixture into whatever shape you please, taking care that the rice filling stays in the middle. Flatten these hamburgers a little and, if you are not going to cook them straight away, keep them in the fridge.

The hamburgers can be grilled or fried on a griddle, with very little oil but a very high heat. Give them 2–3 minutes on each side, turning once only and making sure that both sides are nicely browned. If you prefer the steak well-done, put them in a preheated oven at 180°C/350°F/Gas Mark 4 for 5–8 minutes. Serve hot, as suggested above.

Alternatively, if you like hamburgers with sauce, heat your chosen sauce in a frying pan, put the hamburgers into it, cover the pan and simmer for 5–8 minutes.

Threshing: Bali

Long-Cooked Beef with Compressed Rice
Gulai daging

For a long period of cooking, cuts of beef with plenty of flavour are needed. The choice here is among brisket, skirt and flank, with some oxtail, or a combination of these. They are not expensive to buy, but they take time to prepare. All the fat from the brisket has to be trimmed off and discarded, and sinews cut from the flank and skirt, and the bones from the oxtail. Ask your butcher to give you the bones from the brisket; with the tail bones, these will make plenty of good stock.

Gulai daging is a popular family dish in Malaysia and Indonesia. It is usually eaten with plain cooked white rice, but for a party we serve it with lontong (compressed rice, page 107). This is not only delicious in itself, but it allows the host family to do all the cooking the day before and to enjoy the food with their guests.

Preparation: 1 hour
Cooking: 1 hour 50 minutes

For 10–12 people

1 kg/2 lb 3 oz boned brisket
1 kg/2 lb 3 oz flank or skirt
    steak
1 oxtail

For the paste:

1 large onion, chopped
2 cloves garlic, chopped
1–3 red chillies, de-seeded
    and chopped
2 tsp ground coriander
1 tsp ground cumin
1 tsp ground turmeric
8 candle nuts or 12 blanched
    almonds
2 tbsp peanut oil
2 tbsp water
½ tsp salt

Prepare the meat as described above and cut into cubes about 2.5-cm/1-inch square.

Blend all the ingredients for the paste until smooth. Put the paste in a saucepan, bring to the boil and simmer for 5–6 minutes. Add all the meat and stir it around for 2–3 minutes. Cover the pan and simmer for 5–8 minutes. Uncover, add the kaffir lime or bay leaves and the stock. Bring this back to the boil and simmer for 1 hour. Stir from time to time, and add a little more stock or hot water if necessary. The liquid must always cover the meat.

Add the coconut milk and potatoes. Bring back to the boil and continue cooking, stirring often, for 25 minutes. By this time the meat will be quite tender and the potatoes almost cooked. If you are going to serve the gulai as soon as it is ready, add the beans and continue to simmer for 10 more minutes. Then adjust the seasoning, and serve immediately.

Alternatively, if you are cooking 24 hours before serving, stop before the beans are put in, leave everything to cool and then store it in the refrigerator. Next day, heat the stew slowly and bring it to the boil.

274

Other ingredients:

2 kaffir lime leaves or bay
  leaves
1 stalk fresh lemon grass,
  washed and cut into 2 or 3
  pieces
1.7 litres/3 pints/7½ cups
  beef stock
570 ml/1 pint/2½ cups thick
  coconut milk
More salt to taste
450 g/1 lb small new
  potatoes, scraped and
  washed
450 g/1 lb French beans,
  topped and tailed and cut
  in halves

Put in the beans, cook for 10 minutes or a little longer until the beans are tender, adjust the seasoning and serve.

The gulai and the compressed rice should come to table separately; guests help themselves to rice and then ladle the gulai over it.

Red Stew of Beef
Rogan josh

Plain cooked white rice is by far the best accompaniment to this gorgeous stew. I have always made rogan josh with brisket, but silverside or flank steak would be just as good. You can of course cook it equally well with lamb or goat; I have had several lamb and goat versions of this dish in India, not always called rogan josh but still recognizably the same dish.

I usually make this stew in large quantities for a buffet party, because it takes a long time to cook; but any that is left over freezes very well, and will keep in the freezer for up to 3 months.

Preparation: 1 hour, including cooking on the stove
Cooking: 2–2½ hours in the oven

For 8–10 people, or more as part of a buffet

2–2.5 kg/4–5 lb/8–10 cups brisket, silverside or flank steak of beef, cut into 2.5-cm/1-inch cubes
1 tsp salt
1 tbsp plain/all-purpose flour
112 ml/4 fl oz/½ cup peanut oil or corn oil
2 large onions, finely chopped

For the paste:

4 cloves garlic
1½ tsp chopped ginger root
4–6 large red chillies, de-seeded and chopped
The seeds from 4 green cardamoms
3 cloves
2 tsp ground coriander
2 tsp ground cumin
1 tsp paprika
½ tsp salt
4 tbsp hot water
2 tbsp peanut oil

Other ingredients:

2 curry leaves or bay leaves
5-cm/2-inch stick of cinnamon
112 ml/4 fl oz/½ cup plain yogurt
Salt to taste
850 ml/1½ pints/3¾ cups hot water

Rub the meat with salt and flour, and keep it aside while preparing the other ingredients. Blend all the ingredients for the paste until smooth.

Heat the oil in a wok and fry the meat in batches for about 3 minutes each time. Take it out with a slotted spoon and drain in a colander. In the same oil, stir-fry the onions until lightly coloured. Transfer the onions to a bowl. Pour the paste from the blender into a wok or pan, and simmer, stirring often, for 4–5 minutes.

Add the meat, and stir it around to cover it with the paste. Cover the wok or pan and go on simmering for 3 minutes longer. Uncover, add the fried onions, curry or bay leaf, and cinnamon stick. Stir in the yogurt, a little at a time. When all the yogurt has gone in, continue to simmer for 2 more minutes, then add the hot water. Stir again, and cook for 5 minutes.

Transfer the stew to a large ovenproof dish or casserole with a lid, and cook, tightly covered, in a preheated oven at 160°C/320°F/Gas Mark 3 for 1 hour. Then turn the oven down to 120°C/250°F/Gas Mark ½, take the dish out of the oven and give the stew a good stir. Adjust the seasoning. Put it back into the oven to continue slow cooking for a further 1–1½ hours. Serve piping hot.

Donburi with Beef

A *donburi* is a Japanese porcelain food bowl, about 15 cm/6 inches in diameter, and with a lid. It is also the word for any one-dish meal that you eat from the bowl: rice cooked with vegetables and meat, egg or fish, and whatever sauce or garnish is needed to make it interesting.

Cook the rice while preparing the ingredients for the beef topping (for plain cooked rice, see pages 98-100).

Preparation: 10 minutes
Cooking: 15 minutes

For 4–6 people

450 g/1 lb/2 cups Japanese or
   Thai Fragrant rice, boiled
   or steamed or cooked in an
   electric rice cooker

For the beef topping:

2 tbsp peanut oil or corn oil
285–340 g/10–12 oz rump
   steak or fillet steak or
   sirloin of beef, sliced thinly
   into small strips
4 spring onions/scallions, cut
   into rounds
2 cloves garlic, crushed
2-cm/¾-inch piece of washed
   and peeled fresh ginger
   root, or 1 tbsp of ginger
   juice (page 372)
225 ml/8 fl oz/1 cup hot
   water
2 tbsp mirin
2 tbsp dark soy sauce
Salt and pepper or cayenne
   pepper to taste

Heat the oil in a wok or frying pan and stir-fry the beef for 3 minutes. Add the onions, garlic and ginger. Stir for 1 minute, then add the rest of the ingredients except the salt and pepper. Increase the heat and let the mixture boil vigorously for 1 minute. Taste, and add salt if necessary or black pepper or cayenne pepper if desired.

Divide the rice among the bowls and put equal portions of beef and sauce on top. Serve at once; or reheat in a microwave oven and serve hot.

Rice Dish in the Manner of Damascus with Various Meats
Una minestra di riso alla damaschina con diverse carni

This is my version of an old Italian recipe which my friend Gillian Riley translated for me from a work of Bartolomeo Scappi, published in 1570. I have adapted it somewhat to suit present-day tastes, with about one-twelfth of the quantity of butter that Scappi apparently enjoyed. Don't be put off by the rather lengthy preparation and cooking times. The result is delicious.

The meats and stocks should be prepared the day before the party, for the sake of convenience. The dried chestnuts and chickpeas/garbanzos need to be soaked overnight.

In my opinion, this dish needs a clear sauce, and the best sauce for it is the strained stock. Just heat it up, with 2–3 tablespoonfuls of chopped sorrel or parsley, and a few drops of lemon juice if you wish. But if you are going to use the stock as sauce, cook the chickpeas/garbanzos and chestnuts in water.

Preparation: 2 hours boiling and boning the meat + overnight soaking
Cooking: 2 hours

For 12–16 people

For the rice:

1 kg/2 lb 3 oz/4½ cups
   Arborio or other Italian
   short grain rice
112 g/4 oz/½ cup dried
   chickpeas/garbanzos,
   soaked overnight
112 g/4 oz dried chestnuts,
   soaked overnight
56 g/2 oz butter
Salt and pepper to taste
1 tsp ground cinnamon
2 tsp sugar (optional)

Put all the ingredients in the 'meats' list, except the sausages, into a very large saucepan. Bring to the boil, then simmer for 1 hour, skimming off the froth from time to time. After 1 hour, take out all the meat; as soon as the pieces are cool enough to handle, separate the meat from the bones and set both aside. Discard the skin of the capon or chicken, and the meat fat.

Return the bones to the saucepan and continue simmering for another 30 minutes, then add the sausages and simmer for 15 minutes longer. Remove the sausages and set them aside with the meat. Strain the stock and discard all solids. When the stock is cold, refrigerate it so that next day the fat on top can be thrown away.

On the day of the party, discard the fat from the stock and heat it till it is almost boiling. Put the chickpeas/garbanzos, chestnuts and rice in three different saucepans. Measure the rice in cups, and add to it the same number of cups of stock plus 1 more cup. Use the remaining stock to cover the chickpeas and chestnuts, if you are not going to use it as sauce (see

For the meats:

½ leg of lamb
1.35 kg/3 lb neck of veal
1 capon or free-range
    chicken, quartered
450 g/1 lb small Italian
    cooking sausages or
    cotechino
3 litres/5¼ pints/13 cups –
    or more – water; enough to
    cover the meat
1 tsp salt
2 onions, not peeled but
    washed and quartered
5 cloves garlic
10 whole black peppercorns
2 bay leaves

introductory note); otherwise use water. Cook them all at the same time. The rice will absorb all the stock after about 15 minutes boiling; it should then be transferred into a large bowl. The chickpeas/garbanzos and chestnuts will need to boil for about 35–40 minutes. When they are done, drain them and leave them to cool before taking off the thin skins of the chickpeas/garbanzos and chestnuts. Cut the chestnuts into quarters. Then stir all the butter into the rice, followed by the chickpeas/garbanzos and chestnuts, and season the mix with salt and pepper.

Now cut the meats and sausages into quite thick slices. Butter 2 large flameproof casseroles. Divide one half of the rice between the two casseroles, levelling it with a spoon. Divide the meat mixture equally and lay it evenly over the rice. Sprinkle the cinnamon and sugar (if used) on top of this. Then spread the rest of the rice evenly over the meat. Cover the casseroles with aluminium foil, and bake in a preheated oven at 160°C/320°F/Gas Mark 3 for 1 hour. Serve very hot, with salad or some lightly cooked spinach.

Rice Casserole with Pork
Arroz com porco

For this recipe, and for several other Latin American rice dishes, I must thank Elisabeth Lambert Ortiz. This one is from Brazil.

Preparation: 10–15 minutes preparing the marinade + overnight marinating
Cooking: 75 minutes

For 4–6 people

1 kg/2 lb 3 oz/4½ cups pork:
    shoulder or leg meat, cut
    into 2.5-cm/1-inch cubes
700 ml/1¼ pints/3 cups
    water
½ tsp salt

For the marinade:

112 ml/4 fl oz/½ cup dry
    white wine
112 ml/4 fl oz/½ cup white
    vinegar
2 cloves garlic, crushed
1 medium onion, finely
    chopped
Salt and freshly ground
    pepper
1 tbsp chopped coriander/
    cilantro leaves
1 red chilli, de-seeded and
    chopped; or ½ tsp Tabasco

Other ingredients:

340 g/12 oz/1½ cups long
    grain rice

Mix all the ingredients for the marinade in a glass bowl. Put in the pork cubes and turn them well so all surfaces are covered in the marinade. Cover the bowl and refrigerate for 8 hours or overnight, turning the meat over once or twice.

Lift out the pork cubes and pat them dry with kitchen paper. Strain and reserve the marinade. Discard the solids. Heat the oil in a casserole or saucepan and sauté the pork cubes until they are lightly browned. Add the onion, green pepper, garlic and coriander/cilantro leaves, and sauté for 3–4 minutes more. Add the strained marinade, cover the pan, and simmer for 35–40 minutes, by which time the pork should be tender.

While the pork is cooking, wash the rice, drain it, and cook it in a saucepan with 700 ml/1¼ pints/ 3 cups of water and ½ teaspoon of salt. Cover the pan and simmer on a low heat until all the water has been absorbed – about 20 minutes. Turn off the heat but leave the lid on the pan until everything is ready for the final stage of cooking, in the oven.

Adjust the seasoning of the pork stew, add the ham and 112 g/4 oz grated cheese, and mix well together. Butter an ovenproof serving dish, put half the rice into it, and level the rice with a fork. Spread the cooked meat evenly on top of the rice, and the remainder of the rice on top of it. Sprinkle the rice with the remaining 2 tablespoonfuls of cheese and the butter, cut into small pieces. Put the dish into a preheated oven at 190°C/375°F/Gas Mark 5 for about 10 minutes, until the top is slightly browned. Serve hot

2 tbsp vegetable or olive oil
1 medium onion, chopped
1 green sweet/bell pepper,
   de-seeded and diced
1 clove garlic, chopped
1 tbsp chopped coriander/
   cilantro leaves
Salt and freshly ground
   pepper
112 g/4 oz/½ cup boiled
   ham, diced
112 g/4 oz freshly grated
   Parmesan cheese; 2 tbsp
   reserved for garnish
15 g/½ oz butter

with Tomato Sauce (page 347) or Red Pepper and Tomato Sauce (page 349).

Steamed Pork Stuffed with Vegetables

This is my adaptation of a Korean dish, in which the vegetables are chosen for their colour and then cut into fine julienne strips to give a good-looking presentation. In Korea this would never be served alone but always with a bowl of plain cooked rice, a bowl of soup, some *kimchi* or pickled vegetable, and a small bowl of hot relish. The authentic sauce, poured over the meat before steaming, is made from dried prawns/ shrimp, ginger and chillies. For me, this is delicious, but if dried prawns/shrimp and fresh ginger aren't available, or you don't care for chillies, make the alternative sauce given below – and use plenty of garlic.

If you use dried shiitake mushrooms, soak them in hot water for 10–20 minutes. Drain them but keep the soaking water to go into a stock pot with the mushroom stalks.

Preparation: 2 hours soaking + 20–25 minutes
Cooking: 10–12 minutes

For 4 people

450–570 g/1–1¼ lb
   tenderloin of pork, cut into
   4 portions
2 tbsp peanut oil

Alternatively, for the garlic sauce:

2–3 cloves garlic
2 tbsp fresh breadcrumbs
2 tbsp olive oil
1 tsp sesame oil (optional)
8–10 whole black peppercorns
170 ml/6 fl oz/¾ cup stock or water
¼ tsp salt

For the marinade:
2 tbsp light soy sauce
¼ tsp chilli powder
1 tbsp rice vinegar or
   white wine vinegar
1 tbsp mirin or sherry

For the vegetables:

2 medium carrots, peeled and
   cut into fine julienne strips
2 medium courgettes/
   zucchini, cut into julienne
   strips
4–6 fresh shiitake
   mushrooms, sliced, or dried
   shiitake mushrooms,
   soaked in hot water for
   10–20 minutes, and sliced
8 spring onions/scallions,
   trimmed and washed, then
   cut into julienne strips
Half a mooli/white radish or
   turnip, weighing
   112–170 g/4–6 oz, peeled
   and cut into julienne strips
2 tbsp peanut oil
Salt and pepper

For the dried prawn/shrimp
and ginger sauce:

2 tbsp dried prawns/shrimp,
   soaked in hot water for
   5–10 minutes then drained
1 tsp finely chopped ginger
   root
1 small dried red chilli,
   chopped
1 tbsp light soy sauce
170 ml/6 fl oz/¾ cup stock
   or water

Mix the ingredients for the marinade in a glass bowl, and marinate the meat for 2 hours or longer.

Prepare the vegetables and sauce while the meat is marinating. If you want the vegetables well-cooked, sauté each vegetable by itself for 2 minutes in a little oil, and season with salt and pepper. Use the same pan throughout. Then set them aside. Alternatively, omit this step and stuff the meat with the raw vegetables.

For the dried prawn/shrimp and ginger sauce, put all the ingredients into a blender, blend smooth, and pass through a sieve into a small saucepan. Heat gently and adjust the seasoning before spooning the sauce over the meat.

For the garlic sauce, do exactly the same, except that this sauce does not need to be sieved. Transfer it straight from blender to saucepan, and heat it a little longer – up to 4 minutes – to make the garlic less pungent.

When you are ready to steam the meat just before serving, make 5 deep parallel cuts in each piece, taking care not to cut the meat right through. Place the meat in a heatproof dish, deep enough to hold the juices that will come out during the steaming. Stuff the vegetables into the cuts you made in the meat, a different vegetable in each cut. There will be quite a lot left over; arrange these on top of the meat, so that their colours match those of the stuffing.

Pour the sauce evenly over the stuffed pork, together with the cooking juices from the frying pan. Then steam on a high heat for 12–15 minutes. Serve immediately with rice.

Pork in a Hot Spicy Sauce
Pork vindaloo

I don't eat pork very often, but this vindaloo is my favourite pork dish, because of course I am addicted to the hot chillies that it contains (which you should reduce in quantity somewhat if you do not share my passion for chilli). It also gives me an excuse to help myself to more rice, to soak up the spicy sauce.

This is a dish from western India, a speciality of Goa, a place I have never visited. The recipe came to me via the Philippines, from a recently published book called *Home Chefs of the World: Rice and Rice-Based Recipes*. It was published by IRRI, the International Rice Research Institute, in conjunction with Suhay, a women's welfare organization in Los Baños. IRRI have published innumerable books and pamphlets on every other aspect of rice and evidently thought it was time they got around to cooking some. The compiler, Mrs Inderjeet Virmani, the wife of a senior IRRI researcher, gave me permission to reproduce a recipe or two, so here is one.

Preparation: 20–25 minutes + 2–3 hours marinating
Cooking: 35–55 minutes

For 4–6 people

450–560 g/1-1¼ lb/2½ cups tenderloin of pork, cut into 2.5-cm/1-inch cubes
4 tbsp peanut oil or olive oil

For the marinade:

2 tbsp rice vinegar or lemon juice
½ tsp chilli powder
½ tsp ground cumin
¼ tsp salt

For the paste:

1 small onion, chopped
3 cloves garlic, chopped
2–4 large red chillies, chopped

Mix the marinade in a glass bowl and marinate the meat for 2–3 hours. Blend all the ingredients for the paste together until smooth.

Stir-fry the pork in the oil for 5 minutes. Remove it with a slotted spoon and let it drain. In the remaining oil, fry the onions for 2–3 minutes; then add the paste, stir, and simmer for 3–4 minutes, stirring often. Add the pork and tomatoes, if used, and vinegar. Stir again, and cover the pan. Simmer for 3 more minutes. Adjust the seasoning, add the hot water, and continue to simmer, uncovered, for 12–15 minutes. Serve hot, with plenty of white rice.

A *Variation*. Tenderloin or fillet of pork is an expensive cut, but it is so tender that it needs only a short cooking time. Long cooking, however, suits vindaloo very well, so if you want a large quantity you can use the whole leg, on the bone, or about 2 kg/4½ lb of loin. This will be enough for 10–12 people.

On the day before you make the vindaloo, boil the meat in plenty of water with some salt, 1 onion, 1 carrot and 1 potato, all cut in halves, for 2 hours.

1 tsp chopped ginger root
1 tsp ground coriander
2 cloves
½ tsp ground cumin
¼ tsp ground turmeric
½ tsp ground cinnamon
½ tsp sugar
1 tbsp rice or white vinegar
2 tbsp water

Other ingredients:

1 large onion, chopped
2 ripe tomatoes, skinned,
  de-seeded and chopped
  (optional)
112 ml/4 fl oz/½ cup hot
  water
1 tbsp white or rice vinegar

When the pork is cold, cut off all the fat and gristle, cut up the meat, and marinate it in the fridge overnight. Also in the fridge, keep the stock that the meat was boiled in; you can then skim off all the solidified fat next day, so that you are left with clear stock.

Then proceed as above, doubling all the quantities for the ingredients of the paste and other ingredients. In the last few minutes of cooking, instead of adding hot water, heat your stock and use that. Let it cook for somewhat longer, say 30–40 minutes, so that the sauce is reduced to a thicker consistency.

Sichuan Shredded Pork on Rice

On one of our research trips for this book we arrived in Taipeh after a few days in Hong Kong, where we had had several superb Cantonese meals. Wonderful as those had been, I confess it was a treat for me to find myself in a Sichuan restaurant in Taipeh, enjoying this hot and spicy pork; it was one of a spread of equally robust dishes which occupied the centre of the round table, to which everyone in the party helped themselves. To go with them, we each had a bowl of gleaming white rice.

At home, I serve this as a complete main course, the pork piled on top of plain cooked Thai Fragrant rice, with no other accompaniment. There will probably be a salad afterwards, and the first course and dessert may well be from completely different parts of the world.

Preparation: 25–30 minutes including cooking the rice + soaking time
Cooking: 10 minutes

For 4 people

450–675 g/1–1½ lb/3 cups
   tenderloin of pork, cut into
   julienne strips

For the marinade:

1 tsp peanut oil
1 tsp sesame oil
¼ tsp chilli powder
1 tsp cornflour, dissolved in
   1 tbsp water
1 tsp light soy sauce

For the hot paste:

4–5 cloves garlic, chopped
1 tsp chopped ginger root
2–5 small dried red chillies,
   soaked in hot water for 10
   minutes, then drained
2 tbsp yellow bean sauce
1 tbsp Shaohsing wine or dry
   sherry
1 tbsp rice vinegar
2 tbsp water

Other ingredients:

450 g/1 lb/2 cups Thai
   Fragrant or other long
   grain rice
2 tbsp peanut oil
56 g/2 oz/½ cup dried
   shiitake mushrooms,
   soaked in hot water for
   30 minutes, then sliced
112 g/4 oz/⅔ cup canned
   bamboo shoots, drained
   and rinsed, then cut
   into matchsticks

6–8 canned water
   chestnuts, rinsed and
   sliced
112 g/4 oz/1 cup spring
   onions/scallions,
   trimmed and cleaned,
   then cut into rounds
56 ml/2 fl oz/¼ cup
   stock or water
1 tsp sugar
1 tbsp light soy sauce

Mix all the ingredients for the marinade in a glass bowl, and marinate the strips of pork for 30 minutes. Cook the rice by any of the methods described on pages 98–100.

Blend all the ingredients for the paste until smooth. Stir-fry the paste in a wok or large frying pan for 2 minutes. Add the pork, and stir-fry for another 3 minutes. Add the mushrooms, bamboo shoots and water chestnuts, and continue stir-frying for 2–3 minutes more; then add all the remaining ingredients. Stir and simmer for 3 more minutes, and adjust the seasoning.

Arrange the rice on a heated serving platter, pile the pork on top and serve at once.

Cajun Hot Pork Sausage

In the home of Cajun and Creole cooking, this sausage is called chaurice, and it is a principal ingredient of jambalaya. You will not be surprised to find that it is very similar to the hot Spanish sausage called chorizo, which is essential to many versions of paella. In fact, the two sausages are virtually interchangeable, so, if you don't want to make the sausages yourself, use whichever one you can find in your own local shops.

Preparation: 20 minutes
Cooking: 20–25 minutes

Makes 8–10 small sausages

450 g/1 lb/2 cups pork, from the leg, minced
170 g/6 oz/¾ cup pork fat, minced
3 tbsp rice flour or breadcrumbs
1 tsp roughly ground black pepper
2 tbsp olive oil
5 shallots or 2 onions, chopped
2 cloves garlic, chopped
2 red chillies, de-seeded and chopped, or 1 tsp chilli powder
¼ tsp ground allspice
1 tsp chopped thyme
2 tbsp chopped parsley
1 bay leaf, chopped or crumbled
1 tsp salt and a little more to taste

Stir-fry the shallots or onions in the olive oil for 3 minutes, and add the other ground and chopped ingredients. Continue frying and stirring for 1–2 minutes more. Remove from the heat, transfer to a bowl and leave to get cold. When the mixture is cold, add the pork and pork fat, and the rice flour or breadcrumbs. Mix everything well together, kneading the mix for a few minutes with your hands; or, better still, blend everything until smooth.

Fry or poach a teaspoonful of the mix, and taste it to see if the seasoning is as you like it. Add salt and pepper if needed. Refrigerate for at least 30 minutes, preferably longer, so that the mix becomes firm and easier to handle.

Then proceed as for other sausages in this book, using clingfilm/plastic wrap to wrap the mixture as you shape it. Poach the sausages in boiling water for 15 minutes, then drain them and let them cool. Unwrap them, and store until needed – in the fridge (up to 48 hours) or freezer (up to 1 month).

Rice for Vegetarians and Vegans

Many rice-growing countries in Asia have a strong tradition of non-violence and respect for all life. Whether this is in spite of their history or because of it I wouldn't like to say, but it has had the result of producing a number of vegetarian traditions, particularly in India and in several Buddhist countries – though most Buddhists are not, of course, actually forbidden to eat meat.

The number of vegetarians in Western countries today must be growing pretty rapidly, too, judging by the numbers I meet. Some of them, especially the strictly observant ones, no doubt become vegetarians or vegans as a protest against inhumane treatment of animals or suspected lack of hygiene in abattoirs. But many simply want to eat a healthier diet and to cut down on their cholesterol. As a result, there are a lot of what I call part-time vegetarians about, and indeed I regard myself as one.

Partly for this reason, and partly because I always enjoy the challenge of cooking for people whose choice of food is restricted, I have given this section of the book at least as much thought and care as any of the others. The dishes it contains are all main-course dishes, but none of them is a complete meal in itself. They either need something to accompany them, or they are themselves accompaniments. Vegetarians will find many suitable recipes in the Rice as Accompaniment section for dishes to go with these.

At this point, I should like to say a little about compressed rice or lontong (page 107). Westerners don't always take to this, perhaps because it is served cold and they are not used to eating stone-cold rice. I have introduced it here, however, as something that is very convenient for heating in a microwave oven.

Gado-gado, for instance, if you mix it well with the peanut sauce and slices of lontong, can be easily microwaved and becomes a delicious and satisfying one-dish meal for vegetarians or (if you leave out the eggs) for vegans. The fact that gado-gado is always eaten cold in Indonesia, as a salad, is neither here nor there, though this may tempt you to try it that way. If you don't have a microwave oven, individual plated portions can be heated by steaming each one for 2–3 minutes. The method of steaming is explained on page 387.

Tempeh

The natural partnership between rice and soya beans has already been mentioned (page 15); because their amino acids complement each other, they make a particularly nutritious combination and go a long way to make good any protein deficiency that non-meat eaters might suffer. The soya bean is indeed a wonderful plant, fixing nitrogen from the air to provide its own fertilizer and improve the soil it is grown in; but its beans are difficult for the human digestive system to tackle effectively. This problem has long been known in the East, and various solutions found, most of them depending on some kind of fermentation of the beans; this, as it were, pre-digests them for us.

Soy sauce and tofu are now well known all over the world, and they play important parts in many recipes in this book. Tempeh is Indonesian, more precisely Javanese (there, the word is spelled *tempe*.) It is well known in Holland, fairly well known in North America, and obtainable in some health food shops in Britain. Many people who know it regard it as the best of all soya bean products (though, by the way, it can be made from other beans and nuts as well). Tempeh comes in blocks about 2 cm/¾ inch thick, and consists of cooked soya beans bound together by the microscopic fibres of a mould; there are several suitable ones, but Western tempeh makers usually use *Rhizopus oligosporus*.

The appearance of fresh tempeh has been compared to that of Camembert cheese, its surface to that of a new white tennis ball. In texture and flavour it resembles neither of these. When you cut it, you see the beans inside, still complete (picture below). As a result, it has the firmness and the slight chewiness of beans, a more interesting texture than tofu. It is, of course, rich in fibre.

Tempeh needs to be cooked, and if you simply boil it and eat it plain, it has a mild nutty flavour, not unpleasant but not very interesting. Like rice, however, it absorbs the flavours of whatever it is cooked in. It can take the place of meat in a great many Western meat dishes, even in hamburgers. It can be liquidized and used in sauces, soups, dips and dressings. You can of course eat it with potatoes or noodles or bread just as well as with rice; but since it goes well with rice and ought to be better known, I include here simple directions for making tempeh and a few of my own favourite tempeh recipes. These are not cooked with rice, but they are intended to be served with rice dishes, and I specify the most suitable in each case.

Tempeh

You can buy excellent tempeh in many health food shops in big cities in Britain, the Netherlands and the USA. Most of it is made in small, often local, factories and workshops, and it is usually frozen. It will keep in the freezer for up to three months, or in a refrigerator for about a week. Cooked dishes containing tempeh can be chilled or frozen all over again. If tempeh is kept for too long, the surface starts to go black in patches. A little of this does no harm; if you don't like the look of it, just trim it off. Tempeh does not become toxic until it is really rotten, when it smells of ammonia and no one would want to eat it anyway.

If you become seriously interested in tempeh, the book to have is *The Book of Tempeh* by William Shurtleff and Akiko Aoyagi.

Making tempeh at home

First, find your 'starter'. As with bread-making and brewing, you can use one batch of tempeh to start the next, but airborne moulds can contaminate your culture and could make the tempeh toxic. Commercial laboratories cultivate pure strains of *Rhizopus oligosporus* and some will sell small batches, usually in powder form, to home tempeh makers. A few health food shops sell it, or can give you an address for mail order.

To make 8 blocks of tempeh, each weighing about 400 g/14 oz – that is, about 3.2 kg/7 lb altogether – you will need:

2 kg/4 lb 6 oz pack of dried soya beans
3 tbsp white malt vinegar
1 tsp tempeh starter

You will also need the following:

A large pan, capacity not less than 10 litres/2 imperial gallons/2½ US gallons
8 sealable polythene/plastic bags, 23 cm × 15 cm/9 × 6 inches, pierced with small holes about 0.5 cm/⅕ inch apart; a clean bradawl is a suitable tool
A warm place (from 27°C/80°F to 35°C/95°F) to incubate the tempeh for 24–36 hours

You can of course vary the total quantity and the size of your tempeh blocks, but, as with most home fermenting, you are more likely to get good results with a fairly large batch. If you boil up the beans in the morning (about 30 minutes) and make the tempeh that evening (at least 2 hours, including 1 hour when beans are boiling and require almost no attention), the tempeh should be ready early in the morning of the second day following – that is, the whole process takes 48 hours. The incubation temperature, however, makes a big difference; the lower it is, the more time you need, and the more control you have.

The ideal incubator is a small cupboard through which air can move freely. The cupboard is heated with one or two 100-watt bulbs, wired through a simple thermostat (obtainable from most electrical suppliers). I set my thermostat at about 28°C/84°F, and the tempeh is ready in about 30 hours.

Tip the beans into a large saucepan, wash thoroughly, and drain. Cover with plenty of cold water – at least three times the volume of the beans – and bring to the boil. As soon as the water boils, turn off the heat, and leave to stand for 8–16 hours. The beans will then have expanded to about twice their original volume.

Drain most of the water from the beans. Rub, squeeze and press the beans with your hands vigorously to loosen the outer skins and break each bean into its two halves. Don't worry about splitting every single bean, but try to get most of them.

Now get rid of the skins by filling the pan with cold water and swirling around so the skins rise to the top. Pour off the water with the skins. Keep on doing this till most of them have gone. You don't need to get rid of all of them, but the tempeh is nicer if most of them have gone. This method is, I admit, wasteful of water. You can skim the skins from the surface with a small sieve, or pour the water off through a colander into a bucket – then the water goes on the garden and the skins to the compost heap.

When the water is clear and not many skins float to the top, refill the pan with water, hot or cold, so that the beans are covered to a depth of at least 5 cm/2 inches. Add the 3 tablespoons (approximately) of vinegar. Bring to the boil and simmer, uncovered, for 1 hour.

Drain off all the water. Spread the beans out on an old sheet or tablecloth and let them dry and cool to about body temperature. They should not be bone dry, but should not glisten with moisture. A hair-dryer will speed things up. Keep stirring the beans around so they dry and cool evenly.

Now clean and dry the saucepan and gather all the beans together into it (or, better, into a large wide bowl). Sprinkle about a teaspoonful of starter powder over the beans, and stir them thoroughly with a wooden spoon or your hands to distribute the powder evenly through the mass.

Distribute the beans equally among the polythene bags, seal the bags, and pat each one flat – it should be about 2 cm/¾ inch thick so that the tempeh holds firmly together but air can reach the mould at the centre of the block. Lay the bags on wire racks and put them in the incubating cupboard. Air must be able to circulate all round every block.

Leave them for about 24 hours; some visible signs of the mould should have appeared by then. Don't disturb the bags. Fermentation produces its own heat, and mould then grows rapidly, so once it starts don't leave the tempeh in a hot place. When the whitish mould has almost hidden the yellow beans and the blocks are obviously solid, the best place to 'finish' the tempeh is on the kitchen table, where you can keep an eye on it. (It is by now surprisingly warm, and smells rather like fresh-baked bread.)

Don't worry if one or two blackish patches appear; these, however, are a sign that fermentation has gone far enough. Put the blocks straight into the freezer or the fridge; until they are well frozen, they must stay separate from each other, otherwise 'hot spots' will go on fermenting.

Winnowing: Bali

Hot Mixed Vegetable Salad

Although the dressing of this salad is Oriental, it is not chilli-hot. The vegetables are hot because they come straight from the steamer. I would serve this salad on top of steaming hot plain cooked brown rice or white rice, or with the Basic Risotto described on page 122.

You can vary the combination of vegetables to suit what happens to be in your garden or your local shop. In Britain, the young, thin asparagus from Thailand that I mention below is available almost all year round.

Preparation: 15–20 minutes
Cooking: 8–10 minutes

For 4–6 people

340 g/12 oz young, thin
   asparagus, trimmed and
   washed
225 g/8 oz mangetout/sugar
   peas, topped and tailed
225 g/8 oz baby courgettes/
   zucchini, trimmed and
   washed
112 g/4 oz baby sweet corn

For the dressing:

2 tbsp ghee or clarified butter
2 tsp sugar
2 tbsp finely chopped flat-leaf
   parsley
1 clove garlic, crushed
¼ tsp chilli powder
Seeds from 2 green
   cardamoms, crushed in a
   mortar
1 tsp ginger juice
4 tbsp hot water
3 tbsp rice vinegar or lime
   juice
Salt and pepper

Start heating the water in the steamer while you prepare the dressing. Heat the clarified butter in a wok or wide shallow saucepan. Add the sugar, stir for 2 minutes, then add the rest of the ingredients for the dressing, except the water, vinegar or lime juice, and salt and pepper.

Stir for 1 more minute, then add the water and vinegar or lime juice. Bring to the boil and season with salt and pepper. Simmer on a very low heat while you steam the vegetables, all together, for 3 minutes only.

Then transfer the vegetables to the pan with the dressing. Stir them, cover the pan, take it off the heat, and leave it covered for 1–2 minutes. Serve at once, as suggested above.

Gado-Gado with Compressed Rice

Gado-gado is an Indonesian cooked vegetable salad with peanut sauce, usually eaten as a one-dish lunch and almost always accompanied by compressed rice, which we call lontong (page 107). Both dishes are served at room temperature. However, there is no reason why they shouldn't be heated, particularly if you have a microwave oven. Arrange the gado-gado on a serving platter or individual plates, dress it with the peanut sauce, put the cut-up rice round the edge, and pop the lot into the microwave on full power for about 1–2 minutes for individual servings or 2–3 minutes for the whole platter. Scatter the garnish over the warm gado-gado.

Preparation and cooking: about 50 minutes altogether

For 4–6 people

The vegetables:

112 g/4 oz/1 cup of each of
   the following:
   cabbage or spring greens;
   shredded French beans, cut
   into 1-cm/½-inch lengths;
   carrots, peeled and sliced
   thinly; cauliflower florets;
   bean sprouts, washed

The sauce:

285 ml/½ pint/1¼ cups
   Peanut Sauce (page 352)

For the garnish:

Some lettuce leaves and
   watercress
1 or 2 hard-boiled eggs,
   quartered
Compressed rice made with
   225–340 g/8–12 oz/
   1–1½ cups rice (page 107)
¼ cucumber, sliced thinly
1 tbsp Crisp-Fried Onions
   (page 358)

Boil each vegetable separately in slightly salted water for 3–4 minutes, except the bean sprouts, which need only 2 minutes. Drain each separately in a colander.

Serve as described above. Even if the gado-gado is to be eaten cold, the peanut sauce should be heated in a saucepan for a minute or two before it is poured over the vegetables; if the sauce is very thick, stir in a little warm water.

Rice with Sweet Corn and Coconut

When the Japanese occupied Indonesia from 1942 to 1945, almost everyone found themselves with very little to eat. In particular, rice was in short supply, and this was serious; we are a rice-eating people, and if we haven't had rice we feel we haven't eaten at all.

In this recipe, the sweet corn and coconut were originally intended simply to give bulk. When the war ended and – eventually – rice became plentiful again, this dish was not cooked very often, because no one wanted to be reminded of hard times.

Nowadays, it is becoming fashionable in Indonesia – at least in those parts of society that care about fashion – to eat less rice. As a result, this way of serving it is becoming popular on its own merits, and it deserves to stay popular even when fashions change. I like it best when made with brown rice.

Preparation: 30 minutes
Cooking: 25 minutes

For 4–6 people

225 ml/8 fl oz/1 cup water or coconut milk
½ tsp salt
112 g/4 oz/½ cup long grain brown or white rice
112 g/4 oz/½ cup sweet corn kernels – fresh, frozen, or canned
4 tbsp freshly grated coconut or desiccated coconut

If you are using fresh or frozen corn kernels, boil these first in water or stock with a large pinch of sugar for 8–10 minutes. Canned sweet corn need only be drained and rinsed. Whichever sort you use, break and mash the kernels lightly in a mortar, or in a bowl with the back of a spoon.

Wash the rice in several changes of water. Put it in a saucepan and pour in the water or coconut milk with ½ teaspoonful of salt. Bring the liquid to the boil and simmer until it has almost all been absorbed by the rice. Add the partly mashed sweet corn and mix well. Transfer the mixture into a steamer. (If you are using desiccated coconut, stir this into the mixture now.) Steam for 15 minutes. Turn off the heat and leave the mixture to rest for 5 minutes.

(If you are using fresh coconut, mix a large pinch of salt into it.) Transfer the rice and sweet corn mixture into a warm serving bowl. (Stir the fresh coconut into it just before serving.) Serve hot, with a meat or fish dish for non-vegetarians, and vegetables or salad.

Cabbage Stuffed with Spinach Rice

A cabbage leaf is the obvious edible wrapper for all sorts of stuffings from many different cuisines. A simple extension of this idea is to stuff a whole cabbage; with vegetables and nuts, this makes a very satisfying vegetarian main course. The spinach rice that I use here is the well-known Greek spanakorizzo. To accompany it, I suggest potatoes or pasta, or any of the rice dishes described on pages 108–131, and a sauce of your choice – there is a good selection of them on pages 347–357.

Preparation: 50 minutes
Cooking: 45–50 minutes

For 4–6 people

450 g/1 lb young spinach, the
   stalks removed and leaves
   thoroughly washed
2 tbsp olive oil
1 bunch of spring onions/
   scallions, trimmed, washed
   and cut into thin rounds
140 g/5 oz/⅔ cup risotto rice
   or other short grain rice
285 ml/10 fl oz/1¼ cups
   water
A large pinch of grated
   nutmeg
Salt and pepper to taste
1 cabbage

Roughly shred the spinach leaves. Heat the oil and add the spring onions/scallions, stir, and add the rice, stirring until all the grains are coated with oil. Then put in the spinach, nutmeg and some salt and pepper. Stir again, and pour in the water. Give it one more stir, and bring the water to the boil. Cover the pan, and leave to simmer for 14–15 minutes. Then take the pan off the heat, set it on a wet tea-towel/dishcloth, and leave it to cool.

Separate the outer leaves from the cabbage, and trim the hard stalk from each leaf. (Use the heart of the cabbage for something else.) Boil the leaves in slightly salted water for 6–8 minutes. Drain them in a colander.

Line a circular heatproof bowl, about the same size as the cabbage, with some of these blanched cabbage leaves, arranging them upside-down so that they will be right way up when the cabbage, stuffed and cooked, is turned out onto its serving dish.

Put in the cooked spinach rice, pressing it down gently with a spoon. Go on adding more outer leaves of the cabbage, finally closing them over the top of the spinach rice so that the shape of the cabbage is reconstructed, upside-down, in the bowl. Cover the bowl with aluminium foil and put it into a large saucepan. Pour hot water into the saucepan so that it comes about halfway up the outside of the bowl. Bring this water back to the boil, cover the pan, and cook for

30 minutes, making sure the water does not go off the boil and the pan does not boil dry.

To serve, discard the aluminium foil, lay a large plate upside-down over the bowl, turn the whole thing over, and lift the bowl clear of the reconstituted 'cabbage'. Cut it into portions at the table and serve hot.

Donburi with Tofu and Shiitake Mushrooms

This is a vegetarian donburi, prepared in exactly the same way as the Donburi with Chicken and Mushrooms on page 224, but replacing the chicken with tofu and the chicken stock with a vegetable stock. The recipe for the stock is on page 345. If you use dried shiitake, don't forget to put the stalks and the soaking water into your stock pot.

Preparation: 30–35 minutes (including cooking the rice but excluding making vegetable stock)
Cooking: 10 minutes

For 4 people

340–450 g/12–16 oz/
   3–4 cups fresh, firm tofu
All other ingredients as for
   Donburi with Chicken and
   Mushrooms, but omitting
   the chicken and using
   vegetable stock instead of
   chicken stock

For the marinade:

2 tbsp light soy sauce
1 tbsp mirin
¼ tsp ground white pepper
½ tsp ginger juice (page 372)

Put the slab of tofu in a glass bowl and cover it with water that has just boiled. Leave to stand for 10 minutes, then drain in a colander. Put a plate on top of the tofu, and put something fairly heavy – 1–2 kg/ 2–4 lb – on the plate. Leave it for about 25 minutes to press as much water as possible from the tofu.

Cut the slab of tofu into quarters, and each quarter into quarters again. Brown the tofu pieces in butter, turning them over several times. You may need to do this in 2 or 3 batches.

Mix the ingredients for the marinade in a bowl, and marinade the tofu for at least 10 minutes, making sure that all sides of every piece are coated with the mixture. Then proceed with the donburi as described on page 224.

Mooli/White Radish Steamed Cakes with Spiced Lentils

I commend these to vegetarians and vegans (and indeed to everyone) as a lunch or supper dish. They go well with a green salad. They are also nice as appetizers with a drink before you sit down to dinner, though they are quite filling. Mooli/white radishes are often rather large, but you should be able to find smaller ones weighing, say, a pound or half a kilo. Mooli/white radishes, incidentally, are also eaten raw in salads.

Preparation: 1 hour
Cooking: about 40 minutes

For 4 people for lunch or supper, or 6–8 as a snack or with drinks

For the cakes:

1 mooli/white radish,
   weighing about 450 g/1 lb/
   4 cups, peeled and diced
84 g/3 oz/½ cup rice flour
1 tbsp plain/all-purpose flour
1 tbsp water or a little more

For the spiced lentils:

1 tbsp peanut oil
1 tbsp sesame oil
1 onion, finely chopped
1 tsp ground coriander
¼ tsp chilli powder or ground
   white pepper
½ tsp salt
112 g/4 oz/½ cup red lentils,
   soaked in water for 30
   minutes, then drained
70 ml/2½ fl oz/⅓ cup cold
   water

Put the diced mooli/white radish into a blender until smooth. Sift the two flours together into the blender, add the water and salt, and blend again until you have a thick, smooth batter. Half-fill several well-oiled small ramekins with the batter and steam for about 20 minutes. (You may need to do these in batches.) Alternatively, put the batter into a lined cake tin and steam it for 30 minutes. Insert a metal or bamboo skewer to test the cake; if the skewer comes out clean, the cake is done. Run a small knife round the inside of the tin and tip the cake out. Set it aside to cool.

Heat the peanut oil and sesame oil together in a small saucepan and stir-fry the onions for 2–3 minutes. Add the other ingredients, except the water. Stir-fry for 2 minutes longer, then add the water. Simmer for 3–4 minutes until the water has been absorbed by the lentils. Adjust the seasoning.

If you have made one large cake, slice it through its middle as if you were making a sandwich – as indeed you are. Spread the lentils on the bottom half, and put the top half back in place. You can then cut the cake into as many small slices as you like.

If you have made small cakes in ramekins, slice them and make them into sandwiches in the same way. If you are going to serve them as snacks with drinks, cut each one into quarters.

Serve warm or cold. The cakes can be reheated by steaming them for 3–4 minutes immediately before serving.

Red Pepper, Aubergine/Eggplant and Mooli/ White Radish Cake Kebab

These kebabs can be cooked in the oven, or grilled or broiled over charcoal or on a gas or electric grill. Serve them with brown rice or plenty of compressed rice (page 107), and one of the sauces described on pages 347–357.

The mooli/white radish cake can be made well in advance. Allowing 2 kebabs per person, you will need 8 or 12 long metal or bamboo skewers.

Preparation and cooking: 35–40 minutes altogether

For 4–6 people

1 Mooli/White Radish
  Steamed Cake (page 298),
  cut into cubes about
  2.5 cm/1 inch square
4 red sweet/bell peppers,
  de-seeded and quartered
2 medium aubergines/
  eggplants, each cut into 6
  pieces
2–4 tbsp olive or peanut oil
Salt and pepper

Preheat the oven to 180°C/350°F/Gas Mark 4, light the charcoal stove, or switch on the grill, as appropriate. Put the cut-up vegetables and cubes of mooli/white radish cake on the skewers, lay these on a tray, and brush the oil evenly over the vegetables and the mooli/white radish cake. Season with salt and pepper.

Cook in the oven for about 20 minutes, turning the kebabs over once. If you are grilling or cooking on charcoal, cook them for about 15 minutes in all, turning several times. Serve immediately.

Rice and Vegetable Mould

Made in individual moulds, this looks attractive and is a delicious meal by itself. The parsley and cream – or, for vegans, thick coconut milk – should provide sufficient sauce; however, if you want more, Red Pepper and Tomato Sauce (page 349) or Curry Sauce (page 355) can be poured on to each plate before the rice is unmoulded on top of it, or the sauce can simply be poured over the rice when it is served.

For the quantities shown, you will need 4 moulds, preferably small ramekins or pudding basins about 10 cm/4 inches across and 6–7 cm/2½ –3 inches deep.

Preparation: 40 minutes
Cooking: 35–40 minutes

For 4 people

450 g/1 lb/3–4 bunches parsley, washed, the stalks removed
112 g/4 fl oz/½ cup double heavy cream or thick coconut milk
170 g/6 oz/¾ cup short grain rice, washed and drained
2 tbsp olive oil or butter
2 shallots, chopped
2 cloves garlic, chopped
½ tsp chilli powder (optional)
112 g/4 oz/1 cup button mushrooms, wiped clean and sliced
3 medium-size parsnips, peeled and diced
Salt and pepper to taste
340 ml/12 fl oz/1½ cups water

Boil the parsley in slightly salted water for 2–3 minutes. Drain and leave to cool. Squeeze as much water out as you can, and keep the parsley aside. Heat the cream or coconut milk in a small saucepan. When it is hot, put in the parsley and stir until all the cream or coconut milk has been absorbed into the parsley.

Heat the oil in a medium-size saucepan and stir-fry the shallots and garlic. Add the chilli powder (if used), mushrooms and parsnips. Continue stir-frying for 2 minutes. Add the rice and stir it until all the grains are coated in oil. Season with salt and pepper and add the water. Stir once again and bring to the boil. As soon as the water boils, lower the heat, cover the pan tightly, and leave to simmer undisturbed for 18–20 minutes.

While the rice is cooking, line the bottoms of the moulds with greaseproof paper cut into circles to fit. Butter the sides of the moulds. Divide the creamed parsley among the 4 moulds, and press it down lightly with a spoon. Do the same with the rice mixture.

Up to this point, the dish can be prepared several hours in advance. To serve it hot, cover the moulds with aluminium foil and place them side by side in a wide saucepan. Pour hot water into the pan until it comes about halfway up the sides of the moulds. Bring the water back to the boil, cover the pan and simmer for 5–8 minutes. (Alternatively, remove the aluminium foil, replace with clingfilm/plastic wrap or kitchen paper, and heat in the microwave at full power for 2–3 minutes.) Run a knife around the sides of the moulds and turn out the rice on to individual plates. Serve at once, with or without additional sauce.

Rice and Vegetable Roulade

You will need to pre-cook the rice until it is quite soft. Use muslin, cheesecloth, or banana leaves to roll the roulade. The roulade will be easier to cut when it has had time to cool down a little, so serve it warm, with a hot Red Pepper Sauce (page 349) or Tomato Sauce (page 347).

Preparation: 45–50 minutes, including cooking the rice
Cooking: 20–25 minutes

For 6–8 people as a starter

112 g/4 oz/½ cup short grain rice, cooked in 420 ml/ ¾ pint/2 cups water until all the water has been absorbed by the rice
1 medium-size Savoy cabbage
84 g/3 oz butter
Salt and pepper
4–6 carrots, peeled, cut in halves lengthwise, and boiled
225 g/8 oz/2 cups button mushrooms, sliced
450 g/1 lb/4 cups spinach, blanched and chopped, and the water then squeezed out
2 tbsp chopped parsley

Leave the rice to get cold. Blanch the outer leaves of the cabbage, and shred the inner part. Soften the shredded cabbage in the butter and season with salt and pepper. Set aside to cool.

Lay a large piece of muslin or cheesecloth on a tray. (If you are using banana leaves, make it a double layer.) Lay the outer cabbage leaves on this, and spread over them, first, the shredded cabbage; then the rice; then the spinach; then the mushrooms; finally, the carrots. Pick up the edge of the cloth (or leaf) nearest you and roll the whole thing into a large sausage. Twist the ends of the cloth and tie them with string, or fold the banana leaf to close it and pin the ends with cocktail sticks or bamboo splinters.

Steam for 20–25 minutes. Leave the roulade to cool a little before you unwrap it and cut it into thick slices.

Rice Salad with Asparagus

If, like me, you are an asparagus freak; and if you find yourself, as I too often do, with not quite enough of it to go round your table as an elegant first course, then this salad is an excellent way of stretching the asparagus without losing any of its character. It also goes very well as the accompaniment to a main course of, say, grilled fish, or you can serve it as the complete main course of a light meal, to be followed by a good selection of cheeses.

Preparation: 20 minutes
Cooking: 25–30 minutes

For 4–6 people

1.7 litres/3 pints/7½ cups
   water
450 g/1 lb green or white
   fresh asparagus
225 g/8 oz/1 cup long grain
   rice or brown rice, soaked
   in cold water for 30
   minutes, then washed and
   drained
½ tsp salt
3 tbsp olive or peanut oil
56 g/2 oz/⅓ cup freshly
   made breadcrumbs
2 cloves garlic, chopped
A large pinch of chilli powder
   or ground black pepper
¼ tsp salt
2 hard-boiled eggs, chopped
1 tbsp chopped spring onions/
   scallions or chives
1 tbsp chopped parsley or
   mint
2 tbsp lemon juice

Bring the water to the boil in a saucepan. While waiting, trim the asparagus, peel the stems, and cut them diagonally into 3 or 4 pieces. Then wash them. Keep the tips separate from the stems.

When the water is boiling, add ½ teaspoon salt and put in the asparagus stems – but not the tips. Cook for 4 minutes, then add the tips. Continue cooking on a medium heat for 3 minutes. Take out the asparagus with a slotted spoon, put them in a colander and refresh under the cold tap. Reserve 340 ml/12 fl oz/ 1½ cups of the asparagus cooking water to cook the rice.

Put the drained rice into a saucepan and pour on to it the asparagus water plus 1 tablespoon of the oil. Bring it to the boil and give the rice a stir with a wooden spoon, then cover the pan tightly. Lower the heat and let the rice simmer undisturbed for 20 minutes. Remove the saucepan, place it on a wet towel, and leave it to rest for 5 minutes, still tightly covered.

Now transfer the rice to a bowl and fluff it with a fork. Leave it to cool a little, and while you are waiting heat the remaining oil in a wok or frying pan. Stir-fry the breadcrumbs and garlic until they are just slightly coloured. Add the seasonings, the chopped hard-boiled egg, spring onions/scallions or chives, and parsley or mint. Stir, then add the lemon juice and asparagus. Stir again, and pour the whole lot, including the oil, into the bowl of rice. Mix all well together, adjust the seasoning, and leave the salad to cool further before serving at room temperature. Note that this salad must not be chilled – it would be a shame to lose the crunchiness of the breadcrumbs.

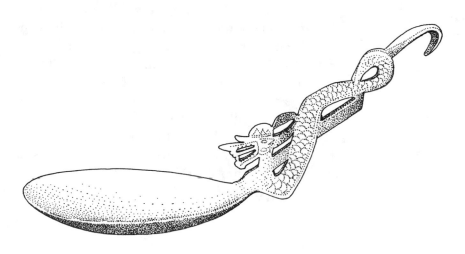

Rice spoon carved from buffalo horn: Indonesia

Glutinous Rice Filled with Tofu and Carrots

The rice can be cooked in coconut milk as described for the Javanese Stuffed Rice Rolls on page 139. The Laotians, however, eat glutinous rice as their staple food, and one of their ways of cooking it is described here. This is without coconut milk.

Because the tofu is to be mashed, there is no need to press the water out of it; you can simply parcel it up in muslin or cheesecloth and give it a good squeeze.

Preparation: 4 hours (or overnight) soaking + 30–35 minutes preparation
Cooking: 40–45 minutes

For 4–6 as a light lunch or a picnic

450 g/1 lb/2 cups glutinous rice, soaked in cold water for 4 hours or overnight, then drained
450 g/1 lb/4 cups tofu
450 g/1 lb peeled carrots
½ tsp salt
¼ tsp nutmeg
½ tsp chilli powder
3 tbsp rice flour or plain/all-purpose flour
3 eggs, beaten
112 g/4 oz/⅔ cup fresh breadcrumbs
2–3 tbsp olive oil or peanut oil

Steam the rice for 20–25 minutes. Then divide it into 2 portions. Line a Swiss roll tin with clingfilm/plastic wrap or foil and fill it with 1 portion of the rice, pressing the rice down to make a thin cake. Remove the rice from the tin, and repeat with the other portion, so that you have 2 rice cakes between which the tofu and carrots will eventually be sandwiched.

Heat the oven to 200°C/400°F/Gas Mark 6. While it heats up, boil the carrots until tender, which takes 8–10 minutes. Cut them up roughly and purée them in a blender until smooth. Purée the tofu in the same way and mix the tofu and carrot in a bowl. Season with salt, nutmeg and chilli powder. Add the flour and eggs and mix well. Adjust the seasoning.

Oil the Swiss roll tin generously and sprinkle half of the breadcrumbs into it, spreading them evenly. Pour the tofu and carrot mixture on top of the breadcrumbs and spread it evenly with a knife. Sprinkle the rest of the breadcrumbs on top, and dribble more oil, as evenly as possible, over the whole. Bake this breaded tofu-and-carrot filling in the oven for 15–20 minutes.

When the filling has cooled a little, turn it out of the tin and sandwich it between the rice cakes. Cut the 'sandwich' into 4 or 6 pieces and serve, hot or cold, by itself or with a sauce of your choice.

Rice Salad, Tabbouleh Style

Tabbouleh, a cracked wheat salad from the Lebanon, has been popular in Britain for many years. It is a delicious salad for summer, especially if you have plenty of mint and coriander/cilantro in your herb garden.

I like to make this version of tabbouleh with short grain brown rice, and to be a little less lavish with the herbs than I would if I were making a really green Lebanese tabbouleh. As with the Malaysian nasi ulam on page 123, the dish is more satisfying if the rice is not smothered by the other ingredients.

Preparation: 30–60 minutes soaking
Cooking: 30–35 minutes

For 4–6 as a lunch dish or 8–10 as a first course or buffet dish

450 g/1 lb/2 cups short grain
    brown rice, soaked in cold
    water for 30–60 minutes,
    washed and drained
1.7–2.3 litres/3–4 pints/
    7½–10 cups water
1 tsp salt
1 tbsp olive oil

For the dressing:

3 tbsp chopped spring onions/
    scallions
3 tbsp chopped coriander/
    cilantro leaves
3 tbsp chopped mint
2–3 tbsp lemon juice
1 tbsp olive oil
Salt and pepper to taste
1 cucumber, quartered
    lengthways, seeds removed,
    then sliced thinly

For the garnish:
4 red tomatoes, skinned,
    de-seeded, and sliced or
    chopped

Heat the water in a large saucepan and when it boils add the salt and oil. Put the rice in a little at a time, so that the water does not go off the boil. Increase the heat a little and cook the rice for 10–12 minutes, stirring once or twice. Strain the rice into a colander, and as soon as the water has drained away transfer the rice immediately to a shallow tray, spreading and teasing it with a fork to get rid of any lumps.

Mix the dressing, including the slices of cucumber, in a bowl. Don't dress the rice while it is still hot, because the heat will make the herbs wilt. When the rice has cooled, mix the rice and the dressing in a large bowl and transfer to a serving platter. Arrange the slices of tomato around the edge, or pile chopped tomatoes on top of the rice. Refrigerate until needed, and serve at room temperature.

Spicy Rice with Aubergine/Eggplant

This is a hot and interesting South Indian pulao that can be made with leftover cooked rice. The baby purple aubergines/eggplants can be replaced by one large one, cut into cubes before frying.

Preparation: cook the rice; 10 minutes
Cooking: 8 minutes

For 2 people

8 baby aubergines/eggplants, fried whole in hot oil for 3–4 minutes
2 tbsp oil
½ tsp mustard seeds
½ tsp chopped fresh ginger root
⅛ tsp turmeric
½ tsp lemon juice
310 g/11 oz/3 cups cooked rice (preferably Basmati)
2 tbsp Gunpowder (page 360)
Salt and pepper to taste

Heat the oil in a wok or large frying pan. Add the mustard seeds, stir for 1 minute, then add the ginger and turmeric. Stir continuously for another 1 minute. Add the aubergines/eggplants and rice and keep stirring and tossing until the rice is hot. Then add the lemon juice and Gunpowder, and salt and pepper to taste. Stir around for 1 more minute and serve hot.

Chilli con Tempeh

Tempeh does particularly well as a meat substitute in this dish. To get the best taste, you really need to marinade the tempeh in very garlicky salted water and then fry it in oil. However, this process can be omitted, especially if you are pressed for time or don't want to add calories. Tempeh and rice go very well together, for reasons explained on page 15, so it is hardly necessary to add that chilli con tempeh is to be served with plenty of plain cooked brown or white rice.

Preparation: 1 hour (including marinating time)
Cooking: 45–50 minutes

For 4–6 people

450 g/1 lb/4 cups tempeh,
  diced

For the optional marinade/
deep-fry:

112 ml/4 fl oz/½ cup hot
  water
½ tsp salt
½ tsp chilli powder
  (optional)
2 cloves garlic, crushed
Vegetable oil for deep-frying

Other ingredients:

3 tbsp olive or peanut oil
1 onion, finely chopped
1 clove garlic, finely chopped
1 tsp chopped ginger root
3–4 large fresh red chillies,
  de-seeded and chopped, or
  1–2 tsp chilli powder
1 tsp ground coriander
  (optional)
675 g/1½ lb fresh tomatoes,
  skinned and chopped, or
  450 g/1 lb/2 cups canned
  tomatoes
Salt and pepper to taste
½ tsp dried oregano (optional)

The marinade/deep-fry option. Mix all the ingredients for the marinade in a bowl and marinate the tempeh for at least 30–60 minutes. Drain and deep-fry the tempeh in vegetable oil in 2 batches, for 4–5 minutes each batch, stirring often. Drain and leave to cool before continuing.

Without marinating/deep-frying. Heat the oil in a wok or saucepan and fry the onion, garlic, ginger and chillies for 3–4 minutes, stirring most of the time. Add the ground coriander, if used, stir for 20 seconds and add the tempeh. Continue to stir-fry for 30 seconds longer, then add the tomatoes.

Simmer for 45 minutes, stirring occasionally. Season with salt and pepper, and oregano if you wish. Stir again and taste. Adjust the seasoning and serve hot with rice.

Biryani with Stuffed Morels

This is my top favourite among biryanis. I watched it being prepared and cooked by Chef Mohammed Rais in the kitchens of the Maurya Sheraton in New Delhi, and wrote down the recipe very precisely. Unfortunately I can't afford to cook it too often, because morels are some of the most expensive mushrooms there are. But for a rather special occasion this makes an excellent first-course dish, to be followed (I suggest) by grilled meat or fish and salad. It is just as good as a main course, but in that case I think it should be the finale to the main course. In fact, as a complete meal in itself it is perhaps best of all, and it seems less extravagant that way.

Choose large morels so that you can get more stuffing into each one.

Before you start, soak the rice in cold water for 30 minutes or a bit longer. If you use fresh morels, rinse them thoroughly to get rid of dirt and sand in their little crevices, and cut off their stems. The same applies to dried morels, which you then soak in hot water for 40–45 minutes. Keep the stems and soaking water to use in stock.

Preparation: 30 minutes soaking + 30 minutes
Cooking: 30 minutes

For 2 people as a one-dish meal; otherwise for 4

For the rice:

225 g/8 oz/1 cup Basmati, Texmati, or other good long grain rice
¼ tsp salt
1.4 litres/2½ pints/6¼ cups water

For the mushrooms and stuffing:

12–16 large fresh or dried morels
112–170 g/4–6 oz hard cheese, grated; or paneer, ricotta, or other soft creamy cheese

Drain the morels that have been soaked, and pat them dry with kitchen paper. Mix well all the ingredients for the stuffing and stuff the morels. There may be some stuffing left over; if so, sprinkle this on top of the sauce during the final cooking.

Boil the water for the rice with ¼ teaspoon of salt. When it is boiling, put in the drained rice, bring back to the boil, and boil for 6 minutes. Drain the rice in a colander.

Preheat the oven to 180°C/350°F/Gas Mark 4. Assemble all the ground ingredients for the sauce together in a bowl.

Heat the ghee/clarified butter or olive oil in a saucepan. Fry the shallots, garlic and ginger in this for 1 minute, then add the cloves and cardamom. Stir once and put in all the ground ingredients. Stir again and pour in the water. Bring to the boil and simmer for 4 minutes. Add the salt and pepper, then the yogurt, a tablespoonful at a time, and keep stirring constantly. Then put the stuffed morels carefully into the pan, cover, and simmer for 3–4 minutes.

2 green chillies, de-seeded
  and finely chopped
2 tbsp finely chopped
  coriander/cilantro leaves,
  or chopped chives
½ tsp ground cumin
A pinch of salt
½ tsp sugar (optional)

For the sauce:

2 tbsp ghee/clarified butter or
  olive oil
2 shallots, finely sliced
2 cloves garlic, finely sliced
1 tsp chopped ginger
1 tsp ground coriander
½–1 tsp ground cumin
2 tbsp ground almonds
2 cloves
2 green cardamoms
¼ tsp ground cinnamon
¼–½ tsp yellow or red chilli
  powder
¼ tsp saffron powder or
  turmeric
170 ml/6 fl oz/¾ cup water
Salt and pepper
8 tbsp (not levelled) plain
  yogurt

Adjust the seasoning. Transfer everything from the pan to an ovenproof dish with a lid. Sprinkle the leftovers of the cheese stuffing, if any, on top of the sauce. Spread the rice on top. Cover the dish very tightly, and cook in the preheated oven for 30–35 minutes, or longer if necessary, but not longer than 1 hour. Turn the oven down to 120°C/250°F/Gas Mark ½ after 35 minutes. Serve hot.

Bibimbab

This Korean rice dish is a very simple concept: rice, with assorted vegetables on top, artistically arranged. Korean restaurants usually serve it with some grilled beef and a bowl of soup, but even without these it makes a very satisfying meal. The best bibimbab is cooked in an iron pot similar to a Japanese *kama* (illustration on page 132); it should come to table very hot, with a raw egg just broken over the vegetables. You eat it with chopsticks, prodding and pushing the egg down into the hot rice so that it cooks and scrambles.

There should be seven different vegetables; one of them must be spinach, and another should be kimchee, the Korean pickled cabbage. If you can't get kimchee, it can be replaced by almost any pickled vegetable, or by some finely sliced gherkins. Each vegetable is cooked separately, and very lightly, in its own mixture of spices. I serve bibimbab with a bowl of pickled green chillies for people to help themselves; you can buy these in jars from any good delicatessen.

When I was in Korea I ate bibimbab in various places, and I have to say that only one, in the brand-new Hilton hotel at Kyongju, was right in every way: piping hot in an iron bowl, on a wooden tray, with the beef sizzling on a hot iron plate beside it and the clear soup in a pretty, jade-coloured bowl.

Anyway, this is how I cook and serve bibimbab at home as a one-course vegetarian meal.

Traditional cooking pots: Japan

Preparation: 50 minutes
Cooking: 30–35 minutes

For 4–6 people

450 g/1 lb/2 cups short grain
Japanese or Korean rice, or
American Calrose or
Kokuho Rose, cooked in
an electric rice cooker or
by the absorption method
(page 98)
4 or 6 eggs

For the vegetables:

450 g/1 lb spinach, stalks
removed, washed
thoroughly
225 g/8 oz/2 cups peeled
mooli/white radish, cut
into julienne strips
225 g/8 oz/2 cups peeled
carrots, cut into julienne
strips
112 g/4 oz/1 cup fresh
shiitake mushrooms, or
56 g/2 oz/½ cup dried ones
(soaked in hot water for 20
minutes), sliced
225 g/8 oz/2 cups courgettes/
zucchini, cut into julienne
strips

For the sauce or marinade:

1 tbsp peanut oil
1 tbsp sesame oil
4 tbsp chopped spring onions/
scallions

2 cloves garlic, finely
chopped
1 tbsp sesame seed,
crushed in a mortar
2 tbsp light soy sauce
Freshly milled black
pepper or ½ tsp chilli
powder
56 ml/2 fl oz/¼ cup
vegetable stock or
water

For the garnish:
A few gherkins, chopped,
or other pickled
vegetables
Pickled green chillies
(optional)

Blanch the vegetables separately, each for 1–2 minutes, drain, and pile them separately on a platter. Do
not refresh them with cold water, but squeeze out
excess water from the spinach, then chop it roughly.

Combine the two oils and heat in a small saucepan.
Stir-fry the onion and garlic for a minute or so, and
add the crushed sesame seeds, soy sauce and pepper or
chilli powder. Simmer for 1 minute, then add the
stock or water. Simmer for 2 more minutes. Adjust the
seasoning and pour this over all the vegetables. Leave
to marinate for 10–15 minutes.

The easiest way to serve bibimbab really hot is to
put the rice, as soon as it is cooked, into fairly large,
heated, individual soup bowls. Arrange the vegetables
on top, still keeping each vegetable in a separate little
pile so that they form a ring on top of the rice. Break
the raw egg into the centre of the ring. Divide the
marinade-sauce among the bowls, and heat each bowl
in the microwave (or steam it) for 1–2 minutes.

Serve straight from the microwave or steamer,
pausing only to sprinkle the garnish on each bowl.
Each guest can then push the half-cooked egg into the
hot rice to cook and scramble it further. As well as
pickled green chillies, put a small bowl or bottle of soy
sauce on the table for those who want it.

Wild Rice Salad with Potatoes, Aubergines/Eggplants and Cheese

This is a delicious and satisfying lunch dish, and is equally suitable as an accompaniment to roast meat or grilled fish. The wild rice is used to give a nutty flavour and a little chewiness to a salad that is otherwise composed of three softer textures. The dressing is a combination of green herbs and yogurt. For the cheese, I would suggest feta or mozzarella, but any mild cheese will do as long as it can be cut into cubes without crumbling.

Preparation: 1 hour
Cooking: about 1½ hours

For 4 people

112 g/4 oz/½ cup wild rice
112 g/4 oz/½ cup long grain brown rice, washed and drained
850 ml/1½ pints/3¾ cups water
½ tsp salt
450 g/1 lb small new potatoes or waxy potatoes, peeled (or well scrubbed), then halved or quartered
2 medium-sized aubergines/ eggplants, cut into cubes
170 g/6 oz mild cheese, cut into cubes
140 ml/5 fl oz/⅔ cup oil for frying

For the dressing:

6–8 tbsp plain ('natural') yogurt
1 tbsp chopped chives

Put the aubergine/eggplant cubes in a colander. Sprinkle 1 tablespoon salt over them and leave to stand for 30–60 minutes. Rinse the salt off, and pat the cubes dry with kitchen paper. Then fry them in the oil in 3 batches for 3–4 minutes each time.

Boil the water with ½ teaspoon salt and cook the wild rice in it over a low heat for 40 minutes. Then add the brown rice, cover the pan with a tight-fitting lid and continue simmering for a further 30 minutes or until all the water has been absorbed. Remove from the heat, and leave the rice, still with the lid on, to rest for 5 minutes before you put it into a bowl. While the rice is cooking, boil the potatoes in another pan until tender.

Mix all the ingredients for the dressing in a large bowl and add the rice, potatoes and aubergines/ eggplants while they are still warm. Mix everything well together, and adjust the seasoning. Refrigerate until needed. Serve at room temperature.

1 tbsp chopped mint
1 tbsp chopped coriander/
   cilantro leaves
1 tsp sugar (optional)
1 clove garlic, crushed
Salt and pepper to taste

Wild and White Rice Pilaf

The wild rice provides a most attractive colouring, and the chilli is just enough to give an intriguing taste.

Preparation: 1 hour soaking
Cooking: about 1¼ hours

For 4–6 people

84 g/3 oz/⅓–½ cup wild rice
225 g/8 oz/1 cup long grain
   white rice (both soaked
   separately in cold water for
   1 hour, then drained)

Other ingredients:

2 tbsp peanut or olive oil
3 shallots, finely sliced
1 clove garlic, finely chopped
   (optional)
570 ml/1 pint/2½ cups cold
   water
½ tsp salt
a large pinch of chilli powder
2 tbsp chopped coriander/
   cilantro leaves (optional)
½ tsp ground coriander
3 tbsp desiccated coconut
285 ml/10 fl oz/1¼ cups hot
   water

In a saucepan, stir-fry the shallots and garlic in the oil for 1 minute, then add the wild rice and continue stir-frying for another minute. Pour in the cold water and add the salt. Bring to the boil and simmer, uncovered, for 30 minutes.

Add the white rice and all the other ingredients, including the hot water. Bring to the boil again, stir once and cover the pan. Continue cooking on a low heat for 15–20 minutes, or in a medium oven (150–160°C/300–320°F/Gas Mark 2 or 3) for up to 30 minutes. Serve hot.

Tempeh Hamburger Steak

Tempeh is less bland than tofu, with a taste of soya beans and a pleasant nuttiness. Cooked in slices or chunks, it keeps its identity while absorbing the flavours it is cooked with. As a hamburger it tastes very good indeed, as long as you don't add ingredients which people might find additionally strange or regard as acquired tastes. The spices I use in this recipe are Indonesian, so if any are unfamiliar to you, by all means replace them with ones which you know and can easily obtain.

I would, of course, eat this with plenty of brown or white rice, plainly cooked, but it will go with any of the spiced and savoury rice dishes in this book, or you can put it in a bun like an ordinary hamburger.

Preparation: 30 minutes
Cooking: 12–16 minutes

For 4–6 people

3 tbsp peanut oil
4–5 shallots or 2 onions, finely sliced
3 cloves garlic, finely sliced
1 or 2 red chillies, de-seeded and finely chopped
1 tsp finely chopped ginger root
1 tsp ground coriander
½ tsp ground cumin
450 g/1 lb/4 cups tempeh, chopped finely or blended
Salt and pepper
2 tbsp chopped flat-leaf parsley or celery leaves
1–2 eggs
4–5 tbsp peanut oil

Stir-fry the shallots or onions until just slightly coloured. Add the garlic, chilli (if used), ginger and the ground ingredients. Stir-fry for another minute and then add the tempeh. Stir this around and season with salt and pepper. Then transfer everything to a glass bowl and leave it to cool a little.

When it is cool, mix in the parsley or celery leaves and the egg. Mix well together, and form into 4 or 6 patties. Shallow-fry these in oil in a non-stick frying pan or skillet for 6–8 minutes each side, turning them over once. I like to serve these hot, with Peanut Sauce (page 352), rice and cooked vegetables.

Tempeh and Tofu Cooked Salad

This is another vegetarian or vegan dish that will make a substantial and satisfying main course if served with rice. It is particularly good if you serve it hot with Wild and White Rice Pilaf (page 313) or cold with compressed rice (page 107).

Preparation: 10 minutes
Cooking: 15–20 minutes

For 4–6 people

390 g/14 oz/3½ cups tempeh
340 g/12 oz/3 cups tofu
112 g/4 oz/1 cup beansprouts
2 green chillies, de-seeded
    and finely sliced
3 shallots, finely sliced
1 tsp very finely chopped
    ginger root
1 clove garlic, crushed
2 tbsp mild vinegar
1 tbsp light soy sauce
½ tsp mustard
1 tsp sugar
6 tbsp water
Salt to taste
112 g/4 oz/½ cup sunflower
    oil for frying

Cut the tofu and tempeh into thin pieces, about 2.5 cm/1 inch square. Wash the bean sprouts and drain them in a colander.

In a non-stick frying pan, fry the tempeh in several batches until it is beginning to turn yellow. Do the same with the tofu. Set these aside on absorbent paper. Discard the oil, except for about 2 tablespoonfulls. Stir-fry the shallots, chillies, ginger and garlic for 1 minute or so; then add the vinegar, soy sauce, mustard and sugar. Stir again and add the water.

Bring to the boil and let this mixture simmer for 2 minutes, taste, and add salt if needed. Add the fried tempeh and tofu, stir them around, and add the bean sprouts. Stir again and leave to simmer for another 2 minutes only. Serve hot or cold, as preferred.

Tofu Hamburger Steak

Many of the ingredients in this hamburger are Japanese. However, if you prefer something spicier, by all means use the Javanese ingredients that are listed in the Tempeh Hamburger Steak on page 314. The method is the same for both. The best tofu to use is the firm, fresh Chinese kind, which you buy from a Chinese shop, or the so-called 'original tofu' that is now sold in large supermarkets and health food shops. More information about tofu will be found on page 382.

This tofu hamburger goes well with brown rice or Rice with Azuki Beans (page 112).

Preparation: 15 minutes
Cooking: 10–12 minutes

For 4–6 people

675–900 g/1½–2 lb/
  6–8 cups firm tofu
56 g/2 oz/½ cup fresh
  shiitake mushrooms or
  button mushrooms
2 tbsp chopped spring onions/
  scallions
1 tbsp unsweetened miso
  paste or yellow bean sauce
  (page 374/364)
1 tbsp light soy sauce
1 egg
2 tbsp rice flour or plain/
  all-purpose flour
Vegetable oil for frying

Put the tofu into a bowl and pour boiling water to cover it. Leave it to soak for 10 minutes. Drain, wrap the tofu in a piece of muslin, and squeeze out the water.

Then put the tofu and all the other ingredients, except the flour and oil, into a blender. Blend for a few seconds only. Transfer the mixture to a bowl and mix it again with a wooden spoon. (Alternatively, you can just mash the tofu in a bowl with the wooden spoon, then mix in the other ingredients.)

Adjust the seasoning – add some pepper if you like. Form the mixture into 4 or 6 patties and coat them lightly with the flour, then fry them in the oil, preferably in a non-stick pan, for 5–6 minutes on each side, turning them over once.

Serve as suggested above, with salad or cooked vegetables and Tomato or Red Pepper Sauce (page 347/349).

Fried Spiced Tempeh

Tempeh cooked this way tastes meaty and delicious. To go with it, I would suggest Coconut Rice (page 109) or vegetarian Fried Rice (page 126). The best vegetable dish to eat with this would be beans, served with Mild Curry Sauce (page 355) – make the sauce with coconut milk instead of yogurt if you are a vegan. This tempeh, cut into small cubes after frying, is also good with drinks before you eat.

Preparation and cooking: about 1½ hours altogether

For 4–6 people

About 700 g/1½–2 lb/8 cups
    tempeh
1 small onion
2 cloves garlic
1 tsp ground coriander
1 tsp finely chopped ginger
    root
1 bay leaf
¼ tsp ground galingale
2 heaped tbsp brown sugar
½ tsp chilli powder
450 g/16 fl oz/2 cups
    tamarind water
Salt
450 g/16 fl oz/2 cups water
Vegetable oil

Cut the tempeh into thick slices and slice the onion thinly. Put all the ingredients, except the oil, into a saucepan, cover, and cook for 50–60 minutes or until dry. Take care not to burn the contents of the pan. Leave everything to cool for a few minutes, then fry in hot oil, turning once, so that the slices of tempeh are well browned on both sides. Serve hot or cold.

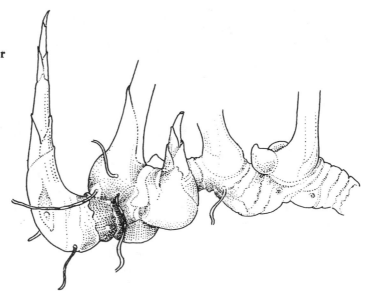

Rice and Beans in Sambal Goreng Sauce

This is a one-pot meal for vegetarians and vegans. It goes well with tofu or tempeh or with any vegetable dish.

Preparation: 10–15 minutes, excluding making the sauce
Cooking: 20–25 minutes

For 4–6 people

450 g/1 lb/2 cups long grain
  rice, washed and drained
570 ml/1 pint/2½ cups water
¼ tsp salt
1 tbsp olive oil (optional)
450 g/1 lb/4 cups French
  beans, topped and tailed
  and cut in halves
570 ml/1 pint/2½ cups
  Sambal Goreng Sauce
  (page 353)

Heat the sauce gently in a small saucepan. Put the rice and water, with the salt and oil if used, in a larger saucepan and bring the water to the boil. When it boils, stir the rice once, then leave to simmer, uncovered, for 10 minutes. Then spread the beans on top of the rice, sprinkled with a little salt, and pour over them one-third of the sauce. Cover the pan tightly, turn the heat as low as possible, and leave everything to cook undisturbed for 10–12 minutes.

Take the saucepan off the heat and put it to stand on a wet towel, still tightly covered, for 5–8 minutes. Then serve at once, with the rest of the sauce in a bowl or sauce-boat for everyone to help themselves.

Spinach, Sweet Corn and Rice Savoury Pudding

This is a very good main-course dish for vegetarians, or for vegans if you substitute coconut milk and plain/all-purpose flour for the eggs. The sweet corn should ideally be taken straight from the young cob, but canned or frozen sweet corn will do perfectly well.

You will need a 1-litre/2-pint/5-cup pudding basin or similar container as a mould.

Preparation: 50 minutes
Cooking: 50–55 minutes

For 4 people

450 g/1 lb/4 cups spinach,
    stalks removed, washed
    thoroughly
4 eggs (or, for vegans,
    112 ml/4 fl oz/½ cup
    coconut milk and 56 g/
    2 oz/¼ cup plain/
    all-purpose flour)
225 g/8 oz/2 cups sweet corn,
    blended until smooth
170 g/6 oz/1½ cups cooked
    rice
Salt and pepper
2 tbsp olive oil or peanut oil
2 onions, chopped
2 cloves garlic, chopped
1 tsp ground coriander
½ tsp chilli powder
56–84 g/2–3 oz grated cheese
    – Parmesan, Cheddar, or
    Gouda (optional)

Boil the spinach in water for 1 minute, drain in a colander and refresh under the cold tap. Squeeze out as much water as possible and chop the spinach. Put it in a bowl and keep aside.

In a frying pan, fry the onion and garlic until soft, then add the ground coriander and chilli powder, and stir. (If you are making the vegan version, stir in the flour and coconut milk at this point, and keep on stirring until you have a thick sauce.)

Add the sweet corn purée and the cooked rice. Mix everything well together, and season with salt. Transfer the mixture to the bowl containing the spinach. Mix the whole thing well. If you are making the non-vegan version, add the eggs and mix them well in with the rest.

Butter or oil the inside of the mould, and transfer the rice and spinach mix into it. Press down well with a spoon, cover with aluminium foil, and place the mould in a saucepan. Pour hot water into the saucepan so that it comes about halfway up the outside of the mould. Cover the pan, bring the water to the boil, lower the heat and let it simmer for 40–50 minutes.

Leave the pudding to cool a little, then run a knife around it, put a plate over the mould and turn it out. Serve warm in thick slices sprinkled with grated cheese if you wish, and with Tomato Sauce (page 347) or another sauce of your choice.

SWEET RICE CAKES AND PUDDINGS

This section has turned out to be quite different from what I expected. I had in mind a selection of the sweet, sticky cakes, made largely of rice flour and coconut milk and often coloured rather bright green with the juice of pandanus leaves, that you are likely to be offered in so many Asian countries if you pay an afternoon call on a friend. Such cakes make perfectly good desserts, although we do not regard them as such.

One or two of these cakes and puddings are indeed included, but most of them were in the end pushed out by dishes which are more Western in style. In their ingredients and flavouring, some are modern, others look back to the traditional ways of cooking rice in the West, using milk, almonds and spices. Many are variations on a rice-pudding theme, though a few may be only just recognizable. But in the course of two years' testing of recipes and entertaining of candid friends, it has become quite clear that these puddings are the ones that go down well in Britain; and a somewhat larger collection of the traditional Eastern sweets can, of course, be found in my other books.

Field temple: Bali

320

Rice and Rhubarb Porridge

Although this recipe comes to me via Finland (from Jaakko Rahola), there are several recognizably similar recipes in this section which are from other parts of the world. Rice porridge or congee can turn up in all sorts of different outfits. You could quite fairly call this a rhubarb fool.

If you have plenty of time, make the porridge in the Oriental way (Caramelized Congee with Berries, see page 327). If you are pressed, by all means follow this Finnish recipe. Finnish jams are extremely good, good enough to put in fine ice-cream, or even rice porridge. This is a real bonus for a cook in a hurry.

To achieve the consistency of porridge you need to cook the rice in at least 4 times its own volume of liquid. It will take over an hour for the rice to absorb so much, and for the rice grains to break up and become soft. For the recipe to be a quick one, as here, you must use a food processor.

You can, of course, make this sweet porridge with any fresh fruit purée. Cook your rhubarb or other fruit with sugar for 2–3 minutes, and put it with the other ingredients into the food processor (some fruits and berries should be passed through a sieve for best results).

Preparation and cooking: 17–20 minutes in all

For 4–6 people

170 g/6 oz/¾ cup short grain or Thai Fragrant rice, washed and drained
450 g/1 lb/1½ cups rhubarb jam, the best obtainable
Sugar if needed
2–4 tbsp double/heavy cream (optional)

Boil the rice in plenty of water at a rolling boil for 10–12 minutes. Drain. Transfer to a food processor with the other ingredients and blend until smooth. Taste, and add sugar if necessary. Chill for about 2 hours. Serve, either chilled or at room temperature, as you prefer.

Stuffed Glutinous Rice Steamed Cakes
Kue bugis

These Indonesian batter cakes are filled with sweetened grated coconut, and are usually wrapped in banana leaves for cooking. As banana leaves, fresh or frozen, are now easily available in many Asian shops in the West, you may prefer to use these instead of ramekins; they give a subtle aroma to the cakes as well as saving the washing up.

Wash your banana leaf well. With sharp scissors, cut it into 20–25 cm/8–10 inch squares. Then soak the squares in hot water for 10 minutes to make them more pliable. Imagine each square divided into nine small squares – three rows of three. In the middle square, arrange the layers of thick coconut milk, porridge, etc., in the order described below, to build up a flattish 'cake'. Making the first folds along the grain of the leaf, fold the two sides over the cake. Then, folding across the grain, fold the ends of the packet downwards and up against the bottom of the cake, so that the cake is completely sealed inside the folded leaf, ready to be steamed.

Preparation: 15–20 minutes
Cooking: 15–20 minutes

Makes 8–10 cakes

225 g/8 oz/1 cup glutinous
  rice flour
340 ml/12 fl oz/1½ cups
  coconut milk
A pinch of salt

For the filling:

112 g/4 oz/1 cup grated
  coconut, fresh or
  desiccated
84 g/3 oz/½ cup brown sugar
1 tbsp glutinous rice flour
225 ml/8 fl oz/1 cup water

Put the rice flour in a saucepan and pour in the coconut milk carefully, stirring continuously. Add a pinch of salt. Cook this mixture, stirring occasionally at first but then, as it thickens, stirring continuously. It will begin to look very like porridge. Go on cooking for 5 more minutes.

Now make the filling. Heat the sugar in the water until it dissolves, then stir in the coconut and let it simmer until all the water has been absorbed into the coconut. Put in a tablespoonful of glutinous rice flour, mix well, and continue cooking for another 2 minutes, stirring all the time.

In another saucepan, boil the thick coconut milk with a pinch of salt. As soon as it is on the point of boiling, this must be stirred continuously for 3 minutes.

In Indonesia, kue bugis are made in banana leaves as explained above, but they can equally well be made in small heatproof bowls or ramekins. Put about 2 teaspoonfuls of thick coconut milk into each ramekin,

For the cream:

225 ml/8 fl oz/1 cup very
    thick coconut milk
A pinch of salt

then a tablespoonful of the thick 'porridge'. Smooth this with a spoon and put on top of it a tablespoonful of the filling, then another tablespoonful of the porridge, and top it off with 2 tablespoonfuls of thick coconut milk. Then steam for 10–15 minutes. Serve warm or cold in the ramekins.

Rice Flour and Chicken Dessert

In 1986 the Culture and Tourist Association of Konya, in Turkey, organized the first of a biennial series of international congresses on food and cookery. It was a great occasion, and hospitality was lavish. Among many delicious things that I tasted there for the first time was this remarkable dessert. You may not expect to find chicken in a sweet dish; I certainly did not, and was duly astonished when I was told about it. But it tastes extremely good.

The version I give here is a combination of two recipes: a Turkish one, from Nevin Halici, and a late fourteenth century Italian recipe for *bramagere*, which is approximately the same word as *blancmange*. The rice ought really to be freshly ground, but rice flour from a packet is perfectly all right.

Preparation: 8 hours (or overnight) soaking + 40 minutes
Cooking: 35 minutes

For 8–12 people

112 g/4 oz/½ cup Jasmine
    rice or Basmati, washed,
    then soaked in 225 ml/
    8 fl oz/1 cup water for at
    least 8 hours or overnight;
    or 112 g/4 oz/½ cup rice
    flour, mixed with 225 ml/
    8 fl oz/1 cup water or milk
1 litre/1¾ pints/4½ cups
    milk
170 g/6 oz/¾ cup granulated
    sugar

Boil the chicken breast in a saucepan, with just enough water to cover it, for 15–20 minutes. If you are using rice grains, put them, and the water they were soaked in, into a food processor and blend until you have a nice runny rice paste.

Take the chicken breast out and refresh it under cold running water for a few seconds. Lay it on a tray, put a tea-towel/dishcloth over it and roll it once with a rolling pin, as if you were rolling pastry. The chicken breast can then be easily torn by hand into very fine shreds.

In a non-stick saucepan, heat the milk slowly. When it is on the point of boiling, pour in the rice paste and stir almost continuously for 15 minutes while it simmers. Then add the sugar, and go on stirring for

1 breast of chicken, without
   skin (about 100 g/
   3½–4 oz)
56 g/2 oz/½ cup ground
   almonds
½ tsp rose water (optional)

10 minutes. Finally add the shredded chicken meat
and the ground almonds and stir for yet another 10
minutes. During this final stir, mix in the rose water if
you are using it.

You can now divide the rice mixture among 8, 10,
or 12 small cups or ramekins, to be eaten, warm or
cold, with a spoon. Alternatively, heat a large, well-
buttered, non-stick frying pan. When it is hot, pour
the rice porridge from the saucepan into it. Give the
pan a shake to level the surface, and then leave it on a
low heat for 7–8 minutes, without stirring. This will
cook the underside of the rice mixture to a lovely
golden brown. Leave it in the pan until it has
thoroughly cooled. When cold, transfer it to a flat dish
and cut it into pieces like a cake.

Coconut Cream Rice Dessert

This is one of many Oriental desserts made with rice flour. It is delicious with a
summer fruit salad (all those juicy red berries) or with my own favourite combination
of mangoes in passion fruit juice.

The rice should really be freshly ground. If you have a food processor, this is no
problem at all.

Preparation: 8 hours or overnight soaking + 40–50 minutes
Cooking: 35–40 minutes

For 8–10 people

112 g/4 oz/½ cup rice, Thai
   Fragrant or Basmati,
   washed, then soaked in
   225 ml/8 fl oz/1 cup water
   for at least 8 hours or
   overnight
570 ml/1 pint/2½ cups very
   thick coconut milk

In a food processor, blend the rice, with the water it
has been soaked in, to a smooth runny paste.

Heat the coconut milk, and cream if used, in a
non-stick saucepan. When it is on the point of
boiling, pour in the rice paste and stir almost continuously for 15 minutes while it simmers. Then add the
sugar and continue stirring for 10 minutes. Finally add
the ground almonds and orange flower water, if used.
Stir continuously for 10 more minutes.

Divide the mixture among 8 or 10 dessert bowls, big
enough to be only half-filled by the creamy rice. Chill

420 ml/¾ pint/2 cups single cream (if you do not want to use cream, use 1 litre/ 1¾ pints/ 4½ cups coconut milk)

170 g/6 oz/¾ cup granulated sugar

56 g/2 oz/½ cup ground almonds

1 tsp orange flower water (optional)

For the mango in passion fruit juice (if required):

2–3 ripe mangoes, peeled and cubed

Juice of 1 lime

2 tsp sugar

10–12 passion fruits

2 tbsp dark rum (optional)

for at least 4 hours before serving, topped with fruit salad or the mango in passion fruit juice described below.

Put the mango cubes in a glass bowl and mix in the lime juice and sugar. Halve the passion fruits and squeeze the juice and seeds into another bowl. Then pass the juice through a sieve into the bowl with the mangoes. Discard the seeds. Add the rum, if used, and taste. You may need to add a little more sugar.

This can also be prepared in advance and chilled, but it should be served at room temperature.

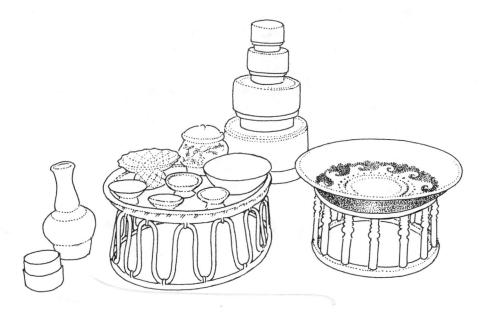

Trays and food stands: Indonesia

Rice Batter Cake with Bananas

This Indonesian batter pudding is traditionally made with coconut milk (page 368), but is just as good with cow's or goat's milk. The pudding will be white or brown, depending on the colour of the sugar.

Preparation: 20–25 minutes
Cooking: 30 minutes

For 4–6 people

170 g/6 oz/¾ cup rice flour
56 g/2 oz/¼ cup cornflour/
    cornstarch
3 bananas
A large pinch of salt
700 ml/1¼ pints/3 cups
    coconut milk or cow's or
    goat's milk
98 g/3½ oz/½ cup palm
    sugar or brown sugar or
    white granulated sugar

Sift the two kinds of flour into a bowl and add the salt. Cut the bananas into rounds about 1 cm/½ inch thick.

Make the batter by blending the flour with about 112 ml/4 fl oz/½ cup of the cold milk so that you have a smooth paste.

Heat the rest of the milk in a saucepan. When it is almost boiling, stir the sugar into it until completely dissolved. Then pour in the batter, a little at a time, stirring it all the while with a wooden spoon so that it becomes a smooth, thick liquid with no lumps.

Spoon this into ramekins, leaving room for the banana pieces. Put two or three banana rounds on top of each ramekin, and then steam the ramekins in a steamer for 25–30 minutes. Alternatively, stand them on the bottom of a large saucepan, pour in boiling water until it comes halfway up the sides of the ramekins, cover the saucepan and cook until the batter is set; this will take 25–30 minutes.

Serve warm or cold.

Caramelized Congee with Berries

Congee may be simply a plain rice porridge, eaten as a cereal at breakfast, or it may become something quite elaborate. When I was a little girl my grandmother would give me congee and nothing else if I had a stomach upset. It made me recover pretty fast, either because I soon got bored with the congee or perhaps because it really did do me good. Since then, I have often experimented with ways to make congee attractive, and I think this recipe does it rather successfully. I hope it will also be welcomed by vegans. You can add as many different kinds of berries in it as you can find, or just stick to one or two.

Preparation: 2–4 hours soaking + 25 minutes
Cooking: 1¼ hours

For 6–8 people

For the congee:

112 g/4 oz/½ cup Thai
  Fragrant rice or any short
  grain rice, soaked for 2–4
  hours or longer, then
  washed and drained
850 ml/1½ pints/3¾ cups
  coconut milk
3 tbsp granulated sugar
A pinch of salt
A few drops of vanilla
  essence (optional)

For the fruit mix:

225 g/8 oz loganberries
225 g/8 oz raspberries
225 g/8 oz strawberries
225 g/8 oz blackberries or
  whatever berries are
  available locally

To finish:

1 tbsp Demerara sugar or soft
  brown sugar for each
  serving

Wash the berries carefully, drain and set aside. Put all the ingredients for the congee in a saucepan, bring to the boil, then simmer, stirring occasionally, until you have a good thick porridge. This will take about 1 hour. You can use the congee as it is, or liquidize it for a smoother texture.

To Serve. Divide half of the congee among 6 or 8 heatproof plates. Distribute the berries equally, arranging them on top of the congee. Divide the rest of the congee among the plates, pouring it on top of the fruit. Sprinkle each serving with brown sugar, and just before you serve put the plates under the grill for 2 minutes or until the sugar is caramelized. Serve immediately.

Rice Flour Pudding with Nuts and Fruit

You can use either cow's milk or coconut milk for this pudding. The best nuts are pistachios; otherwise, use almonds, walnuts, or (in Indonesia) kenari nuts. Whatever kind you use, they need to be blanched or roasted so that the thin skin can easily be removed. The fruit should be either apricots and peaches, or mango and jackfruit. Ideally, the rice should be freshly ground in a food processor, but rice flour from a packet will do.

I suggest you chill the pudding in the bowls or glasses it is to be served in, because unmoulding can be awkward – unless you line the mould with clingfilm.

Preparation: 8 hours or overnight soaking + 40 minutes
Cooking: 30 minutes

For 8–12 people

1 litre/1¾ pints/4½ cups cow's milk or coconut milk
2 tbsp cornflour/cornstarch, mixed with 3 tbsp water or milk
112 g/4 oz/½ cup rice, Thai Fragrant or Basmati, washed, then soaked in 225 ml/8 fl oz/1 cup water or milk for at least 8 hours or overnight; or the same quantity of rice flour, mixed with the same quantity of water or milk
170 g/6 oz/¾ cup granulated sugar
170 g/6 oz/1½ cups peeled fruit (see above), cut into cubes
56 g/2 oz/½ cup skinned nuts (see above), roughly crushed

For the fruit sauce (if required):

340–450 g/12 oz–1 lb/3–4 cups peeled fruit (the same fruit as you are using for the pudding), chopped
1 tbsp lemon juice
1–2 tbsp castor/granulated sugar, dissolved in 4 tbsp warm water

In a food processor, blend the rice and the water it has been soaked in, to a smooth runny paste. In a non-stick saucepan, heat the milk slowly. When it is on the point of boiling, pour in the rice paste, then the cornflour/cornstarch paste, and stir almost continuously while the mixture simmers for 15 minutes. Then add the sugar and go on stirring for another 10 minutes. Finally add the fruit and nuts and stir for another 2 minutes.

Divide the pudding among 8, 10, or 12 small bowls or glasses, as suggested above. Chill, and serve cold, by itself or with a sauce made from the same fruit as you have used in the pudding.

To make the sauce, blend all the ingredients together until smooth. Serve chilled or at room temperature.

Sweet Rice Cake with Raspberries

This pudding is quick and easy to make, but retains the traditional combination of rice, milk and almonds. The fruit topping can be varied: strawberries or red currants in summer, figs or blackberries in autumn, or of course your favourite tropical fruits – jackfruit, perhaps, or durian?

Preparation: 45 minutes
Cooking: 35–40 minutes

For 6–8 people

For the sweet rice cake:

112 g/4 oz/½ cup short grain
　or pudding rice
340 ml/12 fl oz/1½ cups
　milk
112 g/4 oz/1 cup ground
　almonds
A pinch of cinnamon
4 tbsp granulated sugar
2 eggs

For the topping:

450 g/1 lb/4 cups raspberries
1 tbsp castor/granulated sugar
Whipped double/heavy cream
　or pouring cream
　(optional)

Butter a 23-cm/9-inch soufflé dish or Pyrex pie dish and line it with bakewell/wax paper. Turn on the oven to 180°C/350°F/Gas Mark 4.

Wash the rice in several changes of water and put it into a saucepan. Add the milk, stir well and bring to the boil. Simmer for 30 minutes, or until the rice has absorbed all the milk. Set the rice aside to cool.

Beat the egg and sugar until they are quite frothy (this takes about 4 minutes with a hand beater or 2 minutes with an electric one). Add the ground almonds to the mixture and beat for a few more seconds.

Stir the egg, sugar and almond mixture into the rice, and put the whole thing into your lined dish. Bake in the oven for 35–40 minutes. Then take it out, put a plate upside-down on top of the dish and turn the cake out. Peel off the bakewell paper and leave the cake to cool.

Just before serving, spread the whipped cream on top (if you are using it) and spread the raspberries or other fruit on the cream. (Alternatively, put the fruit directly on top of the cake and serve pouring cream in a jug; or forget the cream altogether.) Sprinkle the castor/granulated sugar on the fruit. Cut the cake into 6 or 8 portions and serve.

Italian Rice Cake
Torta di riso

Anne del Conte, who has allowed me to take this recipe from her book *Entertaining all'Italiana*, says that rice cake is as typically Italian as rice pudding is English, and furthermore that there exist as many different versions of it. However, this is a soft cake, not a milk pudding. It must be made at least 24 hours before it is to be eaten, and it should then be wrapped in foil and kept in the fridge. It can stay there for 2 or 3 days if need be. Take it out and let it stand at room temperature for at least 2 hours before serving, so that it warms through again.

Preparation: 45 minutes
Cooking: 45 minutes cooking

For 8–10 people

700 ml/1¼ pints/3 cups
    full-cream milk
170 g/6 oz/¾ cup castor/
    granulated sugar
A strip of lemon peel, the
    yellow part only
2.5-cm/1-inch length of
    vanilla pod, split in half
5-cm/2-inch cinnamon stick
Salt
140 g/5 oz/scant ⅔ cup
    Arborio rice
112 g/4 oz/¾ cup almonds,
    blanched and peeled
56 g/2 oz/½ cup pine nuts
4 eggs, separated
28 g/1 oz candied orange,
    lemon and citron peel,
    chopped
Grated rind of ½ lemon
3 tbsp rum
Butter and dried breadcrumbs
    for the tin
Icing sugar for decoration

Put the milk into a saucepan with 28 g/1 oz/⅛ cup of the sugar, the lemon peel, vanilla, cinnamon and a pinch of salt, and bring to the boil. Stir the rice in with a wooden spoon, and cook, uncovered and stirring often, on a very low heat until the rice has absorbed the milk and is soft and creamy. This will take about 40 minutes. Then set the pan aside to cool.

While the rice is cooking, heat the oven to 180°C/350°F/Gas Mark 4.

Spread the almonds and pine nuts on a baking tray, and toast them in the preheated oven for about 10 minutes. Give the tray a bit of a shake every few minutes so that they don't burn. Let them cool a little, then chop them coarsely with a knife or in a blender. Don't reduce them to powder.

Take the lemon peel, vanilla and cinnamon out of the rice and transfer the rice to a mixing bowl. Work the egg yolks into the rice, one at a time, making sure each is mixed thoroughly. Now stir in the rest of the sugar, and the nuts, candied peel, grated lemon rind and rum, making sure that everything is well mixed together. Whip the egg whites until they are stiff, and fold these in also.

Butter a round spring-clip cake tin with a removable base, about 25 cm/10 inches across. Line the base with greaseproof paper and butter the paper. Sprinkle all over the sides and base with breadcrumbs. Shake off any excess.

Spoon the mixture into the tin. Bake for about 45 minutes; the cake is done when a toothpick pushed into the middle of the cake comes out just a little moist. During cooking, the cake shrinks a little. Leave it to cool in the tin, then unclip the side and turn the cake out on to a plate. Remove the base and the paper, put a round serving dish over the cake and turn it right way up.

Cover the cake and the plate with aluminium foil, and refrigerate as described above. Sprinkle icing sugar all over the cake just before serving.

Black Rice Pudding

This is an East-meets-West variation on black glutinous rice porridge. You can also make it with wild rice, provided you cook the wild rice separately in 340 ml/12 fl oz/ 1½ cups of water for 30 minutes before you start to cook it with the milk.

Preparation: 2–4 hours soaking + 20 minutes
Cooking: 40–45 minutes

For 6–8 people

170 g/6 oz/⅔ cup black glutinous rice or wild rice, soaked for 2–4 hours, then drained
570 ml/1 pint/2½ cups cow's milk or coconut milk
A large pinch of salt
84 g/3 oz soft butter
84 g/3 oz/½ cup sugar
3 eggs
3 tbsp Demerara sugar

Bring the rice, milk and salt to the boil in a saucepan and simmer for 25–30 minutes, stirring often. Leave to cool.

Beat the butter and sugar for 3–4 minutes, then add the eggs. Continue beating for 5–6 minutes longer. Combine this with the cool rice mixture.

Butter a round soufflé dish and pour the rice mixture into it. Sprinkle the brown sugar on top. Bake in a preheated oven at 180°C/350°F/Gas Mark 4 for 40–45 minutes.

Serve hot or warm, with whipped cream if you wish.

Rice Flour and Pistachio Blini

Some years ago I was in Gaziantep, in southern Turkey, a famous centre for growing pistachio nuts. That was where I first met these delicious pancakes – all the more delicious, of course, because the pistachios were fresh off the tree. I have been hunting through Turkish cookbooks for the recipe, but in vain; so after a little experimenting I have made my own pancakes, which I think are pretty close to the ones we had that day.

You can make them as pancakes, in a shallow pan about 18 cm/7 inches in diameter, or as blini in a cast-iron blini pan. I prefer them just as they are, quite sweet already, without anything on them; they are good for breakfast, with maple syrup if you like, but you can eat them at any time of day. For elevenses, or tea, or with coffee after a light supper, spread the blini with jam or spread jam on your pancake and then fold it, in half and in half again, to make a quarter-circle. Stewed or fresh fruit and cream would go well, too.

Preparation: about 30 minutes + 30–40 minutes resting
Cooking: 30–35 minutes

Makes 50–60 small blini or
8–10 pancakes

112 g/4 oz/½ cup rice flour
112 g/4 oz/½ cup plain flour
1 tsp baking powder or
  bicarbonate of soda
A large pinch of salt
5 tbsp icing/confectioners
  sugar
56 g/2 oz margarine, melted
1 egg
285 ml/10 fl oz/1¼ cups milk
2 tbsp peanut or sunflower
  oil
112 g/4 oz/1 cup shelled
  pistachio nuts, boiled for 2
  minutes, skinned, and
  chopped or coarsely ground
  in a blender

Mix the two kinds of flour and the baking powder or bicarbonate. Sift them into a bowl, add the sugar, and mix well with a wooden spoon. Beat the egg and add it, and the melted margarine, to the mixture. Continue stirring with the wooden spoon for a few minutes, so that you get a smooth dough. Then add the milk, a little at a time, stirring constantly so that the dough becomes a smooth, thick batter, able to be poured. Add the oil and stir vigorously to mix it well in. If you are going to make pancakes, add another 56 ml/2 fl oz/¼ cup of milk to make the batter a little thinner. Leave the batter to rest for 30–40 minutes.

Just before you start cooking the pancakes or blini, add the chopped pistachios to the batter and give them a good stir.

Butter or oil the pan and start ladling the batter into it. For blini, fill the compartments in the pan but don't let the batter run over. Cook on a low heat until the batter is set, with little bubbles on top; then turn the blini over and cook on the other side for just 1 minute. For a pancake, use just enough to cover the bottom of the pan thinly, and cook in the same way. Serve hot or warm, as suggested above. If necessary, the blini or pancakes can be reheated quickly in a warm oven.

Creole Rice Fritters
Calas

Almost all rice fritters and croquettes can be turned out in large quantities very cheaply, and calas are no exception. They are delicious either for breakfast, with jam, or at teatime, served like scones with jam and cream. If you make them with salt and pepper instead of sugar, then they go beautifully at breakfast with bacon and eggs.

This recipe is also very quick. Instead of yeast, I use baking powder, so you can fry them straight after their 30-minute rest period instead of leaving the batter to rise overnight. You can, however, keep the batter in the fridge for up to 48 hours, so one batch of batter can provide you with three breakfasts if you time it right.

Preparation and cooking: 1 hour including resting time + time to deep-fry

Makes about 30 fritters

225 g/8 oz/1 cup long grain rice, soaked in cold water for 40 minutes, then drained
570 ml/1 pint/2½ cups water
1 tsp salt
4 tbsp white sugar
112 g/4 oz/½ cup plain/all-purpose flour or rice flour
1 tbsp baking powder
1 tsp cinnamon powder
½ tsp grated or ground nutmeg
4 eggs
Sunflower or corn oil for deep-frying
Icing sugar for dusting (optional)

Put the rice, with the water and salt, into a saucepan and bring to the boil. Stir, reduce the heat and let it simmer for 15–20 minutes or until all the water has been absorbed by the rice. Take the pan off the heat and add the sugar. Stir until the sugar is dissolved, and leave the rice to get cold.

When the rice is cold, sift the flour, baking powder, cinnamon and nutmeg into it. Stir to mix everything, then transfer to a liquidizer or food processor. Break the eggs into the mixture and liquidize the whole lot into a thick batter. Transfer this to a bowl and let it rest for 30 minutes.

To deep fry the calas, heat the oil in a wok or deep-fryer to 160°C/320°F, at which temperature a small piece of bread tossed in turns brown in a few seconds. Each fritter is a tablespoonful of batter; just drop the batter into the hot oil and when there are 5 or 6 of them let them fry for 2–3 minutes or until they are golden brown, turning them often. Drain them on absorbent paper, dust them with icing/confectioners sugar if you wish, and serve, hot or warm, as suggested above.

Black Rice Sorbet

This recipe is my own adaptation of an old family recipe for rice porridge which we used to eat at both breakfast and teatime. Black rice porridge and sorbet are in fact deep purple, as striking in colour as they are in flavour. This version, with coconut milk, is a creamy ice that contains no animal products and is therefore acceptable to vegans.

More information on black glutinous rice and where to buy it is given on page 6.

Preparation: 4–8 hours (or overnight) soaking + 15 minutes
Cooking: 50–60 minutes + freezing time

For 6 people

84 g/3 oz/½ cup black glutinous rice, soaked in cold water for 4–8 hours or overnight, then drained
1.7 litres/3 pints/7½ cups coconut milk, made from 285 g/10 oz/5 cups, firmly packed desiccated coconut
½ tsp salt
1 small stick cinnamon
3 tbsp brown sugar
2 tbsp glucose

Put the coconut milk and the drained rice in a saucepan with the salt and cinnamon stick and bring it to the boil. Simmer gently for 10 minutes and add the sugar. Continue simmering, stirring often, until the porridge becomes thick (this will take 50–60 minutes).

Take out and discard the cinnamon stick and pour the porridge into a liquidizer. Leave it to cool for 10 minutes, add the glucose, and liquidize until the mixture is smooth. Put it into a sorbetière or an ice-cream maker and churn according to the instructions for your machine.

If you don't have a machine, transfer the liquidized porridge, when cold, to a plastic box. Put it in the freezer for 1 hour; it should then be slushy but not quite frozen. Liquidize it again, return it to the plastic box and put it back in the freezer for another hour. Repeat the cycle once more – 3 liquidizings and freezings altogether.

Freeze the sorbet until needed. Before serving, let it stand in the fridge for at least 1 hour to soften.

Rice Ice-Cream

Caroline Liddell and Robin Weir have allowed me to adapt this recipe from their book, *Ices: The Definitive Guide*. It makes an interesting comparison with my own Black Rice Sorbet (page 335). There is nothing new in the notion of making ice-cream with rice; it has been done in Europe for at least 150 years, though the authors say that it is only in Italy that you will find rice ice-cream being regularly made today.

This plain ice-cream tastes very good with a chilled fruit sauce.

Preparation and cooking: 1 hour + about 12 hours freezing

Makes about 1.25 litres/
2 pints/5 cups

112 g/4 oz/½ cup pudding
   rice, washed and drained
505 ml/18 fl oz/2¼ cups
   milk
170 g/6 oz/¾ cup vanilla
   sugar (page 382)
505 ml/18 fl oz/2¼ cups
   double/heavy cream or
   whipping cream, chilled

It is easier to get the right texture if you cook the rice in a double saucepan, but if you don't have one, an ordinary saucepan will do.

Put the rice, milk and vanilla sugar into the top part of a double saucepan and put this directly on the stove. In the bottom part of the saucepan, heat water for steaming. Bring the milk to the boil, stirring constantly. Then put the pan with the milk and rice on to the bottom pan, in which water is now simmering. Cover, and continue cooking for 40 minutes or until the rice is perfectly tender. Then take the pan off the heat and let it cool to room temperature, still covered. Then put the rice mixture in the fridge.

When it is well chilled, stir the chilled cream into the mixture and put the whole lot into the ice-cream machine. (If you don't have a machine, proceed as described for Black Rice Sorbet on page 335.) Churn it for about 15 minutes or until it has the consistency of thick cream. Then transfer it to plastic containers, cover it with waxed paper, put the lid on and freeze. It needs to spend 12 hours in the freezer before it can be served.

Before serving, leave this ice cream in the fridge for at least 1 hour to soften. It contains a lot of starch, so that if you try to thaw it at room temperature it will simply melt on the outside while remaining frozen hard inside.

Baked Rice Pudding

This is Jane Grigson's recipe from *English Food*. I cannot resist the temptation to quote her final words on the subject:

> Three conclusions – a rice pudding must be flavoured with a vanilla pod or cinnamon stick, it must be cooked long and slowly, it must be eaten with plenty of double cream. Like so many other English dishes, it has been wrecked by meanness and lack of thought.

Preparation: 5 minutes
Cooking: 3 hours or more

For 4–6 people

70 g/2½ oz/⅓ cup short grain (pudding) rice
855 ml/1½ pints/3¾ cups full-cream milk, or a little more
28 g/1 oz butter
2 tbsp sugar
1 vanilla pod, split, or 1 cinnamon stick

Put the rice, with about 570 ml/1 pint/2½ cups of the milk and the other ingredients, into a heatproof dish. Leave in a gentle oven at 135°C/275°F/Gas Mark 1 for 3 hours. After the first hour, stir the pudding and add some more milk. After the second hour, do the same thing and, if you like, add some single cream.

By reducing the oven temperature to 120°C/250°F/ Gas Mark ½, you can increase the cooking time and even double it. Add more milk occasionally; Jane Grigson suggests that you may eventually need up to 1.7 litres/3 pints/7½ cups. The advantage of such prolonged cooking is in the rich creamy texture of the pudding and the slight caramelization of the rice grains.

Flemish Rice Pudding with Frambozen

This is a thoroughly modern recipe, for which I have to thank my friend Silvija Davidson. She tells me that Frambozen is a lambic wheat beer – 'lambic' meaning that it ferments spontaneously, without any added yeast – brewed near Brussels, and flavoured with raspberries. You can buy it in London without too much difficulty, and probably in other large towns; but if you cannot find it, or something like it (supposing that there is anything like it), then use any lager beer mixed with 56 ml/2 fl oz/¼ cup raspberry juice, made by passing fresh raspberries through a sieve and sweetened with 2 tablespoons of icing/confectioner's sugar. With the lager and raspberry juice you will also need 285 ml/½ pint/1¼ cups of milk; this is because lager is more bitter than Frambozen, and the milk compensates for this.

Preparation: 30 minutes
Cooking: 3–4 hours

For 6–8 people

125 g/4½ oz/a generous ½ cup Italian pudding rice or other short grain rice
1 litre/1¾ pints/4½ cups Frambozen beer; or lager and raspberry juice (see above) and 285 ml/10 fl oz/1¼ cups milk
A pinch of salt (optional)
100 g/3½ oz/½ cup fruit sugar or castor/granulated sugar
4 eggs, free range, size 2, separated
56 g/2 oz/⅓ cup dry macaroons or amaretti, finely crushed

Place rice, Frambozen (or lager and raspberry juice – but not the milk), salt (if used) and two-thirds of the sugar in a flameproof casserole. Bring the beer to the boil, stir the rice, and transfer the casserole to a slow oven preheated to 150°C/300°F/Gas Mark 2. Bake, covered, for 2–3 hours, stirring occasionally, then remove. If using Frambozen, allow to cool to near room temperature.

If using lager and raspberry juice, stir in the milk at this point and put the casserole on the stove over a low heat. Cook gently, stirring often, until all the milk is absorbed; this will take 15–20 minutes.

Beat the egg yolks in a bowl and stir into cooled rice. Whisk the egg whites until fairly stiff, add the remaining sugar and whisk again until stiff. Stir a good tablespoonful of this meringue into the rice to loosen the mixture, then lightly fold the remaining meringue into the rice. Spoon into lightly oiled baking dish(es): 1 large one (23 × 28 cm/9 × 11 inches) or 2 small ones (18 cm/7 inches square). Sprinkle with crushed macaroons. Bake in a moderate oven at 190°C/375°F/Gas Mark 5 for 40 minutes to 1 hour, or until just firm in the centre.

Serve hot, warm, or chilled. This pudding is good with fresh raspberries, and pouring cream if you wish, but quite delicious even without.

Afghan Milky Rice Pudding
Sheer birinj

In *Noshe Djan*, Helen Saberi describes this as similar to an English milky rice pudding. For me, the taste is surprisingly different, just because of the cardamom seeds and rose water.

Preparation and cooking: about 1–1¼ hours altogether

For 4–6 people

112 g/4 oz/½ cup short grain rice, washed and drained
570 ml/1 pint/2½ cups water
505 ml/18 fl oz/2¼ cups milk
112 g/4 oz/½ cup sugar
2 tsp rose water
¼ tsp ground green or white cardamom seeds
28 g/1 oz/¼ cup finely ground or chopped pistachios or almonds

Put the rice and the water in a saucepan and bring it to the boil. Turn down the heat and simmer it, stirring from time to time, until the rice is cooked and soft and all the water has evaporated or been absorbed.

Add the milk, bring it back to the boil, turn down the heat and continue simmering until the mixture thickens a little. Add the sugar. Go on simmering, stirring often to prevent sticking, until the sugar has dissolved and the mixture has thickened further, though it should remain runny. Add the ground cardamom and rose water and cook for another 1–2 minutes.

Serve the rice on a large flat plate, decorated with ground pistachios or almonds. Afghans like this dish cold, but it can be eaten warm if preferred.

An Indian Milk Pudding with Rice and Saffron
Kesari kheer

This recipe, which I think is a very traditional one, was given to me by Chef Arvind Saraswat, who also showed me how he cooks it in his kitchen at the Taj Palace Hotel in New Delhi. *Kesari* means saffron.

Preparation and cooking: about 1–1¼ hours altogether

For 4–6 people

1.5 litres/2½ pints/6½ cups milk

84 g/3 oz/⅓ cup Basmati rice, washed and soaked for 30 minutes or longer, then drained

15 g/½ oz ghee/clarified butter

112 g/4 oz/½ cup sugar, or more if the dish is to be served cold

¼ tsp ground green cardamom seeds

28 g/1 oz/¼ cup almonds

21 g/¾ oz/⅛ cup raisins

1 g/a small pinch of saffron, dissolved in milk

Boil the milk. At the same time, in another saucepan, heat the ghee/clarified butter and fry the rice for 2–3 minutes, stirring it so that every grain is well coated in butter. Add the boiling milk, and bring this back to the boil. Turn down the heat and simmer gently until the rice is cooked. Add the sugar and continue simmering until the dish is reduced to the desired consistency. Add the remaining ingredients and stir them well in. If you intend to serve the kheer cold, add a little extra sugar.

Serve hot or cold in stemmed glasses.

Blackberry and Apple Cold Rice Pudding

There is nothing traditional about the cold pudding described here; it is just an attractive dessert, made very simply from fresh ingredients. It tastes remarkably good, and is, I feel, true to English taste at its best. It should be chilled in individual stemmed glasses, and served with pouring cream.

Preparation and cooking: about 90 minutes

For 6–8 people

84 g/3 oz/½ cup short grain or pudding rice, washed and drained
56 g/2 oz/¼ cup sugar
28 g/1 oz unsalted butter
700 ml/1¼ pints/3 cups milk
225 g/8 oz/2 cups blackberries, washed and drained
1 eating apple, about 170 g/6 oz when peeled and cored; preferably Cox's Orange Pippin
2 tbsp lemon juice
84 g/3 oz/⅓ cup sugar
285 ml/½ pint/1¼ cups double/heavy cream, lightly whipped
1 tsp gelatine, softened in 1 tbsp cold water
6 or 8 stemmed glasses

Half-fill a largish saucepan with water and bring it to the boil. Add the rice, and cook at a rolling boil for 4 minutes. Drain in a colander. Rinse the saucepan and put the rice back into it. Add the sugar, butter and milk, and cook on a low heat, stirring often, until the milk has been absorbed by the rice. This should take 50–60 minutes; if it takes much less, the heat is too high. Leave to cool.

Peel, core and slice the apple, and put it in a smaller pan with the blackberries and lemon juice. Add the sugar, cover the pan, and cook on a low heat for 4 minutes. Remove the pan from the heat. While the fruit is still hot, add the softened gelatine and stir to dissolve it. Liquidize the fruit mixture for a minute or so, and pass it through a fine sieve into a bowl. Leave it to cool.

When the fruit is cool, mix it into the cool rice with a wooden spoon, stirring everything well together. Leave to cool further before folding in the whipped cream.

Divide the pudding among the glasses, and refrigerate until set. Serve, topped with pouring cream.

Sweet Glutinous Rice with Mango

This sweet glutinous rice is popular, in one form or another, all over South-East Asia. Various fruits can go with it – typically mango, jackfruit, or durian – and it is eaten also with jaggery syrup, or thick coconut milk with a pinch of salt, or with a coconut milk custard called *sankhaya*. When you make it, instead of these rather exotic accompaniments, you may like to try it with sweetened or unsweetened cream, or even with a little crème anglaise.

Preparation and cooking: soaking + 30 minutes

For 6–8 people

450 g/1 lb/2 cups glutinous rice, soaked in cold water for 30 minutes, then drained

570 ml/1 pint/2½ cups coconut milk

A pinch of salt

2–3 tbsp castor/granulated sugar

4 small or 2 large mangoes, peeled, then sliced or cubed

For the sankhaya (optional):

4 eggs, size 2

6 tbsp grated palm sugar or Demerara sugar

A pinch of salt

170 ml/6 fl oz/¾ cup very thick coconut milk

Put the rice in a saucepan with the coconut milk, salt and sugar. Bring to the boil and simmer, stirring occasionally with a wooden spoon, until the rice has absorbed all the liquid and has become very soft. Transfer to a steamer and steam the rice for 15 minutes.

(While the rice is steaming, start making the sankhaya, if you intend to include it. Preheat the oven to 180°C/350°F/Gas Mark 4. Beat the eggs lightly, add the sugar, salt and coconut milk, and stir until the sugar is dissolved. Transfer the mixture to a soufflé dish and cook in a bain-marie in the oven for 20–25 minutes. Serve hot, warm, or cold.)

Let the rice cool somewhat, then mould it. One way is to use individual small moulds, preferably lined with clingfilm/plastic wrap or aluminium foil. Fill each mould, press down fairly firmly with the back of a spoon, then turn the rice out on to the middle of a dessert plate and arrange slices of mango around it.

Alternatively, spread the rice on a tray lined with aluminium foil, then roll it flat with a wetted rolling pin and cut it into diamond shapes with a sharp, wet knife. Serve as above.

STOCKS, SAUCES AND RELISHES

Rice barns: Lombok

This section gives recipes for some basic preparations that rice dishes are cooked in or served with. There are meat, vegetable and fish stocks; sauces, ranging from the mildest curry to hot Indonesian sambal and Moroccan harissa; and dry relishes such as Crisp-Fried Anchovies with Peanuts and the aptly named Gunpowder.

Some of the most interesting sauces are halfway to being dishes in their own right, like Indonesian (or Malaysian) gule or gulai or Persian khoreshta. Claudia Roden, in *The New Book of Middle Eastern Food*, describes khoreshta as 'by English standards, stews rather than sauces', made from 'an infinite variety of ingredients'. I once described gule kambing, an Indonesian lamb (or goat) dish, as 'a liquid lamb stew – or you can think of it as a very meaty soup'. The khoreshta that you will find here, and the Long-Cooked Beef described on page 274, are served in Iran or Indonesia as normal accompaniments to plain cooked rice at any family meal. For a party, several different and more elaborate rice dishes are made, and the meat – usually lamb or goat – is cooked in the same sauce; the difference is that the pieces of meat are larger.

Beef and Chicken Stock

This is a quite simple, but very good stock, suitable for most of the recipes in this book that require meat stock.

It will always taste better if you make it with the whole chicken, and with the brisket together with the bones. Don't discard all the fat from the brisket, even though you will have to remove it from the stock after it has been refrigerated. The meat of the chicken and beef can be used for boiled-meat dishes.

The same method and the same non-meat ingredients are used to make stock from either beef or chicken alone.

Preparation: 20 minutes
Cooking: about 2½–3 hours

Makes 1.1–1.7 litres/
2–3 pints/
5–7½ cups of strong stock

---

1 chicken, preferably free
   range
1 kg/2 lb 3 oz brisket, and
   the bones
About 2.5 litres/4–5 pints/
   10–12½ cups water,
   enough to cover the meat
   in the pan
1 large onion, not peeled,
   quartered
2 carrots, peeled
1 stick of celery, with some
   leaves left on
Mushroom stalks, especially
   those of shiitake
   mushrooms
Soaking water from dried
   shiitake mushrooms
   (optional)
1 tsp salt
10 whole black peppercorns
   (optional)

Cut the chicken in halves or quarters. Wash and clean the inside of the carcass thoroughly. Cut off and discard about half the fat from the brisket. Put the chicken and beef in a large saucepan and add the rest of the ingredients. Bring to the boil, turn down the heat a little, and continue boiling gently for 50 minutes. Skim off the froth as it comes to the surface.

After 50 minutes, take out the chicken pieces but continue gently boiling the beef for 1 hour longer. When the chicken is cold enough to handle, remove the meat from the bones and keep the meat in the fridge for other uses. Put the bones back into the saucepan where the beef is still boiling.

When the beef has boiled for 1 hour 50 minutes altogether, take out the beef, lower the heat, and continue simmering the bones for a further 30 minutes.

Strain the stock into a bowl, leave it to get cold, and refrigerate. The next day, the fat will have formed a solid layer on top of the bowl, and can be taken out in one or several pieces and discarded.

The bones and other ingredients can still be used to make a second batch of stock, quite weak but not altogether without flavour. You can add more fresh root vegetables and salt if you wish.

Vegetable Stock

You may have noticed that I attach great importance to saving the stalks of shiitake mushrooms, and the water in which dried shiitake have been soaked, for the stock pot. Certainly these contribute to my favourite vegetable stock.

The other vegetables should not include too many different kinds, because once you have taken away the stock that you need for your cooking, the remainder, with the vegetables themselves, should make good soup.

Preparation and cooking: about 1 hour altogether

Makes 1.1–1.7 litres/
2–3 pints/
5–7½ cups of stock

2 tbsp peanut oil
1 onion, finely sliced
2 carrots, peeled and diced
2 parsnips, peeled and diced
1 large potato, peeled and
  diced
1 large tomato, left whole
285 ml/10 fl oz/1¼ cups
  shiitake soaking water
  (optional)
A bunch of parsley
2 litres/3½ pints/just under 9
  cups of water
Salt and pepper

Heat the oil in a saucepan and brown the onion slightly, then add the rest of the ingredients. Bring these to the boil and let it all bubble quietly for 30 minutes. Strain, and keep the stock aside until needed.

Vegetable soup   Remove the stalks of the parsley. Add hot water, and/or any unused stock, to the vegetables, adjust the seasoning, and liquidize. Pass the soup through a sieve if you want it very smooth. Reheat, and serve, with a dollop of cream added if you wish.

Fish Stock

The best fish stock I have ever made or used came from the bones, head and trimmings of a magnificent turbot which, for a very special occasion, I had ordered to be delivered express from the quayside in Cornwall. We had turbot sashimi for dinner, and the stock played its part in some very delicious cooked fish dishes thereafter. Of course, you don't have to have fresh turbot; bones and trimmings from all sorts of white fish – plaice, lemon sole, Dover sole – make excellent stock, as do salmon heads and bones. To make it better still, put in, if you can, a little of the flesh as well, or perhaps a small plaice or a bit of a different fish altogether, such as cod or haddock.

Preparation and cooking: about 50 minutes altogether

Makes 850 ml–1.1 litres/
1½–2 pints/4–5 cups of
stock

About 1 kg/2 lb head, bones
and trimmings of white fish
1.4 litres/2½ pints/8 cups
water
1 onion, sliced
1-cm/½-inch piece of ginger
root, peeled (optional)
1 stick of celery, roughly
chopped
A little salt and pepper

Put everything in a saucepan, bring to the boil and let it boil very gently for 20–25 minutes. Strain and leave to cool, then refrigerate until needed.

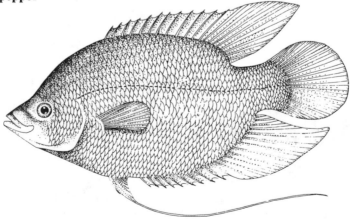

Gurami fish

346

Bonito Stock
Dashi

In a book about rice, there are bound to be quite a few Japanese recipes, so I include this basic Japanese stock. This is the authentic dashi, which is easily made at home. Most Japanese cookbooks will tell you that there is now a widely available instant dashi. They may also tell you that this product contains more monosodium glutamate (MSG) than nature intended; so, for me, it's back to the kitchen.

Preparation and cooking: 18–20 minutes

Makes 1.1 litres/2 pints/
5 cups of stock

About 25 cm/10 inches of
  kelp/konbu
1.1 litres/2 pints/5 cups cold
  water
Additional 112 ml/4 fl oz/
  ½ cup cold water
60–70 g/2–2½ oz bonito
  flakes

The kelp/konbu must not be washed – if it is, it will lose its flavour. Just wipe it with a clean, damp cloth. Put it in a saucepan and add 1.1 litres/2 pints/5 cups of water. Heat it slowly; ideally it should be almost but not quite boiling after 10–12 minutes. The water must not boil while the kelp is still in the pan, so discard the kelp, then bring the water to the boil. As soon as it boils, add 112 ml/4 fl oz/½ cup more cold water and the bonito flakes. Bring back to the boil, skim off the froth, and take the pan off the heat.

Leave it to stand for 50–60 seconds. During this time the bonito flakes will sink to the bottom. Strain the stock through a sieve lined with muslin. Do not squeeze the flakes. Use the clear stock straight away, or refrigerate for use later. It can be kept in the fridge in a closed container for up to a week.

Tomato Sauce

This starts off as a basic sauce which can be made with either fresh or canned tomatoes. You can refine or spice it to your own taste or for a specific purpose. You can also transform it into your own home-made tomato ketchup.

The quantity shown here is, I think, the minimum that you should make in one batch. It will keep in the fridge for at least 10 days.

Preparation and cooking: about 1–1¼ hours

Makes about 570 ml/1 pint/
2½ cups basic sauce

900 g/2 lb fresh ripe
   tomatoes, skinned, or three
   or four 340-g/12-oz cans/
   1½ cups of chopped
   tomatoes
6 shallots or 2 onions, finely
   chopped
2 cloves garlic, finely
   chopped
2.5-cm/1-inch piece of ginger
   root, peeled
½ tsp salt

For Ketchup

2 tbsp light soy sauce
1–2 tsp sugar
2 tsp cornflour/cornstarch or
   potato flour
1 tbsp mild vinegar or rice
   vinegar

Bring all these ingredients to the boil in a saucepan. Simmer on a low heat for 50–60 minutes, stirring occasionally and making sure the mixture doesn't dry out. Add 2 tablespoons of water from time to time. The end result should be quite thick. Take out the piece of ginger. You now have your basic tomato sauce, which can be used in the following ways.

1   Use it as it is, by heating the amount you require in a small saucepan. Add pepper or chilli powder to taste. If you like a little oil in it, add 1–2 tablespoons of the best olive oil you can find, or peanut oil. As soon as the oil is hot, stir the sauce and leave it to cook for 5–8 minutes, stirring occasionally.

2   For a very smooth sauce, add seasoning (and oil, if you wish) as described in the preceding paragraph, and pass it through a fine sieve. You can then add any chopped herbs you fancy: parsley, coriander/cilantro leaves and dill are all good. The solids that remain in the sieve can be discarded or, better, added to the stock pot.

You may say that it would be easier to put everything in the blender. This, however, would not give a rich red sauce but an orange-coloured one with a strong taste of onions. The texture, too, would be much less smooth.

3   To make tomato ketchup, you require the additional ingredients shown.

Mix these together and stir until smooth. Transfer them to an enamelled (that is, a non-reactive) pan. Heat the mixture gently, stirring it all the time. As soon as it thickens, add the smooth red sauce described in paragraph 2 above, but without any herbs. Let it simmer for 2–3 minutes longer, still stirring continuously. Adjust the seasoning. The ketchup can be used while it is still hot, or it can be stored in a jar and refrigerated (for up to 10 days) until required.

Red Pepper Sauce

If you wish, you can make this sauce extremely smooth, as you can the Tomato Sauce on page 348. If you make it with equal quantities of tomatoes and red peppers, it becomes, logically enough, Red Pepper and Tomato Sauce.

Preparation: 15 minutes
Cooking: 50 minutes

Makes 570 ml/1 pint/
2½ cups basic sauce

3 tbsp olive oil or peanut oil
4 large red sweet/bell peppers,
  de-seeded and diced
4 shallots, finely sliced
1 tomato, skinned and
  de-seeded, then chopped
1 tsp ground coriander
  (optional)
Salt and pepper to taste
570 ml/1 pint/2½ cups water

Stir-fry the pepper in the oil for 2 minutes. Add the shallots and go on stir-frying for 3 more minutes. Then add the other ingredients and simmer, uncovered, for 45 minutes. By this time the sauce will be quite thick. Stir, adjust the seasoning, and the basic sauce is ready to serve. It can be made some hours in advance and reheated.

To make a smooth sauce, pass it through a fine sieve. If you wish, add some finely chopped herbs of your choice just before serving.

Soy Sauce with Chilli

This is excellent with satay, and is specially recommended to those who don't like, or want a change from, peanut sauce. It is also recommended with crunchy spring rolls, raw vegetables, and noodles.

Preparation: 10 minutes

Makes about 3
tablespoonfuls

2–4 small chillies, de-seeded
  and finely chopped
2 shallots, finely sliced
1 clove garlic, finely chopped
  (optional)

Juice of 1 small lime or
  lemon
1 tsp olive oil (optional)
1 tbsp light soy sauce
1 tbsp dark soy sauce

Mix all the ingredients together in a bowl, and serve.

Three hot sauces

Crushed Red Chillies with Salt
Sambal ulek

This is the basis of all the sambals that Indonesians use, either as a hot relish or for spicing a cooked dish, and it is an ideal base for harissa and piri-piri sauce (below). You can buy it in jars, usually made in the Netherlands and labelled *Sambal Oelek*. This use of *oe* for Indonesian *u* (pronounced like *oo* in English *school*) is nowadays found only among the Dutch.

However, if you have a food processor this is quite an easy sambal to make at home, and of course it will be much better value. Make plenty, and you can pack it in plastic bags and freeze it, or keep it for up to 2 weeks in an airtight jar in the fridge. For small quantities, see below. If you want the sambal less hot, discard the seeds of the chillies.

Preparation and cooking: about 35–40 minutes altogether

Makes about 450 g/1 lb

450 g/1 lb red chillies, stalks removed
570 ml/1 pint/2½ cups water
1 tbsp salt
1 tbsp vinegar (any kind)
1 tsp sugar (optional)
2 tbsp peanut or olive oil
6–8 tbsp boiled water

Put the chillies in a saucepan and cover them with the water. Bring to the boil and simmer for 15 minutes. Drain, and put the chillies in the blender with salt, vinegar and sugar (if used). (You may need to do this in batches.) Add the peanut or olive oil and the boiled water, and blend until smooth.

Harissa

Like sambal ulek, harissa can be bought in jars or cans from good delicatessens. I personally find the canned sort much too sour. In *Good Food from Morocco*, Paula Wolfert suggests sambal ulek as an alternative to harissa. They are in fact very similar chilli sauces, variations on each other.

To make harissa, put ½–1 teaspoon of roasted cumin seed in a mortar, and add 1 tablespoon of best olive oil. Crush the cumin seeds with a pestle, then add 1 tablespoon of sambal ulek. Mix everything together vigorously while adding a little more olive oil.

Piri-Piri Sauce

Start with 2 tablespoons of sambal ulek, and stir in 1–2 teaspoons of lime or lemon juice. You can also, if you wish, add 2–3 tablespoons of coarsely crushed roasted peanuts. Instead of salt, people in different parts of South-East Asia add fish sauce or shrimp paste to their basic hot chilli sauce.

Making small quantities   If you want just enough sauce for one meal, soak 4–6 dried small red chillies in hot water for 30 minutes, then drain. Cut up the chillies and put them in a mortar with a little olive oil or other oil, and some salt. Add cumin seeds, or fish sauce or shrimp paste, as you wish. Grind all together to make a smooth, or fairly smooth, paste. If you don't eat it all, it will keep in the fridge for 2 or 3 days; the oil and salt help to preserve it.

Rice storage boxes and bins: Indonesia

Peanut Sauce

This is the best-known, best-loved sauce for satay. It is also used for Gado-Gado (page 294), and goes well with any grilled meat or hamburger steak.

If you like your satay sauce chilli-hot, there are several quite passable powdered instant sauces on the market. For making it yourself, there are various so-called short cuts, most of them involving crunchy peanut butter. Avoid these; the method described below is as easy, cheaper, and much nicer.

Preparation: about 40–45 minutes

Makes about 285 ml/
½ pint/1¼ cups of sauce

112 ml/4 fl oz/½ cup
  vegetable oil
225 g/8 oz/1½ cups raw
  peanuts
2 cloves garlic, chopped
4 shallots, chopped
A thin slice of shrimp paste
  (page 380, optional)
Salt to taste
½ tsp chilli powder
½ tsp brown sugar
1 tbsp dark soy sauce
450 ml/16 fl oz/2 cups water
1 tbsp tamarind water (page
  381) or juice of ½ a lemon

Stir-fry the peanuts for 4 minutes. Remove with a slotted spoon to drain in a colander, and leave to cool. Then pound or grind the nuts into a fine powder, using a blender, coffee grinder, or pestle and mortar. Discard the oil, except for 1 tablespoonful.

Crush the garlic, shallots and shrimp paste in a mortar with a little salt, and fry in the remaining oil for 1 minute. Add the chilli powder, sugar, soy sauce and water. Bring this to the boil, then add the ground peanuts. Simmer, stirring occasionally, until the sauce becomes thick; this should take about 8–10 minutes. Add the tamarind water or lemon juice and more salt if needed.

When cool, keep in a jar in the fridge. Reheat as required for use with satay or as a dip for crudités or savoury snacks. The sauce will keep in the fridge for up to 1 week.

Sambal Goreng Sauce

This is a rich, creamy sauce, so it will taste nicer if you make it quite spicy.

Preparation: 20 minutes
Cooking: 1 hour

Makes about 570 ml/1 pint
/2½ cups of sauce

For the paste:

4 shallots, chopped
2 cloves garlic, chopped
3 large red chillies, de-seeded
   and chopped, or ½ tsp
   chilli powder + 1 tsp
   paprika
1 tsp shrimp paste
2 candle nuts or macadamia
   nuts or blanched almonds
   (optional)
1 tsp chopped ginger root
1 tsp ground coriander
A large pinch of galingale
   powder
½ tsp salt
2 tbsp peanut oil
2 tbsp tamarind water
2 tbsp of the coconut milk
   (see below)

Other ingredients:
850 ml/1½ pints/3¾ cups
   coconut milk
5-cm/2-inch stem of lemon
   grass
2 kaffir lime leaves
2 large red tomatoes, skinned,
   de-seeded and chopped
Salt to taste

Blend all the ingredients for the paste until smooth, and transfer to a saucepan. Bring to the boil and simmer, stirring often, for 5 minutes. Add the coconut milk, lemon grass and kaffir lime leaves. Bring everything to the boil again, then simmer for 50 minutes, stirring occasionally.

Add the chopped tomatoes and some more salt. Go on simmering for another 10 minutes. Adjust the seasoning, and serve hot. Alternatively, let the sauce cool and refrigerate it until needed. The sauce will stay good in the fridge for 3–4 days. To serve, reheat the sauce gently almost to boiling point, then simmer for 15 minutes, stirring frequently.

Almond Sauce

Preparation and cooking: about 30 minutes

Makes about 570 ml/1 pint/
2½ cups of sauce

56 g/2 oz/½ cup ground
   almonds
850 ml/1½ pints/3¾ cups
   lamb or chicken stock
Salt and pepper to taste
1 clove garlic, crushed
2 tbsp lemon juice, or more to
   taste

For the garnish:

2 tbsp chopped parsley
1 tbsp roasted pine nuts or
   slivered almonds (optional)

Mix the almonds and cold stock together in a sauce-pan. Bring to the boil, season with salt and pepper. Simmer gently, stirring from time to time, for 20 minutes. Add the lemon juice. Stir and taste, and add more salt and lemon juice if needed. Serve hot, with the garnish sprinkled on top just before it comes to the table.

Terraces: Banaue

Mild Curry Sauce

This sauce goes well with many of the dishes described in *The Rice Book*; where I think it is particularly suitable, I have said so. If you want it stronger and spicier, double the quantities of ground coriander, cumin and chilli, but leave the other quantities unchanged.

Preparation and cooking: 40–45 minutes

Makes 570 ml/1 pint/
2½ cups or a little less

3 tbsp olive oil or peanut oil
2 tbsp water
4 shallots or 1 large onion,
   finely chopped
3 cloves garlic, chopped
1 tsp chopped ginger root
1 tbsp plain/all-purpose flour
   or rice flour
½ tsp chilli powder
2 tsp ground coriander
1 tsp ground cumin
½ tsp ground turmeric
2 tbsp ground almonds
1 tsp salt, or more to taste
720 ml/1¼ pints/3 cups
   chicken stock or water
200 ml/7 fl oz/just under
   1 cup plain yogurt
1 bay leaf
2 cloves
2 green cardamoms
2 tbsp chopped mint
   (optional)

Blend all the chopped ingredients with the oil and 2 tablespoons of water until smooth. Simmer this in a saucepan for 4–5 minutes, stirring often. Then add all the ground ingredients, and stir for 2 minutes. Add the flour, and stir briskly for a minute or two; then put in the stock or water, a little at a time, continuing to stir so that there are no floury lumps. Season with salt, and let the sauce simmer for 15 minutes.

Add the yogurt, a spoonful at a time, stirring vigorously so that it does not curdle. (If it does curdle, put the whole lot into a liquidizer and run the machine for a few seconds before putting the sauce back in the pan.) Add the cardamoms, bay leaf and cloves. Simmer for another 3 minutes.

Up to this point, the sauce can be made up to 24 hours in advance. When you are ready to serve it, heat it gently, take out the cardamoms, bay leaf and cloves, adjust the seasoning, and add the chopped mint if you wish.

Peach Khoresh

Claudia Roden gives this as a variant of apple khoresh, so you can of course make it with apples. I have chosen peaches here because a peach khoresh goes beautifully with any rice and lamb dish that has not been cooked in a sauce. Or, made with chicken, this khoresh goes with any chicken and rice dish that needs more sauce. Any of these variants can be served, as khoresh was originally intended to be, with plain cooked rice.

Preparation and cooking: about 1½–1¾ hours altogether

Makes about 570 ml/1 pint/ 2½ cups of sauce; as a stew, sufficient for 4–6 people with rice

3 tbsp olive oil or peanut oil, or clarified butter
3 shallots or 1 small onion, finely chopped
450 g/1 lb/2 cups lean lamb, or chicken meat, cut into small pieces
¼ tsp cayenne or black pepper, or chilli powder
½–1 tsp ground cinnamon
Salt to taste
4–5 peaches, peeled and sliced
570 ml/1 pint/2½ cups water
2–3 tbsp lemon or lime juice

Heat the oil or butter in a saucepan and fry the shallots or onion until soft. Add the meat and brown all over. Add the ground ingredients and some salt. Stir-fry for a minute or so, then add the hot water. Bring this to the boil. Remove any scum that comes to the surface.

Simmer very gently for 1 hour (if using chicken) or 1½ hours (for lamb), adding more hot water when necessary. When the meat is tender, add the peaches and lemon juice and continue cooking for 4–5 minutes. Adjust the seasoning and serve hot, as suggested above.

Rhubarb Khoresh

In previous books I suggested that Western cooks who couldn't get *belimbing wuluh* for various Indonesian/Malaysian dishes should substitute rhubarb; it has the right sweet/sour balance, with the sourness predominating. It follows that if you live in the tropics and can't get rhubarb for this khoresh, you can use belimbing wuluh (page 364) instead. Another good alternative is tamarind.

Like other khoreshta, this is traditionally served with plain cooked rice. If you prefer the sauce without pieces of meat in it, simply strain it (*before* you add the rhubarb, of course) and use the meat to make Fried Rice (page 126) or Beef and Rice Omelette (page 189). The strained sauce is suitable for any of the moulded rice dishes that are described in this book.

Preparation and cooking: about 1½–1¾ hours altogether

Makes about 570 ml/1 pint/ 2½ cups of sauce; as a stew, sufficient for 4–6 people with rice

---

2–3 tbsp oil or butter

3 shallots or 1 onion, finely chopped

2 cloves garlic, chopped (optional)

450 g/1 lb/2 cups brisket or stewing steak, the fat removed, cut into small pieces

½ tsp chilli powder

1 tsp ground coriander

½ tsp ground cinnamon

1 tsp salt

850 ml/1½ pints/3¾ cups hot water or more if needed

225 g/8 oz rhubarb or belimbing wuluh, or 56 g/ 2 oz/½ cup tamarind pulp

Heat the oil or butter in a saucepan and fry the shallots or onions and garlic until soft. Add the beef and stir-fry for 2 minutes. Add the ground ingredients and salt and continue stir-frying for 1 minute. Add the hot water, bring it to the boil and skim off any scum.

Let the mixture boil for about 10 minutes, then lower the heat, cover the pan and simmer for 1½ hours. Uncover several times to check the water level and add water at the halfway mark or as required.

While the meat is cooking, wash and cut up the belimbing wuluh or rhubarb into small pieces, and keep aside. If you are using tamarind, put it in a small pan, add 112 ml/4 fl oz/½ cup of water and boil for 10 minutes. Then pass the brown water through a sieve and discard the solids.

About 10 minutes before cooking is finished, if you are going to use the meat with Fried Rice, etc., as suggested above, pour the khoresh into a bowl and then back into the pan through a sieve to remove the meat. Then add the rhubarb, belimbing wuluh or tamarind water to the sauce, and cook for the final 10 minutes. Adjust the seasoning and serve as suggested.

Crisp-Fried Onions

Fried onions are suggested as garnish for a number of recipes in this book. You can, of course, buy them ready-made: Scandinavian fried onions are sold in plastic tubs in most supermarkets, and Thai shops make them from the little red onions, not quite shallots, that are found in many Asian countries. These have much less water in them than big European onions, so they fry crisp without the addition of flour. To make crisp-fried onions from your own home-grown shallots, proceed as follows.

Preparation and cooking: 40–45 minutes

Makes about 500 g/1 lb

1 kg/2 lb 3 oz/9 cups
    shallots, thinly sliced
285 ml/½ pint/1¼ cups
    sunflower oil

It is easier to make these fried onions in a wok, but a frying pan will do. Heat the oil until a sliver of onion dropped into it sizzles immediately. Fry the shallots in 3 or 4 batches, stirring all the time, for 3–4 minutes each time or until they are crisp and lightly browned. Remove with a slotted spoon to drain in a colander lined with absorbent paper. Let them cool, then store in an airtight container; they will keep crisp and fresh for about a week.

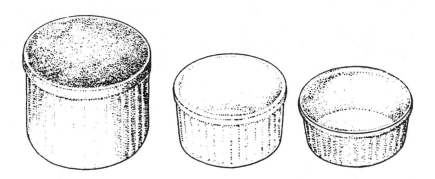

Crisp-Fried Anchovies with Peanuts

In any rice meal in Asia there are always some little relishes, often well laced with hot chilli. This one is not highly spiced, but it is savoury and crunchy and equally good either on the dinner table or as an appetizer to be served with drinks.

Preparation and cooking: 40–45 minutes

Makes about 700 g/1½ lb

450 g/1 lb dried anchovies,
   heads removed
450 g/1 lb/3 cups peanuts
112 ml/4 fl oz/½ cup
   sunflower oil or peanut oil
½ tsp chilli powder
   (optional)

Stir-fry the peanuts in a wok or frying pan in 3 batches, for 4 minutes each time. Remove them with a slotted spoon and drain them in a colander or on absorbent paper. Use the same oil to stir-fry the dried anchovies in 3 batches, for 3–4 minutes each time. Drain these in the same way. Allow peanuts and anchovies to go cold, then mix them well together. Put them in an airtight container, add the chilli powder (if used) and shake well to mix the powder evenly. This relish keeps for up to 2 weeks.

Gunpowder

I have searched many Indian cookbooks for this hot relish, but have not found anything that quite matches it. It is evidently a nickname for a hot kind of *sambhar masala*, or a variation of what some books call *mulagapodi*. My recipe is from a South Indian chef at the Maurya Sheraton Hotel in New Delhi.

I always dry-fry my Gunpowder, but if you prefer you can fry each ingredient separately in hot oil and drain them on absorbent paper before grinding them. The quantities shown here are approximate; in particular, you can reduce or increase the amount of chilli to suit your taste. In the recipe below I have put in the quantity that I enjoy.

Preparation and cooking: about 1 hour

Makes about 340 g/12 oz/
3 cups

112 g/4 oz/1 cup chana dal
112 g/4 oz/1 cup urad dal
112 g/4 oz/1 cup mung dal
½ tsp asafoetida/hing
28 g/1 oz/¼ cup whole red
  chillies
½ tsp salt or more, to taste

Dry-fry the dal and chillies together in a wok or frying pan, stirring all the time, until the dal is lightly browned – this will take up to 10 minutes. You must keep stirring continuously.

Let the dal and chillies cool, and put them into a grinder or food processor. (If your machine is small, you may have to do this in batches.) Grind for a few seconds only; the dal should still be in coarse, crunchy fragments, not actually powdered.

Add the asafoetida and salt and mix everything well together. Store in an airtight jar and use as a relish whenever you feel like it. Gunpowder, as long as it is absolutely dry, keeps indefinitely.

Ingredients, Utensils, Techniques

INGREDIENTS

Page references are to illustrations unless otherwise stated.

ALLSPICE   Not a mixture of spices, but the berry of a tropical American tree (*Pimenta dioica* or *P. officinalis*) whose taste resembles those of several spices. Sometimes called Jamaica pepper.

ANDOUILLE   A smoked sausage, originally from northern France, made of marinated and salted pig's innards in the large intestine.

ASAFOETIDA, HING   This is obtained from varieties of large fennels, whose roots produce a resin which is dried and sold in waxy chunks or ground to powder. It originated in Iran and Afghanistan, but is produced today in many middle eastern countries. It has been used for centuries as a medicine and flavour-enhancer. The strong, unpleasant smell disappears in cooking.

AUBERGINE, EGGPLANT   These glossy purple fruits of *Solanum melongena* are now familiar everywhere, many of them being grown in Holland. They came originally from India, where they are called *brinjal*. Beware the thin but sharp spines on the green stem.

There are also baby purple aubergines, small round white aubergines (below) and pea aubergines (page 363).

Aubergines/eggplants

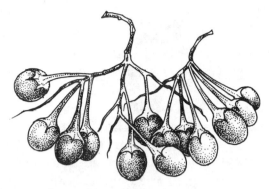

Pea aubergines/eggplants

AZUKI BEANS   These small red beans (*Phaseolus angularis*) are used in many kinds of cooking, and are sold in most Western supermarkets. Don't confuse them with red kidney beans, which are much larger. The anglicized version of the name is sometimes misspelled 'adzuki'.

BAMBOO SHOOT   Canned bamboo shoots (or baby ones in glass jars) are easy to buy almost anywhere, and even in Asia are usually preferred to fresh ones. Fresh shoots are scarcely superior in taste or texture, and are time-consuming and even painful to prepare. Canned ones are already trimmed and pre-cooked, and can now even be bought pre-cut into pretty shapes. When the can or jar has been opened, unused shoots will keep in the fridge for 7–10 days if packed in fresh water which is changed daily.

BANANA LEAF   Young banana leaves are used in most tropical countries for cooking and wrapping food. They can be bought, trimmed into large squares and with the tough midrib cut away, in most Asian shops in the West. In the freezer, they keep for several months.

BASIL   There are at least four kinds of basil in South-East Asia; the two that are most often available in the West are *Ocimum basilicum*, with light green leaves and white flowers, originally from India; this is, I think, what the English call 'sweet' basil. The other is *O. gratissimum*, with purplish stems, from Thailand and Malaysia. Sweet basil is available almost everywhere, but the second type is imported from Thailand and sold mostly in Thai shops.

BAY LEAF The bay is a kind of laurel tree (*Laurus nobilis*); many of its close relatives are poisonous, but a single bay leaf adds a mildly bitter, aromatic flavour to a sauce.

BEAN SAUCE, BEAN PASTE Far Eastern cuisines use several pastes and sauces made of crushed and sometimes flavoured beans. These are usually easy to find in Oriental shops. Yellow and black bean sauces are fermented from soya beans.

BEAN SPROUT The bean sprouts we buy in supermarkets are those of MUNG/ GREEN GRAM BEANS. You can of course grow your own on a piece of damp flannel; it takes them 3–4 days to reach the best size for eating. They consist mostly of water, but they have a nice crisp texture. They must be eaten fresh; when they start to go brown and soft, they cease to be attractive. It is always worth while breaking off the brown root of each sprout, if you can make time to do it, simply for the sake of appearance.

BELIMBING WULUH A tropical South-East Asian fruit (*Averrhoa bilimbi*), smooth-skinned, acid tasting.

BELL PEPPER For all practical purposes, this is an alternative name for PIMIENTO.

BLACK PEPPER Both black and white peppers come from a vine, *Piper nigrum*, native to tropical Asia. White pepper is more highly processed and therefore more expensive, but is less aromatic; it is used mostly in light-coloured dishes where black pepper would look out of place. Whole pepper berries retain their fragrant oils far longer than ground pepper; many dishes require whole black pepper.

BONITO FLAKES The bonito is another name for the skipjack (*Katsuwonus pelamis*), a relative of the tuna. In Japanese it is *katsuo*; its flesh is dried hard and shaved thinly to make *katsuobushi*, essential for Japanese stocks or *dashi*. Bonito flakes are obtainable in the West at Japanese shops and at many good Asian food shops.

BREADCRUMBS If you buy these ready-made, be careful to avoid those that have been artificially coloured, since these may affect the appearance of the food. For the dishes in this book, make your own crumbs from fresh white or brown bread which is a day or two old and rather dry. Remove the crusts, cut the bread into smallish pieces, and give these a quick spin in your food processor. The crumbs should be used while fresh, or else frozen.

BRISKET A cut of beef, taken from the lower part of the shoulder.

BUFFALO MEAT   This is not the North American bison, and certainly not the caribou, but the Asian 'water' buffalo (*Bos bubalus*), called *kerbau* in Malaysia and Indonesia and therefore, by some English writers, the carabao. Before machines entered the rice fields, these animals did virtually all the heavy work that men and women could not do by themselves, but some were also bred for meat. In South-East Asia cows were almost unknown until quite recently, and Hindus in India regard cows as sacred; so 'beef' in many Asian recipes was originally buffalo. The meat is rather coarse and tough, and one reason for cooking rendang for so many hours in coconut milk was to make it more tender. Beef can be substituted for buffalo in any recipe in this book.

BULGUR (or BURGHUL)   The cracked wheat used in the Middle East for making *tabbouleh*.

BUTTER BEAN   Like most dried beans, these must be soaked for 3–4 hours before use.

CANDLE NUT   This is an oily tropical nut, about as big as a large hazel nut but in a much tougher shell. It is a basic ingredient of many Indonesian and Malaysian dishes, and in those parts of the world it is called *kemiri* or sometimes *buah keras* (which, appropriately, means 'tough nut'). Its botanical name is *Aleurites moluccana*. When fresh and raw, it is mildly poisonous, but becomes harmless when cooked. Kemiri are sold in packets in many Asian shops in the West, but if you can't get them then MACADAMIA NUTS are an excellent substitute. If you can't get those either, almonds will do.

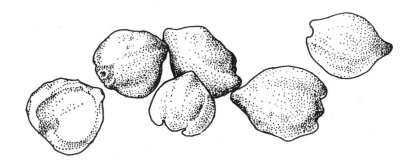

Candle nuts

CARDAMOM Burkill lists six genera which produce seeds of a cardamom type, which explains why people sometimes disagree as to what exactly a cardamom looks like. The best, and therefore the one most often cultivated, is *Elettaria cardamomum*, which produces a dark-coloured seed in an outer layer whose colour depends on how it was processed and prepared for market; starting with the top quality, it may be green, white, brownish, or almost black. Large black cardamoms, however, may also be the fruit of less pungent, cheaper species of the genus *Amomum*, a relative of ginger. The recipe will tell you how to use them – either split open the capsules and crush the seeds, or use whole cardamoms, e.g. in curry. In the latter case, discard them before serving.

CASHEW NUT LEAF The cashew tree (*Anacardium occidentale*) produces not only the familiar nuts but also leaves that are used, in Java and elsewhere, to flavour rice. Unfortunately, they are only available in places where they grow.

CAYENNE PEPPER A powdered form of a very hot red chilli pepper, useful as a kind of standard because its degree of hotness is predictable whereas a fresh or dried chilli may be more or less hot than the cook expects. See CHILLI POWDER.

CHAURICE The French/Louisiana/Cajun name for a smoked pork sausage with chillies and other spices, very similar to a Spanish or Mexican chorizo.

CHICKPEA, GARBANZO *Cicer arietinum* is one of the most nutritious vegetables and has probably been cultivated for at least as long as any other existing crop. Although there are many varieties and a wide range of colours, sizes and shapes (including the small, split Indian chana dal), the ones that are sold in supermarkets all look the same. Canned chickpeas are immersed in water, but dried ones must be soaked, usually overnight. It is said to be almost impossible to overcook chickpeas.

CHILLI See also JALAPEÑO CHILLI. Chillies come in a vast range of sizes, shapes, colours and hotness. All are of the genus *Capsicum*, many are varieties of *C. annuum*, but the very small, very strong ones are usually *C. frutescens*. They were among the first plants to be taken to Europe and thence round the world after Columbus discovered America; it is hard now to imagine how Asia managed for all those years without them. People who aren't used to chillies suppose that they are hot and nothing else, but in fact they have a wide range of smells and tastes; this is why it is important to use the right kind of chilli for your purpose.

Briefly, the things to remember about chillies are: colour has no relation to hotness, but size has – generally, the smaller they are, the hotter they are. Dried chillies are just as hot as fresh ones. The hottest part is the seeds, so remove these if you or your guests are not accustomed to them. People get used to eating chillies, so a sambal that causes real pain to a novice, and even blisters the palate, will taste pleasantly warm to an habitué. Handle hot chillies with respect – wash your hands afterwards, as chilli on your fingers will make your eyes sting sharply if it gets near them, though it will not actually harm them. If you do get chilli in your eye, wash it well with cold water. If you get a mouthful of painfully hot chilli, boiled rice or raw cucumber are the most effective salves; cold water (or iced lager) is not much good.

CHILLI OIL   A reddish-coloured, very hot and pungent oil, sold in small bottles in some Asian shops in the West, and in delicatessens and food halls of department stores.

CHILLI POWDER   A very convenient way to get the effect of chillies when whole ones are not easily obtainable or are for some other reason inconvenient. Chilli powder has the advantage of more or less standard hotness, and of course is easily measured. It is virtually the same thing as CAYENNE PEPPER, but is usually sold in larger packets and is cheaper.

CHINESE LEAVES (also CHINESE CABBAGE, CHINESE WHITE CABBAGE, CHINESE CELERY CABBAGE)   Tall, cylindrical, tightly furled white and green leaves; now generally available in Chinese shops and in many good greengrocers and large supermarkets.

CHINESE MUSHROOM   These are usually shiitake mushrooms which have been dried over charcoal. They are wickedly expensive, but well worth the money, for they are used in small quantities to give a delicious flavour and a wonderfully tender-chewy texture to many dishes. They will keep indefinitely in a dry place. They must be soaked in hot water for at least 20 minutes before cooking.

CHORIZO   See CHAURICE.

CILANTRO   See CORIANDER.

CINNAMON   This is the bark of a tree, *Cinnamomum zeylanicum*, cut very thin and dried and scraped so that it rolls itself up into 'quills'. It is also sold in powdered form. Quills keep their flavour for a long time in airtight storage, but powdered cinnamon should be used quickly. In many recipes, a fragment of a quill is ground or blended into a paste with other ingredients. Most sauces and other dishes described in this book call for a quill of cinnamon to be put in during cooking and discarded before serving. In some countries, cassia bark (*C. cassia*), which has a stronger but less subtle aroma, is sold as cinnamon; this was also done in Britain until fairly recently. 'Cinnamon' and 'cassia' are both semitic words, because these spices were traded between the growers in India and the markets in Babylon and the eastern Mediterranean.

CLAM   Clams come in many sizes. When you buy, make sure none are open or damaged; cook and eat them the day they are bought. Rinse them under the tap (scrub rough-shelled ones) and open them by either steaming for a few minutes or putting in a moderate oven for a short time.

CLARIFIED BUTTER   Butter bought in a shop contains small quantities of sugar and milk protein which can interfere with frying. To get rid of these, heat the butter gently until it stops frothing and a thin sediment has fallen to the bottom of the pan. Strain the butter through muslin.

CLOVE   This is one of South-East Asia's most important spices and trade goods, imported into Europe for at least 2,000 years; the history of the trade is a peculiarly depressing one of human stupidity, violence, envy and greed. The dried flowers of *Eugenia aromatica* are instantly recognizable by shape and by smell; dentists until recently used oil of cloves as an antiseptic, which may be one reason why cooks take care not to make the aroma too obvious. Most cloves now sold in the West are grown in Zanzibar and Madagascar.

COCONUT   Young coconuts, which are full of water and have very soft flesh, do not play any part in this book. Old fresh nuts, which have brown, hard, hairy shells, are easily obtainable almost anywhere and are the best for cooking. Hold the nut to your ear and shake it gently; you should hear liquid sloshing about inside. If you do, the nut is probably all right. If not, it may be very old and stale. To open the nut, tap it smartly all over with a heavy blunt instrument to loosen the shell from the flesh. Then give it a few firm blows to crack the shell. The water will spill out, so do this over the sink or on the back-door step. If the flesh is still sticking to the fragments of the shell, prise it away carefully with a short-bladed, blunt knife. The white flesh has a brown outer skin. For making coconut milk, this is left on when the flesh is grated, but for light-coloured dishes (especially sweets) it must be peeled off and discarded.

Creamed Coconut. This is like a hard, whitish margarine. It has its uses, but I would not recommend it for any of the recipes in this book, unless a very small amount is needed near the end of cooking in order to thicken the sauce.

Desiccated Coconut. Very useful for making COCONUT MILK. Packeted brands bought in supermarkets are good, but expensive if you need a large quantity. Most Asian shops sell unsweetened desiccated coconut in large bags much more cheaply. Sniff the bag before you buy; if it has been in store for too long, it will smell rancid, even through the plastic.

COCONUT MILK   This is not the water that you drink from a fresh nut. It is a white, milky liquid that is easily extracted from coconut flesh with hot water, and it is essential for much South-East Asian cooking. You can buy it in cans from most Asian shops, or you can buy 'instant' powder and simply mix it with water; these are both quite all right, but they do not get results as good as fresh milk you have made yourself from either a fresh nut or (just as good) desiccated coconut.

1   *From Fresh Coconut.* One nut makes about 570 ml/1 pint/2½ cups of milk. Grate the flesh, pour hot water over it and leave it to cool till it is hand-hot. Then squeeze handfuls of the grated flesh through a fine sieve, pressing out the last drop. For thicker milk, use less water, and vice versa. (This can be done in a blender: see below.)

2   *From Desiccated Coconut.* You will find 340 g/12 oz/5 cups of desiccated coconut makes about 570 ml/1 pint/2½ cups of thick 'first extraction' milk. If you then repeat the steps described below, you will get the same quantity of thin milk from the second extraction. If you mix the two, you will have about 1.1 litres/2 pints/5 cups of average milk.

With a blender: The water should be fairly hot. Put the desiccated coconut and half the water into the blender. Blend for 20–30 seconds, then squeeze and sieve the resulting mush. Put the squeezed coconut back into the blender with the rest of the hot water, and repeat.

Without a blender: Simmer the desiccated coconut and water in a pan for 4–5 minutes. Allow to cool a little, then sieve and strain as above.

Storing and Using Coconut Milk. This milk will keep in the fridge for not more than 48 hours, during which thick 'cream' may come to the top; this can simply be stirred back into the liquid below. Coconut milk cannot be frozen. If you are cooking for the freezer, omit the coconut milk until you thaw the dish ready to reheat and serve it. Rendang (page 269) is an exception – the milk is totally absorbed into the meat, therefore Rendang and Kalio can be frozen.

CORIANDER, CILANTRO   The leaves of this plant (*Coriandrum sativum*) are now very familiar even in Britain, and the seeds – whole or ground – are also easily obtainable. For Thai cooking, the roots are also used. Thai shops import fresh plants with roots attached, but at most greengrocers you can find a few stems with at least part of the root still in place. If you don't need these at once, cut them off and freeze them. The leaves cannot be frozen.

CORNFLOUR, CORNSTARCH   The fine white powder made by grinding maize kernels; it is virtually pure starch, and is used in baking and as thickener for sauces. Never put it straight into the sauce – it will simply go lumpy. Stir it into a smooth paste with a little cold water, then stir it into the sauce.

COTECHINO   A large Italian boiled sausage, containing the soft skin of the pig's head and snout.

COURGETTE, ZUCCHINI This is one of the smaller members of the large *Cucurbita pepo* family, easily grown in temperate-zone gardens so you can have stuffed courgette flowers, by themselves or attached to the very young, tender courgettes, at almost no cost. Courgettes should normally be bought, or picked, not more than about 12 cm/5 inches long; for making stuffed courgettes (page 145) larger ones are useful.

CRÈME FRAÎCHE This is cream which has been cultured to make it mildly acid but not sour. Supermarkets sell it ready-made.

CROÛTONS Cubes of white bread, without crust, about 1 cm/½ inch square, are baked in the oven for 10–15 minutes at 180°C/350°F/Gas Mark 4. Alternatively, slightly smaller cubes of bread can be fried in oil or clarified butter, turning them over often so they brown evenly; or toasted sliced bread can be brushed with melted butter on both sides and then cut into cubes.

CUMIN The tiny seeds of *Cuminum cyminum* are used in much Asian cooking; if you use it often, it is cheaper to buy it in an Indian shop, where it is called *jeera*. Not to be confused with caraway seeds, though they look similar.

DAL See also URAD DAL. The Indian word for any kind of split gram – gram being any kind of small pulse except peas and beans. These are rich in proteins, hence their importance in poor Asian countries. Always use the type of dal prescribed in the recipe – different pulses have very different tastes and cooking qualities.

DEMERARA SUGAR Brown sugar with large crystals; it used to come from Demerara in Guyana, but is now a rather vague name for a range of types and qualities of brown sugar. Can be used as a substitute for coconut sugar or palm sugar in Oriental dishes.

DRIED SHRIMP In Britain, these can only be bought in Asian shops, where they are sometimes called dried prawns or *ebi*. They are sold in packets, already shelled, salted and roasted, and they are somewhat expensive; however, a packet will last quite a long time. Use sparingly, as directed in the recipe, otherwise the flavour will be too strong.

EGGPLANT See AUBERGINE.

FENNEL A very common plant (*Foeniculum vulgare*) in Mediterranean countries, California, etc., with a rather pungent smell and taste resembling anise. All the parts of the plant are edible, but in this book we use mainly the swollen leaf-bases of 'sweet' or 'Florence' fennel, which form a kind of spherical bulb. It can be eaten raw or cooked. Waverley Root, by the way, says the ancient Greek word for fennel is *marathon*, and the battlefield was given this name because wild fennel grew on it profusely.

FILÉ POWDER   A fine powder of sassafras leaves, used in Louisiana and along the Gulf Coast of the USA, especially in gumbo soups; not easily obtained elsewhere, and therefore included in this book only as an optional ingredient.

FILO PASTRY, FILA PASTRY   Extremely thin sheets of flour-and-water dough, used in countless Middle Eastern dishes. It is very difficult to make the dough thin enough for use, but very easy in most places to buy it ready-made in packets, either fresh or frozen. Like all thin pastries, filo quickly dries and becomes brittle when exposed to the air, so thaw or unpack only what you need.

FISH SAUCE   In this book, this refers to the pungent sauces used in many savoury dishes in mainland South-East Asia: *nam pla* in Thailand, *nuoc mam* in Vietnam, *patis* in the Philippines. These are easily available in Thai or other Asian shops in the West and are not expensive. They are roughly equivalent to the solid, even stronger smelling SHRIMP PASTE used in Malaysia and Indonesia.

FIVE-SPICE POWDER   A famous stand-by of Chinese cooks, sold in every Chinese shop and many delicatessens that are not Chinese. The five spices are usually cassia bark (see CINNAMON), CLOVES, FENNEL, star anise, and either GINGER or SICHUAN PEPPER. The result tastes somewhat of liquorice and should be used sparingly.

FLOURY POTATO   See also WAXY POTATO. Suggested varieties, which are widely obtainable at least in Britain, are Home Guard, Maris Peer, Maris Piper, King Edward, Pentland Dell.

GALINGALE, GALANGAL   This is the old English name for a plant (*Languas galanga*) whose root or rhizome looks like a pinkish kind of ginger. Fresh and powdered galingale are now fairly easy to buy in Asian shops in the West; it is called *laos* or *lengkuas* in Malaysia and Indonesia, *ka* in Thailand. Dried slices of the root are also obtainable – these should be soaked in cold water before use, and discarded before serving.

GARBANZOS   See CHICKPEAS.

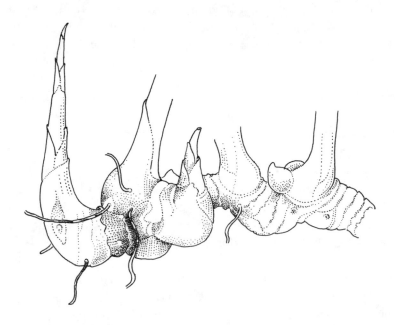

Galingale

GHEE The great Indian cooking medium, very similar to clarified butter but with a stronger flavour. Real ghee, from sour cow's or buffalo milk, is difficult to make at home but easy to buy, in cans or tubs, in Indian shops. Clarified butter is an adequate substitute.

GHERKIN A small pickled cucumber; usually sold in glass jars.

GINGER Fresh ginger is now easily obtainable everywhere, and much to be preferred to the powdered kind. Cut off a piece of root, peel it, and then grate, chop or blend it as prescribed in the recipe.

GINGER JUICE This juice can be pressed from grated ginger. To help the juice to run, soak the grated ginger in a teaspoonful or two of tepid water for a few minutes, then squeeze the ginger in a garlic crusher or through a fine-mesh sieve.

GOAT Many of the tropical Asian recipes in this book call for goat's meat, since the goat is a familiar animal all over the world whereas the sheep is not. Most recipes in this book therefore specify lamb even when the dish is originally intended for goat's meat.

GREEN GRAM BEAN See MUNG BEAN.

HING   See ASAFOETIDA.

JALAPEÑO CHILLI   A type of CHILLI, regarded as hot in North America but by no means among the hottest in the world; these can be bought, usually preserved in glass jars, in European delicatessens. They are prescribed for certain recipes in this book, not so much for their hotness as for their flavour.

KAFFIR LIME LEAF   The leaf of a citrus plant, *Citrus hystrix*, used in many South-East Asian dishes for its bitter flavour. The Indonesian name is *daun jeruk purut*. Packets of fresh and dried leaves are sold in Europe.

KELP   See KONBU.

KENARI NUT   Kenari trees (*Canarium comune*) are often planted for shade along Indonesian roadsides; they grow thick and tall. The nuts are oily, and look and taste much like almonds, so that the cook can substitute either of them for the other.

KONBU   This is a Japanese kelp or seaweed, and one of the essential ingredients in dashi (stock; page 347). It is therefore easy to buy, as long as you are within reach of a shop that sells Japanese foodstuffs.

LEEK   Avoid large, coarse-looking giant leeks; young tender ones should be trimmed of roots and most of the length of their green leaves, then washed very carefully under running water to get rid of any soil that has worked its way in between the layers.

Lemon grass

LEMON GRASS This is now quite easily obtainable almost anywhere. Cooks in South-East Asia have a wide spectrum of subtly sour and bitter flavours, and lemon grass (*sereh* in Indonesian, *Cymbopogon citratus* to botanists) is a particularly useful contributor to this. It can be used fresh, dried, or powdered. You may be able to root a stem of it in a glass of water and cherish it as a house plant. It is sold in stems about 15 cm/6 inches long; for most dishes, about one-third of this length is sufficient. The outer layer is very tough; if the stem is left whole during cooking, remember to remove it before serving. For many dishes, the outer layer is stripped off and the tender inner part chopped.

LOGANBERRY The first of these came from the garden of Judge Logan in California in the 1880s. They were a cross between a wild blackberry and the judge's raspberries – the sort of genetic accident that occasionally works out well. Loganberries should be eaten the day they are bought, and should not normally be washed.

MACADAMIA NUT This originated in Australia, but most of the nuts that come to the West are commercially grown in Hawaii. They are not yet as well known or as easily available in Britain as they deserve to be. They are delicious raw; however, they function in this book as a good substitute for CANDLE NUTS.

MANGETOUT, SUGAR PEA A pea eaten whole with its shell.

MARJORAM This herb (*Origanum majorana*) is very similar to OREGANO, and it is perhaps more accurate to call it sweet marjoram. It is sweeter and milder than oregano, but your local greengrocer or supermarket may not offer you the choice or know the difference, so, in effect, the two herbs can be regarded as interchangeable.

MIRIN Very sweet Japanese rice wine, used only for cooking, easily obtainable in Japanese and many other Asian shops; if you cannot get it, substitute saké or dry sherry, plus ½ tsp sugar for each tablespoon of mirin.

MISO Fermented Japanese bean paste, made of crushed boiled soya beans usually mixed with some other grain; one of Japan's major staple foods. Light-coloured miso is usually fairly sweet; red miso, made with barley, is savoury; so is dark miso. There are many flavours and textures within these three main types. Asian shops and many health food shops sell several types, often labelled 'soya bean paste' or the like. Miso will keep in the fridge for up to 12 months.

MONKFISH Only the tail of this fish is normally ever seen, apparently because fishmongers think that if their customers caught sight of the head they would never want to eat monkfish again, or at any rate would not pay the high prices for it that they do now. Alan Davidson's *North Atlantic Seafood* has pictures of it which are certainly quite alarming, and which also explain why it is called angler-fish or, in parts of the USA, goose-fish, all-mouth, or lawyer. Apparently Americans don't eat it much, which is a pity, because the flesh is excellent, almost resembling lobster, and it has no little bones – instead, a primitive cartilaginous skeleton, easily removed. Remember to cut away also the thin membrane that covers the tail underneath the skin, if the fishmonger has not done so.

MOOLI, WHITE RADISH A large, smooth, cylindrical white radish, with a pleasant, mildly warm taste; it can be eaten raw or cooked, and is now sold in many supermarkets as well as ethnic shops. It is very closely related, if not identical, to the Japanese daikon (which means literally 'great root') – they are both cultivars of *Raphanus sativus*.

MOREL These little mushrooms look rather like tiny, conical sponges. Fresh ones can be bought in autumn in Britain, at a price; dried ones at any time, in the best food halls and delicatessens. They are always cooked, and they are among the best-tasting of all mushrooms.

MUNG BEAN, GREEN GRAM BEAN These little green beans are used for growing BEAN SPROUTS, and when split become *moong dal*. They are also ground for flour. Every Indian shop sells them, and many other Asian and health food shops.

MUSSEL These small shellfish, their shells usually blue-black, are found all over the world and are often farmed. 'Wild' mussels are liable to be contaminated by pollution. When buying them, make sure their shells are clean-smelling and tightly closed, or close when you tap them, and are free of sand. Scrub them well and remove the stringy 'beard' with a knife. Use a knife to open the shell; the mussel must then be eaten or cooked immediately.

NAM PLA See FISH SAUCE.

NORI A species of *Porphyra*, marine algae which form dark brown or green ribbons or sheets, similar to English laver. Nori sheets, cut to standard sizes, are a standard food in Japan, where they are used to wrap sushi. (The shiny side should be outside.) The sheet needs to be toasted by passing one side only over a gas flame a few times so that it becomes crisp; this may be done in the factory, in which case the product is *yaki-nori*. All nori is sold in airtight packets and should be kept, after opening, in sealed containers in a dark place.

NUTMEG This is one of the spices that, growing only in a few remote islands of eastern Indonesia, brought Indians, Arabs and eventually Europeans to fight over the control of the trade routes and the suppliers. Even when it was finally moved to other areas in the tropics, it had a difficult history; in the 1860s plantations in Malaya were wiped out by disease. Much of the nutmeg that is imported to Europe and America today is grown in Grenada. Ground nutmeg loses its aroma quickly, so it is better to buy whole ones and keep a nutmeg-grater in the kitchen drawer. The mace that surrounds the nutmeg has a similar but slightly sweeter flavour; it is sometimes sold in pieces, more often as a powder.

OKRA, LADIES' FINGERS, GUMBO This plant, *Hibiscus esculentus*, came originally from Africa, but because it has been taken to so many places it can be bought, fresh, in both Greek and Indian shops. Its finely tapered pods, although they have a rather slimy texture, are tender vegetables and are an essential ingredient in gumbo, or Creole soup. When you buy them, avoid any that are going brown or are more than about 10 cm/4 inches long, as these may be fibrous. Trim the stalk off without cutting into the pod.

ORANGE FLOWER WATER This is obtainable in some shops that specialize in Middle Eastern or eastern Mediterranean food, or you may be able to buy it at a chemist's.

OREGANO This herb (*Origanum vulgare*) is similar to MARJORAM, and is sometimes called wild marjoram. For practical purposes, the two can be considered the same; if you have a herb garden, you may disagree.

OYSTER SAUCE Sauce made substantially of oysters would be prohibitively expensive, and this is usually labelled 'oyster-flavoured sauce'. It can be bought in any Chinese shop and, increasingly, in supermarkets.

PALM SUGAR Originally a dark reddish-brown sugar, made from the juice of the coconut-palm flower, often called jaggery. Nowadays, as sold in Asian food shops, it is much paler in colour, but still comes in a rock-hard block. Either grate this by hand against a cheese grater, or knock a piece off and dissolve it as directed in the recipe.

PANEER, PANIR A kind of Indian cottage cheese, though Tom Stobart in *The Cook's Encyclopaedia* says 'milk curds that hardly warrant the name of cheese'. You can buy paneer in Indian shops, or make your own with Tom Stobart's instructions:

Bring milk to the boil and add some lemon juice. As soon as the milk curdles, pour it into a clean cloth and hang up to drain overnight. Squeeze out the water by pressing the bag. Press between boards or plates to remove the last liquid. Leave it to dry, then cut it in squares or knead it. Always use *panir* fresh.

He adds that you use only just enough lemon juice to cause the milk to coagulate, and you must not leave it to drain for so long that it goes sour.

PAPRIKA   Powdered dried red chillies from Hungary – made from sweet peppers, it is not particularly hot, but it has the flavour needed for many Hungarian dishes. In this book, it is sometimes suggested as a substitute for chilli powder when you want the colour but not the hotness of chilli.

PICKLING ONION   Small brown-skinned white-fleshed onions.

PIMIENTO   Another name for BELL PEPPER or SWEET PEPPER.

PINE KERNEL, PINE NUT   In Europe, these are harvested from the cones of the Mediterranean stone pine, *Pinus pinea*, and are nicest when fresh and very lightly roasted. They are easy to find in delicatessens and shops that specialize in Middle Eastern food, but they are expensive. They are often used in Korean cooking.

PINTO BEAN   A variety of kidney bean, called 'pinto' (painted) because of its reddish flecks. Soak for 3–4 hours before use.

PISTACHIO   We think of these as Turkish, Persian, or Afghan, but the trees, *Pistacia vera*, now grow in many dry, hot countries – southern Italy, Arizona and elsewhere. Dreadfully expensive, but worth the money.

PLANTAIN   In effect, any variety of cooking banana, often green but sometimes yellow or black.

POMEGRANATE JUICE   In getting the juice out of a fresh pomegranate, the trick is to separate the seeds from the yellow, bitter-tasting pith and membranes. First, slice off the stem end of the fruit. Stand the fruit upright, cut end upwards, and make a series of vertical cuts through the skin. Gently separate the fruit into sections, then bend the skin of each section back so that you can detach the seeds and collect them together in a sieve. You can now crush the seeds to release the juice.

PUMPKIN   A member of the huge family of squashes (the COURGETTE is another), which originated in the Americas. Pumpkins come in many shapes and sizes. All contain a lot of water, and their weight is reduced by about half as they cook. This is one reason why they make such good soup.

QUINCE   The hard, yellowish fruit of a tree, *Pyrus cydonia*, related to the apple and pear; fragrant but sharp-tasting, used in cooking but not eaten raw.

RAISINS   Sun-dried muscatel grapes; raisins, currants and SULTANAS are basically

377

the same thing made (traditionally by rather different methods) from different varieties of grape.

RICE FLOUR This is easily found in any Asian shop and most delicatessens; glutinous rice flour should also be fairly easy to get. The difference between them is important; one will not do as a substitute for the other. Ground rice is relatively coarse, but rice powder is ground even more finely than rice flour, and if the recipe calls for powder (as does that for Rice Flour Crisps, for example, on page 144), then powder it must be.

RICE PAPER There are two kinds: one, made from rice flour, is a fairly thick, brittle sheet, usually cut and packed in discs about 15 cm/6 inches across and used, in Vietnam and elsewhere, to wrap spring rolls. The other is the very thin edible tissue that macaroons are baked on. This is not made from rice but from the pith of a plant such as *Tetrapanax papyrifera* (occasionally grown in English gardens as 'the rice-paper plant') or *Aralia papyrifera*, whose seeds were also considered a delicacy in T'ang China.

RICE POWDER See RICE FLOUR.

RICE VINEGAR China and Japan produce a wide range of vinegars from rice wines; broadly speaking, Chinese vinegars are sharp-tasting, Japanese ones mellow and in some cases positively sweet. It is important to have the right vinegar for the job, and you should have no difficulty finding the limited selection called for in this book. You can, of course, use these rice vinegars to make Western-style vinaigrettes or for general cooking.

RICOTTA An Italian whey cheese, usually sold in its fresh, unripened, creamy-white form, which is how it is used in this book – e.g. as a substitute for PANEER.

ROSE WATER Popular in Middle Eastern sweets, and often used with ORANGE FLOWER WATER, 'when', in Claudia Roden's words, 'it is the weaker of the partnership and can therefore be used less sparingly'.

SAFFRON By weight, this is perhaps the world's most expensive foodstuff in common use; the saffron 'threads' that one buys in little envelopes containing a fraction of a gram are the stigmas of *Crocus sativus*, the saffron crocus. The flavour is unlike anything else, and the yellow colour is extraordinarily strong, so only a tiny quantity is required. Saffron has long been associated with rice dishes in Spain and the Middle East. 'Powdered' saffron, if cheap, is simply a vegetable dye; you would do better to use TURMERIC.

378

SAKÉ   The Japanese word in fact refers to any alcoholic drink, but for the rest of us it is the slightly grainy, slightly perfumed liquor that slips down so comfortably, especially when it is served warm in little porcelain cups, that we don't realize how alcoholic it is: about 15–17 per cent, stronger than most grape wines and much stronger than beer. Yet saké is really a rice beer; the rice grains, instead of being malted, have their starch converted into sugar by a mould, *Aspergillus oryzae*, which in Java is often used to make TEMPEH. Yeast is then added, and turns the sugars into alcohol in the usual way. Saké does not mature; it can be drunk as soon as it is made, and should not be kept for more than a year. It must be stored in a cool, dark place. Once the bottle is opened, it should be drunk within a few days. The etiquette of serving and drinking saké does not concern us here, but because saké contains a number of amino acids it softens food and is therefore much used in cooking. There is no need to buy any particular grade or type; you can cook and drink out of the same bottle, and any saké which the Japanese regard as fit for export will be of at least good average quality.

SALAM LEAF   This is not a 'curry leaf' or KAFFIR LIME LEAF, but, like them, it can be replaced in cooking by a bay leaf. Dried salam leaves are sold in some Asian shops; a single leaf in the cooking pot is sufficient. Botanically, the plant is *Eugenia polyantha*.

SAMBAL   In Indonesia and Malaysia, a general term for hot and spicy relishes. You can buy these ready-made in Asian shops, and some are good – Yeo's and Koningsvogel are examples. It is better, of course, to make your own, and you can then adjust the hotness to your liking by using more or less chilli.

SCALLOP   A shellfish, whose double shell was once associated with pilgrims and is now the trademark of an oil company; there are many species. If they are processed at sea, it is often only the edible muscle that comes to market, but if you buy the complete creature its shell should be scrubbed and opened with a knife, and the muscle cut out with scissors. The reddish-yellow coral is also edible, the rest should be discarded.

SEA LETTUCE   A species of seaweed, *Ulva lactuca*, imported to the UK from Brittany but no doubt harvested on other coasts as well. Available in most good delicatessens.

SERRANO CHILLI   These are quite small, stubby, bright green Mexican chillies.

SHALLOT   Though somewhat expensive in Britain and sometimes hard to find, these are simply a small variety of onion; but their flavour is characteristic. The small red onions sold in Asian shops are very similar. Ordinary small onions will just about do if nothing else is available.

SHAOHSING WINE   A standard Chinese cooking product, easily available in any Asian shop; quite expensive, but it keeps indefinitely. Dry sherry is the usual substitute, but not as 'authentic'.

SHIITAKE   These delicious Japanese mushrooms are now grown commercially in Britain and lots of other places. Dried shiitake keep indefinitely, but fresh ones should be used within a day or two. The stems are tough, so cut them off and use them in the stock pot.

SHRIMP PASTE   The exquisite, delicious, ineffably pungent and salty seasoning for a vast range of savoury dishes in South-East Asia, doing the same job as FISH SAUCE but in a far more concentrated form. It is sold in hard blocks, also labelled *terasi*, *trassie*, *balachan* or *blachen*, and in little 5-gram/⅙-ounce slices. These slices are ready to use. The block, usually about 225 g/8 oz, needs to be sliced about 5 mm/⅕ inch thick and each slice cut into four squares; these should then be roasted on a sheet of aluminium foil in a moderate oven or in a frying pan on the stove for about 5 minutes. This creates a very strong odour, which you eventually come to love but which is a bit of a shock at first. The roasted pieces should be kept in an airtight jar, ready for use; one piece is enough for the average dish. Shrimp paste is very strong; use sparingly. It keeps indefinitely.

SILVERSIDE   An English cut of beef, the lean outer part of the thigh muscle.

SORREL   A sharp-tasting, sour green herb, associated with French cooking but now pretty generally available in Britain. It must be used very fresh. It makes particularly good soup and is delicious in salad, but it should not be eaten in large quantities because of the oxalic acid in its leaves.

SOY SAUCE   In Britain, the best all-purpose soy sauce to go for is probably Kikkoman, but other well-known brands – Amoy, Pearl River Bridge, etc. – are also very good. Several recipes in this book call for light and dark soy. All soy sauce is very salty, but 'light' is saltier, 'dark' is somewhat sweeter. Kikkoman (from Japan) will just about do for both, but a purist will want to use Chinese soy in Chinese dishes. Pearl River Bridge makes both, but has forgotten to make clear, in English on the label, which is which. The easiest way to tell them apart is to remember that 'superior soy' is light, 'soy superior' is dark. The French word *épais* also appears on the dark soy label, and of course the Chinese characters are different. In Indonesia, soy sauce is known as *kecap* (ketjap), and in the Netherlands, and in some shops in Britain, you can buy *kecap manis*, Indonesian-style sauce – this counts as dark sweet soy.

SPANISH ONION, YELLOW ONION   A particularly large variety of onion, fairly mild in flavour.

SUGAR PEA   See MANGETOUT.

SULTANA, GOLDEN SEEDLESS RAISIN   A dried, sweet, seedless grape, first grown in Turkey; modern supermarket sultanas come from Australia and California, but lack the authentic flavour of the originals. Avoid, if you can, sultanas that look very glossy, they may have been coated with mineral oil.

SWEET CHILLI   See SWEET PEPPER.

SWEET CORN   Unless the recipe calls for fresh corn on the cob, canned corn is perfectly satisfactory.

SWEET PEPPER   (also, in Britain, PIMIENTO; US, BELL PEPPER) Any variety of *Capsicum* that is mild-flavoured; there are many of these, and each country has its favourites. In Britain they are usually round and green, red or yellow; in the USA bell-shaped. Spain and Turkey have long, pointed varieties that are also called sweet chillies; they are very light green, sometimes almost white. In Spain they are often fried, in Turkey stuffed or pickled.

SWISS CHARD   A form of spinach beet, i.e. a beet grown for its leaves and leaf-ribs, not its root.

TAMARIND, TAMARIND WATER   The name is Arabic and means 'Indian date', though the tamarind fruits in their pods are nothing like dates. Early Arab traders probably shipped the dried pulp, which was valued for its sourness. This is still the easiest way to buy tamarind today; blocks of the pulp are sold in most Asian shops. Recipes usually call for tamarind water rather than the solid pulp. To make tamarind water, break off a piece of the pulp and put it in a little warm water (as a rough guide, 1 part by weight of pulp to 10 parts water). Squeeze and knead it so that the juice and flavour are expressed into the water; the more pulp you use, and the harder you squeeze it, the darker the water will become. Discard the solids. The water will keep in the fridge for up to a week. It doesn't look very nice, but it helps to make the food taste good.

TASSO   Very highly seasoned smoked ham, made and sold only in parts of the south-eastern United States.

TEMPEH   A fermented soya bean product; see pages 288–292.

THYME Garden thyme (*Thymus vulgaris*) is the species normally used for cooking; other species are good, but many wild thymes are unsuitable.

TOFU, BEANCURD A thick curd made from soya 'milk', very nutritious, very bland in taste and texture but delicious when cooked with flavours that it readily absorbs. In Indonesia it is called *tahu*. Fresh tofu is sold in many Asian shops, certainly in all those that deal in Chinese or Japanese foodstuffs; it is packed and stored in cold water, and must be stored in the fridge and used within 3 days at most. Branded fresh tofu is now manufactured and distributed in UK supermarkets (e.g. Cauldron brand, which may be 'original' or 'smoked'); this, too, has a limited fridge life. Japanese 'silken' or 'everlasting' tofu is easily obtainable, and will keep for a long time as long as it is not opened; it is very soft and smooth, ideal for making creamy soups, dipping sauces and ice cream. Fried tofu is sold in Japanese and some other Asian shops. You can also make your own by deep-frying cubes of plain tofu, about 2.5 cm/1 inch on a side, until the surface is slightly browned. The inside remains white and soft. Fried tofu from a shop may be rather oily. Remove excess oil by pouring boiling water over the cubes and lightly pressing or patting them with absorbent paper. Deep-fried tofu can be stored in the fridge for up to a week, but not frozen.

TOPSIDE An English cut of beef; the lean meat from the top of the inside leg, normally without any bone.

TURMERIC Another rhizome, resembling GINGER; it can be bought fresh in Thai and Chinese shops, but ground turmeric from the supermarket is just about as good and much less trouble. If you want to use fresh turmeric, peel it, chop it, and blend it with other ingredients to make (for example) a curry paste. Turmeric contains a strong yellow dye, which makes it excellent for such dishes as yellow rice. Turmeric juice leaves a stain on cloth which is almost impossible to remove.

URAD DAL Dal is split pulses, whole pulses are gram. Urad dal is made by splitting black gram, which confusingly produces white dal (with perhaps some flecks of black or green seed-coat mixed in). In India it is considered a 'heating' food, best for cold weather. It is usually cooked without any pre-soaking. It is easily found in any Indian shop and many delicatessens.

VANILLA Another expensive flavouring, especially if you buy real pods of the South American vanilla orchid (*Vanilla planifolia*). These are individually pollinated by hand, picked just before they ripen, and are packed tightly so that they sweat, producing aromatic white crystals of vanillin, which give the dark-brown pods a fuzzy appearance. Properly matured pods will keep for a long time. Top-quality essence is made by extracting the flavour from the pods with alcohol, but most commercial products use a synthetic substance which is cheaper and much less subtle. A pod placed in a custard or with a cake will flavour it during cooking, and can be re-used several times.

VANILLA SUGAR   To transfer real vanilla flavour to sugar, keep two or three pods in a large jar of sugar, keeping the jar always topped up as the sugar is used.

VINE LEAF   For making dolmas (page 140), you can use any young and tender vine leaf as long as you wash off it any chemicals it has been sprayed with; or buy packets or cans of leaves, usually packed in brine. Rinse them well, otherwise they will taste very salty.

WATER SPINACH   (also swamp cabbage) This is a creeping, trailing, wet-loving plant (*Ipomoea reptans* or *I. aquatica*); in Indonesia and Malaysia it is called *kangkung*.

WAXY POTATO   See also FLOURY POTATO. Suitable varieties obtainable in the UK are: Asperge, Ausonia, Bintje, Charlotte, Civa, Diana, Maris Bard, Morag, Pentland Javelin, Shelagh, Spunta, Ulster Sceptre.

WHITE RADISH   See MOOLI.

YELLOW BEAN SAUCE   See BEAN SAUCE.

YELLOW ONION   See SPANISH ONION.

YOGURT   Fresh yogurt is a living product, with two active beneficial bacteria (*Lactobacillus bulgaricus* and *Streptococcus thermophilus*) sharing an environment of milk – pasteurized, and usually homogenized, before they are let loose in it. They break down the sugars in the milk to make lactic acid. It is one of the most quickly digested of all foods. For cooking, a 'natural' yogurt is best. It must be used before the date stamped on the container, otherwise the bacteria develop further and the flavour is spoilt. You can of course make your own; instructions are given in Stobart's *Cook's Encyclopaedia* and elsewhere.

ZUCCHINI   See COURGETTE

UTENSILS

You can easily cook perfect rice in an ordinary saucepan, and almost every recipe in this book can be prepared and cooked with basic kitchen equipment. But if you are going to cook rice, and Asian food, on a fairly regular basis, then you will find some or perhaps all of these items useful and labour-saving. Page references are to illustrations.

Pestle and mortar   You can use a European-style pestle and mortar, made of marble or a similar material, or wood; or an Indonesian *cobek* and *ulek-ulek*, made preferably of wood (stone ones can leave small chips in the food). The Japanese *suribachi* is an earthenware mortar with parallel grooves incised on its unglazed interior; this is used with a wooden pestle for grinding sesame seeds. It also has a brush of finely split bamboo to sweep the fragments of seed from the grooves.

Food processor   This can probably be regarded as basic equipment; many of the recipes take its use for granted. I can't imagine being without one.

Electric rice cooker (page 98)   These are quite expensive, but they last a long time and are a tremendous help if you cook rice often and if you serve rice at parties.

Saucepans   Recipes sometimes specify what description of saucepan is needed – extra large, thick-bottomed, deep, or wide and shallow (to allow room to stir-fry). One or two more specialized pans may be useful.
   Wok   Extremely useful, indeed essential for all kinds of Far Eastern and South-East Asian cooking. Ideally, a wok should be used on a gas ring, but if you don't cook with

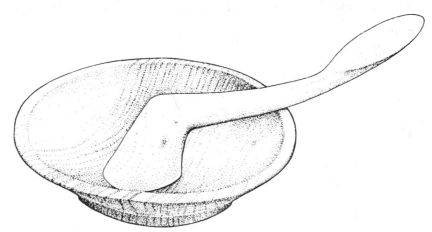

Cobek and *ulek-ulek*: Indonesia

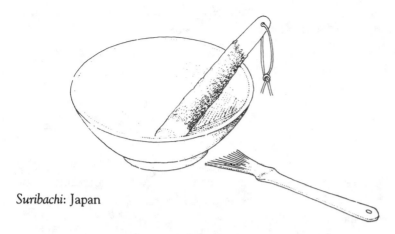

Suribachi: Japan

gas you can still buy a wok designed for use on an electric hotplate, or a wok with its own built-in electric heating element.

Steamer (pages 101 and 188) For notes on steaming, see Techniques, below. A steamer is convenient for 'finishing' rice if you are a regular rice eater but do not have an electric rice cooker. A double- or triple-decker steamer is useful if you know it will be used fairly often; it takes up a lot of space.

Blini Pan (page 146). Useful if you make blini often, but quite unnecessary otherwise; you can cook them on a griddle or in a thick-bottomed frying pan.

Moulds Several types are used in recipes in this book.

Ring Mould. The best is an ovenproof glass one, or a non-stick ring mould; it must be plain, with no embossed patterns.

Ramekins. These small ovenproof porcelain or glass straight-sided bowls are invaluable for soufflés because they can go straight from oven to table, but they have a lot of other uses.

'Golden Cups' Mould (page 147). This is needed for the recipe on page 148. You should be able to get one from a Thai shop; most have either two or four cups.

Swiss Roll Tin. This is a plain, low-sided oblong tin, useful but not essential for shaping flat slabs of sticky rice, etc.

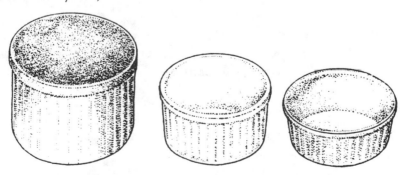

Ramekins

385

Japanese bamboo rolling mat (page 175)   Quite useful when you are making sushi; it combines rigidity in one direction with flexibility in the other.

TECHNIQUES

No recipe in this book demands any operation of great skill or dexterity, and the techniques described here are probably already familiar to you. Where a technique or procedure occurs only once or twice in the book (smoking, for example), it is described as part of the appropriate recipe method.

Preparation

CUTTING JULIENNE STRIPS OR MATCHSTICKS   Both these terms are used in the book, and they both mean the same thing. It is normally vegetables that are treated in this way. Slice thinly, then stack up the slices and slice the other way into matchsticks.

DICING AND CUBING   'Dicing' (usually vegetables, occasionally meat) means cutting into small cubes. For small dice, cut julienne strips or matchsticks, then slice these across; medium or large dice are correspondingly thicker. 'Cubing' (usually meat) means cutting into still larger cubes; the recipe usually suggests a size.

DE-VEINING A PRAWN OR SHRIMP   The black 'vein' is the intestine. Hold the prawn in one hand so that its back is towards you. With a small sharp knife, cut along the centre line of the back, taking care to go deep enough but not too deep. Open the prawn as if it were a book, and cut or pull the vein out. Wash the prawn under the cold tap. De-veining in this way also makes the prawns curl up prettily when they cook. If you want them to stay straight, take off the head of each and pull the vein out without cutting.

PEELING TOMATOES   Fill a small pan or bowl with water that has just boiled. Put the tomatoes in this water for about 2 minutes, and immediately transfer them to cold water. Leave them for a few seconds; the skin can then be easily stripped off.

Cooking

BLANCHING   Cooking (usually vegetables or some types of nuts – e.g. almonds or pistachios) for not more than 2 or 3 minutes.

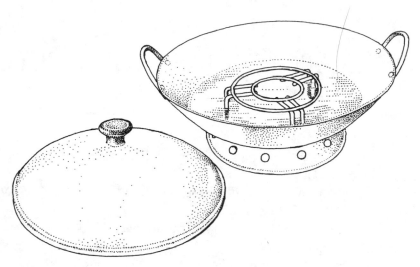

Steaming in a wok

USING A BAIN-MARIE   Cooking in the oven in a reservoir of boiling water. A deep baking tin makes a good bain-marie; put some hot water in the bottom of the tin, and in it place the bowl(s) containing whatever is to be cooked. It may sometimes be necessary to lay a folded tea-towel/dishcloth or newspaper in the water first; the recipe will give directions on this.

STEAMING   (pages 100–101) This is a very healthy and convenient way of cooking. If the food is in ramekins or small cups, these can be cooked in a rice steamer. For larger items, you need, ideally, a big double-decker steamer (pages 101 and 188). But you can also use either a large saucepan or a wok. The saucepan has the advantage of high sides and a close-fitting lid. In the pan or wok, put a trivet or other firmly seated support that will hold whatever is to be cooked above the water level. An upside-down plate is often sufficient. If the food is in a bowl, the water may come part-way up the outside of the bowl; obviously it must not get into the food. The water must of course be boiling when steaming begins. If steaming goes on for a long time, the water may need to be replenished with boiling water straight from the kettle.

BOOKS ABOUT RICE, AGRICULTURE, NUTRITION

Anonymous, ed. Harry J. Carman, *American Husbandry* (New York: Columbia University Press, 1939)

Barker, R., and Herdt, R.W., with B. Rose, *The Rice Economy of Asia* (Washington, DC: Resources for the Future, 1985)

Benedict, Murray R., *Farm Policies of the United States 1790–1950* (New York: The Twentieth Century Fund, 1953)

Bertin, J., and others, *Atlas des cultures vivrières* (Paris: Mouton, 1971)

Bray, Francesca, *The Rice Economies: Technology and Development in Asian Societies* (Oxford: Blackwell, 1986)

Burkhill, I.H., *A Dictionary of the Economic Products of the Malay Peninsula* (1935; repr. Kuala Lumpur: Ministry of Agriculture and Co-operatives, 1966)

Chandler, Robert F. (ed.), *Rice in the Tropics* (Boulder, Colo, and London: Westview Press, 1979)

Chang, K.C. (ed.), *Food in Chinese Culture* (New Haven, Conn.: Yale University Press, 1977)

Department of Health, *Dietary Reference Values for Food Energy and Nutrients for the United Kingdom* (London: HMSO, 1991)

Ente Nazionale Risi, *Rice and Restaurants* (Milan: ENR, c. 1990)

Farwell, George, *Mask of Asia: The Philippines Today* (New York and London: Praeger, 1967)

Freeman, J.D., *Iban Agriculture* (London: HMSO, 1955)

Geertz, Clifford, *Agricultural Involution: The Processes of Ecological Change in Indonesia* (Berkeley, Calif.: University of California Press, 1963)

Geertz, Clifford, *Negara: The Theatre State in Nineteenth-Century Bali* (Princeton, NJ: Princeton University Press, 1980)

Glover, Ian C., 'Some problems relating to the domestication of rice in Asia', in V.N. Misra and Peter Bellwood, eds, *Recent Advances in Indo-Pacific Prehistory* (Oxford University; and New Delhi: IBH Publishing Co., c. 1979)

Gray and Thompson, *History of Agriculture in the Southern United States to 1860* (Washington, DC: Carnegie Institute, 1933)

Grist, D.H., *Rice* (Harlow, Essex: Longman, 1986)

Gourou, Pierre, *Riz et civilisation* (Paris: Fayard, 1984)

Hanks, Lucien M., *Rice and Man* (Chicago: Aldine Atherton, 1972)

Hartley, Dorothy, *Food in England* (London: Macdonald, 1954)

Herklots, G.A.C., *Vegetables in South-East Asia* (London: Allen & Unwin, 1972)

Hill, R.D., *Rice in Malaya: A Study in Historical Geography* (Kuala Lumpur: Oxford University Press, 1977)

Huke, Robert E. and Eleanor H., *Rice: Then and Now* (Manila: IRRI, 1990)

International Rice Research Institute, *Rice Grain Quality and Marketing: Papers presented at the IRRI Conference, June 1985* (Manila: IRRI, 1985)

Jefferson, Thomas, *Papers* (Princeton, NJ: Princeton University Press, 1958; 24 vols)

Kumar, Tuktuk, *History of Rice in India* (Delhi: Gian Publishing House, 1988)

Lawson, Dennis T., *No Heir to Take its Place* (Georgetown, SC: The Rice Museum, 1972)

Leeming, Frank, *Rural China Today* (Harlow, Essex: Longman, 1985)

Leung, Woot-Tsuen Wu, and others, *Food Composition Table for Use in East Asia* (Washington, DC: FAO and US Department of Health, Education, and Welfare, 1972)

Marten, G.G. (ed.), *Traditional Agriculture in South-East Asia* (Boulder, Colo, and London: Westview Press, 1986)

McGee, Harold, *On Food and Cooking: The Science and Lore of the Kitchen* (New York: Charles Scribner's Sons, 1984; London: George Allen & Unwin, 1986)

McGee, Harold, *The Curious Cook* (Berkeley: North Point Press, 1990; London and New York: Harper Collins, 1992)

Mears, Leon A., *The New Rice Economy of Indonesia* (Gajah Mada, Yogyakarta: Gajah Mada University Press, 1981)

Moore, Richard H., *Japanese Agriculture: Patterns of Rural Development* (Boulder, Colo, and London: Westview Press, 1991)

Morgan, Dan, *Merchants of Grain* (London: Weidenfeld & Nicholson, 1979)

Null, Gary, *The Complete Guide to Health and Nutrition* (London: Arlington, 1984)

OECD, *Agriculture in China* (Paris: OECD, 1985)

Oxford Food Symposium, *Proceedings*, particularly the volumes for 1984–5 and 1989 containing papers by various authors on rice, Middle Eastern food, etc. (London: Prospect Books)

Pringle, Elizabeth A., *A Woman Rice Planter* (London: Macmillan, 1913; Columbia, SC: University of South Carolina Press, 1992)

Rassers, W.H., *Panji, the Culture Hero* (The Hague: Nijhoff, 1982; 2nd edn)

Root, Waverley, *Food* (New York: Simon & Schuster, 1980)

Scott, J.C., *Weapons of the Weak* (New Haven, Conn., and London: Yale University Press, 1985)

Tannahill, Reay, *Food in History* (Harmondsworth: Penguin, 1988)

Tasker, Peter, *Inside Japan* (London: Sidgwick & Jackson, 1987)

Vaughan, Duncan A., and Sitch, Lesley A., 'Gene flow from the jungle to farmers', in *BioScience*, vol. 41, no. 1, January 1991

Vergara, Benito S., *A Farmer's Primer on Growing Rice* (Manila: IRRI, 1979)

Visser, Margaret, *Much Depends on Dinner* (Harmondsworth: Penguin, 1986)

Watson, Andrew M., *Agricultural Innovation in the Early Islamic World* (Cambridge: Cambridge University Press, 1983)

Wilson, C. Anne, *Food and Drink in Britain* (London: Constable, 1973)

Wittwer, Yu, Sun and Wang, *Feeding a Billion* (Ann Arbor, Mich.: University of Michigan Press, 1987)

COOKERY BOOKS

Algar, Ayla, *Classical Turkish Cooking* (New York: Harper Collins, 1991)

Bareham, Lindsey, *In Praise of the Potato* (Aldershot, Hants.: Grafton, 1989)

Benghiat, Norma, *Traditional Jamaican Cookery* (Harmondsworth: Penguin, 1985)

Benghiat, Suzy, *Middle Eastern Cookery* (London: Weidenfeld & Nicholson, 1984)

Bhumichitr, Vatcharin, *The Taste of Thailand* (London: Pavilion, 1988)

Bhumichitr, Vatcharin, *Thai Vegetarian Cooking* (London: Pavilion, 1991)

Bissell, Frances, *Sainsbury's Book of Food* (London: Websters International for J. Sainsbury plc, 1989)

Black, Maggie, *Medieval Cookbook* (London: British Museum Press, 1992)

Brennan, Jennifer, *Curries and Bugles: A Cookbook of the British Raj* (London: Viking, 1990)

Chamberlain, Lesley, *The Food and Cooking of Russia* (Harmondsworth: Penguin, 1983)

Chin-hwa, Noh, *Practical Korean Cooking* (Elizabeth, NJ: Hollym, 1985)

del Conte, Anna, *Gastronomy of Italy* (London: Transworld, 1987)

del Conte, Anna, *Entertaining all'Italiana* (London: Transworld, 1991)

Davidson, Alan, *North Atlantic Seafood* (London: Macmillan, 1979; Harmondsworth: Penguin, 1980)

Davidson, Alan, and Knox, Charlotte, *Fruit: A Connoisseur's Guide and Cookbook* (London: Mitchell Beazley, 1991)

Glasse, Hannah, *The Art of Cookery Made Plain and Easy* (1747; London: Prospect Books, 1983)

Grigson, Jane, *English Food* (London: Macmillan, 1974; Harmondsworth: Penguin, 1977)

Halici, Nevin, *Nevin Halici's Turkish Cookbook* (London: Dorling Kindersley, 1989)

Holt, Geraldene, *Recipes from a French Herb Garden* (London: Conran Octopus, 1989)

Itoh, Joan, *Rice Paddy Gourmet* (Tokyo: Japan Times, 1985)

Jaffrey, Madhur, *A Taste of India* (London: Pavilion, 1985)

Jaffrey, Madhur, *Eastern Vegetarian Cooking* (London, Jonathan Cape, 1983).

Kalra, J. Inder Singh, *Prashad: Cooking with Indian Masters* (Bombay: Allied Publishers, 1986)

Liddell, Caroline, and Weir, Robert, *Ices: The Definitive Guide* (London: Hodder & Stoughton, 1993)

London, Sheryl and Mel, *The Versatile Grain and the Elegant Bean* (New York: Simon & Schuster, 1992)

March, Lourdes, *El libro de la paella y de los arroces* (Madrid: Alianza Editorial, 1985)

Norman, Jill, *The Complete Book of Spices* ((London: Dorling Kindersley, 1990)

Ortiz, Elisabeth Lambert, *The Complete Book of Mexican Cooking* (New York: Ballantine, 1967)

Ortiz, Elisabeth Lambert, *The Book of Latin American Cooking* (London: Robert Hale, 1984)

Ortiz; Elisabeth Lambert, *The Food of Spain and Portugal* (London: Lennard Publishing, 1989)

Ortiz, Elisabeth Lambert, *Caribbean Cooking* (London: Penguin Books, 1977)

Ortiz, Elisabeth Lambert, *Japanese Cookery* (London: Collins, 1986)

Owen, Sri, *Indonesian Food and Cookery* (London: Prospect Books, 1980 and 1986)

Owen, Sri, *Indonesian and Thai Cookery* (London: Piatkus, 1988)

Owen, Sri, *The Cooking of Thailand, Indonesia and Malaysia* ((London: Martin Books for J. Sainsbury plc, 1991)

Owen, Sri, *Exotic Feasts* (London: Kyle Cathie, 1991)

Perl, Lila, *Rice, Spice and Bitter Oranges: Mediterranean Foods and Festivals* (Cleveland, Ohio, and New York: World Publishing, 1967)

Prudhomme, Paul, *Chef Paul Prudhomme's Louisiana Kitchen* (New York: William Morrow, 1984)

Ramazani, Nesta, *Persian Cooking* (Charlottesville, Va: University Press of Virginia, 1974)

Roden, Claudia, *A New Book of Middle Eastern Food* (London: Viking, 1985; Harmondsworth: Penguin, 1986)

Saberi, Helen, *Noshe Djan: Afghan Food and Cookery* (London: Prospect Books, 1986)

Salaman, Rena, *Greek Food* (London: Fontana, 1983)

Seoul Hilton International (Food and Beverage Department), *Culinary Heritage of Korea* (Seoul: SHI, 1987)

Sevilla, María José, *Life and Food in the Basque Country* (London: Weidenfeld & Nicholson, 1989)

Shaida, Margaret, *The Legendary Cuisine of Persia* (Henley-on-Thames, Oxon: Lieuse, 1992)

Shurtleff, William, and Aoyagi, Akiko, *The Book of Tempeh* (New York: Harper & Row, 1979)

Shurtleff, William, and Aoyagi, Akiko, *History of Tempeh)* (Lafayette, Ca.: Soyfoods Centre, 1984)

Shurtleff, William, and Aoyagi, Akiko, *The Book of Tofu* (Berkeley, Ca.: Ten Speed Press, 1975)

Simmons, Marie, *Rice, the Amazing Grain* (New York: Holt, 1991)

So, Yan-kit, *Classic Food of China* (London: Macmillan, 1992)

Solomon, Charmaine, *The Complete Asian Cookbook* (Sydney: Hamlyn, 1976)

Stobart, Tom, *The Cook's Encyclopaedia* (London: Batsford, 1980)

Taruschio, Ann and Franco, *Leaves from the Walnut Tree* (London: Pavilion, 1993).

Tsuji, Shizuo, *Japanese Cooking: A Simple Art* (Tokyo and New York: Kodansha, 1980)

Virmani, Inderjeet (ed.), *Home Chefs of the World: Rice and Rice-Based Recipes* (Manila: IRRI/Suhay, 1991)

Willan, Anne, *Reader's Digest Complete Guide to Cookery* (London: Dorling Kindersley, 1989)

Wolfert, Paula, *Good Food from Morocco* (London: John Murray, 1989); also published as *Couscous and Other Good Food from Morocco* (New York: Harper & Row, 1973 and 1987)

General Index

Index to the Recipes

Page numbers in italics refer to illustrations